Working through Memory

Working through Memory

Writing and Remembrance in Contemporary Spanish Narrative

Ofelia Ferrán

Lewisburg
Bucknell University Press

© 2007 by Ofelia Ferrán

All rights reserved. Authorization to photocopy items for internal or personal use, or the internal or personal use of specific clients, is granted by the copyright owner, provided that a base fee of $10.00, plus eight cents per page, per copy is paid directly to the Copyright Clearance Center, 222 Rosewood Drive, Danvers, Massachusetts 01923. [978-0-8387-5658-4/07 $10.00 + 8¢ pp, pc.]

Associated University Presses
2010 Eastpark Boulevard
Cranbury, NJ 08512

The paper used in this publication meets the requirements of the American National Standard for Permanence of Paper for Printed Library Materials Z39.48-1984.

Library of Congress Cataloging-in-Publication Data

Ferrán, Ofelia, 1965–
    Working through memory : writing and remembrance in contemporary Spanish narrative / Ofelia Ferrán.
       p. cm.
    Includes bibliographical references and index.
    ISBN-13: 978-0-8387-5658-4 (alk. paper)
    ISBN-10: 0-8387-5658-1 (alk. paper)
      1. Autobiographical fiction, Spanish—History and criticism. 2. Spanish fiction—20th century—History and criticism. I. Title.
PQ6147.A86F47 2007
863'.6409—dc22

2007012246

PRINTED IN THE UNITED STATES OF AMERICA

A mi madre.
Porque estás conmigo, siempre.

A mi padre.
Porque me sigues enseñando el valor de buscar todo aquello que está
"dentro del alma, en turbio y mago sol envuelto."

For Sachin.
For all your love and support.
For your bad jokes and wonderful sense of humor.

Contents

Acknowledgments	9
Introduction	13
1. Jorge Semprún: Trauma and Memory	66
2. Juan Benet: The *Pharmakon* of Memory	102
3. María Teresa León: The Performance of Memory	142
4. Montserrat Roig: Twilight Memory	182
5. Antonio Muñoz Molina: Memory and Postmemory	225
Conclusion	268
Appendix	281
Notes	299
Works Cited	338
Index	357

Acknowledgments

While doing research for this book over the years, I have had the good fortune to enjoy financial support from various institutions, to which I would like to extend my gratitude. The University of Minnesota has generously supported various stages of this project with a Grant-in-Aid of Research, Artistry and Scholarship, and a Faculty Single Semester Leave from the Office of the Vice President for Research and Dean of the Graduate School. The university has likewise awarded me a McKnight Summer Fellowship and a University of Minnesota Faculty Summer Research Fellowship. Various International Travel Grants from the European Studies Consortium and the Office of International Programs at the University of Minnesota have provided me with financial aid to attend a number of international conferences. The discussions with other scholars arising from papers presented at those conferences have undoubtedly improved my final book project. Furthermore, a Research Grant from the Program for Cultural Cooperation Between Spain's Ministry of Education, Culture and Sports, and United States' Universities enabled me to do research in Spain.

I have had the enormous fortune to have colleagues at the University of Minnesota who have been exceptionally supportive in good as well as trying times, in matters both personal and professional. I am deeply grateful for their friendship, which has made me a better teacher, scholar, and person. A heartfelt thank you, especially, to Fernando Arenas, Ana Paula Ferreira, Amy Kaminsky, Carol Klee, Joanna O'Connell, Connie Sullivan, and Barbara Weissberger. During the year I spent teaching in the Department of Romance Languages and Literatures at the University of North Carolina, Chapel Hill, I was again fortunate to find wonderful colleagues, among whom I would like to thank especially, for their friendship and kindness that year, Lucia Binotti, Marsha Collins, Stuart Day, Frank Domínguez, Alejandro Mejías-López, Rosa Perelmuter, Jose Polo de Bernabé, Alicia Rivero, and María Salgado.

Without the support of my friends and family, I would not have done much of what I have been able to accomplish. We have shared laughter and tears, and your support has always made the journey much more enjoyable. My deepest gratitude to María Bullón, Toni Dorca, Sonia Feigenbaum, and, always, Christine Henseler, as well as so many others over the years, both near and far. Yasmeen and Jim Moody have given me and my family support in ways we will never be able to repay.

One friend, who is no longer with us, was also my mentor. I cannot begin to express my gratitude to John Kronik for everything he taught me, and for all his support throughout the years. I will forever miss his editorial corrections, as well as his smile.

My family has given me love, support and inspiration, the most valuable gifts of all. To my brother Jaime, I thank you for making me laugh. Thank you to my father for instilling in me a love of language and showing me that true strength of character can be gentle, generous, and kind. My mother's spirit inhabits each and every one of the following pages, just as it inhabits all the best things that I do in my life. I now know the true value of memory, "harto consuelo," because there you reside and continue to be my guide. Without the love and care of my husband this book would never have reached completion. Thank you for everything, Sachin. Yes, it is FINALLY finished. Let the A. B. Era begin!

A shorter version of chapter 1 was published as " 'Cuanto más escribo, más me queda por decir': Memory, Trauma, and Writing in the Work of Jorge Semprún" in *Modern Language Notes (MLN)* 16.2 (March 2001): 266-94. A shorter version of chapter 2 was published as "*Memoria de la melancolía* by María Teresa León: The Performativity and Disidentification of Exilic Memories" in *Journal of Spanish Cultural Studies* 6.1 (2005): 59-78. The Web site of the *Journal of Spanish Cultural Studies* is: http://www.tandf.co.uk/journals/titles/14636204.asp.

Working through Memory

Introduction

> The past is not over, it is not even past.
> —William Faulkner

> La memoria no actúa espontáneamente. Es el resultado de una obra, de una elaboración.... Hay dos tipos de pasado: uno que llega hasta ahora y otro que desaparece. El primero es el de los vencedores.... Del segundo, que es el de los vencidos, se ocupa la memoria. La pregunta es cómo hacer justicia a los muertos.
> —Manuel Reyes Mate

[Memory does not act spontaneously. It is the result of work, of an elaboration.... There are two types of past: one that reaches us today and another that disappears. The first is that of the victors.... The second, which is that of the vanquished, is addressed by memory. The question is how to do justice to the dead.]

General Overview

In an article entitled "Lugares de la memoria" [Places of memory] published in *El País* on April 4, 2004, the Spanish philosopher Manuel Reyes Mate describes how, after the March 11 terrorist train bombings in Madrid, people spontaneously created a "place of memory" in a corner of the Atocha train station by leaving candles, flowers, and messages of sympathy to commemorate the victims. One month after the bombings, Reyes Mate notes critically that while station guards discreetly begin to dismantle the offerings, counselors inform the public that the average time span for returning to "normal," inasmuch as this is considered possible, is one year. Remembering and forgetting are inevitably intertwined in the difficult balance between honoring the past, mourning the victims of such traumatic events, and moving on with life.[1]

What is particularly interesting in the article by Reyes Mate is the broader political and historical context within which he frames his observations. The desire to all-too-quickly dismantle the place of memory in the train station, and to comfort people with the idea of a not-too-distant return to "normalcy," are presented as part of a larger political and social issue. This larger problem is Spain's inability, in the recent past, to adequately work through the memory of its civil war, from 1936 to 1939, as well as of the long Fascist dictatorship of General Francisco Franco, from 1939 to 1975. Since the Spanish transition to democracy after Franco's death was based on what has come to be called a collective "pacto del olvido" [pact of forgetting], Reyes Mate claims that Spain still needs to create an adequate "culture of memory," a process whereby society effectively confronts the legacy of its traumatic past of war, exile, dictatorship, and repression. As an example of this lack of a culture of memory, he cites the fact that, unlike other countries where museums exist to commemorate the memory of traumatic historical experiences, Spain does not yet have a similar official museum about its civil war. It is symptomatic that, to this day, Spain has not undertaken any official institutional reappraisal of its past nor produced an official report documenting past repression, such as the Truth and Reconciliation Commission in South Africa or the "Nunca Más" [Never Again] report in Argentina. That Spain has undergone no judicial process bringing responsible parties from the Franco dictatorship to justice has led attorney Carlos Castresana Fernández to complain: "No ha habido ningún tribunal para el general Franco, ni siquiera el de la memoria" (Castresana Fernández 2001) [There has been no tribunal for General Franco, not even that of memory].

One could add other observations: for example, there has been little official governmental aid or support, until 2004, for the work of civic organizations calling for the exhumation of the numerous mass graves still located throughout Spain, mass graves filled with the bodies of people killed during the civil war or in the postwar reprisals by the victors. Spain's traumatic past of war and political repression is still, in a very real sense, buried, and, as Reyes Mate observes, an adequate culture of memory needs to be developed to truly confront and work through this past.

Working through Memory: Writing and Remembrance in Contemporary Spanish Narrative contributes to this project. In this study, I explore various constructions of memory in contemporary Spanish literature that evoke different aspects of that "buried" past of repression. Each chapter analyzes a different text that presents memory and the recuperation of the past as its main theme, each one highlighting a different problematic aspect of such an exploration of remembering. I study not only how every work places memory at center-stage thematically, but how each one presents a meta-narrative reflection of the very process of memory production, of how it is written and rewritten, recounted or repressed, transmitted or forgotten.

These works are read as "meta-memory texts," a term I am coining to highlight their self-reflexive nature. This term also foregrounds the inextricable connection between processes of memory production as well as transmission, and issues of writing and narrative representation, as the resonance with the term "metafictional text" makes clear. In Spanish, this relation is further underscored by the fact that the very term "memoria" [memory] refers both to the faculty of human recall and, as the *Diccionario de la Real Academia Española de la Lengua* [*Dictionary of the Royal Spanish Academy of Language*] defines it, to an "estudio, o disertación escrita sobre alguna materia" [a study, or written dissertation about some subject]. Memory and writing are, indeed, intimately connected. My thesis is that the self-reflexivity of these meta-memory texts, their self-conscious exploration of the relations between memory and representation, is what makes them particularly appropriate models for how to develop a much-needed culture of memory in Spain. Furthermore, I argue that these texts likewise serve as a model for a culture of countermemory, using Foucault's term for a practice of remembrance that recovers historical perspectives marginalized by official versions of the past.

The title of my book underscores the various levels at which this process of working through memory is being undertaken in my study. First of all, each author is shown to be working *through* memory, that is, using memory as the thematic axis around which his or her text is attempting to come to terms with a painful aspect of the past. By bringing these works together, the present study argues that they are part of a larger cultural dynamic by means of which Spanish society is still trying to *work through* its repressive and traumatic history. Each text, furthermore, is seen to highlight the manner in which literature and narrative are crucial elements of that enterprise. On another level, this study demonstrates that contemporary Spanish literature is an appropriate site for *working through* broader issues related to memory in contemporary scholarship.

The theoretical framework within which I analyze such narrative representations of remembrance places this book within a broad field of memory studies that transcends the Spanish context. The past thirty years have seen an unprecedented rise in interest in the study of memory within the humanities and social sciences.[2]

Memory plays a central role in theoretical issues such as the discursive construction of identity (at both an individual and collective level); the place, understanding, and definition of experience within that process of identity formation; the relationship of the present to the past; the question of whether access to the past is a recovery or recreation of events; the manner in which memories of the past serve particular interests in the present; and the way in which a collectivity forges an identity over time and across generations. These issues are explored in all the texts studied in the following chapters. In all these works, memory is shown to be both a central and a destabilizing force. This is due to the very nature of memory, for the term refers both to something remembered and to the *process, or act, of remembering itself,* a dual meaning that underscores the self-reflexivity at the heart of my project.

My study is interdisciplinary, borrowing from a wide range of theoretical discussions on memory that have emerged in fields ranging from sociology to psychoanalysis, from political and literary theory to history, from cultural studies to philosophy. I draw especially from trauma theory, which explores such questions in a manner particularly appropriate for understanding the difficulties in recovering, at both a personal and collective level, a past of violence and repression such as that of contemporary Spain. In fact, the concept of "working through" memory, while originating in the work of Sigmund Freud, has been effectively developed by historians and philosophers, such as Paul Ricoeur, Saul Friedlander, and Dominick LaCapra, among others, in large part as a response to the challenge that the Holocaust has placed on thinking about memory and the possibility, or impossibility, of adequately representing such a traumatic past. My study thus illustrates that theoretical insights gained in recent Holocaust studies are extremely helpful in understanding contemporary Spain's difficulty in confronting its own traumatic history.

The concept of "places of memory" that Reyes Mate highlights in the aforementioned article in *El País,* which is an important element of my analysis here, is derived from the seminal work of French historian Pierre Nora. The development of what he called *"lieux de mémoire"* [places of memory] in his multivolume study of French history and historiography, *Les lieux de mémoire* [*Realms of Memory*], published between 1984 and 1993, has been fundamental in shaping the emerging field of memory studies in the past twenty years.

Finally, the term "remembrance" in my title evokes the work of Walter Benjamin, which has greatly influenced my analysis of representations of memory in contemporary Spanish narrative. The term "remembrance," for Benjamin, reflects a perspective toward the past that is critical of modern conceptions of progress, and that underscores the debt the present has to the *victims,* and not the *victors,* of history. Benjamin calls for this critical approach to the past in several of his writings, including the famous "Theses on the Philosophy of History" and *The Arcades Project*. The original German term Benjamin uses in these texts, "*eingedenken,*" which is translated in English as "remembrance," is not commonly used in Benjamin's native tongue. In fact, as John McCole explains, "the term *eingedenken* is a coinage; it suggests a kind of memory that involves both remembrance and mindfulness (1993, 260). McCole further explains how the word *eingedenken* "plays on the words *gedenken* and *eingedenk*. *Gedenken* (verb or noun) means 'thinking of' some thing or someone, often in a commemorative or memorial sense; *eingedenk* (a predicative adjective that governs the genitive case) means to remember something in the sense of 'bearing it in mind' " (1993, 260). Benjamin's concept of "remembrance," therefore, evokes a special kind of memory. It is a process of remembering that seems to double up upon itself, to be self-reflexive. It is composed of two terms, each of which in itself implies a need to remember, as if one of them alone were not enough for the task at hand. As "an exercise in keeping faith with one who is absent" (McCole 1993, 267), this remembrance that Benjamin calls for clearly evokes a sense of great responsibility toward that which is being recalled. It is a task to be taken up in a mindful, conscientious manner.

Such a practice of remembrance, which "is the result of work, of an elaboration," is precisely what Reyes Mate, following Benjamin, calls for in one of the epigraphs to this introduction, and what I claim the narrative texts analyzed here embody. *Working through Memory* shows that the self-reflexive work of mindful memory, of remembrance, in these narratives does, indeed, attempt to address the urgent question in contemporary Spain that Reyes Mate evokes of "how to do justice to the dead." These dead are, in fact, the absent ones with whom contemporary Spanish society must learn to keep faith. In part, these dead are the victims of the Spanish civil war and of the subsequent Francoist repression whose memory has not been adequately honored in post-Franco Spain.

In Spanish, there are many terms one could use to translate the English " to remember." "Recordar" or "acordarse" are the most commonly used, but there are two other words, less common, that I believe are particularly appropriate to transmit the full implications of Benjamin's concept of "remembrance" as it will be explored in the following chapters. "Remembranza," or "remembrar," and "rememorar" are especially interesting because they each consist primarily of a root, "membrar" and "memorar," which, by itself, already means "to remember." The prefix "re" would thus seem to be unnecessary, for it creates a term that should literally be translated as "to re-remember." The prefix is not at all superfluous, however, if we understand these terms as evoking that doubling-up of memory upon itself, that mindful remembrance, that Benjamin had in mind. It is not insignificant, furthermore, that the use of the prefix "re" in these terms evokes the idea of remembering *again*, thus signifying a process that is forever being taken up anew; a process that is, in fact, never truly finished.

"Remembrar," or "rememorar," can also be seen to translate perfectly the idea for which Toni Morrison had to invent the English term "rememory" in her novel *Beloved*. Like Morrison's *rememory*, these terms work as both a noun and a verb, and they imply a kind of remembrance that, in its eternal return, ultimately haunts, and possesses, the person who is doing the remembering. Toni Morrison's novel tries to "do justice" to the many silenced voices of the victims of slavery in the United States in a manner similar to what the texts studied in the following chapters attempt with respect to Spain's recent history of war and repression. The specters from the past that haunt Sethe, the protagonist of *Beloved*, are spirits akin to those that haunt the protagonists of the works studied here, as well as to the many victims of the civil war and Francoist repression still haunting Spanish society from the depths of the mass graves scattered throughout the country. When Sethe tries to describe her experience of *rememory*, she clearly demonstrates that something long gone can continue to have a presence, even a physical presence, which can confound and confuse as much as it can give solace and comfort, depending on how one is inclined to react to it:

> Some things just stay. I used to think it was my rememory. You know. Some things you forget. Other things you never do. But it's not. Places, places are still there. If a house burns down, it's gone, but the place—the picture of it—stays, and not just in my rememory, but out there, in the world. What I remember is a picture floating around out there outside my head. I mean, even if I don't think it, even if I die, the picture of what I did, or knew, or saw is still out there. Right in the place where it happened.... Someday you be walking down the road and you hear something or see something going on. So clear. And you think it's you thinking it up. A thought picture. But no. It's when you bump into a rememory. (1988, 36–37)

Sethe's *rememory* inhabits places, places of memory, which bear the traces of what is long gone. Bumping into such places, bumping into a *rememory*, will either trigger a sense of fear and denial, or engender a process of remembrance, a process of "rememorar" and "remembrar" that is only a first step toward doing "justice to the dead." The mass graves in Spain can be considered a kind of *rememory* with which Spanish society has certainly collided. Although none of the texts analyzed in the following chapters specifically explores the topic of the mass graves from the civil war and postwar era, a concern with improper burial is nevertheless ever-present. To fully comprehend how these texts can contribute to the development of a proper "culture of memory" more generally in Spain today, it is essential to understand the connections between the problem of the mass graves which has recently erupted with so much force onto the social, cultural, and political scene in recent years, and a broader concern for things improperly buried and inadequately mourned in contemporary Spanish society. The texts studied here, by explicitly thematizing various strategies of remembrance, different ways in which that endless process of "remembrar" and "rememorar" can be put into action, serve as possible models for how to work through a painful and traumatic past that is still "floating around out there," still haunting Spain in the present.

Remembering and Forgetting the Past: the Spanish Context

"En este pueblo hay más muertos fuera del cementerio que dentro" (Silva and Macías 2003, 21) [In this town there are more dead outside the cemetery than inside]. This was the sentence with which an old man on the outskirts of the small town of Priaranza del Bierzo, in the Spanish province of León, responded to a question posed to him in early March 2000 by journalist Emilio Silva. Silva was looking for the mass grave in which he believed his grandfather, Emilio Silva Faba, had been secretly buried, along with thirteen others, after being summarily executed on October 16, 1936, by Nationalist forces during the civil war. The old man's response to Silva's query points to the fact that the mass grave in which the remains of Silva's grandfather were later to be found is unfortunately part of a larger historical, and also current, problem in Spain. At the beginning of the twenty-first century, about 30,000 people were still believed to be interred in mass graves throughout the country. Some of these mass graves were created during the civil war, but many came into existence afterwards, being filled with victims of the Nationalist repression in Franco's Spain up to the early 1950s.[3]

The improperly buried bodies in these mass graves, ghostly reminders of a past of war and repression which have not been given proper burial even through Spain has enjoyed thirty years of democratic rule, are a perfect metaphor for the work of memory that still needs to be undertaken in Spain. This task has been carefully sidestepped, for various reasons at different times, since Franco's death in 1975. These are many of the Spanish dead to whom justice is still due. Once Emilio Silva realized that the task he was facing involved thousands of other people just like himself, looking for loved ones who had been effectively "disappeared" during and after the civil war, he cofounded the "Asociación para la Recuperación de la Memoria Histórica" [Association for the Recovery of Historical Memory] (hereafter referred to as ARMH). As it has organized the exhumation of many mass graves in order to provide an appropriate burial to those found therein, this association has been an important force in creating a greater public awareness of the need for Spanish society to face the consequences of its Francoist past.

The use of the term "desaparecido" [disappeared] to describe the people presumed to be interred in mass graves in Spain, but whose exact location is unknown, is one that Emilio Silva consciously assumed in order to evoke the experience of various Latin American countries, including Chile, Argentina, and Uruguay, that have experienced military dictatorships and massive human rights violations. When Silva began to think seriously of exhuming the mass grave where he believed the remains of his grandfather were located, he wrote an article in a local Leónese newspaper entitled "Mi abuelo también fue un desaparecido" [My Grandfather Was Also Disappeared]. By comparing the repressive Francoist practice of summary executions in Spain with the human rights abuses in various Latin American countries, Silva was clearly indicating that, although the Spanish transition to democracy has long been hailed as a model for transitions to democracy in Latin America, it, in fact, has suffered from problems that are only slowly, and very belatedly, being acknowledged within Spain.

Silva's use of the term "desaparecido" may point to the fact that it was, in part, the Pinochet affair, the process begun in 1998 by Spanish judge Baltasar Garzón's demand for Pinochet to be extradited to Spain to be judged for his crimes against humanity, that made many in Spain become increasingly impatient with the lack of similar measures within Spain seeking accountability for Francoist repression. Whatever the final outcome of the Pinochet affair, it is part of an ongoing process that may eventually hold some promise for the future. The 2005 trial in Spain that sentenced the Argentine military officer Adolfo Scilingo, present at the trial, to 640 years in prison due to his participation in the systematic practice of forced disappearances and torture enacted by the Argentine military Junta in the 1970s and early '80s is particularly important in this respect. In 2005, also, Judge Baltasar Garzón called for the creation of an official truth commission that would investigate and document the full extent of Francoist repression. For now, however, the demand seems to have fallen on deaf ears, and Garzón's own inability to follow up on his demand, when he has proven such a forceful crusader for legal trials involving Latin American military officers, is quite revealing. It remains to be seen if such a truth commission actually materializes in Spain, or if the Spanish legal system will continue to seek accountability for past crimes against humanity committed abroad but not those suffered at home.[4]

Between October 21 and 28, 2000, the first exhumation organized by the ARMH was undertaken at Priaranza, and the remains of Silva's grandfather, as well as of twelve other bodies, were disinterred.[5] In early 2001, the ARMH was officially established. When the organization began to receive hundreds of requests from family members asking for help in locating their "disappeared" relatives, it recognized the importance of undertaking an effective media campaign to create a greater awareness within Spanish society of the problem of the mass graves. This media campaign soon began to have national repercussions. In the summer of 2002 the ARMH organized a work group, with volunteers from all over Europe, to undertake more exhumations, and the article in the newspaper *El País* describing the event became, up to then, the most widely read news item in the history of *El País* online (Silva and Macías 2003, 84).[6]

In 2002, the ARMH presented its findings to the United Nations Work Group on Forced Disappearances. This would allow the association to gain greater national and international recognition for its claim that the exhumation of mass graves in Spain should be covered by International Human Rights Law, and that organizations like the United Nations should put pressure on the Spanish government to address the issue. In November of that year, the United Nations Work Group determined that it would represent the cases of individuals "disappeared" and presumably located in mass graves in Spain, but only those that had occurred after the creation of the United Nations in 1945. Although this left out the majority of the cases that the ARMH had documented up to that point, the resolution was an important victory. Now, for the first time, the Spanish government would face some international pressure to begin to address adequately its past of war and repression.

It is symptomatic, in this respect, that in November 2002 the Spanish Congress presented a declaration, supported by every single party in Congress, including the ruling right-wing party at the time, the Partido Popular [Popular Party], officially condemning the Franco regime. The proposal recognized officially that the transition had not adequately faced the consequences of, and made reparations to those who had suffered, Spain's past of repression. It also urged the government to support the work of organizations such as the ARMH, although it was suggested that such support be provided at the local government level. This was a problematic suggestion, revealing a continued reluctance on the central government's part to fully assume such responsibilities.[7] This congressional resolution emerged partly in response to several proposals put forth by various left-wing political parties, proposals that, in turn, were due in part to the growing public awareness of the work of the ARMH, and other such organizations, throughout Spain. This was the first time since Franco's death that such a unanimous official government condemnation of Francoism was presented, and was thus quite significant. A similar proposal in 1999 had been passed by the Spanish Congress, but without the support of the Partido Popular. That the right-wing party felt the need to support the proposition in 2002, although it had rejected a similar decree three years earlier, is an indication of the growing public awareness during the intervening years of the way in which Spain still has a debt to pay to those who suffered the violence and repression of the civil war and Franco regime.

However, the resistance to fully accepting the consequences of this history of repression continues to be strong. In 2003, for example, the members of the Partido Popular in Congress refused to support a proposal whereby the government not only reiterated its recognition of the need to honor the victims of Francoism, but actually organized an event in parliament to honor them. A party spokesman explained this refusal by claiming that such a proposal represented a "return to the past" which "contributed nothing positive" to contemporary Spanish society (Kolbert 2003, 70).

It is thus unclear if the much-lauded congressional decree of 2002 signaled a change in the attitude that has characterized the transition of not wanting to face the legacy of Francoism in democratic Spain. Perhaps it is merely one more example of a practice in which the memory of the past is invoked, and officially commemorated, in a purely superficial manner, only to disappear when true accountability for that past is faced. This strategy, in fact, perfectly explains the Partido Popular's support of the 2002 proposition, but rejection of the one passed in 2003. As a spokesman explained, the party refused to support the second resolution because "dio ese debate por cerrado cuando aprobó, el 20 de noviembre de 2002, una moción de condena del franquismo" and "el PP cree que con la proposición no de ley aprobada precisamente un 20 de noviembre de 2002 queda cerrado el asunto" (Cué 2003) [it considered the debate closed when it approved, on November 20, 2002, the motion condemning Francoism . . . the PP believes that, with the proposition approved precisely on a 20th of November in 2002, that topic is closed].

Such a practice in which superficial remembering effectively entails forgetting, and where apparent forgetting allows for a past legacy to continue into the present, has, indeed, characterized the way in which post-Franco Spain has dealt with the memory of the civil war and Franco regime. As José Colmeiro explains: "el gran tabú colectivo de la transición ... es que la sociedad española todavía no ha reconocido su complicidad con el franquismo, ... prefiriendo el simulacro de la amnesia colectiva. Por todo ello, el retorno de lo reprimido se vuelve más visible, pero también menos operativo" (2005, 32) [the great collective taboo of the transition ... is that Spanish society has still not recognized its complicity with Francoism, ... preferring the simulacrum of collective amnesia. Because of this, the return of the repressed becomes more visible, but also less operative].

The governmental decree of 2002 may, in fact, prove to be one more example in which the repressed past of the civil war and Francoism returns in a visible, yet not highly operative, manner. As Colmeiro further explains, "se evidencia en la España contemporánea un aparente estado de identidad esquizofrénica, entre la imperante amnesia histórica generalizada y la excesiva gestualidad rememoradora" (2005, 32) [we see in contemporary Spain an apparent state of schizophrenic identity, between the reigning and generalized collective amnesia and the excessive rememorative gestures]. Indeed, with the Amnesty Law passed in 1977, believed to be necessary for a peaceful coexistence and reconciliation between different political groups, many believed the transition effectively instituted a culture of amnesia in which the memory of the civil war and the Franco regime became effectively taboo. The Amnesty Law pardoned those who had been accused of political opposition to the Franco regime, but it likewise guaranteed that anyone who had been part of the regime would not be held accountable for any past actions. Amnesty became amnesia, and the generalized consensus that emerged in the early transition seemed to fly in the face of the celebrated maxim by George Santayana claiming that those who do not remember the past are destined to repeat it. In Spain, quite to the contrary, the only agreement that all political forces seemed able to gather around at the time was that, in order not to repeat the past, it was best to forget it.[8]

However, as Colmeiro and others have noted, this "pact of forgetting" was operative even though novels, films, autobiographies, historical studies, and other works exploring the past of the civil war and Francoism began to appear after Franco's death. This paradox does, indeed, amount to a "schizophrenic" condition which can only be understood if we recognize that memory and forgetting are interrelated in complex ways, often working together instead of representing opposing forces.⁹

The Spanish historian Santos Juliá points to this paradox when he proposes that, instead of talking about a "pact of forgetting," or a collective amnesia instituted by the transition, we should understand this process by using the paradoxical Spanish expression "echar en el olvido" [to throw [something] into oblivion]. As he explains, citing the dictionary definition of this expression: "Echar al olvido, ú en olvido (*sic*). Frase que vale olvidarse voluntariamente de alguna cosa" (2003, 17) [To throw in or into oblivion. Phrase that means to voluntarily forget something]. As Juliá comments elsewhere: "Pero, ¿cómo podría olvidarse nadie voluntariamente de algo si al mismo tiempo no lo recordara, si sufriera amnesia? Se olvida voluntariamente sólo cuando se rescata el recuerdo de lo que se quiere olvidar" (2002, 17) [But, how could anybody voluntarily forget something if they did not at the same time remember it, if they suffered amnesia? One can only forget voluntarily when one rescues the memory of what one wants to forget]. This concept of "echar en el olvido" is useful for understanding some aspects of how post-Franco Spain has dealt with the past, for it holds remembering and forgetting in tension, without fully resolving the contradiction. However, inasmuch as Juliá presents the expression as a way to claim that there was no "pact of forgetting" at all during the transition, it is somewhat problematic, as will be explored later.

One example of the way in which the collective memories of the Second Republic, the civil war, and Francoism were both repressed *and* ever-present in the early stages of the transition to democracy is highlighted by Paloma Aguilar. While the predominant attitude, especially of the political elites, was that it was best to lay a subtle veil of silence over the past in order, supposedly, not to rekindle any violence, it is interesting to note that many of the formal elements of the new democratic system that emerged were consciously chosen to differ from those that had characterized the Second Republic. This demonstrates that the decision-making process during the early transition was, in fact, governed by a pervasive recollection of that earlier time period. As Aguilar explains, in the transition "a bicameral parliament was conceived (unlike the unicameral parliament of the 1930s) together with a different electoral law and a monarchic form of government instead of a Republic.... Consensus and negotiation, which were scarcely practised under the Republic, became the typical means of progressing under the Transition. At the same time, the reforms proposed in the 1970's were debated slowly and implemented gradually and moderately unlike the reforms passed under the Republic, which became the source of its most serious problems" (2002, 165–66). Thus, in the immediate post-Franco era, the memory of the past was ever-present, while, at the same time, the transition was being conceived as a historical tabula rasa, a completely new act in a play in which most major actors did not want to be reminded of their connections with any of the previous scenes.[10]

It is important to recognize, as both Santos Juliá and Paloma Aguilar have done, that there have been different ways in which the traumatic past of the civil war and Francoism has been repressed in post-Franco Spain. In the years immediately following Franco's death a generalized consensus emerged, actively promoted by the political elites and seemingly accepted by society at large, that it was better not to dig up the past for fear that another civil war might erupt. The attempted military coup in 1981 was seen, from this perspective, as a reminder of the very real possibility of such a return to violence.

From 1982 to 1996, however, with the Socialist Party in power, a slightly different justification for letting go of the past was added to that prevalent during the early years of the transition. Led by the Socialists, Spain embarked on a frenzied campaign to become "modernized" and "European," and dealing with the past was simply not compatible with such a forward-looking campaign.[11] During these years, the repressed past of the civil war and Francoism emerged every so often with special force, in dates such as the fiftieth anniversary of the beginning of the civil war in 1986 and the end of the war in 1989. The commemorations of these occasions were carefully contained so as not to produce a strong social demand to revisit the past in any significant manner. As Santos Juliá explains, "con la llegada del Partido Socialista al poder se pensó que la guerra y el franquismo pasaban a ser temas reservados a los historiadores. Se dieron por cerradas las heridas, y a otra cosa" (qtd. in Rojo 2004) [with the arrival in power of the Socialist Party, it was thought that the war and Francoism became topics reserved for historians. The wounds were considered closed, and on to something else].[12]

Attempting to limit any real debate about the past to the sphere dominated by historians was not the only strategy followed at this time to assure, as Colmeiro states, that the return of the repressed past should become "más visible, pero también menos operativo" (2005, 32) [more visible, but also less operative]. The 1992 celebrations in Spain, including the Olympics in Barcelona, the naming of Madrid as "European capital of culture," the "Expo" in Sevilla, and, of course, the grand, ubiquitous commemoration of the "Quinto Centenario del Descubrimiento de América" [Fifth Centennial of the Discovery of

America] achieved this objective by other means. These massive commercial ventures not only showcased Spain's newly acquired modernity to the world, but they managed to do so by presenting the image that Spain was dealing with its past (that of its colonial ventures in the case of the "Quinto Centenario"), yet, in essence, Spain was sidestepping any real confrontation with the most problematic aspects of her history. Despite the benefits gained from hosting these events, therefore, these celebrations reflected a major problem in Spain. According to Colmeiro, "estas grandes conmemoraciones espectaculares son operaciones masivas de olvido colectivo" (2005, 34) [these grand, spectacular commemorations are massive operations of collective forgetting]. With these grand commemorations, again, an apparent act of remembering became, in practice, an exercise in forgetting. The official attempt to frame the 1492–1992 commemoration as an "encuentro de culturas" [encounter of cultures] was particularly revealing in its desire to evade confrontation with the violence and suffering of the experience of conquest.[13]

Almost a decade later, a similar rhetoric evoking an "encounter" of cultures again enacts an official strategy of erasure of a violent past. This time, the violence and repression of the Franco regime within Spain are dismissed along with the earlier violence of Spanish colonial, imperial conquest abroad. In 2001, in an official speech granting the Cervantes Prize to author Francisco Umbral, King Juan Carlos exclaimed that "nunca fue la nuestra lengua de imposición, sino de encuentro; a nadie se obligó nunca a hablar en castellano: fueron los pueblos más diversos quienes hicieron suyos, por voluntad libérrima, el idioma de Cervantes" (qtd. in Marcos and Company 2001) [never was ours a language imposition, but of encounter; no one was ever forced to speak Castilian: of their own free will, the most diverse peoples made the language of Cervantes their own]. Official representatives of the autonomous regions of Spain complained that the statement seemed to deny that Castilian had ever been forcefully imposed during the Franco regime in regions such as Cataluña and the Basque country, and that Catalan and Basque were officially prohibited, as was, in fact, the case. In response to such complaints, the Minister of Education, Culture, and Sports of the then-ruling Popular Party, Pilar del Castillo, further minimized the repression of the Franco regime: "habría que ver cuándo se ha prohibido hablar una lengua en España y con qué intensidad" (qtd. in Espada 2001) [we would have to see when any language has been prohibited in Spain, and with what intensity]. Clearly, on more than one occasion, the official rhetoric of an "encounter of cultures" has effectively served to forget an uncomfortable past.[14]

These strategies of preventing any true confrontation with the past by either circumscribing it to historians' discussions or making it disappear with an ostentatious and commemorative sleight of hand became harder to maintain once the right-wing Partido Popular came to power in 1996. At this point, as Santos Juliá explains, "cuando triunfó el Partido Popular, empezaron a sonar nombres que eran los mismos que habían sonado durante el régimen de Franco. Se pensó que no habían cambiado mucho las cosas, y que la vieja derecha recuperaba su lugar de siempre. La historia volvió entonces a ser de todos y no sólo de los especialistas" (qtd. in Rojo 2004) [when the Partido Popular triumphed, the names that emerged were the same as those from the Franco regime. It seemed that things had not changed very much, and that the old right had recovered the place it had always enjoyed. History then again became something that belonged to everyone, and not only to specialists]. The new leaders of the Right continued to downplay their Francoist legacy (ideological and otherwise: the grandfather of the president of the Partido Popular at the time, José María Aznar, for example, was a close personal friend of Franco). However, the new anniversaries relating to the civil war and Francoism that took place during this time period (for example, the sixtieth anniversary of the beginning of the war in 1996, and the same anniversary of its end in 1999, as well as the twenty-fifth anniversary of Franco's death in 2000) were not so easily limited to historians' deliberations. It is significant, in this respect, that one of the first open debates held in a Spanish newspaper about whether Spain should "forget" or "assume" its recent past emerged in 1999, and marked a noticeable increase in articles of all kinds, from those written by historians to opinion pieces from ordinary citizens, regarding Spain's need to confront its Fascist past.[15]

The debate about how to confront Spain's Fascist past has thus only recently begun to be taken up by society at large in a manner that might lead to a more engaged confrontation with Spanish history. It is only at the beginning of the twenty-first century, after more than twenty-five years of democratic stability, that the return of this repressed past is perhaps occurring in a manner that is not simply superficial, but operative, following Colmeiro's terminology.[16] On a purely symbolic level, an unexpected return of the repressed past occurred at the end of the 2003 Davis Cup tennis championship in Melbourne when, by mistake, the Himno de Riego, the official hymn of the Second Republic, was played instead of the Marcha Real, the current Spanish national anthem. This caused an indignant outcry from the Spanish government, but, quite interestingly, led to many Spanish youth downloading the Republican hymn as the ringing melody on their cell phones (qtd. in Padilla 2004).

Many of these same cell phones may have been involved in an incident several months later in which the specter of the return of the repressed past in Spain had a much more significant impact. In the days between the March 11, 2004 terrorist train bombings in Madrid and the national elections on March 14 which the Socialist Party won, messages sent via personal cell phones contributed to a growing unease among the general population. These messages relayed many people's growing indignation at the belief that the then-ruling Partido Popular was manipulating information about who was responsible for the bombings. The perception that the Spanish government was not presenting accurate information to the people made many recall the censorship practices of the Franco era. The government, in fact, seemed to push the hypothesis that the Basque terrorist group ETA was responsible for the bombings when solid evidence already pointed to the responsibility of Al-Qaeda or some related Islamic terrorist group. Although this was not the only reason (among others, a majority of the Spanish population had opposed Spain's participation in the war in Iraq, and they resented the Aznar government's decision to participate despite that popular opposition), it was surely one of the factors that led to the defeat of the Partido Popular. This is so, in part, because it drove many people who had been planning to abstain from the elections, out of a generalized feeling of disenchantment with politics, to get out and vote for the Socialist Party. The return of the repressed past in Spain has thus recently had quite a real, and not merely symbolic, impact.[17]

The inaugural address of the newly elected Socialist prime minister, José Luis Rodríguez Zapatero, on April 15, 2004, is particularly interesting in this context. The repressed past again returns at the end of his presentation, but this time it is as a creed that Rodríguez Zapatero claims has guided him throughout his life. Spain's new prime minister ended his inaugural speech with a phrase taken from the testament of his grandfather, Juan Rodríguez Lozano, a captain in the Republican army who was executed for remaining loyal to the Republic by Nationalist forces shortly after the beginning of the civil war. The last words of Rodríguez Zapatero's inaugural address were: "un ansia infinita de paz, el amor al bien y el mejoramiento social de los humildes" [an infinite desire for peace, a love of what is good, and the social betterment of the poor]. This phrase not only reflects the weight of the past on Rodríguez Zapatero's personal life, but signals, hopefully, a broader change within Spanish society. The head of the new government was recalling the civil war in his first official remarks instead of evading any recollection of it, and he was subtly admitting the existence of an unpaid debt toward the victims of that past.

It still remains to be seen if the memory of the civil war and Francoism under Rodríguez Zapatero's government will become something more than a superficial commemoration. It is not yet clear whether the memory of the war evoked in his speech will engender a process that will, in some real measure, "do justice to the dead" of Francoist repression, justice to the memory of individuals like Rodríguez Zapatero's or Emilio Silva's respective grandfathers. There are, at least, some encouraging signs. In September 2004, the Socialist-led government passed a decree calling for the creation of an inter-ministerial commission to produce a report that explores ways in which the government could later devise a law to provide "judicial and moral" rehabilitation to the victims of Francoist repression (Cué 2004). This "Law of historical memory," as it is informally called, is a concrete, practical measure that is long overdue. It is believed that the commission will explore, among other matters, ways in which the criminal files of Republican prisoners may be revised retroactively in order to clear their names of the crimes of which they may have been unjustly accused. It may also develop official policies that would guarantee some form of compensation and "rehabilitation" for the victims of Francoism. The commission may propose suggestions for how to devise official policies to support, both morally and economically, the work of organizations like the ARMH in their task of exhuming the mass graves throughout Spain. Such policies may include regulations that provide open access to archives where information about the Francoist repression is found, archives that are still, in many cases, inaccessible to those who need to do relevant research. The law that is expected to be developed based on the initial report by the commission may also propose a policy for dealing in a systematic manner with the many places of memory inherited from Francoism (in the form of statues, plaques, street names, etc.) that still exist throughout Spain, and which are becoming increasingly contested sites, as well as for creating one or more official places of memory to the victims of Francoism.[18] Such a plan may reflect the growing demand from various organizations and institutions that the Valle de los Caídos [Valley of the Fallen] be adapted in some way for this purpose, for example, by creating a permanent museum, exhibit, or learning or research center on Francoism and Francoist repression within the site.[19]

The commission, however, has had to extend the deadline for the presentation of its report several times because of the difficulty in accommodating the different demands from various organizations that have testified before it, as well as in conceiving of practical measures to deal with many of the aforementioned issues. Furthermore, it is particularly significant that, in one of these announced delays, the reason given was that the government wanted to make sure that the final proposed law would accommodate both sides of the civil war, even if the law was still intended to focus primarily on those victimized by the Nationalist side. This need to revert to a supposed "balanced" perspective is a problematic throwback to the rhetoric predominant throughout much of the transition. Such rhetoric continues to hide, under the apparently reasonable logic of a need to represent both sides, the fact that each side has not had equal access to recognition and redress for the crimes committed against it, neither during nor after the Franco regime (Cué 2005a).[20]

This is precisely one of the main points of the 2005 Amnesty International report on Spain: "España: poner fin al silencio y a la injusticia. La deuda pendiente con las víctimas de la guerra civil española y del régimen franquista" [Spain: putting an end to silence and injustice. The pending debt with the victims of the Spanish civil war and the Franco regime]. As the report states, talking about the executions, disappearances, incarcerations, and other such "crimes against humanity" systematically enacted by the Nationalist forces during the civil war and the Franco regime in the postwar era: "el conjunto de abusos y crímenes contra el derecho internacional que fueron perpetrados durante dicho periodo, no fue una dimensión abordada por la transición, como tampoco lo fueron los derechos de las víctimas que fueron privadas de verdad, justicia y reparación, y a contar con recursos efectivos para hacer valer sus derechos" (Amnesty International 2005, 9) [the problem of the abuses and crimes against international law perpetrated during that time period was not an issue which was faced during the transition, neither were the rights of the victims, who were deprived of the truth, of justice, of reparations, and of the effective recourses to implement their rights]. The report further explains "los derechos de las víctimas no pueden ignorarse bajo la noción genérica de responsabilidades atribuidas a ambos bandos. Amnistía Internacional considera que el esclarecimiento imparcial de estos hechos, sus autores y la naturaleza de los crímenes es una tarea pendiente" (Amnesty International 2005, 11) [the rights of the victims cannot be ignored under the generic notion of responsibilities attributed to both sides. Amnesty International considers that the impartial investigation of these acts, of the authors and of the nature of the crimes, is a task that still needs to be fulfilled].

The report further claims that access to concrete knowledge about the perpetration of human rights abuses is a basic human right, and that, in the case of systematic violations by a political regime in the past, governments in the present are bound by international human rights legislation to make such access to knowledge adequately available to society. This has still not been achieved in Spain. Concrete measures are presented that the current Spanish government could take to guarantee this basic human right to Spanish society, and specific suggestions are made for how to implement policies that would likewise provide some form of reparation to the victims of such crimes, or to their families. Such reparations, in fact, can only be implemented once the basic human right to full knowledge about the crimes is ensured. Significantly, the report specifies that such measures to guarantee adequate knowledge and compensation for having suffered human rights abuses due to crimes against humanity cannot be denied in the name of any past amnesty law, as such crimes against humanity are considered "imprescriptible." This clearly indicates that no Spanish government can continue to forego the aforementioned tasks, which it is obliged to undertake according to international human rights law, because of the Amnesty Law of 1977 (Amnesty International 2005, 12, 23). It remains to be seen if the report of the interministerial commission, and the subsequent "Law of historical memory," will, in fact, respond adequately to the challenges posed by the Amnesty International report and finally implement real practical measures that are long overdue, or if they will ultimately provide little more than a symbolic gesture, devoid of any real consequence, as has happened so many times in the recent past in Spain.[21]

Whatever the final, revised law may turn out to be, the fact remains that the ongoing work of the ARMH, and other such civic organizations, has been an important force in creating a greater public awareness of the unresolved human rights problem in Spain. That a civic organization, created by ordinary citizens, may thus ultimately have a significant influence on government policy is perhaps one of the strongest indications of the difference between the current political climate in Spain and that of the early stages of the transition. As Jordi Solé Tura, a member of the first democratically elected Congress during the transition as well as of the committee that drafted the 1978 constitution, explains, one of the greatest weaknesses of the early transition was that the decision-making process was handled by the party elites in a secretive manner which did not encourage a broad-based social and political mobilization. This eventually led to the rapid transformation of society's hopes for change into a generalized "desencanto" [disenchantment] with the political process (1987, 29). Peter McDonough and others likewise highlight the fact that a markedly low level of civic engagement on the part of Spanish citizens not only is a legacy of almost forty years of dictatorship, but is partly due to the manner in which the political elites orchestrated the transition process: "Spain shows signs of Democracy light. Democratic procedures are solidly in place, but participation seems to have stagnated.... The participatory deficit in Spain is a by-product of the ethos of tolerance and bargaining that pervaded the transition from Francoism. The viability of Spanish democracy has been achieved at some cost to its quality" (1998, 1).[22]

It is within this context that the true importance of the work of civic organizations, such as the ARMH and others, must be measured. The active engagement and initiative of so many citizens within these organizations thus reflects not only a growing awareness within Spanish society that the time has come for Spain to confront its past, but also a potentially healthy change in the very functioning of the democratic process itself. As Helen Graham claims, referring to the work of these organizations: "memory work that emanates from civil society is inherently more healing and more useful in terms of building a democratic culture" (2005, 146). These organizations, furthermore, function as "memory entrepreneurs," which, according to Elizabeth Jelin, are essential for what she calls the "labors of memory" to be implemented in a healthy and effective way within society (2003, 33, 5). It is important to stress, however, that the welcome emergence of such a healthy civic initiative does not, in the least, diminish the need for effective governmental policy in these matters.[23]

It is not coincidental that for both Emilio Silva and José Luis Rodríguez Zapatero the need to address the legacy of the civil war and Francoism in today's Spain emerges from a desire to vindicate the experience of their respective grandfathers. This reveals another important change between the present moment and that of the early transition. As Santos Juliá and Paloma Aguilar explain, that Spanish society in the last few years seems to have begun to accept that it has to deal with the past in a way it has not done throughout the transition is in part because a new generation has achieved maturity in Spain. This generation has come to be known as "la generación de los nietos de los vencidos" (Rojo) [the generation of the grandchildren of the vanquished]. As Juliá and Aguilar explain:

> Ahora ha llegado una generación que no vivió la guerra, que ni siquiera vivió la dictadura y que, por tanto, vuelve atrás y responde a los datos de la historia desde otra mirada.... Ahora son los nietos de quienes vivieron la guerra los que toman la palabra. Y lo hacen sin culpa y sin miedo. No pueden ser acusados de connivencia con el régimen de Franco, ni padecen el miedo a la represión que atenazaba a quienes padecieron la dictadura, de ahí que su visión sea más libre.... La generación de los nietos de los vencidos... tiene la imperiosa necesidad de hacer justicia a sus abuelos, de ver reconocidas públicamente su lucha, su sacrificio y también el sufrimiento de sus familiares, que se vieron obligados a guardar silencio durante el fran-

quismo y a muchos de los que aún atenazaba el miedo y la impotencia a la muerte de Franco. (qtd. in Rojo 2004)

[Now there has emerged a generation that did not live through the war, that did not even experience the dictatorship, and that, therefore, looks back and reacts to the events of history from another perspective. . . . Now it is the grandchildren of those who lived the war who speak up. And they do so without any guilt or fear. They cannot be accused of connivance with Franco's regime, nor do they have the fear of repression that tortured those who suffered the dictatorship, and therefore their vision is freer. . . . The generation of the grandchildren of the vanquished . . . has the imperious need to do justice to their grandparents, to make visible their struggle and sacrifice, as well as the suffering of their families, who were forced to be silent during the regime and many of whom were still tortured by fear and impotence after Franco's death.]

According to Juliá and Aguilar, the coming of age of this new generation is one of the factors that have made it possible for a new perspective toward the past to emerge in the last few years. This perspective is no longer caught in the ideological paradigm of the "dos Españas" [two Spains] of earlier generations, and can thus be more open to accepting responsibility towards the past and seeking more information about Spanish history. This new perspective has emerged due to the temporal distance, as well as the generational connection through family ties, between this younger generation and the era of the civil war and Franco's regime.

However, if these observations by Juliá and Aguilar are encouraging, there are other more disheartening indications that point to a disturbing lack of knowledge about the past among many young Spaniards. Armengou and Belis point to a recent poll among Spanish youth that seems much less encouraging than the observations by Juliá and Aguilar: "según una reciente encuesta (*El País*, 19-10-2002), nada menos que el 33.8% de la juventud española de 12 a 18 años cree que una dictadura puede ser necesaria en ocasiones o que tanto da que tengamos dictadura o democracia siempre y cuando haya orden y progreso (eslogan del franquismo)" (2004, 16) [according to a recent poll (*El País*, 10-19-2002), no less than 33.8% of Spanish youth between the ages of 12 and 18 believe that a dictatorship may be necessary at times, or that it does not matter whether we have a dictatorship or a democracy, as long as we have order and progress (a Francoist slogan)]. A third of the youth interviewed had such little consciousness of what a dictatorship entails that they claim they would accept one willingly if it upheld "order and progress." These two terms were, of course, part of the tirelessly repeated slogans of the late Franco regime, and their easy assimilation in the discourse of Spanish youth today highlights a troubling level of ignorance on their part as to the realities of life under Franco. The tenacity of a rhetoric that holds these social factors as desirable qualities, above and beyond political freedom and democracy, likewise points to the way a certain legacy of Francoism persists in contemporary Spanish society.

The echoing by a considerable percentage of this younger generation of the very same slogan used by the late Franco regime to legitimize its power is quite revealing. Santos Juliá explains that, according to polls, many Spaniards do not have as negative a view of Franco as other societies, like Germany and Italy, have of their past Fascist leaders. There are, of course, many reasons for this difference, some of which are of an international and not purely national nature; others are related to Franco's exceptionally long rule, and still others involve the unimaginable horror that characterized the Holocaust. Juliá explains that one such reason for this ambiguous valorization that many Spaniards have of Franco is that most people today, if they lived through the regime at all, remember above all the later years, those in which the political repression was not as harsh as immediately after the civil war (qtd. in Valenzuela 2002). In the sixties and early seventies there was still a lack of political liberties in Spain, to be sure, but this time period also saw the beginning of an economic development that improved the quality of life for a large percentage of the population. The relative weight of this last phase of Franco's rule in Spaniards' recollections of the regime is what makes it all the more important for there to be works of all kinds, fictional and nonfictional, that explore those earlier, and harsher, years of the regime, as well as the civil war. As Juliá exclaims, "por eso son aun más necesarios los ejercicios de ficción o no ficción que recuerden—descubran en muchos casos a millones de españoles—los horrores sobre los que se cimentó aquella dictadura" (qtd. in Valenzuela 2002) [that is why it is all the more necessary to have fictional as well as non-fictional works that remind people of –in the case of millions of Spaniards, that teach them about– the horrors on which that dictatorship was founded"]. All of the texts analyzed in the following chapters are examples of such works.

It is important to note that the Francoist slogan, "order and progress," evoked by the young Spaniards polled in 2002, was originally intended by the regime to have the same legitimizing effect as that of the "25 años de paz" [25 years of peace] which the regime coined in 1964 to celebrate the twenty-fifth anniversary of its victory in the civil war. The massive commemoration that the regime organized in 1964 served a function similar, although by other means, to those that the Socialist government held in the 1990s. In both cases, the very same commemorations that were supposedly intended to remember the past were in reality helping to forget it.

In 1964, the regime wished to subtly shift the rhetoric by means of which it justified its rule. In the years after the war, it had sought an origin-based legitimacy by keeping the civil war ever-present in official proclamations, arguing for the regime's existence as the logical outcome of its victory in what it called the "crusade" against the "anti-Spain" of the Second Republic. By 1964, however, the regime wished to develop a discourse based on a performance-based legitimacy. To this end, it needed to downplay the memory of the war that it had emphasized in its earlier rhetoric, and emphasize the economic development that it was starting to generate. As Aguilar explains, it is quite significant that the massive commemoration "25 years of peace (1939–1964)" organized in 1964 to achieve this change in discourse established the time frame to be commemorated as beginning in 1939. The celebration thus *excluded* the civil war and effectively began a process whereby the war became less and less present in the regime's official discourse. It is especially revealing, in this context, that an original grand commemoration had been proposed for 1961, but was later bypassed in favor of that of 1964. The 1961 celebration, entitled "25 años de vida española (1936–1961)" [25 years of Spanish life (1936–1961)], would have included the years of the civil war within its commemorative enterprise. The 1964 commemoration, therefore, was instrumental in ushering in a change of rhetoric that would make it possible to substitute the traumatic memory of the civil war which marked the beginning of Franco's regime with a more palatable memory of the economic "peace," as well as "order and progress," generated by the regime in its later years (Aguilar 2002, 112–28). The long-term success of this strategy is in part made evident by the poll of Spanish youth in 2002.

It is thus clear that to appropriately understand the paradoxical interrelation of remembering and forgetting the past which has characterized the transition, one must recognize that this process had already begun during the Franco era, particularly with the change of rhetoric evidenced in the 1964 commemoration. This conviction is reflected in my study, as the earliest texts analyzed date from the 1960s. These texts, in various ways, resist the process whereby Spanish society was being encouraged to forget the most traumatic aspects of the past in favor of a more palatable view of "progress" presented by the regime. The explicit reflection the texts provide on the way remembering and forgetting are inextricably connected is, in fact, one of the ways in which they resist the strategy of late Francoism which clothed a process of forgetting in a celebration supposedly meant to remember the past. The rest of the texts studied cover every decade between the 1960s and the 1990s, and the conclusion briefly relates the discussion of these texts to works published in the last few years. The time frame for my study underscores the importance of recognizing the continuities, when analyzing the problem that Spanish society has had with facing its past, between the late Franco regime and the post-Franco era.

Emilio Silva has often highlighted such continuities when describing what led him to found the ARMH, as well as some of the obstacles he has encountered in the process. Many of the elements that have emerged in the previous discussion reappear in Silva's commentary about the work of the ARMH:

> El hecho de que hayamos emergido los nietos reivindicando la memoria de nuestros abuelos desaparecidos ha sido algo inesperado para ciertos sectores políticos, porque representa que tendríamos que estar contentos porque España ha tenido una transición estable que nos permite tener el carro de la compra lleno, y de pronto somos como una especie de mala mutación, vamos a decirlo así, que nos hemos preocupado de esto.... Aquí hay un gran problema de derechos humanos, y en este país se ha tapado la nariz mucha gente, a derechas y a izquierdas. Han hecho la movida madrileña, los felices ochenta, etcetera.... y estaban bailando sobre una España sembrada de cadáveres. (Silva and Macías 2003, 191)

> The fact that the grandchildren of the vanquished have emerged, vindicating the memory of our disappeared grandparents, has been quite unexpected for certain political sectors, since we should have been happy because Spain has had a stable transition that has allowed us to have a full shopping cart, and so suddenly we are like a bad mutation, so to say, because we have cared about these things.... We have here a great problem of human rights, which is that in this country many people have held their noses, on the right and on the left. They have had the "movida" in Madrid, the happy eighties, etc.... and they were all dancing on a Spain strewn with corpses.

To fully assume the exercise of memory regarding Spain's repressive past, one has to counter the discourse of progress that is dominant at the time. This is evoked in Silva's rejection of an ideology in which having a full shopping cart becomes synonymous with a healthy transition to democracy.[24] Manuel Reyes Mate has also stressed the important role that civic organizations like the ARMH have had in pushing an otherwise reluctant political and legal establishment in Spain to accept responsibility for the problem of the mass graves. He further agrees with Emilio Silva that the effectiveness of this new social movement will depend precisely on their going beyond the process of exhumations, tremendously important in itself, to generating a critique of an entire social structure whose well-being is built upon its failure to assume a responsibility for the victims of past repression. As he claims, the members of this new generation "no se van a contentar con llevar los restos a un cementerio, sino que acabarán preguntándose por una civilización que ha montado el progreso sobre una tierra con tantos cadáveres" (Reyes Mate 2003c) [they will not be content with taking the remains to a cemetery, they will eventually question a whole civilization that has created its progress on a land full of corpses]. A similar tension is explored in every one of the texts studied in the following chapters. In fact, it will become clear that such a conscious and explicit resistance to such discourses of progress in the name of practices of remembrance is one of the essential factors that will make memory become an "operative" and not merely superficial practice in these texts.

An example of a member of the generation of the grandchildren whose ideas echo those of Reyes Mate and Silva is a young man interviewed in Montse Armengou and Ricard Belis's book *Las fosas del silencio,* as well as in the documentary on which the book is based. With help from the ARMH, José Antonio Landera, a "guardia civil" [civil guard], has exhumed and given proper burial to the remains of his grandfather's brother, José Landera Cachón, killed early in the civil war by Nationalist forces and left in a mass grave in Prado de Paradiña, in León. Landera is not content, however, with the process of exhumation and reburial, but sees his work as going beyond this task: "si empezamos a desenterrar cadáveres, pero sin recuperar la memoria, sin hacer un archivo de la represión; si sólo metemos una excavadora y un arqueólogo y sólo sacamos huesos, lo estaremos haciendo mal: esa persona desaparecerá otra vez" (Armengon and Belis 2004, 219) [if we begin to disinter bodies, but without recovering memory, without creating an archive of repression; if we only bring in an excavator and an archaeologist, and we only recover the bones, then we are doing a bad job: that person will disappear once more]. He exclaims, furthermore, that helping others of his generation learn about this aspect of history is just as important a task for him as is the exhumation itself: "mi objetivo no sólo era recuperar sus restos, saber dónde estaba, sino intentar recuperar la memoria de este hombre y que la gente de mi edad, que no hemos conocido la historia porque nadie nos la ha contado, podamos saber qué pasó" (2004, 220) [my objective was not only to recover his remains, to know where he was, but to try to recover the story of this man, so that people my age, who do not know this history because no one has taught it to us, may know what happened].

Such a perspective is helpful in its recognition that the exhumations must be understood not only as a problem of proper mourning and appropriate reburial, despite how important these are in their own right. They must become a catalyst for a greater process that seeks to develop appropriate educational measures and critical practices in society to combat social apathy, ignorance, and the multiple forms of resistance to confronting the legacies of the past in present-day Spain, such as a continued reluctance on the government's part to implement appropriate measures of redress for those who have suffered human rights violations, or the continued maintenance of laws that guarantee immunity to those who committed such violations.

Landera's concerns about the need to go beyond the process of proper reburial and mourning to engage in a broader process of social education and critique may be seen to echo the argument presented by Lessie Jo Frazier, in the context of postdictatorship Chile, who calls for a practice of "countermourning." She studies the case of human rights groups in Chile who do not accept the proper reburial and building of official monuments to the victims of the military dictatorship as the end of their work, especially when such efforts are undertaken within the context of official amnesty decrees that guarantee impunity to the perpetrators of the crimes. For these groups, exhumations of mass graves of the disappeared cannot lead solely to a process of mourning whereby one comes to terms with past atrocities, for such coming to terms with the past is impossible for these groups, when no proper *accountability* for past crimes has been sought at an institutional level. As Frazier explains, "rather than politics as mourning, by allowing themselves to be haunted, these orphans of regime transition effect a countermourning that refuses to relinquish the past and gropes toward a politics that might alloy their memories' integrity with a vision for the future" (1999, 105). Like Landera in Spain, such individuals worry that erecting monuments for the proper burial of the disappeared, while necessary and just, may make the victim "disappear once more," if that task is not connected to a broader demand for justice and accountability.[25]

The image that Frazier evokes of a practice of "countermourning" that allows one to be "haunted" by the disappeared, as well as the images that Silva and Reyes Mate presented earlier, in which Spain's grand celebrations of progress and development are seen as taking place on a land strewn with corpses, are particularly important. The corpses evoked emerge as ghosts, whose haunting presence is felt even though they are nowhere to be seen. They interrupt the festivities reminding the living of an unpaid debt to the past. That these corpses have been improperly buried, and have been ignored for so long, is precisely what transforms them into ghosts, and what forces them eventually to reemerge from oblivion. As Jo Labanyi explains, "ghosts are the return of the repressed of history—that is, the mark of an all-too-real historical trauma which has been erased from conscious memory but which makes its presence felt through its ghostly traces" (2002, 6). The image of the ghost, of someone who haunts the living because he or she has not received proper burial, reappears in every one of the following chapters. The practices of memory these texts present engage in various ways with the "ghostly traces" of a previously repressed history of trauma. These traces, however, can only be recognized once the dominant discourses of "order and progress," of "peace," "stability," and "modernization" are shattered, thus allowing those traces of a previously repressed past to emerge through the cracks.[26] All the texts studied in the following chapters thus explore ways to help us stop dancing and celebrating over a land strewn with corpses. They provide much-needed examples of how to appropriately address the ghosts who may be present, even if invisible, at the scene, but who are certainly not part of the celebration.

We may now understand that it is to the power of such ghosts that Aguilar and Juliá were referring when they explained that members of the generation to which Silva and Rodríguez Zapatero belong have an "imperious need to do justice to their grandparents, to make visible their struggle and sacrifice, as well as the suffering of their families" (qtd. in Rojo 2004). This recognition is particularly significant, for it ultimately undermines the use that Juliá himself has made of the expression "echar en el olvido," a phrase he proposes to describe how the past of the civil war and Francoist repression has, in fact, been confronted during the transition. For Juliá, the use of this phrase supposedly invalidates what others claim when they affirm that the amnesty law of 1977 effectively implied a form of collective amnesia. As Juliá claims, "Una sociedad no podrá amnistiar, echar al olvido, un pasado si no lo recuerda con claridad, si carece de la conciencia de lo que ese pasado fue, si lo ha dejado caer en el olvido" (2003, 17) [a society will not be able to amnesty, or throw into oblivion, a past if it does not remember it clearly, if it lacks a consciousness of what that past was, if it allows for it to fall into oblivion]. In support of his claim that in this process of "echar en el olvido" Spanish society effectively confronted its traumatic past, even as it was deciding not to return to it in a way that could ignite old controversies, Juliá points to the many texts of all kinds, fictional as well as historical, that have been published about the civil war and Francoism since Franco's death. He especially seems to refer to the historical investigation to which his own professional work belongs. All these texts, far from having forgotten the past, have been "investigándolo y publicándolo hasta el último detalle" (2003, 24) [researching and publishing it up to the last detail]. He further claims that with this historical work, "Hemos investigado, publicado y hablado de nuestro reciente pasado hasta la saciedad" (2003, 18) [we have investigated, published and spoken of our recent past to satiety].

The hyperbolic element of these assertions is interesting not just because it is, in fact, a highly problematic claim (is it *ever* possible to research the past and publish about it "up to the last detail," and "to satiety"?) but especially because it seems to reveal a somewhat defensive reaction on Juliá's part. This reaction is perhaps based on the fear that any affirmation that the past has not been appropriately confronted in post-Franco Spain does not acknowledge all the valuable historical work that has been published during that time. But in highlighting the undoubtedly meritorious work that such historical investigation has produced, and in claiming that such work proves that the past was in no way "forgotten," Juliá is circumscribing the process of remembering to only one of various levels at which such remembrance must take place in order for there to be an effective practice, in society at large, of working through the past. Javier Tusell, another professional historian, responds to Juliá's argument by claiming that such a process of remembering the past has to function at three basic levels in society: that of the political elites, that of the intellectual class, and that of society at large. One could add here that even within these levels, no one homogeneous process of remembering or forgetting the past exists, either. Whatever would constitute the process of remembering or forgetting the past that is achieved in society at large, for example, is necessarily a combination of many separate practices taken up by various sectors, groups, generations, institutions, each of them with a different level of access to power and capacity to influence others. Despite the fact that professional historians have, indeed, produced much valuable historical research on the civil war and Francoist repression, Tusell believes that the political elites demonstrated too excessive a fear of confronting the most difficult aspects of that past in the name of creating a political consensus during the transition (2003, 37). In this respect, it must be acknowledged that any "pact of forgetting" during the transition, even one that would imply, as Juliá claims, some amount of keeping the past present while it was being forgotten in the name of a peaceful reconciliation, was by no means a pact among equal political forces. The unequal power of the political forces on the Right and the Left during the transition is essential to keep in mind when understanding the unequal effect that such a political pact had on different sectors of society.

Most important of all, however, is the fact highlighted by Tusell that, despite all the historical writings produced in post-Franco Spain, such knowledge has not been adequately disseminated throughout society at large, and thus, according to him, despite the value of such historical work: "esa fuerza purificadora de la verdad no se ha hecho presente en la sociedad española" (2003, 37) [that purifying force of the truth has not been made present in Spanish society]. Indeed, if the past had been researched, investigated, and spoken about "to satiety" in Spain, why would organizations like the ARMH have had to emerge, organizations led by individuals who are moved by the "imperious need to do justice to their grandparents, to make visible their struggle and sacrifice"? If the past had been investigated "up to the last detail," why did Amnesty International have to produce a report in 2005 urging the Spanish government to develop some kind of policy and official institution to help these individuals gain access to adequate knowledge of the crimes against humanity committed during and after the war? Why is that knowledge not already available to them? That knowledge, in fact, is a basic human right that is still unmet, a right necessary for the subsequent guarantee of other rights such as due compensation for having suffered violations, of various kinds, systematically imposed by a repressive regime. Despite its useful ability to keep remembering and forgetting within a dynamic tension instead of seeing them as mutually exclusive, Juliá's expression of "echar en el olvido" is thus problematic, in part, because it does not adequately acknowledge the different levels at which the process of confronting the past must take place within society. In this sense, the very fact that one single, general process of "echar en el olvido" is invoked is problematic, as it would be more appropriate, if anything, to talk about multiple practices of "echar en el olvido," practices that function differently, with very different effects, at different levels, and within different segments of society.

Interestingly, even though Juliá refers to the work of Paul Ricoeur to present examples of practices of "echar en el olvido" (from various national contexts in different historical periods), that supposedly serve to better understand this practice in contemporary Spain, he does not heed a warning that Ricoeur himself presents in the very same work from which Juliá takes those examples.[27]

In *Memory, History, Forgetting*, Ricoeur warns that an excessive concern for achieving political consensus and reconciliation at times of political transition may inhibit the development of appropriate venues for the emergence of a fruitful and healthy practice of controversy to emerge in society at large, where competing claims and views about the past can be presented in the name of a healthy dialogue, and not as political weapons against others. Against such an excessive concern for consensus, Ricoeur calls for the development, also, of an appropriate practice of what he calls *dissensus*. Ricoeur borrows this term from Mark Osiel's study *Mass Atrocity, Collective Memory, and the Law*. Here, Osiel studies various criminal trials of the second half of the twentieth century, such as those in Nuremberg, Tokyo, Argentina, and France, and argues, as Ricoeur explains, for the benefits of "the *dissensus* provoked by the trials' public proceedings and . . . the educational function exerted by this very *dissensus* on the level of public opinion and collective memory" (Ricoeur 2004, 323). Such a practice of *dissensus* would guard against the potentially repressive aspects of a consensus that creates an artificial sense of unity where divisions from the past still exist, and still need to be worked through. Such *dissensus*, in fact, implies an educational process throughout society at large, and the development of an atmosphere in which controversy can lead to greater knowledge of the past and not to conflict among different factions in the present. As Ricoeur explains, "is it not a defect in this imaginary unity that it erases from the official memory the example of crimes likely to protect the future from the errors of the past and, by depriving public opinion of the benefits of *dissensus*, of condemning competing memories to an unhealthy underground existence?" (2004, 455). This kind of healthy *dissensus* is precisely what Spanish society has not developed, in part because there has been no public trial or truth commission to deal with the Franco regime, and its repressive practices, which could have generated this kind of debate. In her book *State Repression and the Labors of Memory*, Elizabeth Jelin makes a similar claim about the dangers of focusing too obsessively on the need for consensus during political transitions, a focus that ultimately does not allow for the development of "legitimate spaces for the expression and controversy about different memories. A democratic order would imply, therefore, the recognition of plurality and conflict more than the hope for reconciliations, silences, or erasures by fiat. This recognition of conflict, however, has to be anchored strongly in the rule of law" (2003, 105).

Juliá's defense of the practice of "echar en el olvido," which may have worked during the early transition to guarantee a policy of consensus and reconciliation, does not leave enough space for practices that allow for a healthy *dissensus* to emerge in Spanish society at large. What is particularly striking is that Juliá's own observation about the changes ushered in by the "generation of the grandchildren" should open the way for a beneficial shift in the focus from the excessive need for consensus toward a recognition of the benefits of *dissensus*. As we saw earlier, Juliá explains that this younger generation "looks back and reacts to the events of history from another perspective.... They cannot be accused of connivance with Franco's regime, nor do they have the fear of repression that tortured those who suffered the dictatorship, and therefore their vision is freer" (qtd. in Rojo 2004). The "new perspective" and "freer vision" of this generation is exactly what may allow them to engage with the past with a healthy level of *dissensus*, and eventually help the rest of society to develop such a healthy attitude to the past. In this sense, Juliá's implicit argument for the continued relevance of the focus on consensus in his defense of the practice of "echar en el olvido" misses an opportunity to shift the debate toward a healthier paradigm in which *dissensus*, as well as consensus, is valued.

In his analysis of the mass graves in Spain, Ulrich Winter argues precisely for the way in which the process of exhumations may help generate a new perspective toward the past that reflects something akin to a healthy *dissensus*, as defined by Ricoeur, and a salutary "recognition of plurality and conflict," as expressed by Jelin. Echoing Jelin's expression, Winter suggests that the mass graves be seen not so much as a place of memory, but as a "lugar de reconocimiento" (2005, 26) [place of recognition]. The expression "lugar de reconocimiento" is particularly felicitous for not only does it evoke a site that enables a process of competing versions of the past to emerge and be acknowledged, in a process of "reconocimiento" [recognition], but it also implies the need for "conocimiento" [knowledge] of the past in the first place. Such knowledge, in fact, is necessary before any process of supposed reconciliation can appropriately be sought at all. It is this knowledge of the past that was not made appropriately available to Spanish society before the reconciliation was supposedly ushered in by the transition. Such "places of recognition," according to Winter, are ones that are "escabrosos y dislocados, pero que posibilitan un proceso social de reconocimento entre memorias conflictivas" (2005, 23) [scabrous and dislocated, but that allow for a social process of recognition of conflicting memories].

The dislocated nature of such places of recognition points to the fact that they are not perfect and unitary, not fixed and stable. They are not so much a place, as a process. They must, therefore, be constantly negotiated and renegotiated. As Winter further explains:

> Acontecimientos, monumentos, símbolos o interpretaciones de éstos que niegan esta dislocación –bien sea por la reconciliación coactiva entre pasado y presente, como se dio en la transición, o por la exclusión del Otro y de la memoria misma, como en el caso del Valle de los Caídos– difícilmente

podrían convertirse en referentes de los múltiples colectivos de un Estado como España. Dentro del marco de una política del reconocimiento, el conflicto entre memorias, lejos de ser un defecto, es constitutivo de las identidades culturales. (2005, 28)

[Events, monuments, symbols or interpretations of these that deny this dislocation—be it in the name of a coerced reconciliation between past and present, as occurred during the transition, or due to the exclusion of the Other and of memory itself, as in the Valley of the Fallen—will not easily become referents for the multiple collectivities in a state like Spain. Within the framework of a policy of recognition, the conflict of memories, far from being a defect, is constitutive of cultural identities.]

If the exhumations of mass graves, and all the work being done around this process such as the recollection of oral testimonies, historical investigation, and archival research, are to be effective in Spain, they must help contribute to an ongoing process in which different and opposing memories are allowed to enter into conflict within a healthy process of *dissensus* that can ultimately be taken up by society at large.

Something similar, in fact, is expressed by two of the young cultural anthropologists who are working with interdisciplinary teams currently performing exhumations in Spain. Francisco Ferrándiz, for example, presents the image of the mass graves, and the very process of the exhumations, as a "resonance box" (2005a, 3) where various different and competing memories come together and are negotiated in an open-ended process. Ignacio Fernández de Mata likewise sees the mass graves and the performance of exhumations as "spaces of mediation for the negotiation of a hidden and convulsive past" (2005, 20). It is very important to recognize this process of negotiation among different memories that emerges with the exhumations, a process that does, indeed, convert these graves into "places of recognition."

In this sense, the exhumation of these graves cannot be seen simply as a "recovery" of memory, and the very name of the most important organization coordinating this process, (Association for the Recovery of Historical Memory [ARMH]), is actually misleading. For there is no memory or history that is simply being "recovered" from the past in this process. There are multiple memories and histories that are emerging, and, more than being "recovered," they are being produced within competing discourses in the present. It is very easy to think that the disinterred bones, because of their very materiality, because they seem to have a history of violence inscribed right *on* them, in the form of fractures, bullet holes, and so both, do, in fact, embody a history and a memory that has been silenced, buried for too long, a history and a memory that are now being "recovered." But, as Ferrándiz explains, "the meaning attached to exhumed bones depends heavily on the junctures and dissonances among diverse memory plots and idioms that emerge and compete around them" (2005a, 1). Fernández de Mata echoes this idea when he states: "despite their definite materiality and impartial existence, once they are in the open bones are not neutral scripts" (2005, 15). The competing "memory plots and idioms" that are creating the very meaning, the script, of the disinterred bones include, among others, the testimonies of witnesses and family members of the victims, the discourses of the various professionals performing the exhumations, the perspectives of the members of organizations like the ARMH and other volunteers helping with the process, the claims made about these events by politicians of all kinds and of various political inclinations, the coverage of the mass media presenting these events to a larger public, the multiple views of that public itself about the exhumations, and the many discourses by critics, professors, historians, and others that will frame these events in different ways. In this sense, the mass graves and their exhumations are, indeed, "places of recognition," places in which multiple forms of knowledge, and of acknowledgment of differences, arise. And the process begun by this practice of "recognition" will, in fact, continue well beyond the reburial of the human remains found in the mass graves. If that practice of proper reburial is essential, and a right that should be guaranteed to all, this process of "recognition," which should continue long after the reburial is performed, is just as important.[28] This "recognition" hopefully will lead to a process of remembrance more than memory, of "countermourning" more than mourning, to an ongoing process that has no easy closure, and that, because of this fact, is all the more important. Such a practice of "recognition" will guarantee that memory becomes a form of "rememorar" and "remembrar," an open-ended process always needing to be taken up again and again, always being re-created and renegotiated, and thus always making us aware that, as William Faulkner used to say, "the past is not over, it is not even past."

Remembering and Forgetting the Past: Theoretical Reflections

It is important to recognize that many of the issues discussed earlier regarding the difficulty in post-Franco Spain of coming to terms with a traumatic past can also be placed within a broader international and theoretical context. At the same time as Spain was undergoing its political transition to democracy, transitions of other kinds were taking place around the world. They implied changing conceptualizations of the nature and practice of memory, and, in the late twentieth century, ultimately led to an unprecedented interest in the study of memory from a variety of disciplines.

It is helpful to remember, for example, that Jean-François Lyotard's seminal study about postmodernism, *La condition postmoderne: rapport sur le savoir* [*The Postmodern Condition: A Report on Knowledge*], was published in 1979, coinciding with the early Spanish transition. The postmodern condition, according to Lyotard, is partly characterized by the suspicion and subversion of master narratives of all kinds. The belief in progress as the guiding force ensuring modern society's continual advancement was one such master narrative that has been radically questioned under postmodernism. The future-oriented perspective of modernism thus shifts, increasingly, in the latter part of the twentieth century, toward an outlook where the past seems to take the place the future once held as an object of reflection. Andreas Huyssen refers to this shift as the change from a modernist concern with "present futures" to the postmodern emphasis on "present pasts" (2003, 11). Within this latter paradigm, the weight of the past is increasingly felt upon the present as the promises of an ever-improving future are recurrently belied by historical experience. As Huyssen observes: "Whatever their specific occasion, cause, or context, the intense memory practices we witness in so many different parts of the world articulate a fundamental crisis of an earlier structure of temporality that marked the age of high modernity with its trust in progress and development, with its celebration of the new as utopian, as radically and irreducibly other, and with its unshaken belief in some telos of history" (2003, 27). Huyssen further explains how many of these memory practices emerged in the 1960s, in the wake of decolonization, as new social movements began searching for alternative histories that questioned, from various perspectives, the patriarchal, Eurocentric models that had prevailed until then (2003, 12).

It is, of course, important to recognize, as Huyssen does, that this emphasis on the past can have very different political implications. It may manifest itself in memory practices (such as the ones to which he refers in the previous quote) that present welcome alternatives to dominant views of the past from the vantage point of previously marginalized perspectives. Yet it may also arise as practices that *reinforce* dominant, conservative historical discourses by effectively presenting a nostalgic longing for an idealized, unproblematized past, such as that generated by an increasingly powerful "heritage industry."[29] In both cases, what becomes increasingly clear during this time period is that such memory practices cannot be understood without considering the interests in the present that are served by them.

This presentist perspective, which recognizes that memory is a practice that occurs in the present and reflects that present context, even though it ostensibly deals with the past, has become ever more powerful in recent approaches to memory, although it builds on a long tradition. This perspective is clearly espoused, for example, by Mieke Bal, in the introduction to an important collection of essays on the subject, significantly entitled *Acts of Memory: Cultural Recall in the Present*. Bal explains that all the essays in the volume understand memory as "an activity occurring in the present, in which the past is continuously modified and redescribed even as it continues to shape the future (1999, viii), and that, furthermore, "memory is active and it is situated in the present" (1999, viii). From this perspective, it becomes ever more important for memory practices to become self-reflexive. Any attempt to recall the past must be aware of the forces in the present that enable, and limit, such recall, as well as the present interests that are served by a particular way of remembering the past. This, for example, is an important perspective to keep in mind when analyzing the exhumations of mass graves in Spain, as they become effective "places of recognition" that generate a healthy *dissensus* throughout society.

In the 1980s and '90s, furthermore, the concern with memory was given a new impulse by several historical, social, and cultural developments. Huyssen claims that one factor in this growing concern with memory is a general anxiety in many cultures at the end of the twentieth century with changing experiences of time and space, what he describes as "a slow but palpable transformation of temporality in our lives, brought on by the complex intersections of technological change, mass media, and new patterns of consumption, work, and global mobility" (2003, 21). The new information and technological revolutions of the last few decades, where ever more information seems to be processed ever more quickly, and geographical distance often seems to collapse in the face of a media culture promising access to everything "here and now," have created a need for some kind of "temporal anchoring" which has been filled, in various ways, by a turn to the past (2003, 28).

An important historical development in the late 1980s and '90s that has also contributed to the obsession with looking at the past is the fall of Communism in various countries in Western Europe, and the problems faced by these societies as they have tried to develop new forms of government under the weight of past repressive regimes. Finally, the concern with memory at the end of the twentieth, and beginning of the twenty-first century is also partly due to a resurgence of interest in the Holocaust in Europe and the United States. This resurgence emerged in part from a series of fortieth and fiftieth anniversaries related to

World War II and the Historians' Debate of 1986 in Europe, as well as from the enormous impact of the 1978 television series *Holocaust* in the United States (Huyssen 2003, 12).[30] The Holocaust, of course, is one of the major historical experiences that radically undermined the belief in historical progress, as it demonstrated how technological advancements could systematically be used for previously unimaginable destruction.

Reflections about the Holocaust have been central to the boom of memory studies since the 1980s in other ways as well. As Carlo Ginzburg explains, the concern over the disappearance of the generation who lived through the Holocaust has been an important element in the growing attention paid to the study of memory in the late twentieth century (1997, 353). As the individuals who personally experienced the Shoah pass on, the need to rethink how memory works beyond the individual sphere has become crucial for guaranteeing that the event is not forgotten.

Along with this growing concern for understanding the dynamics of collective memory, and its interrelation with personal recollection, the advanced age of many who experienced the Holocaust has also spurred an interest in the various ways in which memory, both collective and personal, is passed on from one generation to the next.[31] A similar concern is reflected in several of the novels studied in the following chapters, especially the most recent ones, in which the transmission of memory across generations becomes a major theme. This reflects the fact that, within the last two decades in Spain, the growing awareness of the need to confront the memory of the civil war partly emerges out of a concern over the imminent disappearance of the generation that experienced it. The urgency of undertaking this task in Spain is cited ever more frequently in statements as varied as official government decrees, historical writings, and, within major newspapers, in letters to the editor written by ordinary citizens.

There is another experience of "disappearance" that Huyssen claims has contributed to the late twentieth century boom in the study of memory. The experience of the "desaparecidos" of the military regimes of the 1970s and '80s in Latin America also brought to the fore the problem of finding ways to remember a traumatic historical event which was characterized in large part by the absence, the "disappearance," of many of the people who suffered it most directly. Despite important differences in these various historical traumas, all such experiences have left in their wake a collective resolve that they should be forever remembered so that they never occur again (the post-Holocaust dictum *Never Again* is echoed in the title of the report on Argentina's military repression: *Nunca Más*, for example).

This resolve, however, coexists with a growing fear of forgetting such events. This fear has grown ever stronger with the realization that such remembrance has not helped deter later examples of unimaginable horror, such as in Rwanda and Bosnia in the 1990s. As Huyssen notes: "wherever one looks, the contemporary public obsession with memory clashes with an intense public panic of oblivion" (2003, 17). Huyssen sees this coexistence of contrary impulses as one of the many ways in which memory and forgetting must be understood together, and further explains: "this fear of forgetting articulates itself paradigmatically around issues of the Holocaust in Europe and the United States or the 'desaparecidos' in Latin America. Both share the absence of a proper burial site, so key to the nurturing of human memory" (2003, 18). It is clear that the case of Spain's remembering and forgetting of its civil war must be understood within this larger context. In Spain, as has been seen, the unresolved question of the mass graves from the civil war shows that here, too, the dynamics of remembering the country's traumatic past are intimately related to the problem of "the absence of a proper burial site."

The growing importance of Holocaust studies during the last two decades, as well as the impact of such experiences as those of the "desaparecidos" of the Latin American military regimes of the 1970s and '80s, have also led to productive reconceptualizations of the dynamics of memory, in particular of traumatic memory. In fact, trauma in general has become a major theoretical concern during this time. This interest has emerged in part due to the aforementioned anxiety over the passing on of the generation that experienced the Holocaust. It is also related, moreover, to the postmodern stress on the socially constructed nature of reality, and the fundamental role of narrative in all such constructions.

The postmodern emphasis on the impossibility of any direct access to the past is echoed within the dynamics of trauma, where direct recall of a past experience may not be available, despite the fact that the effects of that traumatic event relentlessly persist. In trauma, the past is, in a very real sense, inaccessible yet it is also forcefully present. This makes it a particularly productive site for reflections about history and memory that uphold the postmodern skepticism of any direct access to reality, but that do not want to fall into a purely relativistic stance in which no truth claims about the past may be upheld. The study of traumatic memory thus necessarily holds in creative tension opposing views that see the past as both accessible and inaccessible to present recall, and it is in part the upholding of this tension that has made the study of traumatic memory so productive.[32] Hal Foster has proposed a similar explanation for the recent interest in trauma:

"Why this fascination with trauma... today? To be sure, motives exist within art and theory. As suggested, there is dissatisfaction with the textualist model of culture as well as the conventionalist view of reality—as if the real, repressed in poststructuralist postmodernism, had returned as traumatic (1996, 166). This creative tension is explored in the texts analyzed in the following chapters, as they each present the inevitable "return of the traumatic real" in various ways. This paradox, furthermore, is only one of many that have made the study of traumatic memory particularly salient in the last two decades. As Huyssen explains, "surely, the prevalence of the concern with trauma must be due to the fact that trauma as a psychic phenomenon is located on the threshold between remembering and forgetting, seeing and not seeing, transparency and occlusion, experience and its absence in repetition" (2003, 8).

The fact that, as Huyssen reminds us, traumatic memory "is located on the threshold between remembering and forgetting" is particularly relevant for understanding the way the past has been simultaneously recalled and repressed in post-Franco Spanish society. We have repeatedly encountered, in our earlier brief overview of this problem in Spain, the dynamic by means of which an apparent process of remembering effectively embodies an act of forgetting. It is no coincidence that a similar phenomenon has been studied by scholars of the Holocaust, such as Paul Ricoeur, Saul Friedlander, and Dominick LaCapra. They have productively analyzed this relation between memory and oblivion with the help of the concepts of repeating, or acting out, and working through taken from Sigmund Freud's 1914 essay "Remembering, Repeating and Working-Through" (1958b).

Freud here describes how many people who have experienced a traumatic event in the past may repress any conscious recollection of it. However, they may *repeat* it through certain actions that effectively reenact it, in a process he calls "acting out." This type of "repetition," or "acting out," may seem to be a way in which the patient is recalling the traumatic event. However, what prevents this act from becoming a healthy form of remembering is that he or she remains oblivious to the forces in the present that are repressing the memory from conscious recall in the first place. In fact, as Freud claims, "the greater the resistance, the more extensively will acting out (repetition) replace remembering" (1958b, 151).

This observation changes Freud's understanding of the goal of therapy, for while originally he believed its objective was to try to make the patient recall the event from the past, he claims in this essay that the focus of therapy should be to make the patient aware of the forces of repression and resistance *in the present* that block such recollection.

Freud claims that therapy should help the patient "work through" this resistance (1958b, 155). Only by "working through" the resistances in the present to such recall of the past can true remembering, instead of mere repeating, take place. Freud summarizes this new approach to therapy by explaining its goals: "descriptively speaking, it is to fill in gaps in memory; dynamically speaking, it is to overcome resistances due to repression" (1958b, 148). There is an important shift in the understanding of memory here. It is no longer seen primarily as the *material* from the past that is to be recalled in order to "fill in gaps," but as a *process* that is hopefully aware of the very manner in which it comes about.

This difference between "repeating" and "remembering," between "acting out" and "working through," is helpful for understanding how post-Franco Spain has approached its traumatic past. That past has, in fact, been repeated but not remembered, acted out in various ways, but not worked through. The texts studied in the following chapters embody various modes of working through that past, and the memory practices they represent thus serve as models for how a truly effective culture of memory may be developed in Spain.

As Dominick LaCapra explains, such a healthy process of working through the past is self-reflexive in various ways, all of which are present in the texts studied in the following chapters. The process of working through must resist any attempt to act out, or repeat, the past in a manner that effectively denies the most painful and disruptive aspects of history (those which, in fact, led to the emergence of resistance and repression in the first place). One way in which the pain and destruction of history are sidestepped is when the process of recalling the past is cloaked in discourses of progress and development that allow for a falsely comforting sense of closure. LaCapra explains that a critical practice of working through memory "places in jeopardy fetishized and totalizing narratives that deny the trauma that called them into existence by prematurely (re)turning to the pleasure principle, harmonizing events, and often recuperating the past in terms of uplifting messages or optimistic, self-serving scenarios" (2001, 78). All the texts studied in the following chapters enact this process of working through memory by explicitly reflecting on the way a traumatic past is recalled. They further explore the forces in the present that conspire to contain the most disruptive aspects of that past within various "uplifting messages or optimistic, self-serving scenarios." These, of course, include the various discourses of "peace," "order and progress," and "reconciliation" that have been dominant in late Francoism and post-Franco Spain.

According to LaCapra, furthermore, such practices of working through memory must also resist the temptation for an all-too-comforting sense of closure over the past. This resistance may be enacted by openly accepting and exploring the "empathic unsettlement" that any confrontation with a traumatic past engenders (2001, 78). Such "empathic unsettlement" reflects an understanding of memory as a practice that must engage the affective as well as cognitive dimension of remembering. This necessarily means accepting the pain and suffering, as well as the destabilizing effect in the present, of remembering a traumatic past. It is, of course, the desire to escape such a destabilizing effect that leads a person, or a society, to act out or repeat the past instead of working through it.

Within the context of postdictatorship Chile, Nelly Richard presents a similar emphasis on the need for the memory of the traumatic past to engage with the most unsettling affective and emotional aspects of history. She refers to this as a process of "practicing" memory. This is contrasted to official governmental discourses that merely "refer to" memory:

> It seems, then, that the political consensus is only capable of "referring to" memory (evoking it as a topic, processing it as information), but neither of practicing it nor of expressing its torments. "To practice" memory implies making available conceptual and interpretative instruments needed to investigate the symbolic density of the narratives; to "express its torments" supposes relying on figurative language (symbols, metaphors, allegories) sufficiently moving so that they enter into a relationship of solidarity with the emotions unleashed by memory. The consensus that represses that emotional unleashing of memory only names the past with words exempt from the convulsions of sense, so as not to alter the minute and calculated formularization of political and mediated exchanges. (2004, 17)

Clearly, this distinction between "referring to" and "practicing" memory echoes that between acting out and working through, and is highly relevant to post-Franco Spain. In contrast to the official discourses that merely "referred to" the memory of the civil war and Francoism, in an attempt to create what has ultimately been a problematic politics of consensus, the texts analyzed in the following chapters present various modes of "practicing," which is to say of working through, memory. Richard highlights the importance of figurative language for an effective "practice" of memory because such language has the capacity to evoke emotion and thus to "express the torments" of a traumatic past. This is in large part why narratives such as the ones analyzed here are particularly appropriate sites for studying the dynamics of an effective "practice" of memory.

All the texts analyzed in the following chapters highlight this "empathic unsettlement" as a vital element in their practice of working through memory. It is the empathic unsettlement that these texts both reflect within themselves and hopefully produce in their readers that is at the heart of their politically transformative potential. The process of working through memory that is evoked in the title of my study thus describes the acts of memory *within* the texts analyzed as well as my own practice of reading these texts, which is intended to show how they serve as models for the way this process might be taken up by Spanish society at large.

It is interesting to note that one of the most common Spanish verbs for remembering, "recordar," is particularly appropriate for envisioning the process of working through memory explored here. Derived from the latin "re," again, and "cor," heart, the verb "recordar" evokes a process that makes something pass through the heart again. In classical times, the heart was considered to be the site where remembering took place (thus the English expression "to know by heart"). In this sense, "recordar" means to feel again, thus creating a space for a necessary empathic unsettlement. This image of remembering as an action whereby something is made to pass through the heart again, an image that necessarily implies a relation of affect as much as of cognition, has a particular resonance with the practices of working through memory presented in the texts analyzed here.[33]

Saul Friedlander, like LaCapra, also emphasizes how the process of working through must always resist the consolation of discourses that provide a comforting sense of closure with regard to the past. Borrowing an expression from Maurice Blanchot, Friedlander warns that, " 'working through' may ultimately signify, in Maurice Blanchot's words, 'to keep watch over absent meaning' " (1993, 134). These words, taken from Blanchot's *The Writing of the Disaster,* imply that any process of working through a traumatic past must ultimately face the possibility of a total collapse of meaning that a traumatic experience often entails. The challenge is to find ways to recall, and transmit to others, such an experience of a total collapse without betraying the radical vulnerability of that experience in the very telling of it, since any act of narration necessarily engenders some sense of order and inevitably carries with it the capacity to engender signification.[34] This is one more way in which a practice of remembrance may ultimately embody a form of forgetting, as any narrative that recalls a traumatic past may from the outset have already betrayed, and effectively forgotten, the most radically destabilizing element of the traumatic experience in the first place. Self-reflexivity is one of the ways in which this danger might be averted, and thus the importance placed in this study on meta-memory texts as productive sites for working through memory. Because any such self-reflexive narrative practice is explicitly aware of its own necessarily arbitrary and incomplete nature, it may manage to "keep watch over absent meaning," inasmuch as any final and complete grasp of the past is recognized as illusory.

Within the context of the exhumations of mass graves in Spain, a poignant example of the process that Friedlander describes as "working through" can be found in Ignacio Fernández de Mata's presentation of his work with one of the interdisciplinary groups organizing several exhumations in the province of León. Fernández de Mata describes an unexpected difficulty he and his team found during interviews with family members of the "disappeared" in the mass graves on which they have worked. He mentions how "many promising and intense conversations that we thought would yield 'unsuspected' data finally ended in nothing but general notes, for the facts that our informants wanted to share had receded and practically vanished behind the memory of the intense pain that was suffered and that was still present" (2005, 4). As an example of this difficulty, he presents the case of a woman who, while sitting next to her friend who was being interviewed about the events surrounding one of the mass graves, kept exclaiming "oh, if only *I* told, if only *I* told," in a manner that implied that she had important information to add to her friend's testimony (2005, 4). When the interviewer finally turned to her and asked for her story, however, she could merely repeat vaguely what her friend had told, adding only that they had been very, very afraid. Frustrated at her own incapacity to recount what she had promised, she broke down in tears (2005, 4). Fernández de Mata also explains the process of interviewing another woman who was recounting how two of her brothers had been killed, and another imprisoned, in 1936. As he notes: "In her testimonies, tears coincide with moments of doubt, absence, or fragmentation of memory more than with the exact moments of capture and disappearance of her brothers—it isn't precisely general pain or sadness that brings tears, but the incapacity to fully express the magnitude of the memory through words" (2005, 5). In both interviews, the tears emerge when words do not. The meaning of what is being recalled and recounted here hinges on an uneasy relation between the present tears and the absent words. The traumatic nature of these memories, compounded by the time that has elapsed since the events, leads to a form of remembrance where working through does, indeed, involve learning "to keep watch over absent meaning."

It is no coincidence that Nelly Richard, analyzing the practices of memory that are appropriate in recalling the trauma of the "disappeared" in postdictatorship Chile, also evokes Maurice Blanchot when she calls for a "memory of disaster" (2004, 29). Echoing Friedlander's concern within the context of post-Holocaust memorial practices, Richard calls for an understanding of memory that is equally open-ended and suspicious of any closure as well as of any fixed and stable meanings: "Memory is an open process of reinterpretation that unties and reties its knots so that events and understandings can again be undertaken. Memory stirs up the static fact of the past with new unclosed meanings that put its recollections to work, causing both beginnings and endings to rewrite new hypotheses and conjectures and thereby dismantle the explanatory closure of totalities that are too sure of themselves. And it is the laboriousness of that unsatisfied memory that never admits defeat, that perturbs the official burial of that memory seen simply as a fixed deposit of inactive meanings" (2004, 17).

This "unsatisfied memory" ("memoria insatisfecha" in the original, *Residuos y metáforas*, 1998, 29) is a most appropriate image for the process of "working through" explored here. The practice of memory presented in the texts analyzed in the following chapters is forever unsatisfied because it is forever provisional. It goes back, again and again, constantly undermining any version of history that pretends to have settled all accounts with the past. Unsatisfied memory relentlessly questions previous approaches to the past, and inevitably generates the empathic unsettlement LaCapra claims is necessary for the process of working through memory to take place. This image of an "unsatisfied memory," furthermore, is not only appropriate for understanding the memory practices embodied in the texts studied in the following chapters. It also characterizes my own interpretative strategy, which likewise goes back, over and over again, to similar insights about memory production and transmission as they reappear in each text. My own reading here is a form of "unsatisfied memory," furthermore, as observations made in one chapter are recalled in later ones, always from slightly different angles. My analysis is presented in a manner that acknowledges, from the outset, that different readings can be added to the ones presented here, that other aspects of the past can always be recovered through new acts of memory, that recollection itself is always destined to be partial as well as plural, selective as well as forever "unsatisfied." In this manner, the practices of remembrance that are being explored here are, indeed, different manifestations of a process of "rememorar" or "remembrar" that is always and necessarily incomplete, always in need of being taken up anew.

It is important to note that Richard's "unsatisfied memory" brings to mind Walter Benjamin's critique of official historical discourses. When Benjamin claims that "there is no document of civilization which is not at the same time a document of barbarism" (1969, 256), he is evoking the need for what Richard will later call an "unsatisfied memory." For both critics, official versions of the past inevitably reflect the interests of the victors of history, and only come about by repressing the suffering of those on the losing side of power. Those official discourses must be resisted, torn apart, in order for the pain and suffering of the victims of the past to be able to emerge through the cracks. Richard describes this process: "If 'giving an account' of what happened means not betraying the memory of what the present leaves behind as pain and affliction in words that carry no scars (not to subject the memory of the victims to the humiliation of seeing their past narrated in the unscathed language of the triumphant narrative of actuality), then the question about memory is concerned with the nexus between memory, language, and fissures of representation" (2004, 6). Again, the pain of the past can only emerge within a practice of memory, a process of working through the past, which eschews any "triumphant narrative of actuality," any rhetoric which inevitably hides the scars of past suffering in the name of so-called progress. In fact, following both Benjamin and Richard, it is clear that to give voice to that suffering one has to first shatter that rhetoric of progress, exposing the fissures within such dominant representations of the past.

Within Spain, Manuel Reyes Mate has recurrently called for a similar practice of memory, explicitly based on a Benjaminian approach to history, which is presented as a "memoria vigilante" (qtd. in *El País* 2003) [vigilant memory]. This "vigilant memory," as in the conceptions of Richard and Benjamin, is an act charged with a moral and ethical imperative to side with those who are on the underside of history. As Reyes Mate explains: "memoria moral es sinónimo de justicia.... La memoria moral no es recordar el pasado, sino reivindicar el sufrimiento oculto como parte de la realidad o, lo que es lo mismo, denunciar toda construcción de presente que ignora la vigencia de una injusticia pasada" (Reyes Mate 2002b) [moral memory is synonymous with justice.... Moral memory does not mean to remember the past, but to vindicate the hidden suffering as part of reality, that is to say, to denounce any construction of the present that ignores the relevance of a past injustice]. This moral and vigilant memory will necessarily be concerned with "the nexus between memory, language, and fissures of representation," since to denounce any constructions of the present that ignore past injustices is to recognize that such constructions are narratives of one kind that could, in fact, always be told in a very different manner.

There are two important images that recur in all the texts studied in the following chapters. These images function as metaphors for a memory practice that tirelessly questions dominant accounts of the past, a practice that forever looks beneath such accounts for the traces of the repressed stories of the victims of history. One such metaphor is the image of the palimpsest, where certain layers of writing are only accessible by looking beyond, or below, other layers of overlaid script. The layers of a palimpsest serve as a metaphor for memory itself, a process that may evoke different times, or layers, of the past. The important role of writing in this image further underscores the intimate relation between memory and writing in all the texts studied here.

Second, the recurring images of fragmentary objects rescued from the past, especially the various forms of ruins that appear over and over again, reflect the necessarily fragmentary nature of what is found beneath the dominant versions of history. These images of fragmentation also reflect the fact that previously repressed aspects of the past can only be effectively recovered in similarly fragmentary narratives that reject any totalizing closure and wholeness. These two images, in fact, are interrelated. The ruins are often imaged as palimpsests, with various layers of history being reflected in their structure, and the palimpsests are often incomplete, fragmentary, as if themselves in ruin. The palimpsestic ruins and the ruined palimpsests that consistently reappear throughout this study become perfect metaphors for the "unsatisfied" and "vigilant" memory at work in all the texts analyzed in the following chapters.

Reyes Mate further underscores the necessarily self-reflexive nature of such a "vigilant" memory: "el recuerdo tiene que ser vigilante, autocrítico, consciente siempre de la distancia entre la evocación y la experiencia. Es en ese estado de vigilia donde se produce el relámpago del recuerdo del pasado que ilumina todo el presente" (1991, 213) [memory must be vigilant, self-critical, ever conscious of the distance between the evocation and the experience. It is in that state of vigil when the lightning-flash of the memory of the past illuminates the present]. This "vigilant" memory is a form of what Walter Benjamin calls remembrance, for it is self-conscious, mindful, keenly aware of its duty to those aspects of the past that are not represented in dominant views of history. These words also clearly echo those of Benjamin in "Theses on the Philosophy of History," when the German thinker explains that "to articulate the past historically does not mean to recognize it 'the way it really was'. . . . It means to seize hold of a memory as it flashes up at a moment of danger" (1969, 255). Both statements present memory as a potentially dangerous enterprise, one that, like a lightning bolt, can rip through the present, creating an electrical charge that shocks us into recognizing the suffering and pain that inevitably lie underneath any self-satisfied view of the present.

Both statements, furthermore, highlight the inevitable distance between memory and the actual experience in the past that is being recalled. The acknowledgment of this "distance between the evocation and the experience" that emerges in any act of remembering is, as has been stated earlier, one of the elements that has most contributed to the interest in memory in the recent past. The recognition that memory is not a process of retrieval but of representation necessarily forces one to acknowledge the role of distortion in all recollective practices. Within such distortion, remembering and forgetting will always work hand in hand.[35] Paul Ricoeur recognizes such distortion as a crucial characteristic of a process of working through memory, a characteristic that can be added to those underscored by LaCapra and Friedlander. Ricoeur explains the importance of narrative and narrativization for this process of working through memory: "It is precisely through narratives that a certain education of memory has to start. Here we can introduce the connection between memory and forgetting because the best use of forgetting is precisely in the construction of plots, in the elaboration of narratives concerning personal identity or collective identity; that is, we cannot tell a story without eliminating or dropping some important event according to the kind of plot we intend to build. Narratives, therefore, are ... the place where a certain healing of memory may begin" (1999, 9). This "healing of memory" is precisely what is at stake in each of the works analyzed here. As narratives themselves, these texts embody such a healing of memory. As stories within which the process of creating, and transmitting to others, a narrative of memory is explicitly thematized, such a healing is doubly present in these texts.

If we remember Benjamin's words, however, which claim that memory always "flashes up at a moment of danger," we are faced with one of the paradoxes that arises in all the meta-memory texts studied here. While the memory-as-narrative that is explored in all these texts may enable a certain healing to begin, as it allows for previously repressed aspects of the past to come to the fore, this process is also dangerous. It can only be taken up by confronting very strong forces in the present that have a vested interest in maintaining such repression. Working through memory is certainly risky business, as every one of the texts studied, each in its own way, reflects. Furthermore, such a "healing of memory" will never be complete, for, as LaCapra reminds us, "working through does not mean total redemption of the past or healing its traumatic wounds" (2004, 119).

There is one other important image that recurrently appears in all the following chapters. The process of working through memory that each text presents is partly enacted through the creation of what Pierre Nora calls *lieux de mémoire* [places of memory]. Such places of memory, according to Nora, are objects of various sorts. They are artifacts, sites, symbols, rituals, and so forth that serve to "codify, condense, anchor... memory" (1989, 25). Monuments, flags, and national holidays are examples of the artifacts Nora defines as *lieux de mémoire*, artifacts around which memory is continually reaffirmed and re-created. Although Nora originally conceived this concept for the study of specifically national memories, it has developed into a useful image for understanding the process whereby all kinds of alternative memories are generated, and it is as such that it emerges in the following chapters.[36]

Nora explains that such places of memory often arise in moments of crisis, when views of the past that may have been dominant begin to be questioned.[37] Places of memory, therefore, are connected to experiences of discontinuity, even though they effectively produce continuity as they serve to "codify, condense, anchor . . . memory." Furthermore, there is a necessarily self-reflexive dimension to such places of memory, as "all *lieux de mémoire* are objects mises en abîme . . . because they complicate the simple exercise of memory with a set of questions directed to memory itself" (1989, 20–21). In each of the works analyzed here, a different place of memory emerges as part of the text's reflection about how memory itself is generated and transmitted. The necessarily self-reflexive nature of the *lieux de mémoire* is part and parcel of the way these texts, also, "complicate the simple exercise of memory with a set of questions directed to memory itself." This is one of the elements, in fact, that characterizes these works as meta-memory texts.

The places of memory that emerge in these works, furthermore, are perfect sites for the practice of working through a tirelessly "unsatisfied" and "vigilant" memory. This is so because, by their very nature, such *lieux de mémoire* also work against views of history that pretend to be complete and whole, thus generating a self-satisfied sense of closure. In this sense, the places of memory in these texts are also paradigmatic examples of what Ulrich Winter has called "places of recognition," as defined earlier. Nora, in fact, explains that places of memory are the product of a continual process of re-definition that has much in common with the concept of working through memory explored here, as well as with the concept of "places of recognition," as defined by Winter: "The *lieux* we speak of, then, are mixed, hybrid, mutant, bound intimately with life and death, with time and eternity; enveloped in a Möbius strip of the collective and the individual, the sacred and the profane, the immutable and the mobile.... the *lieux de mémoire* only exist because of their capacity for metamorphosis, an endless recycling of their meaning and an unpredictable proliferation of their ramifications" (Nora 1989, 19).

The image of the "Möbius strip of the collective and the individual" is particularly significant. It points to the ways in which individual and collective memories are inextricably interrelated, as is illustrated in the following texts. Although each work presents one or two individuals whose process of confronting and transmitting to others their personal memory is the main theme of the work, this process is always shown to be determined, limited, formed and deformed, by social forces and collective needs. The very process of sharing those memories inevitably converts the personal rememorative practice into a social and collective enterprise. Each text, however, underscores how even *before* those personal memories are shared, and thus made collective, they are always already social, since the individuals are never free from the pressures and constraints of the various collectivities to which they belong. Individual and collective memory do, indeed, form a Möbius strip that is forever in motion, always in creative tension.[38]

The process of working through memory that all of the individual characters in the following texts enact becomes a collective enterprise in another way as well. Read together, these texts can be seen to embody a self-reflexive practice that may be a model for how to develop the "culture of memory" that is still lacking in Spanish society as a whole today. If, as Paul Ricoeur has stated, narratives are "the place where a certain healing of memory may begin" (1999, 9), then these particular narratives, these meta-memory texts, are certainly a most appropriate starting point for that healing process. Remembering the observation by Reyes Mate after the March 11 terrorist bombing in Atocha with which this introduction began, we can now understand why the texts studied here are particularly appropriate places for exploring how Spanish society might begin to develop the *lieux de mémoire* it needs. The examples these texts provide for different ways of working through memory transform these works into valuable places of memory, and of recognition, themselves, real and symbolic artifacts where a relentlessly "unsatisfied" and tirelessly "vigilant" memory is continuously created and re-created each time the texts are read and re-read.

Paul Ricoeur has further claimed that "it is good that the wounds of history remain open to thought" (1999, 17). This reflection points to one more way in which meta-memory texts, such as the ones studied in the following chapters, may ultimately serve as models for the process of creating a necessary "culture of memory" in Spain. Such texts may, in fact, embody a practice that guarantees that "the wounds of history remain open to thought" in a manner that ultimately *goes beyond* what political legislation or historical investigation may achieve. It is still of vital importance to understand how these literary texts function within broader practices of political and social legislation, civic activism, and historical investigation, all of which are absolutely essential if a country is to work through a past of war and repression that continues to haunt the present. But perhaps the most radical aspects of that practice of working through memory are inevitably reserved for literary, and other artistic texts. These texts can thus still function as models for what must be achieved within society at large, but models that point to something that is ultimately not fully achievable through other means, despite the fact that all those other means are vitally important. We may recall that Nelly Richard, in the context of postdictatorship Chile, claims that such artistic texts are able to "practice," and not merely "refer to" memory precisely because of the affective force and impact of their symbolic language, which allows for memory to "express its torments." As she explains, "to 'express its torments' supposes relying on figurative language (symbols, metaphors, allegories) sufficiently moving so that they enter into a relationship of solidarity with the emotions unleashed by memory" (2004, 17). It is precisely the fact that meta-memory texts, such as the ones studied here, represent the past in ways that "express its torments," through their symbolic language, in a manner that is ultimately unsettling and does not allow for any facile sense of closure regarding the past, that guarantees their most radical political transformative potential.

As new meta-memory texts of various kinds emerge in Spain, it will be interesting to see which ones among them will continue to take up the challenge of working through the past in a manner that explores the wounds of history without pretending to close them definitively, but allowing them to remain continually "open to thought." The present study emerges out of the conviction that such an ongoing reflection may ultimately be the most effective form of healing, and that literature, as well as other forms of artistic representation of the past, is its most appropriate medium.

STRUCTURE OF THE BOOK

Working through Memory: Writing and Remembrance in Contemporary Spanish Narrative is structured with two organizing principles in mind. First, the chapters are arranged chronologically, covering every decade between the 1960s and the end of the twentieth century. The texts chosen include both works written in exile after the civil war and others written within Spain. This arrangement allows for changes in the very process of remembering the past to be traced over different historical and political contexts, such as under the Franco regime, during the transition to democracy, and at the end of the twentieth century. I explore these differences while also underscoring how certain issues reappear continuously, demonstrating that they remain unresolved over time.

Second, the texts have been chosen to represent a broad spectrum of writings that foreground the act of remembering, from works in which memory is a real individual's attempt to recall a historical past, to texts in which memory is a literary metaphor for the creative reconstruction of history on a collective level. The texts studied, therefore, range from autobiographies to fictional novels, and include works that combine elements of both types of writing in varying degrees. There are works written by both male and female authors, and an exploration of the way gender affects the process of remembrance is seen to be central to some of these texts. The diversity of texts studied serves to showcase the wide variety of narrative forms that have been used to explore the dynamics of memory in contemporary Spanish literature.

As memory is inevitably selective, so is this study. There are many more examples of narrative meta-memory texts that could have been included, some very well known and others less so. The concept of meta-memory text, for example, could also very fruitfully be extended to the study of film, and many of the films by Carlos Saura and Basilio Martín Patino, to name only two directors, could surely be examined as works in which the process of working through memory is explored in particularly interesting ways. Many other names could be added, and many more will emerge in the future, as more meta-memory texts are sure to appear in the coming years. Because of limitations of space, this study focuses on a relatively small number of texts that present particularly interesting explorations of the dynamics of memory production and transmission. For each text, I highlight a different literary figure or narrative strategy that effectively embodies the process of working through memory, and that highlights a particularly challenging aspect of this process. The close readings provided of these texts are intended to reflect not only the richness and complexity of each work, but the way in which the process of working through memory is materialized through intricate processes of narrative disruption and fragmentation that must be explored in detail.

The first chapter, "Jorge Semprún: Trauma and Memory," analyzes *El largo viaje* (1963) [*The Long Voyage*], the first novel by Jorge Semprún, perhaps the contemporary Spanish author who has most consistently used literature to explore a traumatic past in a consistently self-reflexive manner. Published in exile in France, and originally in French, *El largo viaje* is the first of his many texts to deal with his experience in, and survival of, the German concentration camp of Buchenwald during World War II. His work connects that experience with other traumatic memories of his past: that of being exiled from Spain after the civil war, of working clandestinely within the Spanish Communist Party to undermine the Franco regime, and finally of being expelled from the party for his critiques of its Stalinist dogmatism. Drawing on trauma theory, this chapter shows how the radical undermining of the self that trauma entails is reproduced discursively within the text. The narrator incessantly records his own inability to recount adequately the experience of the camps, as well as the difficulty for others to understand his tale. The dynamics of trauma in this text underscore an element present in all the works studied: they all explore memory as a double-edged phenomenon, one that is both liberating and dangerous, a practice that can either help constitute or potentially destroy a sense of identity.

The second chapter, "Juan Benet: The *Pharmakon* of Memory," draws on the concept of the *pharmakon,* which embodies a tense and ambivalent relationship between memory and writing, to discuss the novel *Volverás a Región* (1967) [*Return to Región*] by Juan Benet. The double nature of the *pharmakon,* a term that means both poison and cure, recalls the double nature of trauma as a memory that forces one to re-live a devastating experience while also helping one to overcome it. Benet's novel is the first of a series of works in which he develops an allegorical, fictional representation of post-civil war Spain called "Región" (Region), a barren place where any characters who dare to recall a time before the war are faced with death. The novel's exploration of the benefits and dangers of remembering is analyzed in light of Benet's essays in which memory becomes an epistemological tool for the development of knowledge based on uncertainty and ambivalence. Memory, in Benet's work, is subversive of Francoist ideology not only because it dares to recall a past that was forbidden, but because it presents an alternative way of knowing, one that eschews the dogmatic affirmation of certainty and absolutes imposed by the regime.

In "María Teresa León: The Performance of Memory," I analyze the autobiography, *Memoria de la Melancolía* (1970) [*Memory of Melancholy*], of another political exile after the Spanish civil war, María Teresa León. Through the lens of theories of performance and performativity, this chapter explores how León performs a series of "disidentifications" by means of which she constructs a narrative self through memory. In this narrative construction of self, exile, along both political and gender lines, has an ambivalent and destabilizing function, much like the figures of trauma and the *pharmakon* have in the previous chapters. León, like all the other authors studied, consciously presents her act of remembering as a performance that future generations will learn from, thus making of memory a process that is oriented to the future as much as to the past.

Chapter 4, "Montserrat Roig: Twilight Memory," explores how Montserrat Roig appropriates the dynamics of the fetish, an object that both acknowledges and represses the memory of an experience of loss of power, to structure her novel, *La hora violeta* (1980) [*The Violet Hour*]. The figure of the fetish is shown to be central to Roig's novelistic presentation of a woman's re-creation through memory, many years after her estranged mother's death, of her mother's life during the civil war and postwar period. The protagonist of the novel returns to Spain, after a period of self-imposed exile, to participate actively in the transition to democracy, and unexpectedly realizes there is a more personal transition, involving the memory of her own mother, that she must face. The individual and the collective confrontation with the past reflect and influence each other, as the protagonist's attempt to work through her own personal past is inextricably intertwined with a similar process affecting society at large during the time of the transition to democracy.

The last chapter, "Antonio Muñoz Molina: Memory and Postmemory," borrows the concept of postmemory, developed within the context of Holocaust studies, to analyze the novel *El jinete polaco* (1991) [*The Polish Rider*] by Antonio Muñoz Molina. This novel presents the transmission of memory through several generations within two families, spanning the whole of the twentieth century in Spain. Memory here becomes "postmemory," where later generations bear the burden of the recollections of traumatic experiences, such as civil war, exile, and political repression, that their parents and grandparents experienced. Although they may not have suffered these historical traumas themselves, these younger generations are nevertheless haunted by them. Like Roig's novel, therefore, Muñoz Molina's text thematizes the difficult working through of inherited memory. Like all the texts studied, furthermore, *El jinete polaco* illustrates that the obstacles to working through memory may be daunting, but the dangers of not confronting a traumatic past, at a personal or collective level, are undoubtedly greater.

Finally, the conclusion brings the discussion to bear on various meta-memory texts that have been published since the turn of the twenty-first century. Various open-ended questions are presented to help understand how the working through of the traumatic past of the civil war and Francoist repression in Spain may continue to be practiced in the future. The particular contributions that literature, and other art forms, may make to such a necessary, if difficult, process is stressed.

1
Jorge Semprún: Trauma and Memory

> Only one thing remained reachable, close and secure amid all losses: language. Yes, language. In spite of everything, it remained secure against loss. But it had to go through its own lack of answers, through terrifying silence, through the thousand darknesses of murderous speech. It went through. It gave me no words for what was happening, but went through it. Went through and could resurface, "enriched" by it all.
>
> —Paul Celan 1986, 34

IN *ON ORATORY AND ORATORS*, CICERO EXPLAINS THE IMPORTANCE of good memory in rhetoric. To this purpose, he tells the story of the poet Simonides of Ceos, who first invented an art to perfect memory. Simonides, at a banquet in Thessaly given by the rich patron Scopas, recited a poem in praise of his host. Since the poem also included praise of the twin gods Castor and Pollux, Scopas told Simonides he would pay for only half the poem; the rest of his recompense should come from the twin gods. Shortly afterwards, a messenger arrived to tell the poet that two young men wanted to see him in the garden. Simonides stepped outside and found no one. While he was outside, the roof of the house fell in, killing everyone at the banquet except him. The invisible callers had been Castor and Pollux, who thus paid for their share of the poem by saving the poet's life.

Upon his return to the debris, Simonides realized he was the lone individual who could identify the bodies, for he was the only one who remembered their exact positions around the banquet table. From there he developed an *ars memorativa* based on the importance of finding proper images for what is to be remembered and arraying them in a recognizable order. Cicero goes on to emphasize the importance of choosing well the places—the *loci*—for the images to be remembered.[1]

What has never been adequately emphasized in this anecdote is the importance of the place of the poet himself, of the rememberer, the survivor of the terrible accident. It is precisely Simonides's strategic placement outside the house that permits him to be the single survivor of the banquet, the one who can then save the memory of those who died by exercising his prerogative, a tragic one to be sure, of remembering the others because he had been inside the house with them also. The shifting placement of the survivor is crucial in this story about the invention of a system to develop and strengthen memory. This shifting placement is crucial, moreover, for the lesson the anecdote provides anyone seeking to understand the working of memory in the narrations of those modern-day survivors of one of contemporary history's most egregious atrocities, the Holocaust. Indeed, that the first treatise on memory should have emerged as an answer to an overwhelming experience of death is a significant, if underemphasized, aspect of Cicero's story that will be all too relevant in the present discussion.[2]

Spanish author Jorge Semprún Maura, survivor of the concentration camp of Buchenwald, uses his art, narrative in this case, to evoke, like Simonides, the place in memory owed to many who, unlike himself, did not survive. Semprún's place in the world, even before the Holocaust, has always been a shifting, unstable one. Born in Madrid in 1923 to a well-to-do family (his grandfather was prime minister during the reign of Alfonso XIII, and his father was a civil governor during the Spanish Second Republic), he and his family were forced into exile in 1937. Growing up in France, Semprún became part of the anti-German Resistance until he was caught in 1944 and sent to Buchenwald. His experiences there, or, more exactly, the *memory* of his experiences there, are the subject of many of his novels.[3]

Upon his liberation from Buchenwald, Semprún returned to Paris, where he founded and collaborated on numerous cultural magazines, many organized by groups of Spanish exiles, such as *Cuadernos de Ruedo Ibérico*, and others predominantly French, such as *Les Temps Modernes*. He began to work clandestinely with the Spanish Communist Party to undermine the Franco dictatorship and, in 1953, was elected to the party's Central Executive Committee. He kept this position for almost ten years and was in charge of most underground activities based in Madrid dealing with Spanish intellectuals and students. In 1964, together with Fernando Claudín, he was expelled from the Spanish Communist Party for openly demanding more self-criticism from the party power structures. Years later, from 1988 to 1991, he was Spain's minister of culture under Felipe González.[4] He continues, to this day, to work indefatigably within different venues to keep alive the memory of the various historical experiences that have marked his life, in a manner that underscores their effects beyond national frontiers, and that may hopefully lead to constructing a better future.[5]

Semprún has thus had a life-long commitment to political activism as well as to literature, and both of these enterprises have been profoundly traversed by the instability of his "place" of origin in the world. In 1995, for example, he had to forsake his candidacy to the French Academy of Letters because of his unwillingness to renounce his Spanish nationality. His life and work clearly cross many dividing lines. His texts are often written as hybrid forms, blurring distinctions between autobiography and novel, while his cultural affiliation, which connects him, vitally and intellectually, to France and Germany as well as to Spain, makes it possible to productively read his work within different national and cultural frameworks.[6]

Semprún definitely has an unstable relation to any "place" of origin. He is, in a way, the perpetual exile, the eternal outsider. This sense of displacement is exacerbated by the memory of his survival of Buchenwald, which produces in his writing what one critic has perceptively called a state of "discursive homelessness" (Silk 1992, 58).

In speaking about his sense of national displacement, Semprún in fact projects the notion of nationality onto the only realm in which he can always find, or create, a place for himself: that of language. In "... *Vous avez une tombe au creux des nuages*..." [You have a tomb in the clouds], he claims:

> Du point de vue de la langue littéraire, ou bien je suis apatride—à cause de mon bilinguisme invétéré, de ma schizophrénie linguistique definitive—ou bien j'ai deux patries. Ce qui, en vérité, est impossible.... En fin de compte, ma patrie n'est pas la langue, ni la française ni l'espagnole, ma patrie c'est le langage. C'est-à-dire, un espace de communication sociale, d'invention linguistique: une possibilité de représentation de l'univers. De le modifier aussi, par les oeuvres du langage, fût-ce de façon modeste, à la marge. (1995c, 101–2)

> [From the point of view of literary language, I either have no homeland—due to my inveterate bilingualism, my definitive linguistic schizophrenia—or else I have two homelands. Which is, in truth, impossible.... Finally, my homeland is not a national tongue, neither French nor Spanish, my homeland is language. That is, a space of social communication, of linguistic invention; a possibility of representing the universe, of changing it, also, even if in a most modest, marginal way, through language itself.] (My translation)[7]

Language, beyond any national linguistic delimitations, is where Semprún seems to find a sense of belonging. It is no coincidence that this quotation comes from a speech for which Semprún uses as title ("... *Vous avez une tombe au creux des nuages*..."), part of a verse by Paul Celan from the poem "Death Fugue." Immediately before the verse used by Semprún as his title, Celan's poem, evoking the countless prisoners killed and cremated in the concentration camps, reads: "then as smoke you will rise into the air / then a grave you will have in the clouds there one lies unconfined" (1980, 63). The sense of radical displacement as to one's national origin, which Semprún evokes in his speech, is paralleled by a much more harrowing lack of a stable place of final rest in Celan's poem. Both writers point to an existential displacement, in one's origin as well as in one's death. And both turn to language as the only "anchoring" mechanism available to them. Celan goes on, in the same speech to which the epigraph to this chapter belongs, to define his poetic endeavor as "the efforts of someone coursed over by the stars of human handiwork, someone also shelterless in a sense undreamt-of till now, and thus most uncannily out in the open, who goes with his being to language, stricken by [*wirklichkeitswund*] and seeking reality" (1986, 35).

Like two modern-day Simonideses, Semprún and Celan find themselves recalling the experience of a tragedy to which they almost succumbed. They, too, end up suffering the same unstable relation between having been "inside" and later being "outside," an instability that becomes a devastating form of "shelterlessness." Such an experience is a "wound," as Celan says, and becomes as faltering as wisps of smoke rising from a crematorium and trailing through the air or graves paradoxically "dug" in fleeting clouds. Both writers put memory recurrently into play through language. Language is the place to seek some kind of shelter precisely because it is intimately connected with the "wound" that it is trying to heal. This kind of homeopathic process is at the heart of what Freud called the dynamics of trauma, a term whose original meaning in Greek is, in fact, "wound."

A fundamental characteristic of a traumatic experience is that it usually forecloses any attempt to express it in words. Such an experience usually involves some form of an individual's confrontation with, and survival of, his or her own annihilation, the only experience the psyche cannot possibly register. The unconscious thus represses any memory of such an experience. As Freud states in *Beyond the Pleasure Principle* in reference to the memory traces left behind by traumatic experiences: "Such memory-traces, then, have nothing to do with the fact of becoming conscious; indeed they are often most powerful and most enduring when the process which left them behind was one which never entered consciousness" (1961a, 27).

However, the traumatic memory, with a force all its own, keeps reappearing in an indirect form through an uncanny repetition of events in the individual's life that re-creates the traumatic experience. Freud has called this the "return of the repressed," or "repetition compulsion." He presents the by-now famous example of his grandson's game of *Fort-Da*, with which the child overcomes the traumatic anxiety produced by the mother's departure with a game that endlessly reproduces such absence in the form of a disappearing and reappearing toy. Such an activity is undertaken to gain a sense of mastery, retroactively, over an experience whose traumatic character is based in part on the loss of any sense of control over one's own life. As Freud explains, the child playing the *Fort-Da* game "at the outset . . . was in a *passive* situation—he was overpowered by the experience; but, by repeating it, unpleasurable though it was, as a game, he took on an *active* part" (1961a, 15).

Applying the understanding of traumatic memory gained from Freud to the workings of memory in the discourse of Holocaust survivors, Shoshana Felman and Dori Laub claim: "Massive trauma precludes its registration. . . . The victim's narrative—the very process of bearing witness to massive trauma—does indeed begin with someone who testifies to an absence, to an event that has not yet come into existence, in spite of the overwhelming and compelling nature of the reality of its occurrence" (1992, 57).

Such a view has radical implications for our understanding of the relation of language to its historical referentiality and to its supposed representational function. When an individual finally comes to speak about a traumatic event of the past, he or she is, in a way, not referring *back* to something that occurred before but is reliving the experience in the present. It is not a constative, referential speech act but, in a sense, a performative one. This view of language problematizes its relation to the experience that ostensibly precedes it by making that experience come into being, in a sense, at the time of its articulation in language. Laub's claim that "The 'knowing' of the event is given birth to" at the moment of the narration of the experience (1992, 57) begins to illustrate the way traumatic memory points, as he and Felman sustain, to "a theory of a yet uncharted, nonrepresentational but performative, relationship between art and culture" (1992, xx).[8] This theory tries to explain literature's potential for exploring the wound of a traumatic memory while preserving "the uniqueness of the experience in the face of its theorization, and . . . the shock of the unintelligible in the face of the attempt at its interpretation" (1992, xx).[9]

This rethinking of the ways that literature might put into play the dynamics of traumatic memory is appropriate for a subject like the Holocaust, which, despite having spawned a literary tradition of its own, has always harbored a certain mistrust of fiction. Fiction, in this context, is seen as a medium that might betray the horror of the experience and somehow universalize an irreducibly unique event by giving a meaning to an experience that shattered all possibility of stable meaning. Elie Wiesel, for example, has said: "If it is a novel, it is not about Auschwitz, and if it is about Auschwitz, it is not a novel" (qtd. in Lang 1988, 23). Yet Wiesel himself has written novels about Auschwitz, thus undermining his own condemnation of fiction. With regard to poetry, a similar contradiction can be found in the writings of Theodor W. Adorno. Many are familiar with Adorno's famous dictum exclaiming that "writing poetry after Auschwitz is barbaric," yet fewer people are aware that Adorno himself later retracted this affirmation, stating that "perennial suffering has as much right to expression as the tortured man has to scream; hence it may have been wrong to say that after Auschwitz you could no longer write poems" (1973, 362).

The sense of irreality that many who survived the Holocaust feel perhaps lies at the heart of what *does* make fiction an appropriate medium for the expression of such experiences. As Charlotte Delbo confesses in a postscript to *None of Us Will Return*, the novelized account of her experiences in the camps: "I am no longer sure that what I have written is true, but I am sure that it happened" (1968, 128). Semprún himself addresses the same issue when he claims, in reference to any writing that deals with the Holocaust: "la réalité a souvent besoin d'invention, pour devenir vraie. C'est-à-dire vraisemblable" (1994a, 271) [reality often needs some make-believe, to become real. In other words, to be made believeable (1997, 262)].[10] Trauma theory, which shows how fiction may be the place where the dynamics of traumatic memory are reproduced in writing itself, is thus an important contribution to a discussion that, by exploring an absolute limit case, reflects upon the relation of language and fiction to reality, as well as the crucial role of memory in this dynamic.

The performativity of the writing about the Holocaust that trauma theory highlights, a performativity that guarantees that the uniqueness of that terrible experience is not drowned in an attempt to theorize it, resembles what Maurice Blanchot, in *The Writing of the Disaster,* describes as a writing that "is not knowledge of the disaster, but knowledge as disaster and *knowledge disastrously*" (1986, 3; emphasis added).[11]

The grammatical incongruency in Blanchot's notion that a writing of the disaster produces "knowledge disastrously" is of capital importance. The Holocaust, experienced by survivors as the breakdown of any security in the world, a breakdown of their sense of self, is thus relived in their writing by means of various narrative strategies that reproduce similar breakdowns: of grammar, of sense, of logic, of referentiality, of representability, of chronology, of subjectivity.

Meaning and order disintegrate in a literary strategy that "writes-the-Holocaust," that reproduces a breakdown of sense similar to what the survivors experienced. It is a writing that, like the *Fort-Da* game of Freud's grandson, re-creates a traumatic experience endlessly in an attempt to gain some mastery over a situation that, by its very nature, robbed one of any sense of control over one's life.

This dynamic helps to explain the overwhelming need that Holocaust survivors often have to talk, write, express what they went through, and, at the same time, the real *danger* that such an enterprise entails, for it means reliving what was almost impossible to live through the first time. Many, like Paul Celan or Primo Levi, did not manage to survive such reliving of traumatic memories that their work involved. Many, in fact, never did take up the risk and kept their memories in silence.

Semprún points to the dangerous aspect of such writing when he describes why it took sixteen years after his release from Buchenwald for him to be able to write about his recollection of that experience. Although he did try to write about it shortly after his liberation from the camp, the writing proved more dangerous than therapeutic:

> Dans mon cas, en revanche, chaque page écrite, arraché à la souffrance, m'enfonçait dans une mémoire irrémédiable et mortifère, m'asphyxiait dans l'angoisse du passé. Il me fallait choisir entre l'écriture et la vie et j'ai choisie la vie.... J'ai dû décider d'être un autre, de ne pas être moi-même, pour continuer à être quelque chose: quelqu'un. (1995c, 93–94)

> [In my case, however, every page I wrote, wrestled from suffering, submerged me in an irremediably mortal memory, suffocated me in the anxiety of the past. I had to choose between literature and life and I chose life.... I had to decide to become someone else, to not be myself, in order to continue to be something: someone.] (My translation)[12]

Despite the deathly danger that such traumatic memory implies, there is also, as Freud claimed, an unconscious *need* to re-create it, which is what ultimately led to Semprún's many novels about his experience in Buchenwald. Even after having written one of those accounts in 1980 (*Quel beau dimanche!*), which Semprún thought was the last time he would deal with the topic, the memory, with a force all its own and in a most uncanny way, again imposed itself on him. In an interview, he explains the genesis of *L'écriture ou la vie*, which, published in 1994, almost fifty years after the liberation of Buchenwald, shows how the memories of that experience still have a hold over the writer:

> El libro nació casi contra mí. Era un 11 de abril y estaba ocupado en la redacción de *Netchayeev ha vuelto* cuando, sin darme cuenta, me encontré escribiendo en primera persona una serie de recuerdos de Buchenwald que había

olvidado o había querido olvidar hasta aquel momento. En el plan de la novela todo aquello carecía de importancia, eran datos que servían de telón de fondo para caracterizar un personaje, pero ahora estaban ahí, en primera persona. Luego, al reflexionar sobre ello, también me dí cuenta de que el 11 de abril es el día de la liberación de Buchenwald y que el inconsciente me había jugado una pasada. Al día siguiente, 12 de abril, al poner la radio, lo primero que oí fue que Primo Levi se había suicidado. Entonces supe que tenía que embarcarme en *L'écriture ou la vie* y que de nuevo tenía la muerte ante mí. (Martí 1995, 6)

[The book was born almost against me. It was an 11th of April and I was working on *Netchayeev ha vuelto* when, without realizing it, I found myself writing, in the first person, a series of memories of Buchenwald that I had forgotten, or that I had wanted to forget until then. Within the plan of the novel, none of those memories had any importance, they were merely background information that served to develop a character, but now they were there, in the first person. Later, upon thinking about what happened, I realized that April 11 was the day of the liberation of Buchenwald, and that my unconscious had played a trick on me. The next day, April 12, when I turned on the radio, the first thing I heard was that Primo Levi had committed suicide. Then I knew that I had to embark on *L'écriture ou la vie* and that I again had death before me.] (My translation)

Semprún's novels about his experience of Buchenwald manifest, in their very genesis, the dynamics of trauma. By making such a traumatic memory their recurrent, obsessive theme, each of these novels becomes an example of writing that produces "knowledge disastrously" and that does, despite the consequences, attempt to "write-the-Holocaust."

This very same explanation of the genesis of *L'écriture ou la vie* is found within that text itself.[13] Such a meta-narrative reflection about the very text he is writing is common in Semprún's work, and it extends to his exploration of memory. Just as writing builds upon more writing, one memory builds upon another memory, and as Semprún explores the process by means of which such connections are made, writing and memory themselves often become indistinguishable. His texts, therefore, do not just make traumatic memory their recurrent theme, but become meta-memory texts, self-reflexively exploring the very process by means of which this traumatic memory can, or cannot, be narrated, how it can, or cannot, be received by others. Furthermore, these meta-memory texts recurrently enact a process of working through memory. If Semprún's writing reproduces a series of narrative breakdowns within its very frame, it is important to remember how Semprún, the eternal exile, describes the kind of "homeland" that he envisions in language: "a space of social communication, of linguistic invention; a possibility of representing the universe, of changing it, also" (1995c, 102; my translation). Paradoxically, by working through the traumatic memory of the camps and recreating its endless breakdowns of meaning and communication, the possibility of change is upheld, and a space of social communication is sought, one that in no way denies or belittles the atrocity of the past, but that puts the memory of that atrocity to work towards potentially improving the present and the future.

* * * *

Le grand voyage recounts the five-day, four-night train journey that took Gérard, along with 120 other prisoners packed in one single boxcar, from Compiègne, France, to Buchenwald. Gérard is the name of the protagonist and also one of Semprún's *noms de guerre* in the French Resistance, the one he was using when he was caught by German soldiers and sent to the concentration camp. So Gérard is and is not Semprún at the same time; a fictitious doubling of identity that occurred in real life and that will have much to do, as will be seen, with the doubling of subjectivities emerging in the narration of *Le grand voyage*.

Although the novel is recounted in the present and in the first person from the point of view of Gérard, the reader soon finds out that the real present of the narration is *not* that of the boxcar journey but sixteen years afterwards, when the narrator, who often intrudes into his narrative, is remembering that journey. The narrator first makes this clear when he interrupts Gérard's report about the extreme sense of physical pain that invades him while the train is passing through the Moselle Valley. As he sees people on the outside, he realizes the incommensurability between that "outside" and his situation "inside" the boxcar:

> De toute façon, quand je décris cette impression d'être dedans qui m'a saisi dans la vallée de la Moselle, devant ces promeneurs sur la route, je ne suis plus dans la vallée de la Moselle. Seize ans ont passé. Je ne peux plus m'en tenir à cet instant-là. D'autres instants sont venus se surajouter à celui-là, formant un tout avec cette sensation violente de tristesse physique qui m'a envahi dans la vallée de la Moselle. (1963, 24–25)

> [Anyway, when I describe this feeling of being inside which overwhelmed me in the Moselle valley, seeing these people walking down the road, I am no longer in the Moselle valley. Sixteen years have passed. I can't confine myself now to that particular moment. Other moments have superimposed themselves on that one, forming a whole with that violent feeling of physical sadness which filled me in the Moselle valley.] (1964, 22–23)[14]

The moments of his life acquire a force of their own, for they come together, group themselves around the moment being remembered in the Moselle Valley: "D'autres instants sont venus se surajouter à celui-là" [Other moments have superimposed themselves on that one]. As a consequence of the cumulative effect and weight of these memories from different times of his life, the narrator cannot stop at the moment that he is recounting and calmly tell all he would like about it: "Je ne peux plus m'en tenir à cet instant-là" [I can't confine myself now to that particular moment]. This is a particularly curious acknowledgment of *lack* of power over his own memories, for in the preceding paragraph the narrator was boasting of having complete control over his narrative: "Je ne devrais peut-être parler que de ces promeneurs et de cette sensation, telle qu'elle a été à ce moment, dans la vallée de la Moselle, afin de ne pas bouleverser l'ordre du récit. Mais c'est moi qui écris cette histoire et je fais comme je veux" (1963, 24) [Perhaps I ought to talk only of these people out walking and of this feeling the way it was then, in the Moselle valley, so as not to upset the order of the story. But I'm the one writing this story, I'll do as I like] (1964, 22).[15]

Already the issue of mastery, which was crucial in Freud's understanding of traumatic repetition compulsion, is at stake here. Does the narrator control his memories, or do they control him? The question is all the more important as the memories he is evoking are those of his experience of absolute loss of control over his life. It is that loss of control which he felt upon seeing the people who were "outside" while he was "inside" the boxcar that caused his extreme physical pain in the first place.

Another important aspect of this first meta-narrative intervention on the part of the narrator is that he says all those other moments of his life which will come to join the one he is now narrating will form "*un tout* avec cette sensation violente de tristesse physique" (1963, 25; emphasis added). [*a whole* with that violent feeling of physical sadness (1964, 23; emphasis added)]. It is implied that there exists the possibility of a "wholeness" to such a mnemonic narrative, that it will come to some form of closure: "un tout" [a whole]. Yet this supposed "wholeness" will be undermined, as will be seen, in countless ways, not least of which are the vertiginous anachronies the narrator will plunge into, shifting constantly in his memory to moments before and after the scene recounted. Such a strategy gives his narration a quality of boundlessness which subverts any closure and becomes one way to resist his remembered enclosure in the boxcar.

The same tension between historical experience overwhelming the narrator and the narrator trying to regain some mastery over it is presented at the very beginning of the novel:

Il y a cet entassement des corps dans le wagon, cette lancinante douleur dans le genou droit. Les jours, les nuits. Je fais un effort et j'essaye de compter les jours, de compter les nuits. Ça m'aidera peut-être à y voir clair. Quatre jours, cinq nuits. Mais j'ai dû mal compter ou alors il y a des jours qui se sont changés en nuits. J'ai des nuits en trop; des nuits à revendre. Un matin, c'est sûr, c'est un matin que ce voyage a commencé. Toute cette journée-là. Une nuit ensuite. Je dresse mon pouce dans la pénombre du wagon. Mon pouce pour cette nuit-là. Et puis une autre journée.... Oublie cette journée, ce fut le désespoir. Une autre nuit. Je dresse un deuxième doigt dans la pénombre. Un troisième jour. Une autre nuit. Trois doigts de ma main gauche. Et ce jour où nous sommes. Quatre jours, donc, et trois nuits. Nous avançons vers la quatrième nuit, le cinquième jour. Vers la cinquième nuit, le sixième jour. Mais c'est nous qui avançons? Nous sommes immobiles, entassés les uns sur les autres, c'est la nuit qui s'avance, la quatrième nuit, vers nos futurs cadavres immobiles. (1963, 11)

[There is the cramming of the bodies into the boxcar, the throbbing pain in the right knee. The days, the nights. I force myself and try to count the days, to count the nights. Maybe that will help me see clearly. Four days, five nights. But I must have counted wrong, or else some of the days must have turned into nights. I have a surplus of nights, more nights than I can use. One morning, that much is sure, it was in the morning that this voyage began. All that day. Then a night. In the half-light of the boxcar I raised my thumb. My thumb for that first night. And then another day.... Forget that day, it was a day of despair. Another night. I raise a second finger in the half-light. A third day. Another night. Three fingers of my left hand. And today. So, four days and three nights. We're advancing toward the fourth night, the fifth day. Toward the fifth night, the sixth day. But is it we who are advancing? We're motionless, stacked in on top of one another, it's the night that is advancing, the fourth night, advancing toward the motionless corpses we are destined to be.] (1964, 9)[16]

Gérard attempts to re-create some impression of power by imposing an order, a chronological order, on an experience that insinuates itself as overwhelming precisely because it begins to be limitless, in the pain it can generate as well as in its possible duration. The order the narrator is seeking to impose on his experience is supposed to help him "voir clair" [see clearly] what will ultimately remain beyond his comprehension.

The effort to "clarify," to "see clearly," the number of days and nights this trip entails is a leitmotif in the novel. The memories evoked throughout the narrative range from Gérard's childhood, to his first journey of exile from Spain into France, to his activities in the French Resistance, to his time in Buchenwald and the years after his liberation. These narrated memories go back and forth endlessly, with absolutely no predictable order to their appearance. Yet recurrently interjected into this disorder of memory are reminders of Gérard's attempt to impose some delimiting chronology on this chaos: "Ça fait quatre jours et trois nuits que nous sommes imbriqués l'un dans l'autre" (1963, 12) [This makes four days and three nights that we've been jammed against each other (1964, 10)]; "La quatrième nuit de ce voyage" (1963, 58) [The fourth night of this voyage (1964, 56)]; "C'est la quatrième nuit, n'oubliez pas, la quatrième nuit de ce voyage" (1963, 69) [It's the fourth night, don't forget, the fourth night of this voyage (1964, 68)]; "C'est par là que nous sommes arrivés, au coeur de la cinquième nuit de ce voyage" (1963, 161) [It was by this road that we had arrived, in the middle of the fifth night of that voyage (1964, 162)].[17] Such a narrative strategy proves to be a futile attempt at imposing, or superimposing, temporal order on the memories that resiliently disperse, deflect, fragment themselves and overflow the present of the narration. But, of course, the present moment of the narration is itself double; a double present functions in the novel: that of Gérard during the train ride and that of the narrator remembering Gérard—that is, himself—remembering. A mise en abîme structure emerges, where there is not even a stable, fixed, anchoring present to this plethora of memories within memories. As Kathleen Johnson has said of this unstable temporal structure: "because the present of narration cannot be closed, the chronology that it is supposed to establish becomes instead the contorted temporal disorder (future before past, etc.) which destroys any stable present. Time becomes as confused and imbricated within the 'confines' of a constructed and exclusive present as the indissociable mass of bodies in the boxcar (and the elements of memory)" (1989, 283).

Gérard, from the start, uses memory to re-create his experience and to reposition himself in a situation of mastery before an event that robs him of any control. It is similar to what the narrator himself does, narrating the memory of this trip sixteen years later, trying to prove he possesses a control that is not so evidently in his hands. In contrast to the utter inability of the *remembered* Gérard to alter the forward movement of the train he was imprisoned in, the *remembering* Gérard moves relentlessly forwards and backwards in time as he tells his story, as if to assert indefatigably the power and freedom supposedly afforded him by his new position as narrator. He is no longer just another character living the story, for "c'est moi qui écris cette histoire et je fais comme je veux" (1963, 24) [I'm the one writing this story, I'll do as I like (1964, 22)].[18]

The beginning of the novel, with its attempt at imposing the order of days and nights, enacts the issue at the heart of so much Holocaust literature and of studies that question whether fictional constructs are appropriate to represent the overwhelming experience of such an event. In *Le grand voyage*, fictional constructs such as the imposed "order" of time in the conceivable and familiar units of days and nights are not only appropriate but vitally necessary for survival itself.

The novel's first paragraph is also an example of one of the ways that Paul Ricoeur, in the third volume of *Time and Narrative*, explains the inherent, inexorable dependence of history on fiction. All attempts to understand history as a series of lived events rely on fictional constructions, such as the calendar, that make of universal time a human time. These heuristic structures are inherent in all historical enterprises and demonstrate how any attempt at being "objectively" historical is already traversed by a fictional dimension: "The gap between the time of the world and lived time is bridged only by constructing some specific connectors that serve to make historical time conceivable and manipulable" (1984, 3:182). The beginning of *Le grand voyage*, a novel about a real historical experience and event, thus puts into play this intermingling of history and fiction.

Gérard's difficulties in bridging the gap between the historical time and his lived time, shown by his difficulty in keeping straight the number of days and nights of his trip, already imply that this novel deals with an experience that might prove to make that gap unbridgeable. The story of what happened might never be able to be "set straight," "seen clearly," despite the narrator's attempt to do so. It is obvious that Gérard does not have any sense of mastery over his mnemonic narrative when he asks: "Mais c'est nous qui avançons? Nous sommes immobiles, entassés les uns sur les autres, c'est la nuit qui s'avance, la quatrième nuit, vers nos futurs cadavres immobiles" (1963, 11) [But is it we who are advancing? We're motionless, stacked in on top of one another, it's the night that is advancing, the fourth night, advancing toward the motionless corpses we are destined to be (1964, 9)].[19] That his narration escapes into the future, presenting the image of him and his companions as corpses, at the very moment when he is trying to keep it in line within the limited chronology of the days and nights of the present trip, demonstrates that his control over this recounting is not complete. Death is one of the experiences that will prevent him from imposing a stable order on his memories. Indeed, death, and the recollection of death, is at the heart of the traumatic memory recounted. From the beginning, therefore, Gérard's reminiscence is involved in issues of time caught between order and disorder, narration caught between fiction and history, a character caught between life and death.

It is significant that, in the first paragraph, Gérard uses his body (by raising one finger for every day and night he counts) to help impose the chronology that gives him some semblance of order and power. This use of his own body to help count the days and nights that have passed implies that the difficult gap to bridge between the overwhelming historical experience and the human attempt to live through it is literally embodied. Just as one cannot escape one's own body, the heuristic and narrative challenges characterizing this story are also impossible to escape from. Not even time will help.

The body, especially one that, like Gérard's, is in pain, is closely related to the attempt at imposing some order, or sense, on this experience. The very facticity of the body, especially its pain, may lend a feeling of reality to an experience that begins to be too unreal, that begins to break down everything that had been real before then. As Elaine Scarry claims in *The Body in Pain: The Making and Unmaking of the World*: "The felt-characteristics of pain—one of which is . . . its incontestable reality or simply its 'certainty'—can be appropriated away from the body and presented as the attributes of something else" (1985, 13–14).

Gérard uses his body to uphold his belief in humanity by imposing on his experience the chronology of human time in the form of days and nights. Perhaps because that human time is counted on his own body, with his fingers, its existence is guaranteed. Yet even his body will lose its capacity to guarantee any semblance of safety, for it, too, will be destroyed in this experience. Later in the trip, Gérard explains: "j'ai l'impression que mon corps va se briser en morceaux. Je sens chacun de ces morceaux, isolément, comme si mon corps n'était plus un tout" (1963, 122) [I've been feeling as though my body is about to break into little pieces. I can feel each of these little pieces separately, as if my body were no longer whole (1964, 122)].[20] Before, the narrator's memories had seemed to create "un tout" [a whole], although they ultimately failed in that attempt. Here, it is Gérard's remembered *body* that is no longer "un tout" [whole], and is felt as shattered. This experience is all the more devastating, since the body, from the beginning, had tried to keep in place a sensation of human time, "livable" time, which is itself being shattered in this long train ride of death.

Parallel to Gérard's attempt at imposing the human construct of days and nights on the dehumanizing time of the train ride is his stated intention to use the time to select, order, hierarchize his memories, thus giving a semblance of meaning to his life:

> Il y a une autre méthode, aussi. C'est de profiter de ce voyage pour faire le tri. Faire le bilan des choses qui pèseront leur poids dans ta vie, de celles qui ne pèsent rien. . . . J'ai vingt ans, je peux encore me permettre ce luxe de

choisir dans ma vie les choses que je vais assumer et celles que je rejette. J'ai vingt ans, je peux gommer de ma vie des tas de choses. Dans quinze ans, quand j'écrirai ce voyage, ce sera impossible. Tout au moins, j'imagine. Les choses n'auront pas seulement un poids dans ta vie, mais aussi leur poids en elles-mêmes.... Le poids de ta vie sera peut-être quelque chose d'irrémédiable. (1963, 30–31)

[There's another way. Put this voyage to good use by sorting things out.... I'm twenty, I can still allow myself the luxury of choosing in life the things I'm going to assume and those I reject.... Fifteen years from now, when I write about this voyage, it will be impossible. Or at least I suspect it will. Not only will things weigh something in your life, they'll have a weight of their own.] (1964, 29)[21]

There is again an attempt at imposing an order and, by so doing, to show that he still controls his life and can give it the meaning *he* decides. Yet he acknowledges that in fifteen years, when he will be remembering and writing this story, he might no longer have that power. In the unexpected and illogical shift to the second person in the two last sentences, when Gérard addresses his older self (the narrator who is, in fact, the true first person of this narration), there is a clear indication that the unity of meaning he is attempting to create for his life is shattered, for his own self is irremediably split in two. Part of what accounts for this splitting of his self is precisely the experience that Gérard is living and that the narrator is reliving while writing it. It is, in a way, an experience of his own death, or at least of the death of a part of himself. This is a constantly recurring theme not only in this book but in all of Semprún's accounts of Buchenwald.[22]

What makes speaking of his concentration camp experiences so difficult is the haunting realization that, in a way, he really did *not* survive, that he is telling the story of his own death. That is why, when Semprún explained how the memories of the camp overcame him almost fifty years after the experience, he knew he was finding himself with "la muerte ante mí" [death before me]. In *L'écriture ou la vie* he explains how "Une idée m'est venue, soudain... la sensation, en tout cas, soudaine, très forte, de ne pas avoir échappé à la mort, mais de l'avoir traversée. D'avoir été, plutôt, traversé par elle. De l'avoir vécue, en quelque sorte" (1994a, 24) [I'm struck by the idea... struck by the sudden overwhelming feeling, in any case, that I have not escaped death, but passed through it. Rather, that it has passed through me. That I have, in a way, lived through it (1997, 14–15)].[23]

Quel beau dimanche! again thematizes the desire on the narrator's part to show his control over his life by recounting, in an orderly way, his memories of a single Sunday in Buchenwald. As in *Le grand voy-*

age, the memories are resilient, and the novel overflows: into the past as well as into the future beyond that single day in the camp. The narrator of the later text, however, is fully conscious of the artifice of this temporal structure, as well as of the illusion of control on his part that it reveals:

> J'a vais décidé de raconter cette histoire dans l'ordre chronologique. Pas du tout par goût de la simplicité, il n'y a rien de plus compliqué que l'ordre chronologique. Pas du tout par souci de réalisme, il n'y a rien de plus irréel que l'ordre chronologique. C'est une abstraction, une convention culturelle, une conquête de l'esprit géométrique.... L'ordre chronologique est une façon pour celui qui écrit de montrer son emprise sur le désordre du monde, de le marquer de son empreinte. On fait semblant d'être Dieu. (1980, 113)

> [I decided to tell this story in chronological order. Not because I thought it would be simpler that way—there's nothing more complicated than chronological order. And not because I was striving after realism—there is nothing more unreal than chronological order. It's an abstraction, a cultural convention, a victory for the geometrical mentality.... Chronological order is a way of demonstrating your grip on the disorder of the world, of making your mark on it. You pretend you're God.] (1982, 122)[24]

Again, the power over narrative time is but a fiction that the narrator desperately tries to keep alive, all the while knowing that it is artificial. This later novel, however, brings in another experience of metaphorical "death": the exile and displacement that Semprún suffered since his concentration camp experience. *Quel beau dimanche!* weaves intermittently into his recollection of that one day in the concentration camp his experience of being expelled from the central committee of the Spanish Communist Party in 1964. As his militancy in the party had been one of the main sources of his self-definition for a long time, this expulsion is experienced by Semprún as another form of "death." In *Quel beau dimanche!,* therefore, the narrator also confesses to feeling that death is not something he survived. Referring to his experience in the camps, he writes:

> La vie n'était pas un songe, ô non! c'es moi qui l'étais. Et davantage: le songe de quelqu'un qui serait mort depuis longtemps. J'ai déjà nommé, malgré son innommable indécence, cette sensation qui m'a parfois assailli au cours des ans. Cette certitude sereine et totalement désespérée de n'être que le fantasme rêveur d'un jeune mort d'autrefois. (1980, 138)

> [It was my memory that held me in the unreality of a dream. Life was not a dream, oh no! It was I who was. What's more, it was the dream of some-

one who appeared to have been dead for a long time. I have already named, despite its unnamable indecency, the sensation that has sometimes assailed me over the years. That serene, quite desperate certainty of being no more than a dream of a young man who died long ago.] (1982, 149)[25]

This feeling of not having survived one's own death is common to many who lived through the horror of the Holocaust and is at the heart of why such an experience is so traumatic. Such a dynamic is recurrently encountered in the stories of Holocaust survivors, both videotaped and directly interviewed testimonies, and leads Lawrence Langer, in *Holocaust Testimonies: The Ruins of Memory*, to propose talking of the Holocaust not as a "lived" event but as a "died" event: "For the witnesses, the Holocaust is at once a lived event and a 'died' event: the paradox of how one survives a died event is one of the most urgent . . . topics of their testimonies" (1991, 69). The paradox of how one survives a "died" event, and how one narrates it, haunts all of Semprún's texts about Buchenwald.

When death becomes a part of one's past, chronology is irremediably wounded. Any telling of such an experience must belong to what Blanchot has called the "wounded space" (1986, 30) of the writing of the disaster, which echoes Celan's use of language to overcome the "wound" of reality and which inscribes death in its very articulation. In remembering that death, the narrator at least seeks the all-too-illusory power of being the one to do the remembering, even if what he has to evoke takes him to the verge of lunacy and despair. That is why the narrator of *Quel beau dimanche!* affirms: "La mémoire est le meilleur recours, même si cela paraît paradoxal à première vue. Le meilleur recours contre l'angoisse du souvenir, contre la déréliction, contre la folie familière et sourde. La criminelle folie de vivre la vie d'un mort" (1980, 98) [Memory is the best recourse, even if it seems paradoxical at first. The best recourse against the pain of remembering, against the dereliction, against the unspoken, familiar madness. The criminal madness of living the life of a dead man (1982, 105)].[26]

If in *Quel beau dimanche!* Semprún took up memory as a paradoxical recourse against the remembrance of his (figurative) death and the near lunacy derived from such an enterprise, in *L'Évanouissement* he takes a similar course. There he also tries to recall methodically the events of one day in his life: from the 6th to the 7th of August, 1945—the day, not coincidentally, that the atom bomb was dropped on Hiroshima. In *Quel beau dimanche!* the experience of death in the camps is presented alongside Semprún's experience of "death" upon being expelled from the Spanish Communist Party. *L'Évanouissement* (1967) presents a similar juxtaposition of "deaths": those of the many victims of Hiroshima, merely alluded to in the text yet undoubtedly present, and the metaphorical "death" of the story's protagonist, Manuel (again, Semprún in the guise of another one of his real/fictious pseudonyms). One month after his liberation from Buchenwald, while on a train entering one of the Paris stations, Manuel faints, falls into the tracks, and is almost killed by a train. The novel begins with his struggle to regain consciousness and to piece together his memory. It goes on to be as disjointed, fragmented, and irregular a narrative of scattered memories as Semprún's other novels about Buchenwald.[27] With such an accumulation of deaths, and memories of death, Semprún's *L'Évanouissement* can be seen as a form of what Blanchot calls "demise writing" (1986, 33) that characterizes the writing of the disaster.

Such is the recourse, also, that the narrator of *Le grand voyage* has taken up. Memory verges on demise as it is produced by one who knows that he is somehow dead already, one whose memories are, in a sense, impossible memories from the start. That is why there can be no unity in this narration—neither chronological unity in the sense of the linear progression that would characterize a bildungsroman-type of re-creation of one's life (for here that life has already been traversed by death, has already been wounded from before the moment of its being remembered), nor the unity of the subject, for the subject remembering and the subject remembered here will never be able to unite. They are irremediably divided into an unbridgeable "je" [I] and "tu" [you] since death has, again, shattered the unity of this self. For this reason, the recourse to memory on Gérard's part is, as Sally Silk claims, "the vain attempt to establish a subject position" that produces nothing more than an ever more deeply entrenched sense of "discursive homelessness" (1992, 57–58). It is thus necessarily an "unsatisfied" memory that emerges in Semprún's writing.

Gérard's effort, in *Le grand voyage*, to make this inhuman time of the Holocaust, this "died" event, a "lived" and minimally "human" time by imposing some semblance of order on the experience, comes to naught. He fails to impose the chronological fiction of days and nights on his endlessly haunting memory and likewise fails to create the autobiographical fiction of a life freely chosen and re-created at will. The horror of this experience, a horror that has shattered any possible stability forever, has proven too strong for any narrative counterstrategy.

In his study of narrative strategies used to recount such experiences of horror, Paul Ricoeur presents another way in which fiction is found at the heart of historical understanding. He maintains that certain historical events which are the founding rocks for the creation of a community's historical self-definition are events that give a "figure" (an inherently fictional structure) to history. That ability to create a "figure" is what provides such events with their founding force. He cites Rudolf Otto's concept of the *tremendum fascinosum,* the mixed feeling of veneration and fear that characterizes the sublime, the experience of the sacred. This construct is surely one of the strongest, if most pernicious, "founding" experiences that have anchored the historical identities of entire peoples. Ricoeur proposes, for such events as the Holocaust, the idea of the *tremendum horrendum.* These experiences produce a negative "founding" capacity. If the sacred sublime was the underlying dynamic for the appeal of an epic construction of history (a dynamic that was clearly at work, for example, in Nazi ideology), then the *tremendum horrendum* "constitutes the ultimate ethical motivation for the history of victims" (1984, 3:187). The horror dares to look at the dark, deathly, and deadly underside of the epic constructions of history and tries to let the voices of the victims be heard. But, like the individual before the *tremendum fascinosum* who cannot face, let alone communicate, his experience directly because of its overwhelming nature, one cannot face the horror of the *tremendum horrendum* directly. That is why fiction is necessary.

This same dynamic is encountered in trauma theory, where one is faced with an experience so devastating that the psyche cannot even register it, yet it forever reappears in endless, indirect ways. The horror, like trauma, reduces one to silence but at the same time creates the need to articulate that experience in some way: perhaps, through a special kind of silence. Celan's words in the epigraph to this chapter register how language was the only thing to remain secure amid all losses, but "it had to go through its own lack of answers, through terrifying silence, through the thousand darknesses of murderous speech" (1986, 34).

In *Language and Silence* (1967), George Steiner explores the different ways in which silence might be the most eloquent response to radical experiences of the inhuman, such as the Holocaust. Like Ricoeur, he compares (acknowledging an incommensurable difference) the horrified silence of many victims of the Holocaust and the silence of the witness to that other "sacred" space beyond the human, what some cultures have come to call God. Steiner cites, to illustrate his argument, the verses of Dante's *Divine Comedy* where the traveler, after his descent through hell and his ascent to heaven, finds himself at the end facing that sacred being that will remain beyond his comprehension, beyond words, beyond his memory's capacity to recall:

> ... Da quinci innanzi il mio veder fu maggio
> che'l parlar mostri, ch'a tal vista cede,

e cede la memoria a tanto oltraggio.
(1995, xxxiii, 773)

... Thenceforward, what I saw,
was not for words to speak, nor memory's self
To stand against such outrage on her skill.
(1897, xxxiii, 52–54)

This is a quintessential representation of the *tremendum fascinosum*, an experience that will prove to be an "outrage" on memory's skill because it will be impossible to recall in its plenitude. Its place is far beyond the sphere of the human. *Le grand voyage* presents a similar figure of a traveler who, like Dante, comes face to face with what is beyond words; this time it is the *tremendum horrendum*.

At a certain point in the journey, calls for attention emerge from the mass of bodies in the boxcar, for an old man is feeling sick, and people try to inch him closer to a window to save him. Gérard and the "gars de Semur" [guy from Semur], a young Frenchman with whom he has become friends and with whom he engages in conversation to make the passing time more "livable," take either arm of the old man and hold him up, his face in front of the window:

Le gars de Semur regarde le visage du vieillard et il ne répond pas. Le corps du vieillard se contracte subitement. Ses yeux redeviennent vivants et il fixe la nuit devant lui.
"Vous vous rendez compte?", dit-il, d'une voix basse mais distincte. Puis son regard chavire de nouveau et son corps s'affale entre nos bras. (1963, 63)

[The guy from Semur looks at the old man's face and he doesn't reply. The old man's body suddenly contracts. Life flows back into his eyes, and he stares at the night before him.
—"What do you know about that?"—he says, his voice low but distinct. Then his eyes again falter, and his body slumps into our arms.] (1964, 62)[28]

This old man, at the very moment of his death, looking into the night, has caught a glimpse of the horror, of the *tremendum horrendum*. Like Dante's traveler looking directly at God and experiencing the sight as an "outrage" on his memory, this last glimpse by the old man—at the *death* of God?—is even more than an outrage on memory. Much more.

The question "Vous vous rendez compte?" [What do you know about that?],[29] the weight of which was too much for the frail old man to bear, hovers over the whole text of *Le grand voyage*, causing *it* almost to break under its weight also. Gérard feels the import of the question and responds reiteratively: "Mais oui, je me rends compte. Je ne fais que ça, me rendre compte et en rendre compte. C'est bien ce que je souhaite.... Mais oui, je me rends compte, je ne fais que ça. Je me rends compte et j'essaie d'en rendre compte, tel est mon propos" (1963, 67–68) [I know, of course I know. That's all I've been doing, trying to know and to let others know.... Yes, I know, that's all I do know. I know, and I'm trying to let others know, which is my purpose here (1964, 66–67)].[30]

Gérard, indeed, takes up the challenge of facing this question, even if it leads him to his own death, as facing the night led the old man to his. Yes, "se rendre compte" "darse cuenta" [to know] and "en rendre compte" "dar cuenta de ello" [let others know] are Gérard's purposes.[31] They are why he engages in the enterprise of remembering this long journey to/through death. What gives Gérard the courage to embark on this mnemonic journey, retracing the forced voyage of years back, is the sense of responsibility in the face of the dying man's question. This responsibility is at the heart of what, following Levinas, Loureiro sees as the ethical constitution of the subject that is recurrently enacted in Semprún's texts, and which underscores the ethical nature of autobiographical writing. Following Levinas, for whom the highest form of responsibility is "being answerable for the death of the other" and "not let[ting] him die alone" (qtd. in Loureiro 2000, 166), Loureiro analyzes other moments, in *L'écriture ou la vie,* in which Semprún's writing becomes a way of not allowing others to die alone. According to Loureiro, it is the willingness to take up this fundamental responsibility that makes Semprún's writing become "not a literal memory of the facts, but an ethical memory instead" (2000, 167).

Gérard's response, in *Le grand voyage,* to the dying man's question contains, in fact, two fundamental elements that constitute the ethical memory that characterizes all of Semprún's writing about Buchenwald. "Je me rends compte" [I know] implies an epistemological project to know the reality of what happened, to face it, to assume it in all its horror, even if, or perhaps especially because, it means assuming the ultimate incomprehensibility of the experience, the final breakdown of such an epistemological project. "En rendre compte" [let others know] invokes a narrative commitment to share that knowledge, to find the appropriate means for making that knowledge available to others, even in the face of its ultimate incommunicability. I would add a third expression, following Semprún's own play on words around the term *"compte"* ("cuenta," in Spanish), which reflects the ethical memory based on responsibility toward the other in Semprún's writing. For he takes up writing, as one would say in Spanish, "por su cuenta y riesgo" [assuming personal responsibility and even risk for the project; my translation]. Semprún freely, conscientiously, knowingly assumes the responsibility, and the risk, of the ethical memory that his writing embodies, a self-consciousness and self-reflexivity that is at the heart of the meta-memory texts that he creates.³² Semprún's remembrance thus becomes a perfect example of a relentlessly "vigilant" memory.

The difficult return to the past that Semprún's first novel embodies was, in real life, something the writer undertook many years after his liberation from Buchenwald, forty years after that fated date, to be exact. In 1995, French television made a film of one of Semprún's first returns to the ruins of Buchenwald. During that visit, in an interview, Semprún talks of certain conversations that he and several fellow prisoners used to hold on Sundays, the only days on which the prisoners were allowed some social time. One of the recurrent conversations they had revolved around the sense of responsibility they already felt that, if they ever survived the camp, they would have to find the way to speak of what they were experiencing there:

Uno de los temas de conversación en Buchenwald... era cómo contarlo, ¿cómo podía contarse? Y la otra idea, el otro temor... era ¿pero nos creerán? A partir de ese momento resultaba evidente que sería necesario pasar por el artificio de la escritura, y que por verídico que fuera, el testimonio directo no bastaría. Permanecerían... no los libros espontáneos relatando los acontecimientos, sino los libros escritos, compuestos, es decir: el artificio del arte. (1995a)

[One of the topics of conversation in Buchenwald... was how to tell about it. How could one tell it? And the other idea: the other fear... was will they believe us? From that moment on, it was evident that it would be necessary to pass through the artifice of literature, and that, no matter how true it was, direct testimony would not suffice. What would last... were not the books spontaneously telling the events, but written, composed texts, that is to say, the artifice of art.] (My translation)

Fiction is deemed to be the necessary support for such a dangerous enterprise as trying to recount the real-life experience of deportation. This was something that the prisoners themselves were already anticipating, even while still in the camps, as if permanently haunted, like Gérard was, by the question raised by a dying old man in a boxcar on the way to the camp: "Vous vous rendez compte?" [What do you know about that?].

In *L'écriture ou la vie* Semprún again reiterates the need for fiction, in the form of "l'artifice d'un récit maîtrisé" (1994a, 23) [the artifice of a masterly narrative (1997, 13)] to transmit to others something of the unimaginable horror of the camps.³³ Artifice is needed to attempt to represent the truth of the testimony, and it does so precisely by means of a tale that is "maîtrisé," [masterly], one that gives its author some sense, however fleeting, of control while telling his story. The dynamics of trauma are clearly at work here. However, Semprún also explains that there is an important limit to this use of artifice, and that is: "ne jamais faciliter le travail des critiques négationnistes. Chaque mot est pesé afin que l'on ne puisse pas, sous le prétexte que tel ou tel détail est faux, remettre en cause la véracité de l'ensemble de mon témoignage" [never to facilitate the work of negationist critics. Each word is weighed so that it is impossible to put into question, on the pretext that such and such a detail is false, the veracity of my testimony as a whole (qtd. in Rubin Suleiman 2004, 3–4).

This limit that Semprún acknowledges is particularly important in light of certain recent events in Spain. In 2005, the research of historian Benito Bermejo uncovered the fact that Enric Marco, the man who had just been reelected president of the Amical Mauthausen, the organization representing Spanish deportees to Nazi concentration camps during World War II, had never been deported. Marco had completely invented the story of his deportation to the camps of Mauthausen and Flossenburg. He had, in fact, lived this public lie for almost thirty years, writing and speaking publicly about his interment, receiving such honors as the prestigious Cross of Saint Jorge (offered by the Generalitat, the Catalan autonomous government, in 2001 and quickly revoked when the news was made public), and, most ironically of all, becoming the president of the organization representing real Spanish ex-deportees.[34]

In Semprún's novels about Buchenwald there are many examples of fiction becoming an aid to help the writer survive the "outrage on memory" that his journey into the past embodies. As we the readers of Semprún's texts find out only in his later books, first in *Quel beau dimanche!* published seventeen years after *Le grand voyage,* and then in *L'écriture ou la vie,* appearing fourteen years after that, the "gars de Semur" [guy from Semur] in *Le grand voyage,* who engaged Gérard in conversation all through the train ride and thus helped him survive it, was someone Semprún had to invent. Retracing that journey alone would have been too much for him to bear. The invention of the "gars de Semur" was the artifice that Semprún had to add to the account of his real story to not only make it credible but to make it survivable.

It is a curious paradox that, after the narrator's first claim to have complete control over his narration and to be able to do whatever he desires with the story, he speaks precisely of the "gars de Semur":

J'ai décidé de parler de ce gars de Semur, à cause de Semur, et à cause de ce voyage. Il est mort à mes côtés, à la fin de ce voyage, j'ai fini ce voyage avec son cadavre debout contre moi. J'ai décidé de parler de lui, ça ne regarde personne, nul n'a rien à dire. C'est une histoire entre ce gars de Semur et moi. (1963, 24)

[I decided to talk about the guy from Semur because of Semur, because of this voyage. He died right next to me, at the end of the voyage, I finished this voyage with his body standing beside me. I made up my mind to talk about him, it's nobody's concern, nobody's but mine. It's between the guy from Semur and me.] (1964, 22)[35]

The narrator wants to uphold his power and control, as we have seen before, although it is basically a last attempt to keep from acknowledging his *lack* of control over the story. He says that this story is just between the "gars de Semur et moi" [the guy from Semur and me], as if to buttress himself on some source of human companionship. But that solace and support crumble when the reader realizes not only, as the narrator explains later in the same novel, that the "gars" will die at the end of the trip, but also, as the reader learns in later novels, that the "gars" never existed at all. This story is thus not between the narrator and someone else but between the narrator and himself, or, perhaps, between the narrator and death. Death is the only sure companion the narrator has had during the long journey to and back from Buchenwald. And death traverses every single word. That is what has made every single word so difficult to utter.

This difficulty, this near reduction to silence by so much death, is represented by yet another narrative breakdown in the text. Toward the end, when the train finally arrives at its destination, Buchenwald, Gérard tells of how the prisoners prepare to descend from the train. He has to leave behind the body of the "gars de Semur," a difficult thing, as he still tries to re-create or remember conversation with his friend:

Le gars de Semur est mort et je suis tout seul. Je pense qu'il avait dit: "Ne me laisse pas, vieux", et je marche vers la porte, pour sauter sur le quai. Je ne me souviens plus s'il avait dit ça: "Ne me laisse pas, vieux", ou s'il m'avait appelé par mon nom, c'est-à-dire, par le nom qu'il me connaissait.
  Peut-être avait-il dit: "Ne me laisse pas, Gérard", et Gérard saute sur le quai, dans la lumière aveuglante. (1963, 216)

[The guy from Semur is dead and I'm alone. I think that he had said: "Don't leave me alone, pal," and I walk toward the door to jump onto the platform. I don't remember whether he had said that: "Don't leave me alone, pal," or whether he had called me by my name, that is, by the name he knew me by.

Maybe he had said: "Don't leave me alone, Gérard," and Gérard jumps down onto the station platform, into the blinding light.] (1964, 217)[36]

There is a linguistic break in the middle of the last sentence, which ends part 1 of the book. The phrase changes suddenly, in mid-sentence, from first- to third-person narration, almost imperceptibly. The second, and very brief, section of the novel, which is the end of the book, continues to talk of Gérard in the third person and describes the arrival to the camp of the prisoners who survived the train ride. The shattering of the self that had already been highlighted between Gérard's "je" ["I"] and the "tu" ["you"] of the narrator is here emphasized by the radical inability of the narrator to identify with the protagonist once he enters the camp. The memory now becomes too painful, the wound so great that the narrator must completely break with the character (himself) he is remembering in order to survive his narration. We may recall Semprún's own words, in ". . . Vous avez une tombe au creux des nuages . . . ," when he describes why he could not write *Le grand voyage* for sixteen years and had to "décider d'être un autre, de ne pas être moi-même, pour continuer à être quelque chose: quelqu'un" (1995c, 94) [decide to become someone else, to not be myself, in order to continue to be something: someone (My translation)].[37]

Although this shift from first to third person is clearly related to the dynamics of trauma in Semprún's writing, it is important to note that such shifts are also found in other autobiographical narratives, such as those analyzed by Philippe Lejeune in his study "Autobiography in the Third Person." Lejeune explores the way many autobiographies present a similar shifting point of view, and how this narrative strategy underscores the fact that any stable and unitary sense of self is always necessarily an artificial construct that hides "the tension between impossible unity and intolerable division and the fundamental schism which turns the speaker into a fugitive" (1977, 32). The speaker in any autobiographical narrative is always a fugitive, because the identity that is being presented, or re-created, throughout the text is always inevitably escaping the constricting space of the first person, as it is caught in an endless tension between sameness and difference over time. In texts such as Semprún's, however, the traumatic nature of the memory recounted makes the speaker become a "fugitive" in a very special sense, since the difference that traverses identity in such narratives is the radical break that death itself implies when it is felt to have been "experienced" in life.

The simultaneous existence and nonexistence of the "gars de Semur," as well as the simultaneous survival and nonsurvival of the narrator of *Le grand voyage,* are two elements of the text that evoke, in interesting ways, the Simonides anecdote with which this chapter began. Although the twin gods Castor and Pollux did indeed save Simonides, they were never really present at any time. When the poet stepped out to answer their call, he found no one. They are, therefore, somewhat like the "gars de Semur"; they are invisible companions who engage the poet/writer so that he may survive and then go on to practice an art of memory to evoke all those who were not saved.

It is important to remember that Castor and Pollux were twin sons of Zeus, alike in most respects except in one essential trait: one was immortal (Pollux) while the other was mortal (Castor). In one version of their story, upon Castor's death, Pollux asked Zeus to make him die, too, so he could be with his brother. Zeus, moved by such fraternal love, made them both share Pollux's immortality, and thereafter they both lived, together, one day in heaven, in life, and one day in Hades, in death. Castor and Pollux thus ultimately combine mortality and immortality, demise and survival, life and death. They are two who become as one, but one being of an inherently dual nature. Likewise, the narrator in Semprún's texts is often a person who becomes two, as he has to "décider d'être un autre, de ne pas être moi-même, pour continuer à être quelque chose: quelqu'un" (1995c, 94) [decide to become someone else, to not be myself, in order to continue to be something: someone (My translation)].[38] Furthermore, in *Le grand voyage* Gérard specifically needs to invent a kind of "twin," a brotherly companion to save himself on his journey back into his past. The question remains, however, which of the two "brothers" in this story is the mortal one and which the immortal one, or more appropriately for nondivine beings, which is the brother who dies and which the one who survives. Within the text, of course, it is clearly the "gars de Semur" who dies and Gérard the one who outlives him. Extratextually, however, as we know that Gérard is a version of Semprún himself, it is he who is unquestionably mortal while the "gars de Semur" ["guy from Semur"] is immortal inasmuch as he is a purely fictional character. Of course, this distinction does not hold perfectly, for no matter how closely we may associate Gérard with Semprún himself, from the moment that we meet him in the pages of a book, he is also a fictional character. Life and death, mortality and immortality are inextricably intertwined here; they are irremediably destabilized in a narration that itself borders on its own demise.

A text such as this one, therefore, presents a whole series of narrative breakdowns and shake-ups. The unified self that is often presented in traditional autobiographical narrations is shattered and fragmented here, as is any illusion of linear progression or ultimate closure to the memories recounted. These are the different strategies by means of which the traumatic memory explored in this narrative presents a non-referential, performative relation to history, to the history of the horror of the Holocaust. The historical reality of the Holocaust becomes an event that is not *referred to* but that is *written directly into* these various narrative breakdowns. What is represented, or better yet, endlessly repeated in these various breakdowns is the traumatic experience of the loss of power, control, and meaning inherent in this experience of the "disaster," to use Blanchot's expression. However, this endless repetition of various breakdowns is not solely an example of acting out, but also one of working through the ethical memory of the Holocaust, for they are presented as a process whereby the self takes on the responsibility of facing the past as part of assuming the challenges of the present and the future.

An important aspect to reiterate, when dealing with issues such as these, which are crucial to current debates in literary theory, is that the dynamics of trauma never come to a point of complete resolution. The traumatic memory recurs inevitably and thus has to be dealt with forever in new contexts, in new situations where we might have thought the problem had been finally settled. It is, inevitably, a most "unsatisfied" memory. Narratives of traumatic memories help us realize that the interdependence of history and fiction, of truth and artifice, of remembering and forgetting, are issues that will eternally return, that will be compulsively repeated over and over again at different times.

A poignant image of this never-ending process appears in *L'écriture ou la vie*. Semprún describes the ceremony where *Le grand voyage* was awarded the Formentor Literature Prize in 1964. The various editorial houses of the different European countries that had translated the book presented him with a commemorative copy of the novel. As Carlos Barral handed him the Spanish edition, the Spanish editor had to explain that, because of problems with the Franco censorship in Spain and difficulties with the printing in Mexico, the commemorative Spanish copy had the cover of the book as it would appear when published, but the rest of the book was blank. Every single page, a blank one. Semprún meditates on the symbolic appropriateness of this fact. He had, indeed, "blanked out" his mother tongue when writing the book, for it was a language he felt, at the time, exiled from, just as he had been exiled from Spain. But the symbolism had another welcome dimension, on which he comments: "J'en aime l'augure et le symbole: que ce livre soit encore à écrire, que cette tâche soit infinie, cette parole inépuisable" (1994a, 285) [I love the promise and symbolism of it: that this book yet remains to be written, that the task is infinite, the tale never-ending (1997, 276)].[39] Indeed, Semprún's novels evoking his memories of Buchenwald are part of an infinite task; infinite, in part, because they deal with a kind of memory that will never be exhausted, that must, on the contrary, be written through till exhaustion, and beyond.

This blank book can, paradoxically, be interpreted as a palimpsest. The traumatic memory narrated in Semprún's novels is one that can be characterized by what Derrida describes as the "traces of a past that has never been present" (1986, 58). This book made of void pages, full of absent traces, is the one that best represents the accumulation of memory traces that are the legacy of a traumatic concentration camp experience. The lack of traces really points to the fact that there will be an endless proliferation of marks, of writing, that, as Semprún states in *L'écriture ou la vie*, are still to come, destined to be inscribed in what is, for now, a void, a blank book.

This same image evoking implicitly a palimpsestic writing, a layer upon layer of writing that will never exhaust what he has to recall of his experience, comes up again in the documentary of one of Semprún's first visits to Buchenwald after his liberation:

> Al cabo de tres libros, me queda más por decir que antes de empezar a escribir el primero. Se produce un doble fenómeno, como si la escritura ordenara y despertara la memoria a la vez.... La escritura despierta la memoria. Me da la impresión, tal vez no lo haga, de que tengo más que decir ahora que antes de empezar a escribir *Le grand voyage*. Cuanto más escribo, más me queda por decir. Se forman asociaciones, interconexiones, referencias, que se nutren de la propia experiencia y de lo sucedido después. (1995a)
>
> [After three books, I still have more to tell than when I started to write the first one. A double phenomenon takes place, as if writing ordered and awakened memory at the same time.... Writing awakens memory. I have the impression, maybe I won't do it, that I have more to say now than before I started writing *Le grand voyage*. The more I write, the more I have left to say. Associations, interconnections, references are formed that are nourished by the experience itself and by what has happened afterwards.] (My translation)

These endless "asociaciones, interconexiones, referencias" [associations, interconnections, references] will, indeed, become the palimpsestic traces that Semprún will endlessly write and rewrite into those void, blank pages of the award-winning Spanish edition of his first book, his first meta-memory text, about his concentration camp experience.

* * * *

Although the first Spanish edition of Semprún's novel was blank, an image that obviously points to the way that the Franco regime attempted to "erase" and "blank out" what it was not interested in having people know, it is important to highlight the contribution and relevance of this text, as well as of all of Semprún's Buchenwald novels, to the Spanish literary tradition.

First of all, there is the moral imperative behind recuperating in Spain the literary writings by the numerous Spaniards exiled after the Civil War. Within such exile literature, however, there is an added reason to recapture the voices of the Spaniards who experienced the horror of the Holocaust. These survivors, though not silenced by the event itself, were then silenced by a relative lack of interest in their stories back home. It is known that there were Spaniards in Mauthausen, Auschwitz, Buchenwald, Flossenburg, Neuengamme, Sachsenhausen, and Ravensbruck, at least, but the interest in incorporating into the Spanish tradition any literature or testimonies that emerged from these experiences has been meager.[40]

Furthermore, there are important reasons to contextualize a novel like *Le grand voyage* within the tradition created by other Spanish novels of its time. Appearing in 1963, the same year as Martín-Santos's *Tiempo de silencio* [*Time of Silence*], *Le grand voyage* fits in with the literary innovation beginning to take hold in Spanish fiction at that moment, as well as with part of what characterized the previous trend of social realist novels. As David Herzberger explains, one of the ways to read social realist novels of the 1950s, a reading that emphasizes their contestatory value vis-à-vis Francoist ideology, is a perspective that *Le grand voyage* also invites. Many social realist novels demythify Francoist ideology by counterposing to the Francoist mythic construction of the past as epic grandeur an implicit exploration of what Ricoeur calls the *tremendum horrendum*. Herzberger states: "Social realist fiction is thus placed in the service of the unforgettable (i.e., of poverty, isolation, alienation, and the like), which the State plainly set out both to annul and to forget" (1995, 45). Social realist fiction evoked the dark underside of the Spanish past that the epic myth of the Spanish tradition erected by Francoist historiography wanted to obscure. This concept of the *tremendum horrendum* was developed by Ricoeur to study Holocaust literature, and, as has been seen earlier, it is precisely what *Le grand voyage* explores. Thus, *Le grand voyage* presents, in a different context, an undermining of mythic, epic constructions of history similar to that which, according to Herzberger, was undertaken by much of Spanish social realist narrative.

Yet *Le grand voyage* is not a social realist novel at all. In fact, the strategies of narrative breakdown and traumatic memory it highlights point to a questioning of such "realist" literary models. These breakdowns in narrative logic and construction, created by the exploration of traumatic memory, are what make *Le grand voyage* an excellent example of the kind of literary production that Herzberger claims followed after the decline of the social realist novel, what he calls the "novel of memory."

In these novels, the past is presented subjectively, often recreated in an individual's memory. That memory then "serves to sap the roots of myth-producing narrations and to shed the thick wrapping of narrative closure" (Herzberger 1995, 85). This subjective exploration of the past sounds very much like a description of the effects of retracing traumatic memory in *Le grand voyage*. Furthermore, the following description of the subversive potential of the Spanish novel of memory in the face of a mythic and oppressive construction of history defines *Le grand voyage* perfectly: "the novel of memory lays out history as a series of disruptions—of time, of self, of narration, and most importantly, of the referential illusion of truth and wholeness" (1995, 85).

Written at just the time when the Spanish literary scene was turning from social realism to such "novels of memory," *Le grand voyage* can be seen to reflect this shift in representational strategies, albeit within a different context. This view of the novel underscores how *Le grand voyage* relates to the novels written before it in Spain and how it resonates with the new literary tendencies emerging at the time of its publication.

The "disruption . . . of the referential illusion of truth and wholeness" that characterizes the Spanish "novels of memory" is presented in Semprún's work through a particularly poignant image. In *L'écriture ou la vie*, Semprún tells of how, only days after the liberation of Buchenwald, he is put in charge of guiding two young women from the French liberating mission through the camps. Upon seeing the ashes covering the mountains of corpses piled near the crematorium, he reflects upon the utter impossibility of explaining, at that moment, the meaning or truth of that scene. In an articulation of what may be seen as the essence of the traumatic dynamic that has been extensively analyzed here, he observes:

> ces morts horribles et fraternels n'avaient pas besoin d'explication. Ils avaient besoin que nous vivions, tout simplement, que nous vivions de toutes nos forces dans la mémoire de leur mort: toute autre forme de vie nous arracherait à l'enracinement dans cet exil de cendres. (1994a, 133)

> [these dreadful and fraternal dead needed no explanation. They needed us to live, quite simply, to live with all our strength in the memory of their death: any other kind of life would uproot us from this exile of ashes.] (1997, 122)[41]

That the exile from explanation, from a referential attempt to represent the truth or meaning of this historical event, takes the form of *"cendres"* [ashes], of the cinders of so many bodies that, as Celan has also exclaimed, only found their "grave . . . in the clouds" (1980, 63), is significant. Derrida has seen in cinders the most powerful image of that structure of the trace that attempts to deconstruct the metaphysics of presence upon which all referential illusions are based. By being an image of what in its very presence implies absence, "Cinders is a destruction of memory, one in which the very sign of destruction is carried off. . . . Cinders is a trope that comes to take the place of everything that disappears without leaving an identifiable trace. The difference between the trace cinder and other traces is that the body of which cinders is the trace has totally disappeared. . . . And forgetting itself is forgotten" (1995, 389, 391).

The ashes of the burned corpses covering the mountains of yet unburned bodies in Buchenwald do indeed testify to an attempt on the Nazis' part to erase all memory of this historical event. The memory of this image will thus have to be one of forgetting and absence itself. We may recall Freud's description of the memory left behind by a traumatic experience and notice its similarity to the working of the trace of cinders: "Such memory-traces, then, have nothing to do with the fact of becoming conscious; indeed they are often most powerful and most enduring when the process which left them behind was one which never entered consciousness" (1961a, 27). In order to recover that memory, Semprún enters, again, into that exile of cinders. He relives the deaths of so many by a process of putting into play multiple disappearing traces in his narrative: the disappearance of entire characters invented only to be acknowledged as fictions; the disappearance of his own coherent narrative identity as it is ceaselessly fragmented and broken down into the many possible combinations of narrative personae; the disappearance of that illusion of temporal wholeness in the form of an attempted stable chronological figure governing his narratives; the disappearance, ultimately, of the very possibility of a referential truth and meaning to his texts beyond these narrative strategies of disappearance. The blank copy of *Le grand voyage*—that palimpsest without writing—is one more image—perhaps the most powerful—of the disappearing trace governing Semprún's narration.

All these texts, therefore, arise out of a willing reentry into the exile of cinders from which Semprún came out half alive/half dead. Like the twin gods Castor and Pollux, dividing their time between the land of the living and that of the dead, Semprún, with each novel about Buchenwald, revisits that scene of the dead bodies covered with ashes to live through it again. Semprún makes a place, not just in the stories he tells, but in the very narrative strategies used to tell them, where he can relive the memory of the death of so many companions. This is particularly significant for, as Simonides (that other survivor of a tragic event) once learned, making an appropriate place for things is one of the best ways to guarantee their being remembered.

In fact, Semprún literally seems to take up Simonides's task when he narrates, in *L'écriture ou la vie,* his very first return to Buchenwald after liberation, in 1992, to make a documentary for German television. Semprún, after entering the gate of the compound and seeing how many of the buildings in the camp have disappeared, begins to explain to those accompanying him where each building had been, as he remembers where they each stood in relation to one another, just as Simonides had done at his banquet with respect to the other guests.[42] Semprún reflects on the significance of this empty space that he must re-create through memory: "Le résultat était d'une force dramatique incroyable. L'espace vide ainsi créé, cerné par l'enceinte barbelée, dominé par la cheminée du crématoire, balayé par le vent de l'Ettersberg, était un lieu de mémoire bouleversant" (1994a, 305) ["The effect was unbelievably powerful. The empty space thus created, surrounded by barbed wire, dominated by the crematory chimney, swept by the wind off the Ettersberg, was a place of overwhelming remembrance" (1997, 296)].[43]

It is no coincidence that Semprún here uses the French term *"lieu de mémoire,"* evoking Pierre Nora's concept for a real event or symbolic structure that evokes a particular memory and around which a collectivity creates its identity. For Nora, the fundamental purpose of such a *"lieu de mémoire"* is to "block the work of forgetting, to establish a state of things, to immortalize death, to materialize the immaterial" (1989, 19). This is what the empty space in the courtyard of Buchenwald becomes in Semprún's text, a place of remembrance, a *"lieu de mémoire"* upon which he must bring his personal memory to bear lest it become an empty space bereft of traces of the past. By means of his remembering, however, this space becomes a reminder of a past that must not be repeated by future generations, a place for the forging of a collective identity built upon the knowledge of the horror of the past, not its forgetting. Nora further states that a "place of memory" functions to preserve "the presence of the past within the present" (1989, 20). The place of memory that Semprún sees in Buchenwald, however, is characterized in large part by absence, by the disappearance of many of the buildings of the camp. Like Semprún's blank copy of *Le grand voyage,* a palimpsest made of blank pages that will continuously need to be filled, this place of memory is also one that must continuously be re-created. In highlighting the process of mental reconstruction of the camp that he has to undertake to turn it into a place of memory, Semprún foregrounds that the creation of places of remembrance is always a process that must be engaged in actively, not passively received.

It is important to indicate that the "lugar de memoria" that Buchenwald becomes through Semprún's remembering is one that evokes multiple histories of horror, a multiplicity that Semprún is particularly well suited to evoke, since his life was likewise traversed by them. For not only was Buchenwald a German concentration camp, but, soon afterwards, from 1945 to 1952, it was used as a Soviet internment camp for victims of Stalinist repression. Semprún thinks that Buchenwald is thus a particularly important place of memory. In fact, by embodying different histories of oppression, not always acknowledged to have been present in the same site, it is also a perfect example of the kind of "place of recognition" discussed in the introduction. It is a reminder, located in the heart of Europe, of two different histories of oppression, and can thus now become, if acknowledged adequately, "un lieu de mémoire et de culture internationale de la Raison démocratique" (1994a, 316) [a place of remembrance, an international center of Democratic Reason (1997, 306)].[44] Any future of democracy in Europe must thus be constructed in full awareness, in full remembrance, of the various histories of horror in its past. Semprún's conviction that memory is important for constructing democracy leads him to state in an interview that "toda [mi] obra intenta luchar contra el olvido" (Chapa 1989) [all [my] work tries to fight against forgetting] and that "no basta con recordar sino que es necesario saber contrar lo que se recuerda para que la memoria sea útil" (Chapa 1989) [it is not enough to remember, it is necessary to know how to tell what you remember so that memory may become useful].

By highlighting that the place of memory at Buchenwald evokes not only the Nazi past of the setting, but also the Stalinist repression that is not commonly associated with the camp, Semprún puts into play a double dynamic at the heart of Nora's concept of *lieux de mémoire*. Peter Carrier defines this as a process of both "construction" and "deconstruction" (2000, 50). Places of memory construct a symbolic object around which a community develops a sense of identification, but they also deconstruct previous associations in order to make that identity emerge anew out of a series of "disidentifications," in which the past is continually perceived in a new light.[45] It is this combination of construction and deconstruction at the heart of the creation of places of memory that makes such a process, according to Carrier, become "a heuristic tool for understanding the present-day political instrumentality of memory" (2000, 51), a quote that recalls Semprún's own concern for finding ways to present his recollections in a manner that "may become useful."

The desire to make memory useful in constructing the future makes Semprún reflect often on the role of younger generations, born after the Holocaust, who may all too easily forget this past when those who have lived through it have disappeared. *Le grand voyage,* for example, is dedicated to a young Spanish boy, Jaime, "parce qu'il a 16 ans" [because he is sixteen years old]. Within the text, the narrator reflects on the fact that he is writing his book exactly sixteen years after his liberation from the camp, in the hopes that someone of the age of that young boy, born after the experience, might hear and be moved (and moved to action, perhaps?) by that story (1963, 162, 191). The novel further presents, in its last page, an anguished reflection on the narrator's part about how some day there will be no one left who will have lived the experience of deportation, of "the long voyage" he has so carefully re-created in his text.

In *L'écriture ou la vie* the same concern for the transmission of memory to a younger generation is present. The book is dedicated to a young girl, Cécilia, daughter of Semprún's friends, and, as we may surmise from the text, the sister of two boys who accompany Semprún on his first trip back to Buchenwald in 1992 to shoot a German documentary. Semprún had, in fact, dedicated *Quel beau dimanche!* to one of these boys, Thomas. At the end of *L'écriture ou la vie,* as he is overcome by emotion upon entering the courtyard at Buchenwald, he explains "J'ai posé une main sur l'épaule de Thomas Landman, qui se trouvait près de moi. Je lui avais dédicacé *Quel beau dimanche!* pour qu'il pût, plus tard, après ma mort, se souvenir de mon souvenir de Buchenwald.... J'ai posé une main sur l'épaule de Thomas, comme un passage de témoin" (1994a, 301) [I placed a hand on the shoulder of Thomas Landman, who was by my side. I had dedicated *Quel beau dimanche!* to him so that later, after my death, he might remember my memories of Buchenwald.... I placed a hand on Thomas's shoulder, as though calling him to witness in his turn (1997, 292)].[46] Semprún is here explicitly passing on the responsibility of witnessing to the next generation. He is creating a role for a second-generation Simonides, who may not have lived the experience of the camp, but who is witnessing Semprún's re-living of that experience, both by being with him during his return to the site, and, presumably, by receiving all the re-creations of Semprún's experience in his writings. Immediately following this moment in the text, Semprún again thinks of the inevitable disappearance of all those who have lived through the Holocaust, and the danger of it then becoming only a vague, theoretical, cold and distant fact in a history book.[47]

Not only is the empty courtyard of Buchenwald evoked at the end of *L'écriture ou la vie* an important "lugar de la memoria," or "lugar de reconocimiento," but all of Semprún's meta-memory texts about the camp become such "places of memory," and particularly effective ones at that. There are several reasons for this. First of all, Semprún's life story, as has been seen, is deeply marked by several of the most tragic events, and histories of repression, of the twentieth-century that we still need to work through at the beginning of the twenty-first. Semprún is especially well situated, therefore, to make important connections among these events, which are often considered separately. Semprún's life and work connect the reality of exile after the Spanish civil war with that of the much more radical exilic experience of surviving the Holocaust. He faced both the horror of Stalinist oppression and the devastation of Francoist repression in his political activism after Buchenwald. His work, to this day, continues to highlight how, as links among European nations become ever stronger, it is all the more important to understand the connections among the various national histories, and the various traumatic events marking those histories.

However, it is precisely the fact that Semprún's writing about the past takes the form of meta-memory texts that makes them particularly appropriate "lugares de la memoria" today. For they consistently, and self-reflexively, thematize the very process of the creation of a *"lieux de mémoire"* itself. They recurrently enact, and consistently reflect on that very process of enacting, the task of working through the past. If Semprún's texts incessantly re-create numerous breakdowns and traumatic ruptures within their very writing, they also explicitly reflect on how to make such a literary endeavor serve a forward-looking project. This is present in the explicit reflection at the end of several of his texts on how to guarantee that his memory is taken up by future generations, who are hopefully those that will build the new Europe of "Democratic Reason" (1994a, 306).

The *"lieu de mémoire"* [place of remembrance] that Buchenwald becomes in Semprún's texts, all his writings about the camp, in fact, can be seen as examples of the kind of "lugar de la memoria" [place of remembrance] that Manuel Reyes Mate calls for in the article "Lugares de la memoria" mentioned in the introduction to this book. Reyes Mate calls for the creation of "lugares de la memoria" to develop an effective "culture of memory" in Spain today, one that would adequately confront the traumatic experiences of the civil war and Franco repression, something that still needs to be done, despite Spain's having enjoyed almost thirty years of post-Franco democracy. Semprún's explicit reflections on the process of creating effective "places of memory" within an extreme-limit case such as that of the Holocaust thus have much to contribute to the current state of affairs in Spain where a similar process of working through the past is still under way.[48]

Semprún's work seeks a balance between presenting his process of working through memory, and presenting memory itself, as both a gift of sorts and a burden, a responsibility being passed on to his readers, especially to younger generations. At the end of *L'écriture ou la vie*, when Semprún describes how, upon returning to Buchenwald after almost forty years, he placed his hand on the shoulder of the young Thomas (as if christening him as a new, second-generation Simonides), he describes his own hand in that gesture as "une main légère comme la tendresse que je lui portais, lourde comme la mémoire que je lui transmettais" (1994a, 302) [a hand as gentle as the affection I felt for him, as weighty as the memory I entrusted to him (1997, 293)].[49] Enacted between the gentle effect of a touch on the shoulder and the weighty responsibility of a memory being transmitted, Semprún's meta-memory texts certainly have much to contribute to the much-needed development of a "culture of memory" in Spain.

2
Juan Benet: The *Pharmakon* of Memory

Determinada manera de pensar que siempre ha partido de un estrecho paralelismo moral entre el contenido del discurso literario y el contenido del pensamiento, día a día más alimentado por sus raíces científicas, ha pretendido salvar el escollo de la plurivalencia de aquél mediante el destierro de una buena parte a una zona aislada de la cultura. Así el irracionalismo se ha constituido como un campo de concentración de todo aquel discurso que no conviene a las leyes de la razón dominante.... [E]ste discurso literario del que hablo no se propone una rebelión contra los principios dominantes de la razón cuanto la trasposición del pensamiento a un terreno donde toda suerte de certeza es quimérica, cuestionable y estéril; donde no valen las acotaciones de racionalidad e irracionalidad y donde—gracias a la apertura que introducen la contradicción y el misterio—impera el espíritu de lucha de los contrarios. Es el imperio del oxymoron: sólo lo fugaz dura y permanece, todo lo verdadero muestra su falsedad, todo lo evidente encierra su misterio.

[A certain mode of thinking that has always been based on a tight moral parallelism between the content of literary discourse and the content of thought, increasingly fed by its scientific roots, has tried to surmount the obstacle of the multivalence of literary discourse by banishing a good part of it to an isolated zone of culture. Thus, irrationalism has been constituted as a concentration camp for all discourse that is inconvenient for the dominant laws of reason.... This literary discourse of which I am speaking does not so much propose a rebellion against the dominant principles of reason as a transposition of thinking itself to a terrain where all certainty is quimerical, questionable and sterile; where the boundaries between rationality and irrationality do not prevail, and where—thanks to the opening provided by contradiction and mystery—the spirit of the battle of opposites reigns. It is the domain of oxymoron: only what is fleeting endures and remains, everything true reveals its falseness, everything obvious contains its mystery.]

—Juan Benet 1976d, 52–53

IN PLATO'S DIALOGUE "PHAEDRUS" SOCRATES RECOUNTS AN EGYPTian myth about the origin of writing as an aid to memory. Derrida's reading of this myth in "Plato's Pharmacy" is illuminating for an understanding of the role of memory and writing in the works of Juan Benet.

Plato tells of how the god Theuth, inventor of numbers and calculation, of geometry and astronomy, as well as of the calendar, offers several of his new inventions to his superior, the divinity Thamus. Among these is the art of writing, which he enthusiastically extends to Thamus, exclaiming: "This discipline, my King, will make the Egyptians wiser and will improve their memories: my invention is a recipe for both memory and wisdom" (qtd. in Derrida 1981, 75). Theuth affirms that, by writing things down, people will remember them better and learn more easily. The term Plato uses for "recipe" is *pharmakon*, which means more than a recipe: a remedy, a cure.

It is interesting, as Derrida points out, that this same word, *pharmakon*, also harbors the opposite meaning: poison. If writing is to serve as the remedy that will help make memory better, it is at the same time the poison that will endanger it. This is, in fact, the way that Thamus understands his gift, for he rejects it saying that people will not improve their memories but see them deteriorate with such an invention. By having things written down, their own faculty of recall will atrophy. They will come to rely on the external aid of writing and forget to develop their own mnemonic skills through oral repetition. Thus Thamus concludes: "So it is not a remedy for memory, but for reminding, that you have discovered" (qtd. in Derrida 1981, 102).

Writing as the *pharmakon* for memory is thus a highly ambiguous gift, truly an oxymoron. As the epigraph to this chapter implies, Benet believes that literary discourse must both subject itself to and also help create an "imperio del oxymoron" [domain of oxymoron]. That "imperio" [domain] is characterized by the sovereignty of "la contradicción y el misterio [donde] impera el espíritu de la lucha de los contrarios" [contradiction and mystery [where] the spirit of the battle of opposites reigns]. It is the highly contradictory nature of the *pharmakon*, a word that epitomizes such a "lucha de los contrarios" [battle of opposites], that makes it particularly appropriate for understanding the way Juan Benet explores the relationship between writing and memory. This is especially true since memory itself is a recurrent, one might even say obsessive, theme in all of Benet's writing.[1]

Benet has elaborately developed, in a series of critical articles, the views on language and memory that infuse his novelistic world. He has acknowledged the continuity between his creative and critical writing: "Les diré que en el fondo es lo mismo. . . . yo creo que son la misma obra." [I will tell you that they are really the same thing. . . . I believe they are all the same work) (Dyson and Rozlapa 1977, 21). It is thus revealing to extract from his theoretical writings the clues they provide for adequately understanding the dynamic of the *pharmakon* in his creative works.[2]

It is well known that Benet represented a clear break from the social realist narrative tradition in vogue when he began writing in the middle of the twentieth century. In fact, Benet was one of the earliest, most outspoken, and polemical critics of that literary movement.[3] He rejects the view that literature should, or can, reflect the world. He has developed an understanding of the opacity of language which is manifested through a dense and complex writing style. Benet has further proclaimed the artist's engagement not to the social reality around him but only to the literary value of his work. These characteristics, among others, have made many critics see him as one of the most ardent and radical promoters of a "new novel" in Spain, influenced by the French *nouveau roman*.[4]

Benet's view of literature grows out of a deep-seated mistrust for the illusion of the transparency of language. In his opinion, realism in literature shares this conception of language with science in its desire to illuminate and understand the world. The literature that interests Benet, and that he will produce, should not try to explain the world, as science supposedly does, but, quite to the contrary, should try to keep, and foment, the mystery of the unexplained and unexplainable: "por cuanto esa literatura se ha liberado del demonio de la exactitud . . . [deberá] fomentar la invención de esa clase de misterio que por su naturaleza se encuentra y se encontrará siempre más allá del poder del conocimiento" [inasmuch as such literature has been liberated from the demon of exactitude, . . . [it should] foment the creation of that kind of mystery that by its very nature is found, and will always be found, beyond the power of knowledge] (1976d, 48–49). What lies "más allá del poder del conocimiento" [beyond the power of knowledge] is what he repeatedly calls a "zona de sombras" [zone of shadows], a realm beyond that which is clarified by scientific knowledge and reason, which is, for Benet, the realm that literature must explore: "Pero para el hombre de letras en ese mismo punto empieza su zona de sombra, su ámbito de trabajo, su fuente de estímulos e inspiración" [But for the man of letters it is at that very point where his zone of shadows begins, his work space, his source of stimulation and inspiration] (1976d, 51). In an image, borrowed from Faulkner, that is emblematic of Benet's literary project, literature should be like a match that "no despeja las tinieblas, sino tan sólo muestra su horror" [does not dispel the darkness, but only shows its horror] (1976d, 77).

One of the factors that produces this sense of "horror" is that the language used in any literary enterprise already makes it impossible to enter fully that "zona de sombras" [zone of shadows], the "tinieblas" [darkness] that Benet wants literature to explore. Language itself imposes a certain amount of reason and order onto experience. The chaos and contradictoriness of lived experience is inevitably subjected to a minimum of rational order as it is encapsulated in words. This is precisely why, for Benet, the writer must exploit the *pharmakon*, or contradictory nature of writing:

> De ese hombre [de letras] surge entonces una literatura que es antagonista con la ciencia. . . . Y utilizará su razón para oponerse a la razón . . . haciendo uso de las mismas reglas que utiliza la ciencia pero cargándolas—digámoslo así—de una polaridad distinta, al igual que el cambio de signo en la carga del electrón convierte a la materia en la antimateria. (1976d, 50)

> [From that man [of letters] emerges a literature that is antagonistic to science. . . . And he will use his reason to oppose reason . . . making use of the same rules that science utilizes but charging them—so to say—with a different polarity, just as the change of sign in the charge of the electron converts matter into antimatter.]

Writing is both the instrument that will allow the man of letters to explore the mysterious, chaotic, contradictory nature of his experience in the world *and* the barrier that will keep him from doing so. Writing is both the desired remedy and the feared malady.

It must not be forgotten, furthermore, that Theuth invented writing as a means to improve memory, for memory is also, in Benet's work, the ultimate goal of literature. Time, and the capacity of human beings to live in time and to try to express that experience in words, is a major concern in his novels. As he himself has expressed, defining his narrative world: "La idea principal quizás sea medir el tiempo. O calificarlo, tal vez" (Campbell 1971, 266) [The main idea is perhaps that of measuring time. Or of qualifying it, perhaps].

The Bergsonian interest in exploring the disorder of memory as a way to counter the imposed order of scientific, supposedly objective time is a main theme of most Benetian narrative.[5] In Bergson's mistrust of language to capture adequately the fluid and heterogeneous experience of pure *durée*, Benet recognizes his own apprehensions about language's capacity to explore fully the "zona de sombras." The Bergsonian *durée* is a vital experience of time in which memory and perception are linked, creating a lived experience in which past, present, and future are inextricably and simultaneously imbricated. Any attempt to explain such an experience in words, by virtue of language's linear nature, foregoes that simultaneity by forcing the three different temporal realms of past, present, and future to be successive.[6]

Bergson sees that the pure *durée* of lived time is betrayed by an imposition of chronological time as soon as it is put into words: "Au lieu d'une *durée* hétérogène dont les moments se pénètrent, nous aurons alors un temps homogène dont les moments s'alignent dans l'espace" (1970, 178) [Instead of a heterogeneous *durée* where all moments penetrate each other, we would then have a homogeneous time where all moments align themselves in space]. Bergson's description of the *durée* as an experience of time in which the different heterogeneous moments "se pénètrent" [penetrate each other] is particularly revealing. The sexual overtones of this expression will become manifest in Benet's appropriation of the Bergsonian *durée*. Benet will recurrently present characters that try to recapture that heterogeneous time of pure *durée* through memory, in particular the memory of sexual experiences and instinctive pleasure.

Furthermore, for Benet, there is an important distinction to be made between what he calls "tiempo instintivo" [instinctive time] and "tiempo intelectualizado" [intellectualized time] (1976a, 98). By means of their exploration, through memory, of their past (in particular their past experiences of instinctive pleasure), characters in Benet's novels attempt to regain the sense of pure *durée*. However, inasmuch as these experiences have to be transcribed through language, and Benet himself has to present them to us, the readers, by means of words, that "tiempo instintivo" will always be unattainable, always caught underneath the web of the "tiempo intelectualizado" that language inevitably imposes.

In this process, memory itself will also turn out to be a contradictory, oxymoronic entity: a *pharmakon*. Following the Bergsonian approach, memory for Benet is the faculty that allows one to escape the imprisonment of rational, orderly thought: "[el hombre de letras] que ha comprobado para sí mismo cómo la experiencia logra desmentir las leyes más inconclusas y socavar la axiomática más rigurosa, en lo sucesivo sólo confiará en su memoria" (1976d, 61) [[the man of letters] that has seen for himself how experience manages to belie the most inconclusive laws and undermine the most rigorous axiomatic will henceforward only confide in his memory]. However, memory will also be allied with everything that imposes order as soon as one tries to share that experience with others: "La pasión explora, la memoria coloniza" [passion explores, memory colonizes] and "poco a poco la memoria va colonizando el terreno explorado por la pasión" (1970a, 100, 105) [little by little memory colonizes the terrain explored by passion].

This is the trap that Benet's characters face. They turn to memory as an escape from the colonization of rational thought and social order only to find that memory then becomes a colonizing, ordering agent itself. For this reason, Benet's novelistic world, Región, is forever submerged in a state of paralysis, forever longing for something that is lost to it; ever more lost, the more it is sought.[7]

In the quotation that serves as an epigraph to this chapter, Benet talks of how the "escollo de la plurivalencia" [obstacle of ... multivalence] and the "irracionalismo" [irrationalism] that, in his view, characterize the best literature have been pushed aside by science and culture as if into "un campo de concentración" [a concentration camp]. Here we have a glimpse of how the *pharmakon* of memory in Benet might prove to be akin to the trauma of memory in Semprún, raising similar issues of the interrelatedness of history and fiction. Indeed, as seen in the previous chapter, trauma itself functions as a kind of *pharmakon*, being both the illness and the cure, continually repeating and re-creating the very thing that one was trying to escape from. Semprún's "wounding" of chronology in his novels was seen to be a re-creation of the wound inflicted on him by his concentration camp experience. Benet will present a similar wounded chronology in his works. Yet, because of Benet's radical rejection of realism and of the transparency of language altogether, much more is wounded in his novels than just chronology. Almost every traditional narrative structure is broken down: from temporal linearity, to plot and character development, to coherence in terms of point of view.

Robert Spires has defined the antirealist literary strategy of Benet as a challenge to representation that is based on a "poetics of open spaces" (1984, 1). Spires sees that Benet's highlighting of the opacity of language, his exploration of that "zona de sombras" beyond secure knowledge, is based on an unbridgeable gap, or "open space," between signifier and signified. I propose, following the medical metaphor that the term *pharmakon* implies, that those "open spaces" be seen as "wounded spaces," similar to the "wounded spaces" at work in Semprún's novels. Such a term is particularly appropriate for the analysis of *Volverás a Región*, a novel in which one of the main characters is a doctor who lives in an old house/clinic, and where images of illness and remedy, poison and cure, abound. The expression "wounded spaces," borrowed from Maurice Blanchot in *The Writing of the Disaster* (1986, 30), shows that Benet's narrative is also a kind of "writing of the disaster," somewhat like Semprún's. In this case, it is a writing of the disaster imposed on Spain by that terribly wounding experience that was the civil war, and it emerges in a meta-memory text in which the relationship between memory and representation is recurrently, and often explicitly, explored.

It must be noted that, despite the fact that the civil war, and its devastating effects on Spanish society, are ever-present in Benet's texts, his writing, with its self-referential (and often antireferential) bent and narrative complexity, cannot be made to fit neatly into a rhetoric of recuperation of memory and political reparation. Benet's writing will always go beyond, and overflow, such a task. Benet himself was adamant in upholding his belief that literature and politics do not mix well, and that the first could not be made to serve the latter, through a function of social critique, without running the risk of debasement.[8] Benet's demanding writing, which, as Epps claims, is, in certain respects, "about inaccessibility," is perhaps far removed from much of the writing of the other authors studied here, even though all of them also explore narrative complexities in various ways (Epps 2000, 381). However, none of this means that Benet's writing ultimately remains *completely* "inaccessible," nor that a politically subversive dimension in his texts, in particular in his complex explorations of memory, does not exist. It is precisely because of Benet's tireless explorations of the limits and difficulties in literature's attempts to access reality that his meta-memory texts provide such valuable reflections of the complex process of working through a traumatic past, and on the particularly valuable, yet never simple, place of literature in such a task.

* * * *

Volverás a Región is the first of a series of novels in which Benet presents his fictional world: Región, a metonymic reflection of the whole of Spain. The novel begins with a lengthy and highly scientific-sounding presentation of Región dictated from a third-person omniscient point of view. This impersonal narration introduces a highly realistic, almost scientific, narrative which presents excruciatingly concrete geological and geographical data describing Región, an ominous mountainous region with a barren, dreary, and deathly air about it. This section also presents detailed historical information, which reads like a military manual, about the military maneuvers undertaken in the area during the civil war.

After many pages of this scientific, manual-style description of Región, the reader is introduced to the characters. One is a woman in her forties whose name we only come to know on page 161 of the text: Marré Gamallo. She is the daughter of the Nationalist military leader, General Gamallo, who invaded the Republican Región during the war. She arrives in a black car, sometime in the early 1960s, to the ruinous house of Doctor Daniel Sebastián. The doctor, since the war, has closed himself off from the world in his clinic/home with the sole company of an older boy, or young man, a deaf mute who is his patient.

Most of the novel presents the night-long conversation that doctor Sebastián and Marré entertain. Their dialogue, as has been amply noted, is more like a series of monologues, each rambling for pages on end, with a style that more closely resembles the scientific voice of the beginning than any real conversational tone. In fact, their "dialogue" is interspersed with long sections of the omniscient third-person voice, and their own monologues include lengthy philosophical digressions. Consequently, the supposedly different narrative points of view blend to such a degree that it is often almost impossible to know who is speaking: Marré, the doctor, or the omniscient narrating voice. This confusion is heightened by the fact that quotation marks are frequently missing, and the change of narrative point of view occurs without any diacritical warning to help keep the reader oriented. Any narrative verisimilitude is thus flagrantly subverted, there being no stylistic distinction between the first- and third-person narrations. Julia Lupinacci Wescott comments on this narrative ambiguity and how it reflects Benet's subversion of reason: "Thus while *Volverás a Región* initially appears to be a third person narration, its modulation toward a triple first person narration is both medium and message: attempts to order human reality are based on misplaced faith in reason. No perspective on human reality is more privileged than any other in offering the ability to order that reality" (1984, 79).[9]

The conversation between Doctor Sebastián and Marré revolves mostly around their memories of the war, as well as of periods before and immediately after it. Marré is hoping to obtain some information from the doctor about his godson, Luis I. Timoner, with whom she had a brief affair during the war, before he died. Luis, in turn, was the son of María Timoner, the woman the doctor had been in love with years before the war but who stood him up on the day that they were supposed to elope. Both Marré and Doctor Sebastián, therefore, are subject to the dynamics of the *pharmakon* of memory: trying to recapture the plenitude of the past but losing it in the attempt. Lost in their rememorative dialogue, too, is any sense of chronological order, of any order whatsoever. Their reconstruction of the past, together with the impersonal omniscient narration, presents the events recalled in such narrative disorder that by the end of the novel, at least by the end of a first reading, it is virtually impossible to have understood exactly what happened to whom, when, and where.[10]

What ultimately results from this fictional encounter in which these two ghostly characters come together to recall their past is a complete subversion of any narrative certainty and a radical questioning of the possibility of ever coming to terms with, or even knowing, the past. In

Benet's novelistic world, working through the past is not easy and success is never guaranteed.

The novel presents early on a realistic literary paradigm only to subvert it, as is clear from the very first sentence: "Es cierto, el viajero que saliendo de Región pretende llegar a su sierra siguiendo el antiguo camino real—porque el moderno dejó de serlo—se ve obligado a atravesar un pequeño y elevado desierto que parece interminable" (1967, 7) [It's true, the traveler leaving Región who wishes to reach the mountain range by following the old king's highway—because the modern one has ceased to be such—will find himself obliged to cross a small, high desert that seems endless (1985, 1)]. The very first words of the text, "Es cierto" [It's true], seem to be an unwavering affirmation of the possibility of secure knowledge, of certainty. Interestingly, each of the four sections of the novel begins with a phrase that becomes less and less certain: "Es cierto" ["It's true"] introduces the first section; "Ciertamente era" (1967, 91) [It certainly was (1985, 79)] the second; "No sé si sería cierto" (1967, 180) [I don't know whether it was true or not (1985, 162)] the third; and "No lo sé" (1967, 259) [I don't know (1985, 236)] is the beginning of the last segment. Within the representation of a seemingly objective voice describing Región, uncertainty becomes more and more pronounced. This amplification of doubt implies that the path into Región is, in fact, a path into the "zona de sombras" that Benet has talked so much about in his essays.

Returning to the beginning of the novel, however, we find a phrase completely riddled with a significant ambiguity (which is, unfortunately, lost in the translation) immediately following the self-assured exclamation of "Es cierto": "Es cierto, el viajero que saliendo de Región pretende llegar a su sierra siguiendo el antiguo camino real..." (1967, 7) [It's true, the traveler leaving Región who wishes to reach the mountain range by following the old king's highway...(1985, 1)]. The word "real," used to describe the path that the visitor to Región will take, could mean "royal" ("the old king's highway," as it appears in the translation). However, that same word, "real," could also mean "real" (in English), meaning that it is a real, and not invented, path that is being described. It has been noted that the hypothetical "viajero" [traveler], who will be mentioned recurrently throughout the novel, may be understood as a representation of the reader, who also has to traverse the Región made of words before him or her (see esp. Costa 1979). The ambiguity in the description of the path the visitor/reader is to take shows that, despite the self-assured certainty in the first expression of "Es cierto" [It's true], this text might not be as realistic as may seem. In fact, the desert that the visitor must cross to get to the mountains of Región "parece interminable" [seems endless], much like the convoluted syntax of the novel itself, which often leaves the visitor/reader wondering if s/he should not desist in continuing this journey.

The second sentence of the novel implies that the journey may, indeed, be forsaken: "Un momento u otro conocerá [el viajero] el desaliento al sentir que cada paso hacia adelante no hace sino alejarlo un poco más de aquellas desconocidas montañas. Y un día tendrá que abandonar el propósito y demorar aquella remota decisión" (1967, 7) [At one moment or another [the traveler] will get to know the discouragement of feeling that every step forward is only bringing him a little farther away from those unknown mountains. And one day he will have to give up his intent and put off that remote decision (1985, 1)]. Within a narration that seems terribly realistic, therefore, we already have a very unrealistic, even fantastic, element, as the laws of nature turn on this Kafkaesque visitor/reader to Región, making the mountains seem ever farther away the closer he or she comes to them. In Benet's narrative world, therefore, just when one thinks one is getting close to the truth, one finds oneself being pulled further and further from any certainty.

Another element that subverts the supposed scientism of the narrative beginning of the novel is that, interspersed within the dry, objective descriptions of the landscape, are personifications that suddenly make the rigorous scientific discourse bloom into metaphorical lyricism: "La sierra de Región se presenta como un testigo enigmático, poco conocido e inquietante, de tanto desorden y paroxismo: un zócalo y unos alrededores cársticos y permeables inducen a pensar en una tardía mudanza, un viaje al exilio" (1967, 39) [The Región range shows itself like an enigmatic witness, little known and disquieting, of all that disorder and those paroxysms: a base and some karst and permeable surroundings lead one to think of a delayed change, a trip into exile (1985, 31)]. The mountains of Región, the desired goal of the visitor on his trip through the area, are themselves enigmatic witnesses. The "desorden y paroxismo" [disorder] and [paroxysms] the mountain range is witness to apparently refer to the tortuous and tortured scenes of fighting during the civil war that have just been recounted. But perhaps the mountains are enigmatic witnesses to enigma itself, that is, to the enigma that is reflected in the narrative strategies that bring them before our eyes. Those narrative strategies re-create, in their breaking down of distinctions between certainty and uncertainty, between scientific and fantastic discourse, the same "desorden y paroxismo" [disorder] and [paroxysms] they are referring to. Therefore, if the mountains represent "un viaje al exilio" [a trip into exile], the language that creates them will do the same. The "camino real" [old king's highway] that the visitor/reader of Región must follow will ultimately become "un viaje al exilio." The reader will unexpectedly find him/herself exiled from a world of certainty and crossing the threshold into a world of shadows. As Herzberger has observed, "Within this mysterious zone the reader must make his way through contradiction and ambiguity, and in the end hesitancy emerges not only as a fundamental narrative determinant, but also as a way of knowing the world" (1984, 195).

Perhaps the most significant element of the fantastic in the novel is the figure of Numa, the guardian of the woods of Mantua, the area bordering Región. Mantua is a realm into which many a visitor has ventured but from which none has returned alive. Curiously enough, one example that is recounted repeatedly in the novel is of a party of Belgian scientists in a car filled with "muchos aparatos científicos" (1967, 251) [a lot of scientific apparatuses (1985, 229)] who tried to enter Mantua only to be killed by the feared Numa. It is clear that Mantua, and Numa, represent something quite antithetical to science. The fear that Numa has instilled in all of Región permeates the novel and is one of the first things recounted in the text.

At the beginning, the voice that is describing Región and portraying its history during the war tells of a certain ritual that has developed since the conflict. Every September, the survivors of the war congregate at a specified time around the town church and wait for shots to ring out from Mantua, which they do, unfailingly. These shots are understood to be Numa claiming his yearly human sacrifice, "su tributo humano" (1967, 9) [its human tribute (1985, 3)], of whatever poor soul had dared to transgress the limits of his territory.

Numa is a figure that produces hesitancy, as Herzberger expresses it, not just because of his mandate to make everyone hesitate in their desire to enter his dangerous kingdom. His very nature embodies hesitancy, for it is enigmatic and contradictory; another oxymoron in this text which proves to be, indeed, an "imperio del oxymoron" [domain of oxymoron].

There are numerous legends about the origin of Numa, from a belief that he is a survivor of a group of "Carlistas" who fled into the mountains long ago, to the hypothesis that he is General Gamallo himself, escaped into the woods after his invasion of Región during the civil war. Doctor Sebastián begins to describe Numa to Marré by saying: "Su historia—o su leyenda—es múltiple y contradictoria" (1967, 251) [His story—or his legend—is multiple and contradictory (1985, 228)]. The omniscient voice exclaims: "En realidad no hay una sola noticia exacta con referencia a aquellos fugitivos" (1967, 90) [In reality there is no single exact piece of information regarding those fugitives (1985, 76)] when describing a band of Republican rebels who escaped into Mantua during the war and who some people believe are the group out of which Numa emerged. Numa and his realm thus represent an enigma, one that is obviously opposed to rationality, for in Numa's kingdom those who, like the Belgian scientists, come armed with instruments to measure and define reality are destined to die. With respect to Numa's origins, therefore, even the supposedly omniscient voice has to admit its limited knowledge. The limited omniscience of the narrative voice is, of course, a contradiction, one that is particularly appropriate for the description of the contradictory being that Numa is.[11]

* * * *

The enigmatic nature of Numa, and his contraposition to reason and rationality, is related in important ways to the story of the *pharmakon* of writing and memory with which this chapter began. In the "Phaedrus" Socrates extends King Thamus's argument against writing as an aid to memory to a rejection of writing altogether. He asserts that writing is but a weak copy of the real word, the spoken word, that which is divinely inspired and which, he claims, "is written in the soul of the learner" (qtd. in Derrida 1981, 148). Derrida, in his reading of the myth, notices that although writing is rejected as a weak copy of an original *spoken* word, that same spoken word, which is supposedly primary, is itself defined in terms of writing (for it is "*written* in the soul of the learner," emphasis added). Writing, which is assumed to be the copy, here antecedes the original. This inversion is a curious subversion of order and a harsh blow to the supposed precedence of the oral word as guarantor of the presence of the divine Logos in the soul of the speaker. The guarantee of presence that the oral word presumably exemplified was meant to be a guarantee of the primacy of reason, allegedly founded on the Logos, the divine, living, spoken word. Therefore, the questioning of the precedence of the spoken word is also a questioning of the primacy of reason itself. This subversion represents a radical blurring of boundaries, where what was being rejected as dangerous is really already *inside* what was trying to be protected.

A similar blurring of boundaries is what Numa represents by his very nature. This collapsing of distinctions will become all the more significant since Numa's official role is supposedly to *guard* and *uphold* boundaries; among others, those territorial boundaries between Mantua and Región.

It is well known that Numa is an intertextual echo of a similar figure with which Sir James George Frazer begins his book on mythology, *The Golden Bough*.[12] That character is a composite of two figures.

One was a fierce priest in Roman mythology who was in charge of the sacred grove of Diana at Nemi. Like Numa, he was forever on guard, ready to kill those who would enter the grove, yet aware that one of them would eventually kill him and become the next priest. The other figure was benevolent King Numa, the second king of Rome, renowned for his championship of law and order and for his worship of Terminus, the god of boundaries. If one of the two men worshipped law and order, the other represents brute force. The combination of the two becomes a mixed figure that blurs the boundaries between instinct and reason. He is thus a liminal figure perfect for Benet's exploration of the "zona de sombras" ["zone of shadows"] between passion and rationality, between the "tiempo instintivo" ["instinctive time"] and the "tiempo intelectualizado" ["intellectualized time"]. In fact, following Derrida's reading of the *pharmakon* myth, he is also the figure that shows that society often works by excluding what is menacing, without recognizing that the menace is already at the heart of what is being protected from it. It is the oxymoronic logic of the *pharmakon* at work once more.

Stephen Summerhill presents such an interpretation of the function of Numa, where the dangerous force of passion or instinct

> is feared so much that it has been projected imaginatively outside society in the form of a supernatural gunman protecting a prohibited zone.... In consequence, Numa has an ambiguous role. As threat, he induces the people to stay in place because of the potential harm that could come to them were they to transgress the barriers to this world, that is, were they to give in to their own urge to passion. On the other hand, he also protects them, not only because he, as passion, is neutralized through exile, but also because he is presumed to eliminate those who might threaten society by allowing nature to dominate their lives. This explains why he is described in a contradictory manner as both a source of peace and as a menace, for in fact he is both a protection and a threat. (1984, 53–54)[13]

Numa's Mantua is similar to that area of culture that Benet described as "un campo de concentración" [a concentration camp] into which society "exiles" all its feared irrational passions, its uncontrollable contradictions. The creation of this space represents a strategy supposedly to save the rational spirit by excluding from that spirit whatever may undermine it. But by the logic of the *pharmakon* this strategy also shows that what was feared because of its potential for undermining reason is already within reason itself. Numa, the keeper of boundaries, is created as a violent, forceful character. Yet the real violence he represents is that he is but a projection that exiles out of society what is really at the heart of society. Although the inhabitants of Región want to be protected from the violence of the passions that Numa supposedly guards them against, they also recognize that such passion is the only thing that will ultimately save them.

This ambiguity is why Numa is feared by all the inhabitants of Región, but it is also hailed as "nuestra postrer esperanza" (1967, 250) [our last hope (1985, 227)], as Doctor Sebastián says. Trying to cross the boundary that Numa guards so well is an attempt to enter that "zona de sombras" where what society claims to be certain and established is shown to contain uncertainty and mystery. It is a dangerous enterprise, as the deaths of those who become Numa's "tributo humano" [human tribute] attest. But it is an enterprise that Benet, in his writing, is continually attempting.

The importance of writing versus oral speech, which was essential to the myth of the *pharmakon,* has a role to play here, too. It is important that the prohibitive law that Numa imposes forbidding any trespassing into his territory is presented in terms of writing, never orally. In fact, the enigmatic Numa hardly ever speaks. His law is expressed by means of a weathered old sign on which there is written the following, in capital letters to underscore the tone of authority: "SE PROHIBE EL PASO/PROPIEDAD PRIVADA" (1967, 9) [NO TRESPASSING / PRIVATE PROPERTY (1985, 3)].

Writing is what Numa uses to enforce his law. However, the citizens of Región believe that it is orally that he imposes his will, a will on which they have come to depend. Of course, since Numa himself hardly speaks, his speech is replaced by his gun. The perfectly regular, yearly shots around which the inhabitants of Región have organized their lives enforce Numa's control. Despite the supposed "orality" of his prohibition, however, Numa is never seen. In his case, orality does not guarantee presence. Perhaps because of this, the order he imposes is ambiguous. As Doctor Sebastián explains, when speaking of how his fellow inhabitants of Región depend on that supposed "order" that Numa imposes: "Por eso acostumbran a ir allí cada año, a escuchar los disparos celestiales de un Numa que por lo menos, no se equivoca nunca.... El Numa no es más que el pródromo" (1967, 221–22) [For that reason they were accustomed to go there every year, to hear the celestial shots of a Numa who, at least, never misses.... Numa is nothing but the prodrome" (1985, 200–201)].

The shots they hear regularly are taken as the maximum representation of order. At least they are dependable, unfaltering. But that order is really the exclusion, the exiling into a "campo de concentración" of any uncertainty. And uncertainty is precisely where Benet sees life can be lived at its fullest. Excluding uncertainty only makes life less interesting, even, following the medical metaphor of the *pharmakon,* less healthy. That is why the doctor says that Numa is only the "pródromo" [prodrome], the beginning of an illness. And this, despite the fact that he is supposedly there to keep the people of Región safe and "healthy." The boundaries between health and illness are surely being collapsed.

This problem of blurring boundaries will also arise in the *pharmakon* of memory operative in the novel. Jo Labanyi has made this connection: "The conflict between the urge to transgress Numa's boundary and the urge to defend it is repeated within memory. The suppressed memories of the inhabitants of Región are triggered off by the intrusion of a series of motor cars (symbolizing the desire for transgression) bound for Mantua; in order to protect themselves from the pain caused by this involuntary reawakening of desire, they appeal to Numa to cut short the journey to the past" (1989, 117).

Marré will be one such character entering Región in a motor car whose journey to the past in an attempt to reawaken desire will be cut short by Numa. At the end of the novel she leaves the doctor, after their night of conversation about their past loves, and continues her car journey until "el eco de un disparo lejano vino a restablecer el silencio habitual del lugar" (1967, 315) [the echo of a distant shot came to reestablish the habitual silence of the place (1985, 288)]. These are the last words of the text, showing that Marré has probably become one more "tributo humano" [human tribute] that Numa has claimed. If she is sacrificed, it is precisely because, in her trip, she was trying to remember and re-create the only moments of true passion in a life otherwise ruled by society's "reasonable" strictures. She was trying to reenter that realm of the passions, through memory, and for that she must be punished.

The doctor had warned Marré that her trip was a dangerous one: "antes de seguir adelante deseo que comprenda el riesgo que corre (1967, 102) [before you go any further I want you to understand the risk you're running" (1985, 89–90)]. He then reiterates: "El viaje es una locura, por supuesto. No hay curación, si eso es lo que desea saber" (1967, 103) [The trip is madness, of course. There's no cure, if that's what you want to know (1985, 90)]. The mention of a cure raises the specter of the logic of the *pharmakon*, of course, and that specter is what guides Marré's trip. She herself repeatedly states that she is looking for a cure. In response to the doctor's warning that this trip of hers in search of a lost past, a lost happiness, is a "locura" [madness], Marré explains that what she longs to re-create from her past, what she considers the most "sane" and healthy experience of her life, is what society considers most "insane" and unhealthy. As she tells the doctor: "Tenía entendido que esta casa era el lugar a propósito para curar . . .

tales dudas (1967, 104) [I was given to understand that this house was just the place for curing . . . such doubts (1985, 91)]. Later, she asks: "¿Quién puede creer, por consiguiente, que vine aquí en busca de una curación? ¿No será más bien el abandono a las fuerzas de la enfermedad?" (1967, 116–117) [Who can believe, consequently, that I came here in search of a cure? Isn't it rather an abandonment to the forces of the illness? (1985, 103)].

It is clear that Marré's trip implicates a blurring of the distinctions between what is sane, or rational, and what is not; between what is a true cure and what is a malady. Because this trip into the past has so much to do with blurring boundaries, it is particularly significant that most of the conversation takes place at the "umbral" [threshold] of the doctor's clinic/house, the boundary between inside and outside, and that the "threshold" is constantly described as being "en la penumbra" (1967, 92) [in the shadows" (1985, 81)]. That penumbra, furthermore, is the product of a liminal time, dusk, at which the conversation begins, when the remains of the day give way to nighttime.[14] Labanyi has remarked on the "Janus-like nature" of the doorway, which combines the "promise of liberation" symbolized by the threshold and the "containment" represented by the frame (1989, 102). One could see this as a composite of opposites that functions as a *pharmakon,* both alluring and threatening at the same time.

Marré claimed that what the doctor called "una locura" [madness] was for her perhaps the only form of "cordura" [sanity]. She further implies that what society calls "cordura" ("lo que llaman ustedes la parte cuerda)" (1967, 103) [what you people call the sane part (1985, 91)] was for her the most feared form of madness. She here points to the fact that what she is trying to recapture in her rememorative trip is something subversive of society's standards of morality, for it is the only time of her life in which she gave free rein to her passions, her instincts.

Marré tells the doctor of her rigorous moral upbringing under her father's guidance. In that upbringing, anything related to passion, feelings, or sexual instincts was radically forbidden. During the war she was taken hostage by the Republican forces. At one point, her captors called her father to determine if he would surrender to the Republicans in exchange for her freedom. General Gamallo refused, telling her that she must learn to sacrifice herself for the good of the Nationalist cause. She, however, ended up not sacrificing her freedom but finding the only freedom she ever knew through a brief love affair with one of the Republican soldiers guarding her, Luis I. Timoner, as well as through sexual encounters with other soldiers. If she was to sacrifice anything, it was a moral order that had been imposed on her, which she quickly relinquished in favor of an exploration of the realm of the passions and instincts. As she explains (talking of herself in the third person), a woman who, like her, had entered that forbidden territory of the passions "en lo sucesivo aborrecerá las leyes, el orden y la decencia para vivir conforme a un credo que sólo en las faltas encontró su verdadera razón de ser" (1967, 158) [in what follows ... will hate laws, order, and decency in order to live in conformity with a credo that will find its real *raison d'être* only in sins (1985, 142)]. Marré rejects order and reason and accepts as the only form of "sanity" a surrender to the passions.[15]

With the anecdote of General Gamallo's refusal to surrender in order to save his daughter, Benet is evoking one of the events of the civil war that was converted by the Nationalist army, and later by the Franco regime, into the greatest example of a rhetoric of sacrifice for one's country that underpinned Franco's fascistic ideology. During the 71-day siege by Republican forces of the Nationalist Military stronghold in Toledo, the Alcazar, the Republican soldiers supposedly called General Moscardó in the Alcazar with a similar plea to save his son, whom they held prisoner, in exchange for the General's surrender. Moscardó, like Gamallo, allegedly told his son to prepare to sacrifice his life for the good of Spain, a sacrifice that the son, unlike Marré, supposedly embraced as he was about to be executed. The rhetoric of personal sacrifice for the good of Spain, as well as of unwavering obedience to one's parents, that the anecdote embodies became a central tenet of all Francoist ideology.[16] The family became a model for the nation, and sacrifice and obedience to one's superiors the only permissible behavior, as the following quote from Franco's end-of-the-year message to the nation in 1953 attests:

> Por la elevación de sentimientos que el orden familiar entraña, ... que de padres a hijos se transmiten con la antorcha del deber, de los honores, del trabajo o del sacrificio, no solo es semejante a lo que puede establecerse entre la familia y la Patria, sino que la familia constituye un modelo, un arquetipo para la Nación. (qtd. in Granados Nieto 2004, 2)

> [For the exaltation of feelings that the family order embodies, ... which are transmitted from parents to children along with the torch of duty, of honor, of hard work and of sacrifice, is not only similar to what can be established between a family and the homeland, but [it guarantees that] the family is a model, an archetype, for the Nation.]

Marré's behavior during the war, therefore, radically undermines the unquestioning acceptance of duty and sacrifice that children were supposed to display under Francoism. This becomes one of the ways in which the attempt on the part of characters in the novel to re-create through memory their past experiences of desire and pleasure becomes subversive of what became the dominant ideology and social order after the civil war. Benet's explorations of the blurring of boundaries of time, and of concepts of morality and immorality, sanity and madness within memory, thus have an important subversive ideological dimension.

In fact, Marré's rejection of the social order is so complete that, having been separated from Luis Timoner after their brief affair, she takes up prostitution for some time, living, significantly enough, in a hotel called Terminus. Terminus, not coincidentally, was the god of boundaries that the good King Numa of Rome (one of the figures on which the character of Numa is based) worshipped in his attempt to establish law and order in his domain. By being a prostitute in the Hotel Terminus, Marré becomes a figure that subverts established boundaries, thereby undermining the distinction between "morality" and "immorality" once again. This subversion that Marré's story represents is, in fact, reflected in her very name. Marré is the past tense conjugation, in the first person, of the Spanish verb "marrar." The *Diccionario de la Real Academia Española* presents the following two meanings of the verb: "faltar, errar" [to err] and, in a figural sense, "desviarse de lo recto" [to deviate from the straight path]. Marré's name, therefore, highlights the fact that everything about her is subversive of, and a deviation from, the dominant moral order.

Marré further realizes that the "locura" [madness] she was living in the Hotel Terminus had always been latent in her previous life, that is, repressed. One continues to encounter the subversive workings of the *pharmakon*. Within the nature that a moral upbringing had tried to impose on Marré, there existed, already, the subversive capacity to enjoy the body, the instincts.

There is yet another relevant aspect of the *pharmakon* myth in *Volverás a Región*. Derrida explains how the subversive nature of the *pharmakon* is related to the *pharmakos*, the scapegoat, the sacrificial victim. The *pharmakos* is sacrificed in order to purge society of the danger that the poor victim supposedly represents. The sacrifice is "the expulsion of the evil, its exclusion out of the body (and out) of the city" (1981, 130). Furthermore, because it represents a questioning of what is acceptable and unacceptable in society, "The ceremony of the *pharmakos* is thus played out on the boundary line between inside and outside, which it has as its function ceaselessly to trace and retrace" (1981, 133).

After her conversation with the doctor, Marré will become Numa's *pharmakos*, his sacrificial victim. She will be punished for all her attempts to cross boundaries. As has been mentioned before, her conversation with the doctor took place at the "umbral" [threshold], the boundary between the inside and outside of the home. This liminal placement is highly symbolic. What Marré has come to re-live, through memory, is the experience she had of being, for a time (the only happy time of her life), on, or beyond, the boundary between what was "inside" the accepted norms of society and what was "outside" those laws; what was "una cordura" [sanity] and what was "una locura" [madness].

Marré is particularly dangerous because she has, after all, returned to Región of her own free will, *seeking* this reenactment of a boundary-defying experience. It will be recalled that the people of Región, after the war, had adopted the ritual of congregating every September to hear Numa's shots and to witness his regular slaying of the yearly *pharmakos*. As Labanyi notes, this ritualizing of the sacrificial practice had a containment function: "The fact that his [Numa's] shots can be expected in September contains disaster by reducing it to an orderly seasonal pattern" (1989, 98). It should come as no surprise that such a containment function is at the heart, as Derrida explains, of the ritual sacrifice of the *pharmakos*, guaranteeing some semblance of control on the part of society of nature's uncontrollable forces by "the regularity of repetition, by fixing the date" of the sacrifice at the same time every year (1981, 133).

The narrative voice with which the novel begins, as it tells the anecdote of this strange ritual, also explains: "La gente de Región ha optado por olvidar su propia historia" (1967, 11) [The people of Región have opted to forget their own history (1985, 5)]. Marré's very desire to remember, therefore, becomes a subversive act in itself. Her determination to do so whenever *she* wants, not when that action falls into a plan established by society, proves that she is willing to transgress what others are not. Because of her affirmation of her own will, she must become the new *pharmakos*. For this autonomous action, she must be killed.[17]

It is significant, furthermore, that, when explaining her telephone conversation with her father, in which she is told to sacrifice herself for the sake of a higher moral order, Marré makes an allusion to the mythological figure Iphigenia: "Porque la guerra sólo era un pretexto, el ardid que el destino impone, como a Ifigenia, para probar el apego a su padre" (1967, 158–59) [Because the war was only a pretext, a wile that destiny imposes, as on Iphigenia, in order to test her closeness to her father (1985, 142)]. Iphigenia was to be sacrificed by her father, Agamemnon, so that the Trojan war could be won. And Iphigenia obediently complied. Marré, however, did not become the Iphigenia her father wanted her to be. If anything, she became the executioner of the moral order to which she was supposed to surrender. For her rebellion against her father's order, and against the order of reason, she was later to be sacrificed by that other, more enigmatic keeper of order: Numa.[18]

Although Marré herself says that "la guerra sólo era un pretexto" [the war was only a pretext], it is no coincidence that Marré's experience of passion, which undermines the rules of the social order she had grown up with, is something she enjoys during the war. She specifies that what allowed her story of passion to emerge was that any ordinary linearity of time was broken down in the temporal chaos of war: "había nacido y debía su existencia a un estado de cosas que por fuerza no podía durar" (1967, 160) [it had been born of and owed its existence to a state of affairs that would of needs not last (1985, 144)]. It was an experience that renounced, from the beginning, any pretense to be incorporated into an orderly life, for it was an act that emerged "decidido a no prolongar la representación más allá de aquella situación efímera y renunciando de antemano a una ulterior y falsa continuidad que tarde o temprano había de adulterarlo" (1967, 160) [having decided not to prolong the show beyond that fleeting situation and renouncing ahead of time an ulterior or false continuity that sooner or later would adulterate it (1985, 144)].

That "representación" [show] of her fully explored sexuality takes place in a "situación efímera" [fleeting situation] because it represents, however contradictory it may sound, an example of the Bergsonian *durée* in which the heterogeneous moments of past, present, and future are disarrayed and "*se pénètrent*" [penetrate each other], creating a certain sense of simultaneity. And simultaneity cannot last. Any attempt to make it last will "adulterate" it. The war provided Marré with an escape from "normal" chronological time, which made the simultaneity of *durée* possible.

After the war, with a "normal" time reestablished, Marré returned to an "acceptable" life, getting married and outwardly assuming the moral order she had rejected fleetingly, while feeling a growing inner sense of alienation, sadness, and frustration. That ephemeral experience of *durée* was lost after the war, which ended "para dar paso al transcurso de las horas bajo cuyo imperceptible oleaje se sumerge el podría-haber-sido que a sí mismo se sucede y se destruye" (1967, 95) [giving way to the passage of the hours under whose imperceptible wave the might-have-been that follows and destroys itself is submerged" (1985, 83)].[19]

Marré's return to Región is an attempt to take up that "podría-haber-sido" [might-have-been] after it had been "adulterated" by her reintegration into a normalized time. Furthermore, that normalized time, after the war, is characterized by "el transcurso de las horas" [the passage of the hours], that is, by a chronological linearity that reimposed an order onto her adventure of rebellious dis-order.

Just as her enjoyment of freedom and *durée* were predicated on a loss of order, on a certain temporal as well as moral "disarray," her rememorative venture, her dialogue with the doctor, will reproduce that same sense of dis-order. It is, perhaps, a desperate attempt not to let those memories become "adulterated" again by being related in an orderly fashion. That is why the whole story, the *histoire,* of her experiences (which, in my discussion here, is re-created in a deceivingly clear and linear fashion for the benefit of the reader) is presented in the *discours* of the novel in a completely fragmented, disorganized manner. The same elements of the story are introduced numerous times at different moments in the text, yet are never completely elaborated. Foreshadowings of other elements constantly anticipate a development of the plot that Marré will only provide at some unexpected later moment of the dialogue, and sometimes not at all. The temporal disorder that made possible her experience of *durée* during the war is thus reproduced in the chaotic, nonlinear presentation of her dialogue with Doctor Sebastián. Consequently, the time that marks the beginning of their conversation, that liminal moment in which day turns into night, is described as one in which the

> última coloración de un fluido inestable pierde su estructura diurna para descomponerse en mil fragmentos de un tiempo caótico y gaseoso, en cada uno de los cuales está alojada—como el germen en el grano de pollen—palabras, trozos de memoria, inicios de recuerdos abortados y falsos y engañosos ecos que la noche y el día borrarán al restablecer el equilibrio de las horas. (1967, 114)

> [the last coloration of an unstable fluid loses its diurnal structure to break up into a thousand fragments of a gaseous and chaotic time, in each of which is lodged—like the germ in a grain of pollen—words, bits of memory, indications of aborted and false recollections and deceptive echoes that night and day will erase with the reestablishment of the balance of the hours.] (1985, 101)

Because Marré is now ready to forego, once more, any pretense to "integrity" (moral or otherwise), her remembrances are presented as "trozos de memoria" [bits of memory], fragments in a disorderly, chaotic time. Yet these memories, like her previous experiences, are evanescent. Just as her original story of sexual freedom was adulterated by the "paso al transcurso de las horas" [the passage of the hours] that was reestablished after the war, her conversation with the doctor in the "tiempo caótico" [chaotic time] of twilight will also eventually succumb to the "equilibrio de las horas" [the balance of the hours]. It is the inevitable victory of the "tiempo intelectualizado" [intellectualized time] over the "tiempo instintivo" [instinctive time].

The preoccupation of this text with the struggle between these two incompatible "tiempos" [times] is an obsessive one. Following the preceeding quotation describing the chaotic nature of the time during which the conversation between Marré and the doctor takes place, the omniscient voice continues to describe that moment of interlocution:

> Y es un instante en el que—en presencia de un catalizador de la memoria . . . —se produce una fisura en la corteza aparente del tiempo a través de la cual se ve que la memoria no guarda lo que pasó, que la voluntad desconoce lo que vendrá, que sólo el deseo sabe hermanarlas pero que—como una aparición conjurada con la luz—se desvanece en cuanto en el alma se restaura el orden odioso del tiempo. (1967, 114)
>
> [And it's an instant in which—in the presence of a catalyst of memory . . . —a fissure is produced in the apparent outer layer of time through which it can be seen that memory has not kept what happened, that the will doesn't know what will come, that only desire knows how to equate them, but that—like an apparition conjured up by the light—it disappears as soon as the soul restores the hateful order of time.] (1985, 101)

Gonzalo Sobejano finds in this quotation an expression of a fundamental theme in Benet's work: "Se trata de la expresión incidental de un principio que gobierna la narrativa de Benet: la imaginaria anulación del orden crónico por un 'tiempo caótico' " (1983, 18) [This is the incidental expression of a principle that governs Benet's narrative: the imaginary annulment of chronic time by a chaotic time]. Yet what Sobejano does not emphasize is that such an "imaginaria anulación" [imaginary annulment] will never be complete, for "el orden odioso del tiempo" [the hateful order of time], that "orden crónico" [chronic time], will always be restored. That is why Marré's rememorative task is one that is destined to fail. That is why Marré exclaims, "la memoria—ahora lo veo tan claro—es casi siempre la venganza de lo que no fue" (1967, 115) [memory—I can see very clearly now—is almost always the vengeance for what it was not (1985, 101)].

There is yet another "order" that is being subverted in Benet's narrative, a much more political one. It must be remembered that Benet finished writing the novel around 1964 (although it was not published until 1967, due to the notorious difficulty he faced in finding an editor willing to publish his difficult prose). The year 1964 is approximately when, within the novel, Marré returns to Región and engages in conversation with the doctor. It is also the year in which the Franco regime unleashed a massive propaganda campaign to celebrate the "25 años de paz" [25 years of peace] after the end of the war. This campaign attempted to subtly shift the argument for the regime's legitimacy from that of waging a crusade against the "anti-Spain" of the Republic to that of being a purveyor of peace and order for Spain since the war. It is not surprising that the new rhetoric of peace maintained the emphasis on the need for sacrifice from all Spaniards to uphold that cherished order. This is evident in the words of the Minister of Information and Tourism, Manuel Fraga Iribarne, when inaugurating the official state exhibit "España '64" [Spain '64] that year: "La paz exige, por otra parte, sacrificios; tiene su precio, lo mismo en la vida del hogar que en las de las naciones" (Junta Interministerial 1964, x) [Peace demands sacrifices, equally in the life of a home, as in the life of a nation].

This is why it is significant that Marré returns to Región at this particular time. She not only wants to re-create, through memory, that experience during the war by means of which she had rejected a repressive rhetoric of sacrifice, but she now rejects, years later, in her very rememorative project, the dominant rhetoric of peace, stability, order, and progress of the mid-1960s, especially its implicit desire to forget the past of the war. Benet's novel thus undermines the Francoist rhetoric of peace and order in many ways, not least of which is the disorder of the very narrative and the epistemological uncertainty that it creates. In this manner, as Herzberger explains, Benet's writing becomes a powerful "countervoice to the historiography of the Regime" (1995, 107).

At a certain point, Numa, the guarantor of order in the novel, breaks his usual silence and proclaims that, through his actions of killing all transgressors of his terrain, peace is enforced, and "Una paz, por muy ruin que sea, es siempre una paz" (1967, 252) [A peace, no matter how awful it may be, is still a peace (1985, 229)]. It is implied that the peace that is being "enjoyed" in Región is "ruin" [awful]. This is something that the narrative constantly reinforces, and which is clearly at odds with the exalted view of peace and order the regime is trying to portray in the mid-1960s. The violence with which such "peace" was forcefully imposed is highlighted by Doctor Sebastián: "Y en cuanto a la violencia le diré que, aun cuando en apariencia no exista, en esta tierra siempre la hay; es un estado latente... pero que puede ponerse en erupción en cualquier momento" (1967, 126) [And as for the violence I'll tell you that even when it doesn't seem to exist, it's always there in these lands, it's a latent state... which can pass into eruption at any moment (1985, 112)].

References to the fear and repression governing life in postwar Región are numerous in the text, and we are told that, after the war,

"Ya no era cosa de memoria porque la radio no dejaba recordar nada" (1967, 181) [It was no longer a matter of memory because the radio wouldn't let anything be remembered (1985, 163)]. In this context, remembering itself becomes a subversive act. Rejecting the falsely positive view of recent history imposed by the campaign for "25 years of peace," Marré's depiction of memory as "la venganza de lo que no fue" (1967, 115) [the vengeance for what it was not (1985, 101)] takes on added meaning. It evokes all that was suppressed by the victors of the war; everything that the victorious radios did not let people remember; all that was cut short by the war; the quiet suffering of the victims of that war and of the ensuing "peace." Ken Benson has emphasized this ideologically subversive role of memory in the text: "la memoria adquiere una gran carga ideológica . . . 'vengándose' de la 'realidad', copada por el discurso panfletario del poder fascista, para conformar una realidad interior *(lo que no pudo ser)*" (2004, 192) [memory acquires a great ideological charge . . . "taking revenge" of the "reality" cut off by the pamphletary rhetoric of fascist power, in order to create an interior reality *(what could not be)*].

This stance toward the past that does not rejoice over what has happened, but despairingly acknowledges what has been repressed, is shared by the doctor, who confirms Marré's view of memory, claiming, "todo lo que nos queda es lo que un día no pasó; el pasado tampoco es lo que fue, sino lo que no fue" (1967, 245) [all that's left for us is the fact that one day hasn't passed; the past isn't what it was, either, but what it wasn't (1985, 223)]. Because of this, he adds, later on, that time "es la dimensión en la que la persona humana sólo puede ser desgraciada, no puede ser de otra manera. El tiempo sólo asoma en la desdicha y así la memoria sólo es el registro del dolor" (1967, 257) [is the dimension in which a human being can only be unfortunate, it can't be otherwise. Time only appears in misfortune and therefore memory is only a register of pain (1985, 234)]. The doctor, significantly, happens to be a most appropriate interlocutor for Marré because he, too, has had an overwhelming experience of loss. He also has a story of a "podría-haber-sido" [might-have-been] that has remained, forever, "lo que no pasó" [what hasn't passed].

Interspersed in a most chaotic and intermittent manner throughout their dialogue are clues to a failed love story that the doctor himself lived long before the war. The doctor had suffered a morally rigid upbringing similar to Marré's. When he was young, before the war, he was asked once to watch over María Timoner, the lover of a young military officer, Gamallo (Marré's father, before her birth), while Gamallo plays an endless card game with an unnamed "jugador" [player]. Finally, Gamallo, in an outburst of male pride, uses María herself as a token for the game, and the "jugador" wins her. Meanwhile, as the doctor is taking care of her, he falls in love with María, finally getting up enough courage to ask her to escape with him the day before the game was supposed to end. He arranges for them to meet at a certain crossroads only to find, at the appointed time, that María had run off with the "jugador." The doctor thus loses the only "gamble" of his life. Terribly injured from his failed attempt to break out of the mold of society's established norms and to engage the world of the passions, he married a woman he did not love and, until her death, kept up a semblance of a married life that turned out to be as empty and lifeless as his old, ruinous clinic/home. That his meeting with María was to take place at a "crossroads" shows that the doctor did, in fact, manage to come to the crossroads between reason and passion. However, unlike Marré, he did not get to *cross* that boundary. Perhaps that is why, for him, "la memoria sólo es el registro del dolor" (1967, 257) [memory is only a register of pain (1985, 234)], for it can only evoke a failed attempt at being happy.

It is important to note that Marré had called her affair with Luis Timoner a "representación" [representation], and that the doctor's attempt to have an affair with María Timoner occurred during a card game. Furthermore, in one of the instances in which that card game is described, metaphors from the theater are employed: "se diría que habían estado ensayando una escena mil veces repetida, y que, alcanzada una cierta perfección, podían pasar a la siguiente" (1967, 244) [it could have been said that they'd been rehearsing a scene repeated a thousand times and that, having reached a certain perfection, they could go on to the next one (1985, 222)].

Both Marré's and the doctor's historical experiences, which are being re-created through memory, are described in terms of theatrical metaphors. Underneath history lies play: play as theater, play as a game, play as chance, play as the "podría-haber-sido" [might-have-been] that is inherent in the "playful" world of the possible that fiction exemplifies. As Benson emphasizes, however, such play is connected to the very serious ideological undermining of established order in the novel, for "Muy relacionado con el 'deseo', cobra gran importancia en la escritura benetiana el 'juego'. La literatura es un proceso lúdico que subvierte el orden establecido por el 'Estado' y por la 'sociedad' " (2004, 19–20) [Related to "desire," "play" takes on great importance in Benetian writing. Literature is a ludic process that subverts the established order of the "State" and of "society"].

Marré explicitly acknowledges, several times, the possibility that what she is seeking is a fiction: "No sé si he vuelto o he venido por primera vez a comprobar la naturaleza de una ficción" (1967, 115) [I don't know whether I've returned or come for the first time to test the nature of a fiction (1985, 102)]. She later reiterates: "He venido, pues, cuando he alcanzado ese límite para saber hasta qué punto he sido impura e hipócrita o en qué medida he sido víctima de una ficción" (1967, 311) [I've come, then, at a time when I've reached that limit in order to know to what point I've been impure and hypocritical or to what degree I've been the victim of a fiction (1985, 285)].

Acknowledging that underneath history lies fiction may have a certain liberating effect for the main characters of this novel. It is perhaps what allows both of them to articulate views on memory in which remembrance is seen not only as a passive receptacle for the tragic events of the past (that "registro del dolor" [register of pain], as the doctor called it) but also as a creative force engendering new events. The doctor recognizes this creative aspect of memory when he declares: "Es cierto que la memoria desvirtúa, agranda y exagera, pero no es sólo eso; también inventa para dar una apariencia de vivido e ido a aquello que el presente niega" (1967, 247) [It's true that memory adulterates, enlarges and exaggerates, but it's not just that; it also invents in order to give an appearance something that had lived and gone away to what the present denies" (1985, 225 *sic*)]. Marré also presents a qualified view of this creative nature of memory: "Hay cosas que como no sirve de nada recordarlas la memoria las guarda en un cajón de sastre, convencida de que nunca más volverán a tener un uso o que sólo han de servir para un remiendo" (1967, 294) [There are things that since there's no use in remembering them memory keeps in a ragbag convinced that they'll never be of any use again or that they'll only be good for patchwork (1985, 269)].

It is particularly significant that Marré sees the creative capacity of memory in its ability to serve as a "remiendo" [patchwork], something used to mend what is in need of repair. This image points to the convergence between the *pharmakon*-nature of memory, the dual function of remembrance as both cure and malady, with the dynamics of trauma. As Derrida explains, "The *pharmakon* is that dangerous supplement that breaks into the very thing that would have liked to do without it" (1981, 110). The image of memory as a "remiendo" [patchwork] perfectly embodies the dynamic of the supplement that Derrida sees as characterizing the *pharmakon*. A "remiendo," or patch, is something which is added to an object to fix it, to make it "whole," while serving as a constant reminder of its broken or incomplete state. As in the dynamics of trauma, an experience of lack or loss is overcome, "patched," by a process that inevitably highlights that very loss. The recollection presented in Benet's novel is thus a form of "unsatisfied" memory, as it is necessarily incomplete, never whole. This aspect of memory is best represented by the character in the novel who has till now gone unnoticed, perhaps because that is the nature of his role: the young deaf-mute boy who is under Doctor Sebastián's care.

* * * *

Of the three characters' narratives, the boy's past story of suffering is recounted first, early on in the novel. In one of the imperceptible slippages of the omniscient voice (in which it surreptitiously shifts from the description of the military history of the war in Región to that of the personal story of an individual character), the reader is introduced to the past drama of the boy's family history. Although his story is narrated in an oblique way and, as in all the other cases of a character's past, in a fragmented, disorganized manner, the reader can piece together its components. There is a scene, at the beginning of the war, in which the boy is confronted with the incomprehensible (for him) fact that his mother leaves him. After telling him that she will be back the next day, the mother disappears in a black car, never to return. The boy seems to deal with the anxiety produced by his mother's departure by giving himself over completely to a curious game: "y él, con pantalones cortos, que arrastraba su soledad en un jardín recoleto en compañía de unas bolas de barro y unas chapas de botella de cerveza" (1967, 15) [and he, in short pants, dragging his solitude about in a graden retreat in the company of some clay marbles and beer-bottle caps (1985, 9)].

Furthermore, this scene of the boy playing ball to overcome the anxiety over his mother's disappearance is repeatedly, even obsessively, presented throughout the novel. At the end, Marré is explaining to the doctor how she had returned to Región a previous time and, visiting the boy's house, found that "en el pasillo en sombras el chico jugaba a las bolas con la misma atención que en el año 36. . . . [N]o hacía sino jugar con las bolas y de tanto en tanto alzaba hacia mí una mirada muy singular, una mirada que procedía de un temor olvidado, pero no resuelto" (1967, 309) [in the dark hallway the boy was playing marbles with the same attention as in the year 1936. . . . all he did was play with the marbles and from time to time he would raise a very singular look toward me, a look that came from forgotten but unresolved fear (1985, 283)].

Significantly, this game holds an enormous resemblance to the young boy's game of *Fort/Da!* with which Freud explains the dynamics of trauma.[20] The continual reenactment of the disappearance and reappearance of the toy is a way for the boy to gain a sense of mastery that was completely lost when he was abandoned by his mother.

2: JUAN BENET: THE *PHARMAKON* OF MEMORY 129

Lacan provides an interesting extension of Freud's explanation of the anecdote. It is not only through the manipulation of the toy itself that the boy reenacts the traumatic moment of loss implied by his mother's disappearance. The use of the phonemes *Fort* and *Da*, the boy's use of language as something that is pure sound and that has lost a connection to meaning, is what reenacts the real sense of loss in this game. For Lacan, this scene of loss, therefore, is the moment "in which the child is born into language" (1977, 103).

This view of language as a manipulation of phonemes that lose their direct connection to any meaning bears a resemblance to what Spires called the "open spaces" in Benet's writing, in which the unbridgeable gap between signifier and signified is endlessly underscored. Lacan's insight into how this manipulation is a strategy to overcome the shattering experience of loss represented by the disappearance of the mother points to why these "open spaces" might really be considered, as I proposed, "wounded spaces" in this text.

The surprising aspect of the version of the *Fort/Da!* game that Benet presents is that the boy is deaf-mute. He *cannot* take up language to recreate, and thus overcome, the loss he has experienced. Perhaps this is why his suffering is so strong. Perhaps this is why memory remains only a malady for him, never developing that other aspect of the *pharmakon:* the cure. Not only does the boy not develop any sense of cure, but he ends up killing the person in the novel who supposedly has the power to cure: the doctor.

At the beginning of the novel, when Marré arrives in her black car, the boy, probably believing, erroneously, that it is his mother, becomes so overexcited that the doctor has to tie him down to his bed and administer an injection to sedate him. During the night-long conversation between Marré and the doctor, the boy is confined to his room, suffering in silence. When Marré leaves the next morning, and before Numa's shot that presumably kills her rings out, the boy frees himself from his restraints, kills the doctor, and then, in a mad frenzy, runs around the locked house, yelling in anguish and throwing himself against walls and doors in a futile attempt to escape. Thus the doctor, too, becomes a *pharmakos* in this story of multiple sacrifices. The boy, most likely, also dies at the end, although this cannot be asserted with complete certainty due to the ambiguity characterizing the text. The last line of the novel, claiming that "el eco de un disparo lejano vino a restablecer el silencio habitual del lugar" (1967, 315) [the echo of a distant shot came to reestablish the habitual silence of the place (1985, 288)], seems to suggest this possibility. The "silencio habitual del lugar" (1967, 315) [habitual silence of the place (1985, 288)] that is reestablished seems to suggest that both Marré and the boy have, in the end, fallen equally, deadly silent, and this silence weighs over the end of the novel like a terrible, tragic tombstone.

There is another aspect in which the boy's muteness throughout the text becomes significant. As has been noted before, because of the imbrication of narrative voices in the text, the omniscient voice has, in many parts, become completely enmeshed with that of the various characters. If the boy himself has not been able to overcome his trauma by putting into play the game of language as a mechanism of perpetual loss, perhaps the omniscient voice, as well as the other narrative voices of the text, have done so. And, as we have seen, loss has, indeed, been recurrently enacted in the text.

Marré and the doctor have tried to use their memory to re-create the experience of *durée* they once had, but they both fail. Their very language imposes once again the temporal order from which they had tried to escape. Their conversation, as it is spoken, should have provided the sense of presence that the oral word implies, yet by its lack of differentiation from the extremely writerly style of the omniscient narrative voice, any sense of immediate presence is also lost. That omniscient voice itself, at the beginning, seemed to introduce a strictly realistic, scientific description of the area of Región, only to have that realism subverted, lost, in different ways.

One of the examples, mentioned earlier, of the presentation and subsequent subversion of realist detail in the novel is the metaphorical description of the mountains of Región at the beginning as "un testigo enigmático . . . de tanto desorden y tanto paroxismo" (1967, 39) [an enigmatic witness . . . of all that disorder and those paroxysms (1985, 31)]. As has been mentioned before, the "desorden y paroxismo" [disorder and paroxysms] referred to could be just as much the havoc wrought on Región by the civil war as the language in the novel used to provide that historical description. That metaphor, therefore, refers both to the historical reality it is supposedly describing *and* to the language that constitutes it as a description. Language here thus embodies a split reference that Paul Ricoeur explores in his analysis of metaphorical language by indicating that the literal sense is, in a way, destroyed by its metaphorical meaning. As he expresses it, "Just as the metaphorical statement captures its sense as metaphorical midst the ruins of the literal sense, it also achieves its reference upon the ruins of what might be called . . . its literal reference" (1975, 221).

The literal reference is in ruins so that the metaphorical may emerge. That obliteration, that ruining of the literal reference, is what Benet has constantly called for in his advocacy of literature as an exploration of a "zona de sombras" [zone of shadows]. Echoing Ricoeur's view of a double reference to reality, Benet has stated: "Porque la literatura . . .

maneja una segunda realidad. . . . En definitiva, la literatura lo único que hace es investigar, crear una segunda realidad" (qtd. in Campbell 1971, 260–61) [Because literature . . . deals with a second reality. . . . Finally, all that literature does is investigate, create a second reality].

What makes Ricoeur's expression particularly appropriate for Benet's work is that the direct reference to reality that metaphoric language leaves behind is said to be in *ruins*. Benet himself has asserted the following about his first novel: "*Volverás a Región* es una novela sobre la ruina; pretende dibujar la ruina no de una manera meramente descriptiva, sino introduciendo una serie de dimensiones que provocan la ruina" (qtd. in Campbell 1971, 258) [*Volverás a Región* is a novel about ruin; it pretends to draw the ruin not in a merely descriptive manner, but introducing a series of dimensions that provoke ruin].

Benet's novel, in this respect, is similar to Semprún's, for they both present a different version of what Blanchot calls a "writing of the disaster." Blanchot advocates a practice of writing that does not *describe* disaster but *inscribes* it in its very language. For the French critic, such writing should present not "knowledge of the disaster, not knowledge as disaster, but knowledge disastrously" (1986, 3). This scriptural practice was enacted in Semprún's text by his wounded chronology, among other narrative strategies. In Benet, it is the wounding of much more than chronology that produces a "knowledge disastrously," that "provokes ruin." Benet's language presents a wounding of a whole series of traditional narrative conventions, from the coherence of point of view, to stable character and plot development, to any sense of linear chronology. All these "wounds" function to "provocar la ruina" [provoke ruin] as he said, of a referential language that Benet, in his novelistic as well as his critical work, has tirelessly critiqued.

In *Volverás a Región* Benet has recourse to a curious metaphor in describing the emergence of the civil war, that experience which has produced so much "wounded memory":

> El telón de una anacrónica comedieta de costumbres se levanta para dar lugar a un escenario en ruina y en el intermedio, mientras los comparsas se cambian los disfraces y los actores fuman en los pasillos, estalla la guerra civil. Los que hemos llegado tarde a la representación apenas nos hemos hecho cargo de la clase de comedia que nos ha tocado presenciar. (1967, 245)

> [The curtain of an anachronistic light comedy of manners rises to reveal a set in ruins, and during the intermission, while the extras change disguises and the actors smoke in the hallways, the civil war breaks out. Those who have arrived late for the performance barely realize what kind of play we've been called upon to see.] (1985, 223)

Beneath a supposedly realistic representation of reality, such as that of a "comedieta de costumbres" [light comedy of manners], lies a scene in ruins. But those ruins are necessary for representation to occur. All hope of developing a view of the world must be based on the loss implied by ruins. This image embodies Ricoeur's notion that any symbolic reference to reality emerges only out of the ruins of a direct, referential language. It is particularly important that a metaphorical image, an enigmatic one at that, underlies a realistic representation of the world. The perplexity of the spectators, trying to understand their role in the history/story they are witnesses to and participants in, is revealing. It shows that the metaphorical representation underlying the realistic one is the best way to enter that "zona de sombras" [zone of shadows] where all certainty is lost. That perplexity is what, Benet believes, paradoxically best represents our "true" way of being in the world. He has claimed that "sólo la ambigüedad tiene capacidad para hacer historia" (1976a, 56) [only ambiguity has the capacity to create history].

Benet's claim that ambiguity constitutes history underscores how radically subversive his view of historiography is with respect to that of the Franco regime, since the latter was based on supposedly unquestionable, infallible and unambiguous truths about the redemptive role of the regime in history. As Herzberger explains: "Benet's emphasis on the oxymoronic and the contradictory . . . shakes the foundational solidity of Francoist historiography in the way that it rejects narrative certainties . . . [and] undermines at every point the rigid assertions of the Regime" (1995, 95). The difference, furthermore, cannot be greater between the regime's exalted rhetoric of a divinely inspired crusade against the enemies of the "true Spain" and Benet's image of a civil war that haphazardly emerges in a ruinous theater during the intermission of a comedy that leaves its spectators bewildered. This points to one of the politically subversive dimensions of the ruins so pervasive in Benet's text. As Benson explains, referring to Benet's recurrent images of ruins: "La ruina puede interpretarse en consecuencia como una respuesta a la supuesta superioridad del pueblo español que transmite el discurso oficial. Frente al ridículo y anacrónico enaltecimiento, la realidad muestra un pueblo en ruinas" (2004, 160) [The ruin can thus be interpreted as a response to the supposed superiority of the Spanish people transmitted by official discourse. In the face of such a ridiculous and anachronistic ennobling rhetoric, the reality shows a nation in ruins].

However, there is another dimension to the subversive function of ruins in Benet's novel. It must be pointed out that the ruins that Benet portrays are inherently related to his exploration of memory. He has affirmed that "la esperanza o la no esperanza es materia de memoria: todo lo que se hace en literatura es materia de memoria. En definitiva, lo que arruina una cosa es la memoria, no la intemperie" (qtd. in Campbell 1971, 259) [hope or lack of hope is a matter of memory: everything that is done in literature is a matter of memory. In the end, what ruins something is memory, not bad weather]. All of Benet's novelistic world, in fact, has been defined as "la ruina de la memoria" (Guelbenzu 1969, 48) [the ruin of memory]. The images of ruins throughout the novel, and the dynamic of memory they evoke, embody the most subversive aspect of Benet's understanding of the relationship between fiction and history. For ruins in Benet's work present a view, very similar to that developed by Walter Benjamin, of history itself as catastrophe. From this perspective, Benet's ruins evoke a view of history that rejects not only the Francoist exalted rhetoric of the regime's supposedly "sacred" role in Spanish history, but a more general master-narrative underlying the regime's, and many other oppressive political regimes', view of history as progress.[21]

Benjamin's famous depiction, in his "Theses on the Philosophy of History," of the figure of the "angel of history" in a painting by Paul Klee presents a view of progress as being, in reality, one eternal catastrophe: "His face is turned towards the past. Where we perceive a chain of events, he sees one single catastrophe which keeps piling wreckage and hurls it in front of his feet. The angel would like to stay, awaken the dead, and make whole what has been smashed. But a storm is blowing from Paradise. . . . This storm is what we call progress" (1969, 257–58).

Progress is seen as a storm that keeps piling up wreckage, ruin, at our feet. And the reason why "progress" is but a series of ruins is that it is usually defined by the victors of history, and it inevitably emerges out of ruins, which represent in large part the experience of the victims. This radical undermining of the concept of progress grows out of Benjamin's awareness that "there is no document of history which is not at the same time a document of barbarism" (1969, 256). If we are to try to find a way to look at history, to remember or work through the past, that does not reproduce that barbarism, we have to learn to "brush history against the grain" (1969, 257). One way to do this, according to Benjamin, is to engage with events or objects from history in order to understand them anew while rejecting the whole narrative of progress in which those events or objects had previously been embedded. This would mean remembering events or objects in a way that manages to "blast open the continuum of history" (1969, 262) on which that notion of progress is based. Ruins are perfect sites for such a process, and it is thus no coincidence that it has been said that, for Benjamin, "knowledge grows . . . out of the ruins" (qtd. in Frisby 1986, 213). As David Frisby defines Benjamin's proposal, the historical object must be "snatched from the false context of the historical continuum in which it is embedded and placed in our present. The wresting of the fragment from its encrusted context requires a destructive intention in so far as the false continuum is reduced to rubble" (1986, 216).

This is exactly what Benet does in *Volverás a Región*. History as catastrophe is often invoked in the text, and the concept of progress is radically undermined. Doctor Sebastián claims that "el así llamado progeso se consigue a costa de algo, quizá de lo que no puede progresar" (1967, 222) [so-called progress is attained at the price of something, perhaps of what can't progress (1985, 201)]. The concept of progress is questioned ("el así llamado progeso" [so-called progress]) and the doctor highlights that it always emerges at the expense of something, of someone, that does not participate in that same experience or rhetoric ("que no puede progresar" [can't progress]). He further describes those remaining after the war as "unos muertos, unos supervivientes desesperados, . . . incrédulos testigos de una edad catastrófica" (1967, 124) [some dead, some desperate survivors . . . unbelieving witnesses of a catastrophic [age] (1985, 110)]. These ghostly survivors, these living-dead, are somewhat like the "angel of history" that Benjamin described, looking back at what others call "progress" and, in an "unbelieving" stance, seeing only "catastrophe." Labanyi has claimed, along these lines, that, in Benet's text, "The ruins left by the war are emblematic of the permanent record of devastation that is history" (1989, 120).

But there is more to the ruins so prevalent in Benet's novelistic world. Doctor Sebastián goes so far as to state that it was perhaps necessary to lose the war in order to finally give up any vestige of belief in progress: "la guerra había que perderla, costase lo que costase, . . . para perder definitivamente toda confianza en la historia y en el porvenir" (1967, 176) ["the war had to be lost, no matter what it cost, . . . to lose once and for all any confidence in history and its future (1985, 159)]. In this sense, the devastation of the war might prove to be a defense against the greater devastation of a rhetoric of progress that would continue long after the fighting. Perhaps this is why, as his text exclaims, and as Benet loved to repeat frequently, only a Ruin (with capital R) can save us from more ruin: "la propia Ruina . . . , como decía el Viejo Temístocles, nos preserva siempre de otra mayor" (1967, 121) [Ruin itself . . . , as old Themistocles said, always keeps us from a worse one [ruin] (1985, 107)]. The logic of the *pharmakon* is thus at work among the ruins of Región, for only that which is dangerous can ultimately save; only by acknowledging the wreckage left behind by "progress" can one be protected from the devastating effects of that very concept.

One of the most important images of ruin in *Volverás a Región,* a text filled with ruinous images, is the one that Doctor Sebastián presents when he tells Marré that, somewhere nearby, she will find "el tabernáculo de la ruina" (1967, 249) [the tabernacle of ruin (1985, 227)]. The religious image of the tabernacle is ruined here, and this becomes one way in which Benet's writing manages to "blast open the continuum of history," as Benjamin advocated, for it blasts apart, and leaves in ruins, a religious image that could be seen as emblematic of the religious rhetoric underpinning the Francoist ideology of history. This "tabernacle of ruin" is intimately related to all the ways, which have been described in this chapter, in which Benet's novel undermines the rhetoric of sacrifice, as well as of peace and order, upon which the regime's concept of historical progress was based. Ruins are always fragmentary, bits and pieces left over from a shattered whole. This is why ruins are the perfect image with which to undergo the working through of the past that Benjamin advocated, for they are an image of fragmentation that one can come to terms with only if one engages in a shattering of the "continuum of history," or ideology of progress, that created those ruins in the first place.

There is another recurrent image in Benet's text that could be interpreted as a particularly interesting kind of ruin. It is also an image of a fragmented, shattered, dispersed object, a vestige of what was previously whole, and, more importantly, of a previously whole object whose task it was to disseminate and impose a view of the world that was, in a sense, similarly "whole." Throughout the text there are images of rumpled, weathered pages torn from old newspapers and scattered about, their writing often partly erased by the elements. They are anachronistic and dismembered ghosts from previous times. Sometimes these fragments of newspapers are menacing:

> hojas de periódicos envueltas en un gran rollo y que al llegar a su puerta se abrían insinuantes ... golpeándose contra los cristales, remolineando por los balcones y obturando las chimeneas ... para terminar, descoloridas y agujereadas por la lluvia, deshechas por los golpes del viento, colgando de las ramas de los arbustos y espinos" (1967, 140)

> [pages from newspapers rolled up into a large bundle and which, when they reached his door, opened up insinuatingly ... beating against the windowpanes, swirling across the balconies and plugging up the chimneys ... to end up faded, with holes from the rain, torn by the wind, hanging from the branches of the underbrush and brambles.] (1985, 125)

We can, of course, see newspapers themselves as agents of the ideology of progress and history that Benet's text is trying to undermine, which is perhaps why they are so menacing here. Newspapers are mechanisms for the imposition of order, in the epistemological, temporal, and political sense, on reality. They provide description and explanation of the world within a chronological frame.[22] Presenting the image of free-floating and loose pages from old, dated newspapers is a most appropriate way to "blast open the continuum of history," as Benjamin advocated, for it breaks up, "blasts open," another agent of the dominant ideology of progress and history. Such free-floating pages from outdated newspapers whose referent is long past can also be seen as another image of that unbridgeable gap between signifier and signified that Spires sees as central to Benet's "poetics of open spaces" (1984, 1) or what I call Benet's "wounded spaces." It is no coincidence that Blanchot, shortly after mentioning the "wounded space" that the "writing of the disaster" embodies, also mentions that such writing emerges from the "ruin of words . . . the fragment" (1986, 33). The ruins embodied by these fragmented newspapers are, indeed, a "ruin of words."

Another related image in the text presents "unas hojas de periódico diseminadas por el suelo. . . ." and "un calendario farmacéutico [que] colgaba todavía en la pared y conservaba algunas hojas de un año atrasado" (1967, 105) [newspapers [that] were spread over the floor . . . [and] a pharmaceutical calendar [that] hung on the wall and still held some pages of a year long gone by (1985, 93)]. The calendar, another agent of the ideology of temporal order and progress, is here as fragmented and anachronistic, because out of date, as the menacing newspaper pages. Yet another image presents "unos antiguos patrones cortados en hojas de periódico con las notas de sociedad y actualidad de treinta años atrás" (1967, 119) [a few old patterns cut from newspaper pages with the society news and events of thirty years ago (1985, 106)]. This last image of scattered, outdated newspaper pages is particularly interesting, because such pages have been ripped out, "blasted open" from their original context, a whole newspaper, and then have been used to create patterns for sewing something new. This new object to be sewn will thus emerge out of the shattering of the order of time and explanation that a whole, complete, newspaper represents. We are reminded here of Marré's view that memory may only serve "para un remiendo" (1967, 294) [for patchwork (1985, 269)], a sewing metaphor that complements that of the sewing patterns made of newspaper fragments. The patterns made from old newspapers subvert the order that the original newspaper represented. Inevitably, however, that order does not completely disappear, for it is partly reflected in the writing that remains on the patterns, however incomplete and anachronistic. The subversion of order may never be complete, yet the patterns remain, ready to be made into something ever new, to be assembled in unprecedented and unexpected ways.

These images of the ruins made of newspaper fragments, the "ruins of words" in Benet's text, can be seen as embodying the different levels of subversion of order that Benet seeks with his writing. Newspapers are supposedly paradigmatic examples of the kind of realistic, referential use of language that Benet hopes to subvert with his poetics of "open" (or wounded) spaces. They represent the temporal order and the "tiempo intelectualizado" [intellectualized time] to which Benet opposes the "tiempo instintivo" [instinctive time]. They embody a linear, chronological time frame that underlies any rhetoric of progress. Furthermore, they are agents of the dominant ideological order of the Franco regime, presenting the official view of history. All of these "orders" are partially subverted when Benet presents the newspapers as fragmented, dispersed, tattered, and out-of-date.

Because they embody multiple levels of subversion of order, these ruinous newspaper fragments, as well as the ruins of Región in general, may be the most appropriate image for the "places of memory" that Benet's writing provides for a working through of the memory of the civil war and postwar period in Spain. The ruins of Región are "ruined" places of memory akin to the "place of memory" of the almost empty courtyard of Buchenwald in 1992 that Semprún presents in his writing. In both examples, as Pierre Nora claims is the case for all places of memory, a process of construction of a symbolic image requires a simultaneous deconstruction of previous interpretations of that image. Construction and deconstruction are necessarily intertwined, in a process that is akin to that described by David Frisby when explaining Benjamin's proposal for how to work through the past without re-creating the "barbarism" he so forcefully rejected: "The wresting of the fragment from its encrusted context requires a destructive intention in so far as the false continuum is reduced to rubble" (1986, 216). The ruined place of memory that Buchenwald embodies in Semprún's writing reflects the various exiles that the author suffered. The ruined places of memory scattered throughout Benet's Región reflect the "inner exile" suffered by the protagonists of his novel. Paul Ilie has coined the term "inner exile" to describe the experience of those who, after the civil war, did not, or could not, leave Spain despite ideological disagreement with the regime, and thus suffered tremendous alienation and repression. That sense of alienation from the dominant ideology permeates Benet's novel, and leads Ilie to see Benet's text as "perhaps the embodiment of inner exile: a locality is in exile from the rest of Spain; the personages are in exile from time's triple dimension: past, present, future; even, time is in exile from itself since Benet distinguishes between "el tiempo" and "el Tiempo" (1980, 163). The ruined places of memory in Benet's writing thus reflect an "inner exile" whose destructive force is ever-present.

These ruins of memory that Benet's novels embody also have a similar function to that of the image of ashes in Semprún's work. Derrida sees ashes as a "destruction of memory" (1991, 389). He further explains: "the difference between the trace 'cinder' and other traces is that the body of which cinders is the trace has totally disappeared" (1991, 390). This seems to be the case with the disappearance of the poor souls killed by Numa in *Volverás a Región*. Describing one of the occasions in which Numa destroyed his yearly *pharmakos,* or human sacrifice, the text explains how after that shooting "no quedó ningún resto ni explicación alguna" (1967, 15) [nothing was left over nor was there any explanation (1985, 8)]. This lack of any explanation may remind one of Semprún's reaction to the mountain of corpses outside the crematorium in Buchenwald as he was guiding the French women who were inspecting the camp immediately after its liberation. At that moment, Semprún feels that he cannot say anything to the women, and thinks to himself that those corpses "no necesitaban ninguna explicación. Necesitaban que viviéramos, sencillamente, que viviéramos con todas nuestras fuerzas con la memoria de su muerte" (1995b, 138) [needed no explanation. They needed us to live, quite simply, to live with all our strength in the memory of their death (1997, 122)]. The disappearance of so many people in Región, including Marré, may likewise have no "explanation," but the text as a whole, with the many ways in which it puts the "ruins of memory" to work on multiple levels, works to constantly re-create the loss that their death implies. As in the dynamic of trauma and the *pharmakon,* such a re-creation of loss can also serve to keep their memory alive. Their death, without explanation, haunts the survivors who, in Doctor Sebastián's phrase, are "unos muertos, unos supervivientes desesperados, . . . incrédulos testigos de una edad catastrófica" (1967, 124) [some dead, some desperate survivors . . . unbelieving witnesses of a catastrophic war [age] (1985, 110)].

The image of the living-dead that Doctor Sebastián evokes is only one of many images of ghostly beings haunting Región. The stories of the victims of history implicitly return, like the return of the repressed, with these ghostly presences. The region is said to be haunted by an "orden fantasmal" (1967, 17) [phantasmal order (1985, 11)], and traversed by "caminos fantasmales" (1967, 42) [phantom roads (1985, 33)]. The Republican forces defending the region are described as an "ejército fantasmal" and a "regimiento espectral" (1967, 89) [a ghost army, a ... spectral regiment (1985, 77)]. The survivors of the war are depicted as "los supervivientes, los espectros de un ayer tantalizado" (1967, 246) [the survivors, the specters of a tantalized yesterday (1985, 224)]. Benet's "places of memory," embodied in the multiple ruins of Región, serve as sites for the return of the repressed of official Francoist history in the form of these ghostly beings. His whole novel, therefore, could be seen to serve the same function as the wild flower that grows in the area: "la flor de la inquietud, de la desazón del alma, de los contrastes del espíritu.... Porque nace siempre donde descansa un resto humano, un hueso o un escapulario que está pidiendo venganza, recuerdo, y redención al mundo de los vivos." (1967, 190) [the flower of uneasiness, of unrest of the soul, of the contrasts of the spirit.... Because it is always born where human remains are resting, a bone or a scapular that calls for vengeance, recall, and redemption from the world of the living] (1985, 171–72). This flower of the "contrates del espíritu" [contrasts of the spirit] is the perfect image to bloom from within the " imperio del oxymoron" [domain of oxymoron] that Benet wants his writing to be, for it represents a veritable "lucha de los contrarios" [battle of opposites]. In this sense, the flower is an embodiment of the epistemological ambiguity and mystery that Benet seeks in literature. The fact that the flower grows where there are human remains and that it "está pidiendo venganza, recuerdo, y redención al mundo de los vivos" [calls for vengeance, recall, and redemption from the world of the living], makes of this flower an embodiment of the ethical dimension of Benet's novel. Like the flower, this meta-memory text as a whole remembers the victims of official history whose ghostly presence can be felt among the many ruins of Región, and it does so while explicitly reflecting on the always ambivalent and multivalent nature of memory itself.

Because of their nature as a *pharmakon* in Benet's texts, the ruins of memory evoke not only "destruction" but also "reconstruction." They are elements to be employed as "remiendos," to use Marré's expression, "patches" to console, cure, perhaps even provide redemption for, the damaged and wounded ghostly souls populating Región. Benet highlights the never-ending nature of such a curative/painful "remiendo" or "patchwork" process of memory in working through a traumatic past: "Esa memoria es y será siempre un palimpsesto y cada nueva inscripción borra la anterior" (1987, 135) [That memory is and will always be a palimpsest and every new inscription erases the previous one]. The image of the palimpsest appears. It is reminiscent of Semprún's image of the palimpsest that his first Spanish copy of *El largo viaje* became. The words in that copy, absent because of Francoist censure, would have to be forever added in new layers that would never exhaust Semprún's memory of the camp. Memory, in Semprún as in Benet, will always be multilayered. In Benet, as a *pharmakon*, it will also be multinatured. Memory, whether the painful remembrance of loss (the illness) or the hopeful reminder of what is still possible (the cure), will always be multiple. And the multiple traces it leaves behind will always become a palimpsest, a forever-incomplete surface to which new traces can always be added. This is perhaps why it is said in *Volverás a Región* that "la memoria mantiene abierta la cuenta" (1967, 18) [memory keeps the account open (1985, 11)]. One could add, also, that "la memoria mantiene abierto el cuento" [memory keeps the story open]. For, just as the possibility of adding new traces to the palimpsest of memory is endless, the possibility of interpreting those traces is likewise infinite. The reading of this text in which the palimpsest of memory is presented will always itself be a palimpsest.[23] The endless proliferation of Benet criticism, with multiple readings, some completely at odds with others, attests to this.

Reading will be just one more trace added onto this text made up of so many traces which all, together, present what I have called the *pharmakon* of memory. Interestingly enough, Ricoeur has compared reading itself to a *pharmakon:* "Reading is the pharmakon, the 'remedy,' by which the meaning of the text is 'rescued' from the estrangement of distanciation and put in a new proximity, a proximity which suppresses and preserves the cultural distance and includes the otherness within the ownness" (qtd. in Valdés 1991, 337). It is significant that Ricoeur decides to translate *pharmakon* only with its positive meaning. He clearly wants the reader to be able to understand and appropriate the text completely. But the *pharmakon* has its other, darker side, too.

A more appropriate image of the *pharmakon* of reading is provided in Benet's own text. The "viajero" [traveler] who is mentioned throughout the novel also struggles with distanciation and proximity. As he travels toward the mountains of Región, he finds that "cada paso hacia adelante no hace sino alejarlo un poco más de aquellas desconocidas montañas" (1967, 7) [every step forward is only bringing him a little farther away from those unknown mountains (1985, 1)]. This is the truly ambiguous *pharmakon* of reading, and of memory, that Benet's work embodies. The closer we as readers feel we are to "grasping" the meaning of his novelistic world, and the meaning of the traumatic past of civil war and postwar Spain portrayed in that world, the more distanced we truly are from fully understanding Benet's writing. A definitive reading of *Volverás a Región* may elude our grasp, thus guaranteeing that it forever embody the enigma that Benet sought so ardently to foment with his writing. However, the text, with its ruins and ghosts, emerges also as a powerful political act, enbodying, as Marré so eloquently phrased it, "la venganza de lo que no fue" (1967, 115) [the vengeance for what ... was not (1985, 101)].

In this sense, even if we as readers never manage to decipher fully the meaning of this enigmatic novel, we have become the bearers of an important memory presented in the text, the memory of the victims of the war and postwar, of those suffering an endless "inner exile"; a memory all the more important because it was one that was never truly allowed to flower. We, as much as the mountains of Región, have become "witnesses" (perhaps confused and lost at times, but "witnesses" nonetheless) to the "desorden y paroxismo" of history as it is constantly reenacted in the text and presented as an offering to us through the "wounded spaces" of its enigmatic *pharmakon:* memory.

3
María Teresa León: The Performance of Memory

> La memoria puede tener los ojos indulgentes . . . memoria melancólica, a medio apagar, memoria de la melancolía. No sé quién solía decir en mi casa: hay que tener recuerdos. Vivir no es tan importante como recordar. Lo espantoso era no tener nada que recordar, dejando tras de sí una cinta sin señales. Pero qué horrible es que los recuerdos se precipiten sobre ti y te obliguen a mirarlos y te muerdan, y se revuelquen sobre tus entreñas, que es el lugar de la memoria.
>
> [Memory may have indulgent eyes . . . melancholy memory, almost extinguished, memory of melancholy. I don't remember who, at home, used to say: one must have memories. To live is not as important as to remember. The horrible thing was not to have anything to remember, leaving behind an unmarked ribbon. How horrible it is when memories assail you, force you to look at them, bite you and wallow in your entrails, which is the place of memory.]
>
> —María Teresa León 1998, 130

THERE IS AN INTERESTING WEB SITE, ENTITLED "PORTAL DEL EXILIO" [Exile Portal], dedicated to remembering the Spanish Republican exile(s) of 1939. The site presents a series of sections with images of the different chronological stages of the Republican exile(s), the last being: "los retornos" [the returns].[1] Here, among photographs of other illustrious figures returning from exile in the seventies, there is one of poet Rafael Alberti descending from the plane, face smiling, hand waving to all who greeted his return in 1977, after thirty-eight long years of absence from Spain. I came across this site after I had been steeped in readings about Alberti's first wife, María Teresa León, for a long time, and thus after having read over and over again about this moment of their return together to Spain. My initial reaction to the picture was thus quite strong, and a certain misrecognition came over me: "this isn't right, where is León?" For, although she arrived on that same plane with

Alberti in 1977, she is strikingly absent from the picture, even from its caption. Present at the time, absent in the present. Her presence/absence haunts that picture, which thus turns her into a ghost, hovering just beyond the edge of the picture, the edge of the visible.

After my initial reaction, I realized that this experience was in fact quite revealing. First of all, it is symptomatic of the gaps in any and all practices that pretend to recover or represent the past, even those that pretend to fill in the gaps of *earlier* historical narratives. Historical memory is inevitably connected to historical forgetting. In this case, the Web page purposefully presents information about the experience of exile that had been repressively silenced during the Franco regime, and then, to a large degree, sidestepped during the "pact of amnesia" that conveniently emerged during the transition to democracy.

As was mentioned in the introduction to this book, with the fundamental democratic right of equality before the law that was recovered with the transition to democracy in the mid 1970s, a more problematic "equality before the past," to use Gregorio Morán's expression, was implicitly assumed (1991, 75). Morán explains: "Desde los primeros días de diciembre de 1975 se inicia un proceso de desmemorización colectiva. No de olvido, sino de algo más preciso y voluntario, la capacidad de volverse desmemoriado" (1991, 75) [From the first days of December 1975, a process of collective disremembering begins. Not of forgetting, but of something more precise and voluntary, the capacity to become someone who disremembers]. He claims that the transition created a "Reino de desmemoriados" (1991, 75) [kingdom of disremembering subjects] in which everyone was expected to give up any serious and concrete reevaluation of their past during the civil war and then during the Franco regime, either as part of it or as part of the opposition to it, because of the supposedly destabilizing effects such a reevaluation would have. As he explains: "la ingenua convención de igualdad ante la ley fue sustituida por la retorcida presunción de que todos los pasados eran igualmente perjudiciales y por tanto convenía instalarlos en el armario de los cadáveres" (1991, 77) [the naïve convention of equality before the law was substituted for a distorted belief that all pasts were equally damaging, and therefore, they should all be installed in the skeleton closet].[2] The Web site on the Spanish exile(s) of 1939 is highly commendable for its stated intention of combatting such a strategy of "disremembering," yet it unwittingly re-creates a certain "desmemoria" [disremembering] of its own in its failure to mention María Teresa León's return to Spain along with her husband, as if placing her, unintentionally, I am sure, in the "armario de los cadáveres" [skeleton closet] once again.

It should be noted that the singular term "exilio" [exile] of the Web page is symptomatic in itself of a problematically simplified view of a historical experience that was not the same for all who suffered it. This difference is fundamental to keep in mind when analyzing this historical experience.[3]

Of course, that the woman was left "out of the picture," quite literally, is no surprise, since those gaps, silences, and omissions that are inevitable in all representations of the past are more often than not gendered, being produced around, and at the same time producing, woman's invisibility. Furthermore, María Teresa León's ghostly presence/absence in the picture could be seen as an extension of an important aspect of her own writing in her autobiography *Memoria de la melancolía* (originally published in 1970) [*Memory of Melancholy*], traversed as it is, haunted throughout, by the memories of so many fellow compatriots that exile seemed to have relegated to the category of ghosts, of living-dead. Moreover, my sense of misrecognition upon beholding the picture can also be seen to echo another prevailing aspect of her text, the misrecognition, or "disidentification," which I will analyze as being central to León's autobiography, and to the multiple levels of exile reflected therein.[4]

Finally, a picture such as this one, which, still today, presents an image of exile in which key players are erased from memory raises important questions as to what our task as scholars of literature, including that of the Republican exile(s) of 1939, should be. Is it enough to understand our task as one of "broadening the picture," enlarging the frame, so to speak, in order to recover texts and characters from the oblivion and silence to which they have been reduced by being positioned beyond the edge of that all-powerful "frame" called the canon? This is, indeed, an important task, and still much needs to be done in this respect.[5]

But we cannot assume that such a task is the only one to be undertaken, or even that it is clear what it means to adequately "recover" such material from oblivion and neglect. Mari Paz Balibrea's proposal in "El paradigma exilio" [The exile paradigm] opens up a very suggestive course of analysis, recognizing that, in this process of "recovering" the formerly excluded bibliography of the 1939 exile(s), "lo que falta abrumadoramente es el sitio donde ubicarla" (2003, 17) [what is overwhelmingly missing is the place in which to put it]. That is, we cannot simply pretend to "enlarge" the canon to include previously excluded material, without critically exploring the dynamics underlying that very process of canon formation, inextricably related to the dynamics of nation formation, and without recognizing, furthermore, that the very writing of many of those texts from exile radically calls into question, destabilizes, such dynamics. Instead of trying to "stabilize" the position of such texts within the history of contemporary Spanish literature by simply incorporating them, we should perhaps learn to assume, within our very manner of approaching them, the "destabilizations" they often embody. As Balibrea states: "esa desestabilización debe inscribirse en la crítica misma que busca relacionar la cultura del exilio con la del interior. . . . Antes de recuperar de forma duradera el exilio, su crítica deberá demostrar cómo esta literatura saca de quicio a España, dinamitando su canon y sus presupuestos político-narrativos" (2003, 19–20) [That destabilization should be inscribed in the very criticism that seeks to relate the culture of exile with that of the interior. . . . Before recovering exile in a permanent way, the criticism with which it is studied should demonstrate how this literature throws Spain out of kilter, dynamiting its canon and its political-narrative presuppositions].

Meta-memory texts, such as that of María Teresa León's autobiography as well as the texts by Semprún and Benet that have been analyzed in the previous chapters, are particularly appropriate writings to study in this light, because the strategies of memory they present, and critically reflect about, can serve as models for this task. Semprún's autobiographical novels about Buchenwald self-consciously explore the very manner and possibility (or impossibility) of recounting the trauma of exile and deportation without reducing or minimizing the horror that of that experience, all the while recognizing the difficulty in finding an appropriate place in the present for such traumatic memories. Benet's novels about postwar Spain, although not written in exile, portray the realities of inner exile during that time period and do so through the use of narrative strategies of memory that self-consciously counter both the rhetoric of progress and that of an imposed oblivion of the past predominant during the Franco regime. Benet's *Volverás a Región* highlights the lack of a place in postwar Spain for such subversive rememorative ventures, for the characters who attempt such explorations of memory in the novel all die in the end. Both of these texts thus use memory not only to explore a dangerous past, but to vindicate a silenced history as well as to reflect upon the role of memory in creating an identity in the present at odds with official discourses intent on forgetting that history. Such texts embody a process of working through the past that does, indeed, "brush history against the grain," something that likewise characterizes the dynamics of memory in León's autobiography, and which is essential for understanding the manner in which this text "saca de quicio a España" [throws Spain out of kilter], as will be analyzed in this chapter.

Two of the issues mentioned above which I explore in *Memoria de la melancolía* are particularly important in this regard. The ghostly presences that haunt León's text, as well as her own ghostly absence/presence in the picture on the Web, can be examined within a "philosophy of the phantasm" which, as Joan Ramon Resina explains, following Foucault, is a critical practice that "call[s] into question the cozy categories of modern thought: body, state, reason, image, inside and outside, the imaginary" (2000a, 3). Furthermore, the "disidentification" characterizing much of León's narrative, with the fragmented and disjointed construction of self it develops, could be seen as one element that may productively "destabilize" our own critical engagement with her text, as well as with other exilic memoirs and autobiographies, if such a "disidentification" is strategically appropriated as a critical tool in itself. Finally, I want to underscore another element of León's memoirs that has been mentioned in previous studies, but that I believe has not been sufficiently analyzed, and which will be seen to be inextricably related to the previous two issues: the influence on her narrative of León's work in, and passion for, theater. This leads to a constant foregrounding of the performativity and thus instability of any and all identities. In this manner, León's autobiography can be seen as an exploration of an individual past that becomes what Mieke Bal calls an "act of memory." Texts become such "acts of memory" inasmuch as they are actions having a deep impact on the present as well as in the sense that they are "performed" (1999, vii), a term that, in León's text, will take on its full theatrical implication.

The constant foregrounding of theater and all things theatrical, as well as of the performative nature of identity and politics, in *Memoria de la melancolía* is not surprising, given the great passion and devotion León had for the theater. Much of her political activism before and during the civil war was tied to theater projects, and, aside from the novels and collections of short stories she published in her lifetime, she wrote several plays and articles dealing with theater.[6] Performance and performativity will, indeed, be inextricably related to León's use of memory in her representation of the various levels of exile she suffered throughout her life, and to the dynamics of gender underlying such exiles.

León was born in 1903, in Logroño, and spent her childhood moving from city to city, living in Logroño, Madrid, Burgos, and Barcelona. Her father, in the military, and her mother, from an aristocratic family, imposed a conservative education on León, one destined to prepare the young girl for a quiet life as part of the Spanish upper class. She married at a young age and had two children, but, finally, resisting much family and social pressure to remain married, she divorced her husband and concomitantly lost her rights over her two young sons. Later, she met and married Rafael Alberti and began an indefatigable trajectory of political activism, heavily marked by the couple's membership in the Spanish Communist Party.

Many of the projects León undertook reflected her interest in theater. Before the war, for example, she participated in the Misiones Pedagógicas [Pedagogical Missions], a project with an educational goal similar to Lorca's "La Barraca" which represented well-known Spanish plays in rural villages. León and Alberti received a grant from the Republic's Junta de Ampliación de Estudios [Council for Developing Education] to study European theater, and thus they both traveled throughout Europe in 1932, bringing back to Spain a new perspective on the importance of politically engaged theater. They later attended the I Congreso de Escritores Soviéticos [I Congress of Soviet Writers] in Moscow in 1934 and returned there in 1937. During the war, León and Alberti helped found and run the Alianza de Intelectuales Antifascistas [Alliance of Anti-Fascist Intellectuals], which coordinated much of the support that intellectuals from all over the world came to offer the Spanish Republic. Within that institution, León directed the Comité de Agitación y Propaganda Interior [Committee for Activism and Interior Propaganda]. As part of this project, she created and was the director of the Guerrillas del Teatro [Theater Guerrillas], a theatrical troop in charge of taking theater representations to the war front, as well as of Nueva Escena [New Scene], the theater section of the Alianza. Here, she created the Escuela Técnica Teatral [Technical Theater School], which organized courses on different aspects of theater, such as directing, acting, and so forth. León was named vice president of the Republic's Consejo Central del Teatro [Central Theater Council] (the president was Antonio Machado), and she was named director of Teatro de Arte y Propaganda [Theater of Art and Propaganda]. In this capacity she was in charge of directing numerous plays. She was also active in the Junta de Incautación del Tesoro Artístico [Council for the Preservation of Art], organizing, with Alberti, the movement to Valencia of major works from the Prado museum during the war. At the end of the war, León and Alberti began their long exile, first in France, then spending many years in Argentina and Italy before finally returning to Spain in 1977. All of these events are recalled in León's autobiography. Although her active engagement in theater was much reduced in exile, her understanding of theater and of the many theatrical elements of life is present in all of León's writing, including *Memoria de la melancolía*.[7]

* * * *

In *Black Sun: Depression and Melancholia*, Julia Kristeva writes, "For those who are racked by melancholia, writing about it would have meaning only if writing sprang out of that very melancholia" (1989, 3). Angel Loureiro's analysis of *Memoria de la melancolía*, in *The Ethics of Autobiography: Replacing the Subject in Modern Spain*, develops this insight. He keenly observes a significant difference between the second section of the text (depicting the years of the Spanish civil war) and the first and third (the first tracing León's life before the war, the third presenting the long years in exile). Loureiro claims that the second section springs out of a sense of "political melancholy," as León longs for the lost homeland and political ideals of the Republic, while the first and last hinge on what he calls a much deeper and less easily definable "melancholy of transience" (2000, 94). According to Loureiro, these first and last sections frame the incessant loss and displacement that León obsessively depicts in her text not just within the realm of the ideological or political, but within a more general "theological" preoccupation with transience and the passing of time. Loureiro sees this as being the main concern underlying the many images of ruins that appear in León's text: "León's imperative need to return to the ruins has to do with time and meaning, with giving meaning to time, with rescuing things from the destructive passage of time" (2000, 91). This, according to Loureiro, is the much more terrifying sense of loss in León's text that underlies the more evident political loss of the civil war and experience of exile. Therefore, the ruins within León's writing, according to Loureiro, "dissimulate some unspeakable, unrepresentable fear, the terror of a primary loss that León seems reluctant to confront because its threat is more powerful than any political oppression" (2000, 90).

I believe that Loureiro is quite correct in pointing to "a primary loss" in León's text, but I think that this experience cannot be understood without fully acknowledging the way the text foregrounds the gendered nature of such loss, the manner in which the problem of gender is inextricably intertwined with the problem of exile, of the several levels of exile that traverse León's autobiography, and with the narrative strategies of memory used to depict such exile(s).[8] Furthermore, I believe the ruins in León's text do have a very important political function within her narrative, one having to do with the politics of memory, or more appropriately, of "disremembering," which were predominant in Spain at the time she was writing her autobiography and which would perdure during the transition to democracy.

3: MARÍA TERESA LEÓN: THE PERFORMANCE OF MEMORY 149

León's autobiographical voice shifts throughout the text, alternating between first, second, and third person narration. This extreme division within the narrative voice can be seen as a textual manifestation of "disidentification." According to Teresa de Lauretis, this is a narrative strategy whereby women often express the difficulty inherent in their efforts to reconcile images of themselves that they want to forge with the images of femininity that patriarchal society imposes on them (1990). Through an analysis of this "pronominal disjunction" in the retrospective narrative of León, it will become clear that her remembrance re-creates not only the experience of exile that the author suffered after the civil war, but also another type of exile that emerges from the fact of being a woman in a patriarchal society. As Felicity Nussbaum claims, " 'Disidentification' in text or in the world may make visible the previously invisible aspects of ideology that produce subjects, and new positions may be made available through which change may be affected" (1998, 164). It is important to note that such "disidentification" characterizes not only the *content* of the memories of her past that León presents in her autobiography, but the very narrative *process of remembering* through which that past is represented.[9]

Such "disidentification" is at the heart of how León narrates her childhood and adolescence, and it is presented in a narrative saturated with theatrical imagery. From the beginning, León presents this image of herself: "Niña de militar inadaptada siempre, no niña de provincia ni de ciudad pequeña con catedral y obispado y segunda enseñanza" (1998, 73) [Daughter of a military officer forever maladjusted, not a girl from the province nor from a small city with cathedral and bishopric and higher learning], and she does so in the third person. It is important, moreover, that in this first depiction of her childhood she describes herself not so much as what she *was,* but as what she *was not,* as if to highlight her "disidentification" with the way of life being imposed on her. The descriptions of the cities and towns she lived in are presented as if they were annotations for the staging of a play, like the one previously mentioned, or: "Pueblo pequeño. Treinta mil habitantes, catedral y cartuja" (1998, 84) [Small town. Thirty thousand inhabitants, cathedral and monastery], and, "Vida de una ciudad española, con catedral, arzobispo, audiencia, gobernador civil" (1998, 165) [Life of a Spanish city, with cathedral, archbishopric, courthouse, and civil governor]. In these mises-en-scène of her childhood there is an implicit acknowledgment of the way power is staged and performed in society. The buildings serve the function of the backdrop of a stage, and they are always those that represent patriarchal power (church, school, courthouse, town hall).[10]

León describes, again in the third person, various aspects of her life at that time, like the typical "paseos" [walks] through town, an act meant to stage, once again, a sense of belonging to the right social class as well as to perform a correct gender identification, a performance that the young León does not live up to perfectly: "la pasearon.... Pareciera que la sacaban en procesión.... Y la niña sigue su paseo flanqueada por los bigotes y las barbas, por los sombreros a la moda que su madre trajo de la capital.... ¿No tiene tus ojos azules? No. La niña se siente humillada" (1998, 84–85) [they took her for a walk.... It would seem that they were showing her off in a procession.... And the girl continues her walk flanked by the moustaches and the beards, by the fashionable hats that her mother brought from the capital.... She doesn't have blue eyes? No. The girl feels humiliated].

"La niña" [The girl], by the mere fact of not having blue eyes, is already beginning to fall short of what is expected of her, something that caused her embarrassment at first, but that would later become a source of pride. The "bigotes," "barbas," and "sombreros a la moda" ["moustaches," "beards," and "fashionable hats"] are presented as props for this performance of social exhibitionism that not only guarantees one's identification with the right social class and gender behavior, but actually creates the very identities of social class and gender one is aspiring to portray. On a later occasion, upon her criticism of the exaggerated ostentation of a party she attends, León recalls how her attitude marked a clear desire to transgress and rebel: "empezaba pronto su rebelión. A la niña se le iba a desarrollar junto con las trenzas un principio de crítica. Esta niña terminará mal" (1998, 92) [her rebellion started early. The girl would develop, along with her braids, a critical attitude. This girl will come to a bad end].

León's rebellion continues, and soon revolves around her desire to learn, to read, to think for herself. In contrast to her own home and her school run by nuns who were more interested in what she *shouldn't* learn than in what she should, León remembers the freedom and the joy in learning she experienced when visiting the home of her uncle and aunt, Ramón Menéndez Pidal and María Goyri. She recalls how, in their house, she grew to cherish an atmosphere in which there were no taboos on learning: "Aprendí en ella que los libros pueden tapizar de sabiduría las paredes ... y que todo en el mundo puede comprenderse y admirarse" (1998, 65) [I learned there that books can cover the walls with learning ... and that everything in the world can be understood and admired]. She further learns there that knowledge should never be a source of shame: "No bajaban la voz para hablar del arte, aunque estuvieran llenos de desnudos los museos" (1998, 65) [They didn't lower their voice to speak about art, even though the museums were full of nudes]. Above all, she envies her cousin, Jimena, who not only enjoys such a desirable freedom, but can look up to her mother as the first woman in Spain to receive a doctorate in "Filosofía y Letras" (1998, 23) [Philosophy and Letters].

One day, while at her religious school, the young León finds herself fighting with a classmate who, desirous of obeying unflinchingly the moral codes imposed by the nuns, tells on León for reading supposedly prohibited books. León re-creates the dialogue with her classmate:

Pero, ¿tú lees a Dumas?
Asombro y consternación. . . . la chica contó que María Teresa León leía libros prohibidos. ¡Pero no! ¡pero sí! ¿Y Víctor Hugo? También lo he leído. Claro, como tu madre te vigila tan poco. . . . Y ese tío tuyo. Yo les grité ¡Y mi tía! Mi tía fue la primera mujer de España que estudió en una universidad. Peor para ti. Por ahí entra el diablo. ¡Madre, madre, venga! Esta chica . . . Impusieron silencio. Se acercó la maestra. "¿Por qué llora usted, María Teresa?" Yo me levanté como una dolorosa: "Porque leo a Alejandro Dumas." ¿A quién? "A Alejandro Dumas." "Bueno, siéntese." Le preguntaron al confesor si era pecado. (1998, 141)

[But, you read Dumas?
Wonder and consternation. . . . the girl said that María Teresa León read prohibited books. But no! But yes! And Victor Hugo? I've also read him. Of course, since your mother supervises you so little. . . . And that uncle of yours. And I shouted: And my Aunt! My aunt was the first woman in Spain who studied in a university. All the worse for you. That's how the devil takes over. Mother, mother, come! This girl. . . . They imposed silence. The teacher approached. "Why are you crying, María Teresa?" I got up like a crying Virgin: "Because I read Alejandro Dumas." Who? "Alejandro Dumas." Fine, sit down. They asked the confessor if it was a sin.]

Underneath the humor with which this anecdote is told lies a fierce critique of a society that makes a girl feel guilty for the mere fact of reading adventure novels. In such a society, imagination itself, especially in a girl, becomes a sin. León's response to her teacher clearly portrays a desire to identify with a world very different from that of her school, one where a woman is encouranged not only to read, but to study in a university. Beneath the humor with which León tells many of these anecdotes lies, also, the pain of feeling that "disidentification," stronger every day, with respect to the society she supposedly belongs to. Upon recalling these anecdotes, the pain resurfaces. Splitting herself in two, at one point she wants to stop her process of remembering and talks back to herself: "No me gusta que me hablen de esto, calla, es demasiado triste" (1998, 191) [I don't like to hear about that, shut up, it's too sad]. At another point, she splits herself three ways to express the pain she feels while remembering her past: "La niña sigue oyendo frases enteras.... Las voces solas se le han quedado dentro. Mejor no oirlas. Tapizarse los oídos, subirse las sábanas, hasta los ojos, huir de aquello que amorató su vida. Por favor, cierra la puerta. No quiero oir mi infancia" (1998, 12) [The girl continues to hear complete phrases.... The lone voices have remained inside her. Better not to hear them. Cover your ears, raise the sheets, up to the eyes, flee from that which bruised her life. Please, close the door. I don't want to hear my childhood].

Many of these anecdotes are dialogical, as they incorporate into León's own narrative those other voices ("Esta niña terminará mal," "Claro, como tu madre te vigila tan poco," "Peor para ti" [This girl will come to a bad end, Of course, since your mother supervises you so little, All the worse for you]) which represent the patriarchal authority that is demanding the performance and staging of appropriate feminine behavior.[11] The threat of an inescapable and unspecified punishment for León's incipient "rebelión" [rebellion] is, of course, one of the ways in which the patriarchal society of the time enforced rigid gender identifications, so firmly based on a supposedly natural separation of public (male) and private (female) spheres, as well as the cult of female domesticity encoded in the image of the "angel del hogar" [angel of the home], an angel who, suffice it to say, should never be found reading "prohibited" books. As Mary Nash explains: "Any woman who contravened the norms of nature by adopting transgressive gender conduct was implicitly threatened with disaster.... Transgression in this symbolic vision opened up fearful threats of chaos, disorder and unhappiness" (1999b, 30). Such terrible threats are all encapsulated in that one anonymous, authoritative exclamation "Esta niña terminará mal" [This girl will come to a bad end] echoing within León's memory.

The "stagings" of correct femininity, of which the "paseos" [walks] mentioned earlier are only one example among many in the text, clearly point to the performativity of all gender identity, for, as Judith Butler reminds us: "The acts by which gender is constituted bear similarities to performative acts within theatrical contexts" (1990, 272). It is important to remember, however, that Butler's notion of the constituted and performative nature of gender does not mean it is simply an "act" that an individual can willingly and consciously take up. The difference between "performance" and "performative" is essential to keep in mind: "In no sense can it be concluded that the part of gender that is performed is therefore the 'truth' of gender; performance as bounded 'act' is distinguished from performativity insofar as the latter consists in a reiteration of norms which precede, constrain, and exceed the performer and in that sense cannot be taken as the fabrication of the performer's 'will' or 'choice.' . . . The reduction of performativity to performance would be a mistake" (1993, 234). If León uses the language and strategies of theater and theatricality to represent her childhood, it is not to present gender as an "act" or "disguise" that she could turn, or take on and off, at will, but to highlight the social structures and norms that such behavior necessarily repeated and in doing so, upheld. The theatrical language serves to de-naturalize, and thus question, those norms and structures, and the performativity of individual identity is shown to be an ongoing process that is always inextricable from them.

Furthermore, by means of the dialogical nature of her narrative, León is performing another de-naturalizing strategy that Bakhtin saw as the product of the dialogical nature of the novel, here emerging in an autobiography: a "verbal and semantic decentering of the ideological world," leading to a "certain linguistic homelessness of literary consciousness" (1981, 367). Thus, the "homelessness" that exile imposes, whose terrible psychological effects León will explore and express in the narration of her life after leaving Spain in 1939, is already at play *before* political exile, in her gender "disidentification" with her original "home."[12] This depiction of a sense of exile due to gender experienced before León suffered her long exile after the civil war is an example, as Shari Benstock claims, of the fact that "for women, the definition of patriarchy already assumes the reality of expatriate in patria; for women this expatriation is internalized, experienced as an exclusion imposed from outside and lived from the inside" (1989, 20). León's memory is thus traversed by multiple exiles. One is reminded of the multiple levels of exile depicted in Semprún's novels about Buchenwald, exiles that, although not specifically related to gender, also created a radical sense of "homelessness" in his writing.

The theatrical elements in León's narrative bring to the fore the performativity, and thus constructed nature, of all identity. Her autobiography becomes a scriptural practice in which, as Sidonie Smith explains, "the autobiographical subject finds him/herself on multiple stages simultaneously, called to heterogeneous recitations of identity. The multiple calls never align perfectly. Rather, they create spaces or gaps, ruptures, unstable boundaries, incursions, excursions, limits and their transgressions" (1998, 110). Those "multiple calls" of identity that "never align perfectly," and that lead to gaps and ruptures within the performance of identity, are further highlighted by León as she thinks of the lineage she comes from. While remembering her childhood, León also evokes her distant family past, recalling members of earlier generations of her family that had been to Cuba and profited from Spain's relationship with its colonies. A contradiction emerges, one that is constant in León's text, between wanting to both identify and "disidentify" with an identity that supposedly is her own. After evoking recurrent family conversations in which "se cruzaban las miserias coloniales de España" (1998, 184) [the colonial miseries of Spain were entangled], a contradictory attitude toward her family past emerges. León at first seems to desire a continuity with that past: "La verdad es que yo guardo con cariño dentro de mí tantas cosas como me transmitieron. Creo en la cadena que nos enlaza. Creo en la canción que se teje con las canciones que llegan de tan lejos" (1998, 185) [The truth is that I affectionately hold within me so many things that they transmitted to me. I believe in the chain that connects us. I believe in the song that is woven with the songs that arrive from so far away]. Yet she immediately distances herself from it: "Me ha dado pena el ver que mis recuerdos de infancia están llenos de recuerdos coloniales" (1998, 185) [It saddens me to see that my childhood recollections are full of colonial memories].

This sadness, this sense of "homelessness" that a re-creation of "home" evokes, as León highlights the "disidentifications" that made up her childhood, echo the argument made by Biddy Martin and Chandra Talpade Mohanty of how feminism often deconstructs unitary and unproblematic notions of "home" and "belonging," relying on "the tension between two specific modalities: being home and not being home" (1997, 296). As they explain: " 'Being home' refers to the place where one lives within familiar, safe, protected boundaries; 'not being home' is a matter of realizing that home was an illusion of coherence and safety based on the exclusion of specific histories of oppression and resistance, the repression of differences even within oneself" (1997, 296). By bringing to the fore the constant tension between the identifications and "disidentifications" upon which her identity is based, León's autobiography shows that not only is any stable sense of *individual* identity necessarily based on strategic "exclusions of specific histories of oppression and resistance," but that a *family* and *national* identity is as well.[13]

León's writing will constantly bring to light those previously hidden "histories of oppression and resistance," and the instability of point of view in her text, the vertiginous fluctuations between first, second, and third person is a way of making visible, instead of repressing, the "differences even within [her]self." As Sidonie Smith explains, "this process of identification and disidentification is ongoing. As a result there can be no fixed or essential preconstitutive identity" (1998, 111). An ongoing process of construction of the self is what León's autobiography performs, and the dialogical nature of the self that is performed is one that is shot through by multiple ideological tensions that point to a characteristic of woman's autobiographical writing that Shari Benstock describes as foregrounding the "fissures of female discontinuity" (1998, 153). Highlighting these fissures, this discontinuity, becomes an important political statement as it frames the process of forging an individual self embodied by all autobiography within the social forces that mold, even deform, the individual. León explicitly reflects on the process whereby such a multidimensional self comes about:

> Nos traemos adentro una carga inquietante de gustos y de gestos ajenos que se nos van quedando enganchados. . . . Yo siento que me hice del roce de tanta gente: de la monjita, de la amiga de buen gusto, del tío abuelo casi emparedado. . . . Todos, todos. Somos lo que nos han hecho, lentamente al correr tanto años. Cuando estamos definitivamente seguros de ser nosotros, nos morimos. ¡Qué lección de humildad! (1998, 146–47)
>
> [We have inside ourselves a disquieting burden of other people's tastes and gestures that cling to us. . . . I feel that I have been formed by the contact with so many people: the little nun, the girl with good taste, the great-uncle, nearly entombed. . . . All of them. We are what they have made us, slowly, through the years. When we are definitely sure of being ourselves, we die. What a lesson in humility!]

We are, indeed, the product of our encounters and interactions with others. Our most personal, supposedly intimate narration, autobiography, thus always comprises a full chorus of other people's voices. As León elsewhere states: "estamos llenos de frases ajenas" (1998, 185–86) [we are full of other people's phrases]. For Bakhtin, as mentioned earlier, a narrative, such as this one, that foregrounds heteroglossia by highlighting the multivoiced nature of any individual identity ultimately serves to de-naturalize the ideological and discursive structures of power in society within which that identity is forged by showing the cracks, the tensions in those structures, and thus, "depriving [them] of [their] absence of conflict" (1981, 368).

This recognition of the social constitution of one's identity also applies to the very way in which León is remembering her life. Those "frases ajenas" [other people's phrases] that so often emerge in her memories point to the fact that even one of the most personal expressions of our individuality, our memory, is inescapably social and collective. This was, of course, Maurice Halbwachs's famous claim, that all personal memory is irreducibly collective. He claimed this is so, among other reasons, because we live our lives as part of social groups that determine, by reinforcing or countering, what we remember, and because as soon as we put our memories into words, we are using the inherently social medium of language.¹⁴ That León's memory is governed by the dynamics of "disidentification" shows that this most individual act of remembering one's life, of one's most personal memory, is inextricably social and collective, since that memory emerges from the beginning as a response to the social conditions in which one grew up. Within memory, it seems, the personal is clearly political, the individual is inevitably collective, and León's autobiography highlights these facts at every turn.

Always willing to show the cracks and tensions within identity, León continues to present the ongoing process of identification and "disidentification" while narrating the devastating effects of her political exile from Spain after the civil war. There is no progression in this process. There is no stage at which León leaves behind the strategy of self-division enacted in the refraction of her self into different pronouns pretending to reach a final point of plenitude or stability in the first person.¹⁵ After all, as León states, "Cuando estamos definitivamente seguros de ser nosotros, nos morimos" (1998, 147) [When we are definitely sure of being ourselves, we die]. The divisions of her self continue to emerge as political exile imposes another level of estrangement, creating yet again a feeling of separation from her self, from her country, and from her fellow compatriots, all at the same time as she strives to hold on to a feeling of connection to all three markers of identity.

There are numerous moments in her autobiography in which León recounts the estrangement she feels, while in exile, upon reading Spanish newspapers or talking with people still living in Spain. She feels so connected, yet at the same time so disconnected, from that homeland for which she fought with so much enthusiasm during the civil war:

> Es como si yo no perteneciese a ese país del que leo los periódicos... Siento todo fuera de mí, arrancado... Estoy como separada, mirándome. No encuentro la fórmula para dialogar ni para unirme. Una muchacha se me aleja. ¿Sabe adonde va? Siento angustia. (1998, 82)¹⁶

> [It is as if I didn't belong to that country whose newspapers I read... I feel everything outside myself, wrenched from me... It is as if I were separated, looking at myself. I cannot find the formula either to dialogue or unite with people. A girl walks away from me. Does she know where she is going? I feel anguished.]

The internal division that León feels ("estoy como separada mirándome" [It is as if I were separated, looking at myself]) produced by the estrangement of exile is very similar to that internal division she felt while growing up. This is why, on many occasions, like this one, in which León is recalling the estrangement of political exile, she does so by evoking the image of herself as a young girl ("Una muchacha se me aleja" [A girl walks away from me]), suffering from that previous experience of "exile," of "disidentification," from all that was supposed to be her "home." The various exiles that León suffered are thus intimately connected.

Recalling exile upon exile, the memory that this text presents is one that is forever fragmented, divided, faltering and unstable, never reaching a final point of "identification," or rest. From the very first line of the text, León explicitly reflects on this very unstable nature of her recollection: "Todos son palabras y colores dentro de mí que ya no sé muy bien qué representan" (1998, 69) [They are all words and colors inside of me and I no longer know what they represent]; "Todo sumergido en pequeños fragmentos que a veces no fraguan bien ... las imágenes se le han desordenado, encimándose unas a otras" (1998, 79) [Everything is submerged in small fragments that do not coalesce well ... the images have become disordered, some on top of others]; "Esto se habla con palabras sorbidas, truncadas, rotas o interminables" (1998, 94) [This is spoken with shriveled, truncated, broken or interminable words]. Her memory is fragmented and disordered, and at a certain point she herself suffers a similar fragmentation: "Se le había caído el alma, la había perdido, la encontró diseminada y rota" (1998, 80) [Her soul had fallen, she had lost it, she found it disseminated and broken]. Just as her memory, and her very self, are irremediably fragmented, León envisions a similar disorder and fragmentation invading the book of memories she is writing, as the disordered pages seem to take on a life of their own: "Estas cuartillas que voy escribiendo se me han volado todas dispersándose, jugando a la mala pasada de huirme.... Hoy todas se me han dispersado con vida propia y no con la que yo les impuse al escribirlas" (1998, 393–94) [These pages that I am writing have flown out of my hand and dispersed, playing a trick on me by escaping from me.... Today, all of them have dispersed around me with a life of their own and not with the life that I imposed on them in writing them].

These dispersed pages moving with what seems to be a life of their own recall the numerous images of newspaper fragments scattered menacingly by the wind in *Volverás a Región*. In Benet's novel, as we saw in the last chapter, these images subvert the dominant Francoist ideology of progress by blasting apart one of the major tools for the reproduction of such an ideology, the newspaper. León's fragmented memory, and the dispersed pages of her autobiography, likewise contribute to a subversive quality of her writing, one that counters the Francoist ideological rhetoric of progress as well as the patriarchal presupposition that an autobiography is an ordered, linear re-creation of a life that ultimately leads to a recognition of the meaning and sense of that life. León rejects both these constructs, "disidentifies" from them, for, as a woman and as an exile, her story does not fit such constructs, in fact, her story is the one that must be expelled, repressed, for those constructs to be upheld.

Her "disidentification" with the Francoist rhetoric of progress may be seen, as mentioned earlier, in the images León presents of her estrangement upon seeing newspapers from Spain while in exile and not recognizing herself, or her country, in them. At a certain moment she explains: "Cuando ahora abro los periódicos que me llegan de aquel país pienso que todo se ha petrificado.... Y la niña vuelve a pasar el dedo por las hojas que le han traído, deletreando, y en ninguna de ellas encuentra los relieves de la palabra Patria" (1998, 93) [When I now open the newspapers that arrive from that country I think that everything has become petrified.... And the girl again runs her finger over the pages that they have brought her, spelling out words, and in none of them can she find the contours of the word Homeland]. Here, as elsewhere, León reverts to the image of herself as a child, in the third person, to describe such feelings of estrangement from Spain in the present. In this manner, the "disidentification" that characterized her memories of childhood is reproduced now to explain the pain of political exile. The "petrified" newspapers with equally "petrified" news within them in León's quote are similar to those old, outdated, also "petrified," newspapers flying around Benet's Región. Both images highlight a sense of estrangement with the rhetoric dominating those Spanish newspapers. The fact that the girl in León's quote cannot find the contours of the word "Patria" is yet another image of the political "disidentification" produced by exile.

It is important to remember that Marré's return to Región in Benet's novel occurs in 1964, and thus her attempt to remember the civil war is subversive of the Franco regime's rhetoric of progress and of its belief in the need to forget the past proclaimed throughout the propaganda campaign for the "25 year of peace." León most likely wrote a large part of her autobiography throughout the 1960s (although she incorporated fragments from earlier writings). She was thus writing at the time in which the regime was implementing its new strategy of forgetting the war. Unlike Marré, however, León could not "return" to where she experienced the civil war in order to counter the regime's call to forget, so she had to return through her writing. The very project of writing her memoirs, therefore, becomes a subversive "act of memory," akin to Marré's physical and rememorative "return" to Región.

It should also be noted that in the earlier quote in which León sees the pages of her autobiography disordered around her, she feels that the pages seem to have been dispersed "con vida propia y no con la que yo les impuse al escribirlas" (1998, 393–94) [with a life of their own and not with the life that I imposed on them in writing them]. We see, here, an element that will become increasingly important as her autobiography progresses: an uneasy feeling that her memory has a life of its own, a force she cannot control. A fear takes hold of León when it becomes unclear to her whether she controls her memory or whether it controls her. Memory will become increasingly painful and uncontrollable, while at the same time remaining necessary and therapeutic.

León's text thus reproduces in numerous ways the division, fragmentation, "disidentification" that León had suffered through the various forms of exile she experienced. In her very writing, León recreates the experience of loss of a stable identity, the insecurity created by a perpetual sense of non-belonging, in a process that, like the Derridean *pharmakon* analyzed in the previous chapter, proves to be both an illness and its only cure. When talking about the physical pain produced by her memory, León states "Dios, Dios, cómo escuecen en los ojos los recuerdos!" (1998, 275) [God, God, how my memories burn my eyes!]. Memory may be physically painful, but it is necessary. Reflecting, again, on the suffering that writing her autobiography engenders, León thinks: "Tal vez yo no debería haber escrito este libro, pero escribir es mi enfermedad incurable" (1998, 8) [Maybe I should not have written this book, but writing is my incurable disease]. We here encounter the logic of the *pharmakon* of writing once again.

It should come as no surprise that, along with the depiction of memory as a double-edged *pharmakon*, León should evoke the figure of the *pharmakos*, or scapegoat, with which the *pharmakon* is intimately related. Memory is both an illness and cure for León precisely because, through her exile, she has been made into a *pharmakos* by Spanish society, that same conservative society from which she has felt distanced throughout her life. León describes the pain of exile by evoking the image of herself as someone, or something, expelled, rejected, (abjected would be an appropriate term), by that conservative society to which she never quite belonged: "Luego, sintió que la expulsaban de la sociedad como un objeto maligno debajo de la piel de los muy bien sentados" (1998, 80) [Later, she felt that they expulsed her from society like a malign object from under the skin of the very well established].

Interestingly, Spanish philosopher María Zambrano has evoked a similar image of the exiled person as an element expelled from society in a sacrificial rite which, like that of the *pharmakos*, is intended to ensure the homogeneity of a society threatened by what is different. For Zambrano, the exile is transformed "en el estorbo, en lo que se arrojaría de la fiesta cívica, en lo que se relegaría al cuarto oscuro de los trastos" (1990, 34) [into a nuissance, into what should be expelled from the civic feast, into what should be relegated to a dark room full of junk]. As if echoing this image, León, toward the end of her autobiography, dejectedly describes herself as "un trasto inútil que permanece" (1998, 539) [a useless piece of junk that remains]. If Marré, a representative of an internal exile within Spain, was sacrificed at the end of *Volverás a Región* in order to uphold the "peace and order" of the regime, León, as a political exile, likewise feels that she has been made into the *pharmakos* of that same regime. By writing her memoirs, she is fighting so that, despite having been expelled from Spain, she will not also be completely expelled from its collective memory.

If writing is an illness for León, one that, as we have seen, re-creates many of the painful aspects of exile she experienced, it may perhaps also help her to overcome them. Alongside the painful nature of reliving the internal divisions, the "disidentification" at the heart of her recollections, her writing also enables her to re-create herself through the act of narration, a process that provides some sense of empowerment, no matter how disjointed, fragmented, and unstable the self that is being re-created may be. Pointing to such a therapeutic nature to her narrative project, she again splits herself in two as she reflects on the very process of retelling her life and now thinks of some of the experiences that she takes pleasure in remembering, such as the work she undertook with the Guerrillas del Teatro during the civil war: "Lo he contado muchas veces. Bueno, María Teresa, basta, ya lo has contado veinte veces. Pero yo sigo porque es el regreso de la felicidad que dura un instante. Y vuelvo a reconstruirme como hacen los niños con sus juegos de piececitas de madera, recobrando la dulzura de jugar" (1998, 114) [I have recounted it many times. Okay, María Teresa, enough, you've recounted it twenty times. But I continue because it is the return of happiness that lasts an instant. And I again reconstruct myself like children do with their games of wooden blocks, recovering the pleasure of playing].

Narrating her past is a "game," "un juego," by means of which León again reconstructs herself ("vuelvo a reconstruirme" [I again reconstruct myself]) even as the narrative she is telling is one of her very fragmentation. This "juego" León evokes could be understood as a version of the "repetition compulsion" of trauma, illustrated by Freud's example of his grandson's game of *Fort-Da* which we have seen to be an important element of the dynamics of memory in the writing of both Semprún and Benet. What has not been highlighted yet is that Freud uses a theatrical term to describe this game with which the young child overcomes the traumatic anxiety produced by his mother's departure. Freud explains: "he compensated for this, as it were, by himself *stag-*

ing the disappearance and return of the objects within his reach" (1961a, 14; My emphasis). The repetition compulsion inherent in trauma is performative, as the very action or event that caused overwhelming anxiety is "staged" again and again. All of León's autobiography could be seen as a traumatic process of "*staging* the disappearance and return," appropriately enacted within a language suffused with theatrical references. What keeps disappearing and returning, only to disappear again, is the sense of a stable, whole, and secure self.

As seen in the previous two chapters, trauma involves a problem of mastery. One repeats an event, often in memory, that imposed a feeling of lack of control and by that repetition, that "staging," one gains a certain sense of control, retroactively, over the event. Such a dialectic between power and powerlessness within traumatic memory is enacted by León in the quote that serves as an epigraph to this chapter in which she reflects on the role and nature of memory itself. Here, León begins by providing a positive, comforting view of memory: "La memoria puede tener los ojos indulgentes" (1998, 130) [Memory may have indulgent eyes]. Memory is even seen as being more important than living itself, perhaps because memory can help overcome many of the painful experiences of life: "Vivir no es tan importante como recordar" (1998, 130) [To live is not as important as to remember]. Yet, immediately after this, León presents a very different view of memory, one that is painful, harmful, and menacing: "Pero qué horrible es que los recuerdos se precipiten sobre ti y te obliguen a mirarlos y te muerdan" (1998, 130) [How horrible it is when memories assail you, force you to look at them, bite you]. This could be seen as a paradigmatic expression of the dynamics of traumatic memory, in which there is an unresolved tension between memory being a comforting action that the subject undertakes, and it being a painful assault on the subject, threatening its very integrity.

A similar doubt as to whether León is truly in control of her memories or not emerges when she describes the pages of her autobiography as disordered and scattered around her and she feels that "se me han dispersado con vida propia y no con la que yo les impuse al escribirlas" (1998, 393–94) [[they] have dispersed about me with a life of their own and not with the life that I imposed on them in writing them]. In fact, immediately after this quote, León goes on to emphasize the lack of control she has on her memories, stating: "No sé ya qué me cuentan" (1998, 393) [I no longer know what they tell me] and that they produce "una verdad que jamás comprenderemos" (1998, 394) [a truth we will never understand"]. The memories seem to have a life of their own, one that León does not seem to control or even completely understand. This is typical of traumatic memory, for, as Cathy Caruth explains, traumatized people "carry an impossible history within them, or they become themselves the symptom of a history that they cannot entirely possess" (1995, 5). Such is the nature of León's traumatic memory. The different exiles that she has suffered are re-created in her very narrative as she remembers them, in a process that she doesn't quite control, but that still helps her deal with the many levels of loss she experiences.[17]

It should not be surprising that León often enacts the process of "*staging* the disappearance and return" of identity through images borrowed from theater. At one point, she remembers the representation of the play *Numancia,* which Alberti had adapted from Cervantes's play and which León was directing during the civil war in besieged Madrid. She recalls "Eso sí. Muchas noches, mientras representábamos *Numancia,* María Teresa León lloraba entre bastidores viendo subir a su pueblo hacia la hoguera de la muerte común" (1998, 135) [Yes. Many nights, while we represented *Numancia,* María Teresa León would cry behind the scenes seeing her country march towards the pyre of its death]. The boundaries of the theatrical and the real are blurred here, as the story of Numancia, a town resisting a fierce military onslaught, is represented during the desperate Republican defense of Madrid. Just as León had used theatrical metaphors while narrating her childhood to show the ideological de-centering of the subject (herself), here, in a real anecdote about her theater experience, León presents herself as fragmented and de-centered again, not only because the narration is in the third person, but because she presents herself "entre bastidores," that is, "behind the scenes" or "offstage."

Although it is impossible, due to lack of space, to adequately analyze here all the examples in which León makes use of theater images as part of her performative strategy of deconstructing a stable identity, it is important to note that such images function at various levels of the narrative. Sometimes they work as meta-narrative devices framing the narration itself or introducing different narrative strategies, and at other times they are presented as historical anecdotes or as metaphors for other issues dealt with in the text (such as war, death, or political activism).

One of the anecdotes in which León dialogically presents the experiences of "disidentification" during her childhood, for example, explicitly involves theater: "¿La niña, cómica? ¡Jamás! En nuestra familia todas las mujeres han sido decentes" (1998, 113) [The girl, an actress? Never! In our family, all women are decent]. When León presents the story of her involvement with the Guerrillas del Teatro during the war, she begins the section by addressing the reader: "Os lo voy a contar" (1998, 112) [I will tell you the story], and ends the section with the exclamation "Y aquí cae el telón" (1998, 138) [And here the curtain drops]. In another meta-narrative commentary, she equates the process of remembering her friends in exile with a play they are all rehearsing together: "¿Cómo serán todos hoy? Y si me vieran ¿cómo sería yo para ellos? Hemos separado los caminos. ¿Y si diera dos palmadas? ¡Ensayo, ensayo! ¿no han leído en la tablilla que hay ensayo?" (1998, 134) [What must they all be like today? And if they saw me, what would I be like for them? Our paths have separated. And what if I clapped my hands? Rehearsal, rehearsal! Haven't you read that we have a rehearsal?]. León, furthermore, is constantly equating theater with war: "En aquel teatro conocí el pacto secreto que los escenarios dan a los que allí trabajan, pacto que se parece al que las trincheras enseñan, pues es el del peligro común" (1998, 133) [In that theater I discovered the secret pact that the stage provides for those who work on it, a pact similar to that which the trenches provide, for it is that of a common danger]. She further claims that, for the members of the Guerrillas del Teatro, theater "fue nuestra pequeña guerra" (1998, 112) [was our small war].

León repeatedly refers to the experiences she and others underwent as "roles," for example, in the following statement in which, as in so many cases, she talks about herself in the third person: "Le cuesta siempre darse cuanta de que vive en la calle del destierro . . . creyendo que es entonces y han distribuido mal los papeles y le han dado por equivocación el de vieja" (1998, 103) [It's hard for her to realize that she is living on the street of exile . . . believing that it is then, that they have distributed the roles wrong, and that they have mistakenly given her the role of an old woman]. She does the same thing when talking about the particularly harsh experience of exile for women: "En esta dispersión española le ha tocado a la mujer un papel histórico y lo ha recitado bien" (1998, 432) [In this Spanish exile woman has been given a historic role and she has played it well]. This last statement is very important in the text, for one of the stated objectives of León's narrative is to recall the "papel histórico" [historic role] that women have played during the war and in exile, a "papel" [role] that is often not a visibly heroic one, but that is made up of the "pequeñas historias" (1998, 118) [small stories], "las *no* hazañas" (1998, 295) [the *non*-feats]. As León exclaims, talking of the quiet, unsung heroism of Spanish exiled women: "Algún día se contarán o cantarán las pequeñas historias, las anécdotas menudas. . . . . Y se contará la pequeña epopeya diaria, el heroismo minúsculo de los labios apretados de frío, del hambre, de los trabajos casi increíbles" (1998, 432) [One day the small stories, the little anecdotes, will be recited or sung . . . And the small daily epic will be told, the miniscule heroism of the cold clenched lips, of the hunger, of the almost incredible tasks]. Clearly, memory is both performative and a performance within León's text, as images of the theater govern not just many of her recollections, but the very manner in which those recollections are presented.

In another particularly significant example, León stages a theatrical dialogue with an unnamed interlocutor, within an equally theatrical setting, which is a meta-narrative commentary on the testimonial function of her autobiography:

> Nos están llamando: ¡Eh, váyase! Su papel no da para más. Salga de la escena. Está concluyéndose el último acto. Sí, sí, aún puede decir un parlamento más, pero de prisa. Retírese, por favor, tienen que entrar los otros. Qué insistente es usted. ¿No ve cómo bosteza el público? Basta. ¿Por qué insiste? El quedarse es un abuso de confianza, confianza en usted misma. Es que estoy triste. No se enfade, ya me marcho. Pero "¿quién podrá contar esta triste historia" si yo no lo hago? (1998, 325)

> [They are calling us. Hey, go away! Your role is over. Leave the stage. The last act is coming to an end. Yes, yes, you can still say your last lines, but hurry. Leave, please, the others have to come in. How insistent you are. Don't you see the audience is yawning? Stop. Why do you insist? Staying is an abuse of trust, trust in yourself. The thing is that I'm sad. Don't get angry, I'm leaving now. But "who will tell this sad story/history" if I don't do it?]

Loureiro accurately sees how, in this imagined dialogue, "León aptly foregrounds her irreplaceable ethical responsibility" (2000, 96), which is the responsibility of giving testimony to the tragedy of the Spanish civil war and exile that she, and so many with her, have suffered. Loureiro highlights, furthermore, that this responsibility is presented, due to the dialogue form, "as response to another" (2000, 96). This responsibility of testimony, is, indeed, the ethical imperative behind León's autobiography, and the desperate need for an addressee is one of the leitmotivs of León's text. Yet the importance of the fact that this is presented as if León were rehearsing a play is not underscored by Loureiro, nor does he mention the continuation of the anecdote, which is quite significant. In this continuation, the "triste historia" [sad story/history] that León is a witness to, and which she must recall in the face of so many other people's willingness to forget, is no longer just the Spanish civil war, or the plight of the many Spanish exiles from that war. The "triste historia" [sad story/history] has now become plural, incorporating many of the atrocities suffered by other peoples after the Spanish civil war, in a "despreciable siglo XX de los inventos espantosos" [despicable twentieth century of dreadful inventions]:

¿Piensa que me lamento porque tengo que salir de escena? No, no, es porque he leido el diario de esta mañana y me duelen los huesos y me crujen. ¿Usted no lo lee? . . . Tienen que enterarse los que no leen. . . . ¿Sabe lo que es el napalm y la bomba X, y la H y la V? . . . Despreciable siglo XX de los inventos espantosos. ¿Que me vaya? ¿Para que venga quién? Hable más bajito, como el apuntador debe hacerlo. Que salga otro, ande, diga usted que si otro va a hacer el elogio de la opresión, de la violencia . . . yo me retiro. (1998, 326)

[Do you think that I am complaining because I have to leave the scene? No, no, it is because I have read the newspaper this morning and my bones ache and creak. Don't you read it? . . . Those who don't read have to find out. / . . . Do you know what napalm is and the X and the H and the V bombs? Despicable twentieth century of dreadful inventions. You want me to leave? So that who should come? Talk a little more softly, like the prompter should. Let someone else come on, and let them know that if someone else is going to praise oppression and violence. . . . I will leave.]

Given the strategy of "disidentification" that León has consistently used in her self-representation throughout the text, at this moment, in which she presents herself as being onstage, it is not inappropriate to think of a similar strategy applicable specifically to acting, namely, the Brechtian style of acting characterized by the famous *verfremdungseffekt* (estrangement, or alienation, effect).[18] As Richard Schechner explains: "In Brechtian theater, the actor stands beside herself and beside the events enacted—doing and showing at the same time. The Brechtian performer is not lost in the role, or entirely empathetic with the situation" (2002, 128). This "standing beside herself" and "beside the events enacted" is exactly what León has been doing throughout her text, in this last anecdote self-consciously, and literally, as a person onstage. Furthermore, the political implications of such an acting technique are underscored by Elizabeth Wright as she explains the *verfremdungseffekt:* "It goes beyond the concept of 'defamiliarization': it sets up a set of social, political and ideological interruptions that remind us that representations are not given but produced. Contrary to popular belief, *Verfremdung* does not do away with identification but examines it critically, using the technique of montage, which shows that no representation is fixed and final. It is political through and through, for it shows that the spectator is never only at the receiving end of representation, but is included in it" (1989, 19).

The active role of the audience is explicitly sought in León's text. She, in fact, brings the readers into her text in this anecdote, as the audience listening to the recitation of her "triste historia" [sad story/history]. As in a Brechtian play, this active participation is based not, as is commonly misunderstood, on a *doing away* with all empathetic identification with the performer and performance, but on a *critical engagement* with them, a critical stance made possible for the public by the acting, in which the actor does not try to create a complete identification with the character. Clearly, León's representation of herself throughout her autobiography has not tried to reflect a seamless, perfectly stable identity, being based, precisely, on what Sidonie Smith calls an "ongoing process of identification and disidentification" (1998, 111).

This dialectic of proximity and distance could also be applied here to the very topics that León includes in her "triste historia" [sad story/history]. It is now one in which the "problema de España" [problem of Spain] has been de-centered, in a move that underscores the fact that it should not be understood in isolation, but as part of a larger historical context of political struggle and oppression throughout the twentieth century, one that includes the realities of "el napalm y la bomba X, y la H y la V [en este] Despreciable siglo XX de los inventos espantosos" (1998, 326) [the napalm and the X, H, and V bombs [in this] Despicable twentieth century of dreadful inventions]. As León herself explains, evoking the writings of Galdós in which he tries to present the history of Spain: "ahora no son episodios nacionales los que hay que escribir, porque son internacionales" (1998, 390) [now it is not national episodes that we have to write, they are international]. Acknowledging how such exile texts function as "episodios internacionales" [international episodes] forces the readers/audience of León's text to make historical connections that might otherwise be all-too-easy to overlook.[19]

León's text, in fact, does not only connect her experience of exile after the Spanish civil war with later tragic events from other national contexts, thus providing a more general argument against political oppression, but it provides an important historical perspective of her own exile experience which frames her story within a broader conception of exile in Spanish history. At one point she exclaims: "De pronto me parece que estoy contando una historia vieja, la de aquellos españoles que emigraron en 1813, en 1823, en 1832. Goya murió en el destierro" (1998, 464) [Suddenly it seems like I am telling an old tale, that of the Spaniards who emigrated in 1813, in 1823, in 1832. Goya died in exile]. By acknowledging such a connection between these different historical exiles and her own, León is implicitly making a much broader claim, recognizing that exile is constitutive of the nation itself, that all attempts to create a sense of collective identity inevitably produce some form of exile, some manner of expelling an unwanted *pharmakos*. This is the tragic point made by Ernest Renan in his classic essay "What Is a Nation?" when he claims that national "unity is always effected by means of brutality" (1990, 11). Furthermore, he explains that this brutality, this expelling of the element that threatens such unity, must be forgotten in order for the national unity to be effectively upheld. Thus, he claims, "Forgetting . . . is a crucial factor in the creation of a nation" (1990, 11). It is against the brutality of this forgetting that León decides to remember not only her own experience of exile, not only the experience of so many other exiles of her own time, but the connections between their current experience of banishment and so many other experiences of exile throughout the history of Spain. León thus willingly evokes the ghosts of these previous exiles in order to prevent herself and her comrades in exile from becoming ghostly beings themselves, the latest casualties in a long line of "forgotten brutalities" throughout Spanish history.

Such an evocation of ghosts is part of what could be called the "philosophy of the phantasm" (Resina 2000a, 3) traversing León's text. León, in fact, recurrently presents the experience of exile as a sort of living death, something that becomes more and more acute as the text progresses.[20] As *Memoria de la melancolía* approaches its end, it presents what could be seen as a litany of loss, an endless recounting of the death of one exiled friend after another. Ghosts, of course, are partially characterized by the fact that they can find no stable resting place, and thus are obliged to haunt the living forever. For the exiled Spaniards that León dutifully remembers as they pass on, it is this inability to find an appropriate resting place that seems to convert these errant beings in life into errant beings in death.

León often remarks on the fact that the harshest punishment of exile is this inability to find an appropriate resting place: "Estoy cansada de no saber donde morirme. Ésa es la mayor tristeza del emigrado. ¿Qué tenemos nosotros que ver con los cementerios de los países donde vivimos? Habría que hacer tantas presentaciones de los otros muertos, que no acabaríamos nunca" (1998, 97) [I am tired of not knowing where to die. That is the biggest sadness for the immigrant. What do we have to do with the cemeteries in the countries in which we live? We would have to start introducing ourselves to so many of the other dead that we would never end]. The lack of an appropriate cemetery for the Spaniards who lost the civil war, particularly the inability to have such a final resting place in their homeland, is a recurring, haunting, image throughout León's text: "¿Cuántas tumbas hemos ido dejando por el mundo en estos casi treinta años de vida desterrada que vivimos los españoles? . . . ¡Cuántos, cuántos, y cada día un nombre más, España madre de todos nosotros, cada vez un nombre que añadir a los que no podemos dejar sobre tu suelo!" (1998, 128) [How many tombs have we left behind all over the world in these almost thirty years of exiled life that we Spaniards have lived?... How many, how many, and every day another name, Spain, mother of us all, each time another name to add to those that we cannot lay to rest in your soil!]. León sadly notices how a cemetery that had been created in Madrid for members of the International Brigades that died during the civil war has since been destroyed: "Los que buscaron el cementerio de las Brigadas Internacionales, en Madrid, no han podido encontrarlo" (1998, 369) [Those who looked for the cemetery of the International Brigades in Madrid have not been able to find it]. She recalls how only a flag of the Spanish Second Republic marks the place where many Spaniards died in Auschwitz, "En Auschwitz está izada hoy en memoria de los allí desaparecidos la bandera de la República" (1998, 388) [In Auschwitz there is a flag of the Republic raised today in memory of those who disappeared there]. She further mentions how, in a tiny town in the Soviet Union, there is a tombstone for a Spaniard fallen during the Second World War that does not even record his name: " 'Al camarada español que salvó este pueblo.' ¿Cómo se llamaba? No lo supimos nunca. Llegó, combatió y lo mataron. Nada más" (1998, 463) ["To the Spanish comrade that saved this town." What was his name? We never knew it. He arrived, he fought and they killed him. Nothing else].

This preoccupation with the lack of an appropriate cemetery to preserve the memory and lay to rest the remains of so many exiled Spaniards, along with León's deep sense of responsibility to keep their memories alive, transforms her text into a kind of cemetery itself, a *lieu de mémoire,* a place of memory, in which the function of creating and channeling a collective memory is taken up by her writing since it has not been taken up by Spanish society. Alda Blanco has commented on this function of León's text: "María Teresa León hace funcionar este texto como un sitio de memoria simbólico en sustitución de lo que tendría que haber sido un sitio de memoria concreto y material: un cementerio con sus monumentos fúnebres" (1991, 48–49) [María Teresa León makes this text function as a symbolic place of memory in substitution for what should have been a concrete and material place of memory: a cemetery with its funereal monuments]. León's very text functions as a *lieu de mémoire* in the form of a cemetery, and her writing recurrently takes on the function of an elegy, tirelessly mentioning the death of fellow exiles, remembering them as she does so and thus ensuring that they will not be forgotten. Hers is undoubtedly a most "vigilant" memory. In this, León takes on one of the functions of Simonides of Ceos, who, as seen in the first chapter, invented an art of memory that was originally used to remember the poet's companions who had died while attending the same banquet as he. One of the various professional activities of Simonides of Ceos was, in fact, that of being "a poet of elegies and grave inscriptions, paid to remember the deceased and to keep their memory present" (Grobbel 2004, 14). Like Simonides, therefore, León's writing symbolically takes on the responsibility of providing epitaphs for so many of her friends who are dying in exile, far from what should have been their deserved resting place, their homeland. In this sense, León's writing also fulfills the same function as the wild flower growing in Región within Benet's writing. That flower grows where there are human remains and it "está pidiendo venganza, recuerdo, y redención" (1967, 190) [calls for vengeance, recall, and redemption (1985, 172)] for the memory of the dead. We could further say that Leon's text, in a manner similar to those of Semprún and Benet, not only serves the function of a symbolic cemetery for those who have not had a proper burial, but the act of remembrance itself put into play through her very writing enacts a continual *process* of proper burial. Paul Ricoeur has described such a process as the act that we must continually take up, through history and memory, when we accept "the responsibility for the dead of the past, whose heirs we are" (2004, 499). This process, furthermore, "can then be considered an act of sepulcher. Not a place, a cemetery, a simple depository of bones, but an act of repeated entombment" (2004, 499). The act of memory that is exercised in all the meta-memory texts studied here does, indeed, put into play a "repeated entombment" through writing, a process that grows out of a deep sense of "the responsibility for the dead of the past, whose heirs we are."

It is particularly striking to recognize that this function of León's text not only shows the terrible reality of the experience of exile when she was writing, in the 1960s, but is uncannily relevant today. The difficult process being undertaken currently in Spain, laden with pain and fear, of exhuming the numerous mass graves from the time of the civil war shows that Spanish society still needs to create the appropriate *lieux de mémoire* for many of the victims of the war.[21] Jo Labanyi reminds us that "ghosts, while they require remembrance in human consciousness, have an objective existence as the embodiment of the past in the present" (2000, 78). While León consciously takes up the responsibility of having her writing embody the function of "remembrance in human consciousness" for the "ghosts" of exile she evokes, the symbolic cemetery, the *lieu de mémoire*, that her text becomes, like the mass graves today in Spain, is, indeed, an "embodiment of the past in the present." Both the textual and symbolic cemetery, as well as the "act of repeated entombment," that León's narrative becomes, and the mass graves of the civil war in Spain today, function to show that the Spanish society of the present has not adequately dealt with the past, and that the predominant narrative of Spanish history that has evolved in post-Franco Spain does, indeed, need to be re-articulated. León's autobiography, along with other texts from the Republican exile(s) of 1939, has much to contribute to this process of re-articulation, and can thus be seen as a text that not only reflects a time period that has passed, that of political exile during the Franco regime, but anticipates issues that are all too current today.

Remembering Balibrea's claim that "antes de recuperar de forma duradera el exilio, su crítica deberá demostrar cómo esta literatura saca de quicio a España, dinamitando su canon y sus presupuestos político-narrativos" (2003, 20) [before recovering exile in a permanent way, the criticism with which it is studied should demonstrate how this literature throws Spain out of kilter, dynamiting its canon and its political-narrative presuppositions], we can now see one way in which León's text anticipates this challenge. Against the predominant narrative of post-Franco history as one inevitably destined to the recuperation of democracy through a successful and peaceful transition, León's text, and the mass graves still being exhumed today in Spain, are ghostly embodiments of an uncomfortable past *in the present*, reminders, most uncomfortably of all, that the transition to democracy has been uneven and incomplete, that Spanish society still has great debts with its past, that the appropriate *lieux de mémoire* still need to be created. They will not be able to be created, however, until that predominant narrative of recent Spanish history is questioned and undermined, and an acknowledgement is made of the ways in which the transition was precisely *based on,* and *built upon,* the negation of a true engagement with the past.[22]

As Labanyi further reminds us, "Ghosts are, precisely, the 'might-have-beens' of history that return as an actualizable, embodied alternative reality" (2000, 79). To create that "alternative reality" we, as critics, will have to learn to "disidentify" with the presuppositions of the dominant narrative of contemporary Spanish history mentioned earlier. It is here, too, that León's autobiography can serve as a particularly relevant model today, with its foregrounding of strategies of "disidentification" on so many levels. Balibrea's expression of the need to understand how the literature of exile "saca de quicio a España" [throws Spain out of kilter] finds an echo in an image that León herself presents in her autobiography. The sadness she feels in exile upon having lost her homeland makes León cry out for another kind of "patria" [homeland]: "Una patria, Señor, una patria pequeña como un patio o como una grieta en un muro muy sólido" (1998, 81) [A homeland, God, a homeland small as a patio or as a fissure in a very solid wall]. The term "quicio," usually referring to a door frame, is, according to Joan Corominas in his *Diccionario crítico etimológico*, derived from the older term *rescrieço*, which means, precisely, "grieta" [fissure]. León's image of a patria as a "grieta en un muro muy sólido" [fissure in a very solid wall] is, indeed, a conception of the "patria" that "saca de quicio a España" [throws Spain out of kilter], as much as it is a longing plea to find a final place of repose endlessly denied her, even if that place be nothing more than a crack in a wall. We could thus see León's narrative, like so many of the texts of the 1939 exile(s), as works that create, or better yet, embody, multiple fissures, "grietas," in that "muro muy sólido" [very solid wall] that is the predominant narrative of post-Franco history which presents the transition as a successful and peaceful recuperation of full democracy that adequately dealt with, and put to rest, issues related to the civil war and the Francoist past.[23]

The image of the fissure, or "grieta," is precisely one of the metaphors used by Cristina Moreiras Menor in her study *Cultura herida: literatura y cine en la España democrática* to analyze a series of texts appearing in post-Franco Spain in the 1970s and 1980s that counter the new democracy's attempt to establish itself on the basis of a "clean" break with the past, a break that created, as explained at the beginning of this chapter, a "Reino de desmemoriados" (Morán 1991, 75) [Kingdom of unmemoried subjects]. Moreiras Menor explains that, in the face of this official erasure of memory and history upon which the new democracy attempts to establish itself, certain texts in post-Franco Spain foreground the exploration and recuperation of the silenced memory of the civil war and Franco era, allowing that memory to emerge from within the fissures, gaps, "grietas," of the dominant discourses. Such texts are subversive in that they maintain open the wound of history that the official discourses of the new democracy want above all to present as fully and finally sutured and closed: "la política de consenso que organiza la producción cultural a partir de sus narraciones hegemónicas de tachadura de la memoria ... presenta brechas, espacios de fisura por los que sale a escena la urgencia del afecto cancelado" (2002, 40) [the politics of consensus that organizes cultural production according to the hegemonic narratives of the erasure of memory ... presents breaches, fissures through which the urgency of the cancelled affect emerges]. These texts, furthermore, "dan entrada en la escena de la realidad cultural, con fuerza transgresora, a los afectos y efectos de la memoria y del recuerdo de su olvido" (2002, 40) [open up cultural reality, with transgressive force, to the affects and effects of memory and of the remembrance of its oblivion]. In this sense, we can understand how *Memoria de la melancolía* anticipates this dynamic and presents, in 1970, an embodiment of such a narrative fissure, a "grieta en un muro muy sólido" [fissure in a very solid wall].

This wall can be interpreted as the official Francoist rhetoric bent on forgetting the past and celebrating the "25 years of peace" in Spain that was predominant at the time León was writing much of her autobiography, but it also can be interpreted as the call to forget the past that governed the later transition to democracy, which León seems to anticipate in her writing. It thus becomes clear that León's meta-memory text, like many others written in exile in which the memory of the civil war and of exile is tirelessly presented, is in fact a precursor to a whole series of texts that will likewise take up memory as a politically subversive strategy in post-Franco Spain.

There is yet another way in which León's text "saca de quicio a España" [throws Spain out of kilter], as Balibrea envisions the term. The constant presence in the text of the ghosts of fellow exiles produces the effect that Derrida analyzes in *Specters of Marx: The State of the Debt, the Work of Mourning, and the New International,* when he explains that the ghost "unhinges" and "disjoins the living present" (1994, xix). Based on Hamlet's famous cry, when confronted with the ghost of his father, that "the time is out of joint," Derrida remarks that the ghost, by forcibly introducing in the present a recognition of our debt to the past, wounds that very present, causing a state in which "time is disarticulated, dislodged. . . . Time is off its hinges, time is off course, beside itself, disadjusted" (1994, 18). León's autobiography effectively "saca de quicio a España" by relentlessly foregrounding the existence of the ghosts that show that the present has an unpaid debt to the past, and this debt "unhinges," that is, again, "saca de quicio" any narrative, during the later part of the Franco regime or throughout the transition, that pretends to have put the past to rest.

The image of an open wound is particularly significant with respect to León's text. Freud in fact claims that melancholia "behaves like an open wound" (1958a, 253). For Freud, melancholia is a pathological response to loss which, unlike mourning, does not manage to let go of a lost object, or the ideal that such an object represented, and adjust to a new reality in which that object is accepted as lost, as part of the past. León's autobiography presents a melancholy memory, a "memoria de la melancolía," precisely because it refuses to accept the loss of the ideals of the Republic, the loss imposed by exile of the relevance of the lives of so many Spaniards to the continuing development of Spain. Rejecting the supposedly normal accommodation to reality that mourning entails by letting go of the past, León's melancholia becomes a political act of defiance. Melancholia, here, can be seen not as pathological but as politically necessary. The texts that Moreiras Menor analyzes in post-Franco Spain are likewise subversive inasmuch as they are also melancholic. The memories embodied in them "surgen a modo de fisuras sin suturar cuyas cicatrices se imprimen con fuerza desestabilizadora (2002, 29) [emerge in the form of unsutured fissures whose scars are imprinted with destabilizing force]. The open wound that such melancholic texts embody is politically transgressive. León's text can be seen, again, as an early meta-memory text that will, like the later texts that Moreiras Menor analyzes, present mourning as suspect, inasmuch as it ultimately and implicitly accepts the dominant rhetoric of the need to put the past to rest. León's melancholic writing, like these later texts, emerges

> desde una fundamental, e incluso fundacional, experiencia de pérdida y de vacío y, en este sentido, la escritura y las narrativas se constituyen como lugar donde realizar un duelo inacabado cuya escena sintomática señala a una memoria herida por su insimbolizable recuerdo. Son narrativas que recuperan el trauma que las posee desde un afecto en duelo o desde su imposibilidad, constituyéndose así en melancólicas. Sus escenas se abren a relatos olvidados para la Historia. (Moreiras Menor 2002, 123)

> [from a fundamental, and even foundational, experience of loss and emptiness and, in this sense, writing and narrative are constituted as a place to realize an unfinished mourning whose symptomatic scene points to a memory wounded by its unsymbolizable recollection. These are narratives that recover the trauma that possesses them from an affect in mourning or from its impossibility, therefore becoming melancholic. Their scenes open up to stories forgotten by History.]

This is why, far from letting go of the past, León continuously holds on to it, in a traumatic repetition within a melancholic memory that will not allow the past to be ultimately swept under what will eventually be a new and very appealing democratic rug.[24]

Not only does León's writing become a subversive "act of memory," but she is continuously calling for others to participate in such a defiant act of remembrance. Her text is full of calls to other exiles to tell their story, to tell the pain inflicted by their exile: "Contad vuestras angustias del destierro. No tengáis vergüenza. Todos las llevamos dentro" (1998, 402) [Recount your anguishes of exile. Don't be ashamed. We all carry them inside us.]. This call to tell their story is explicitly meant to counter the "disremembering" of the official discourses within Spain: "Sí, desterrados de España, contad, contad lo que nunca dijeron los periódicos, decid vuestras angustias y lo horrorosa que fue la suerte que os echaron encima. Que recuerden los que olvidaron" (1998, 404) [Yes, exiles from Spain, recount, recount all that the newspapers never told, recount your anguishes and how horrible was the fate that was imposed on you. Let those who have forgotten remember]. Furthermore, one of the ongoing themes throughout the text is the desire to tell her story so that future generations of Spaniards, those who have not undergone exile, will remember the experience of the generation devastated by exile. Despite the "disidentification" she has so often felt with these young Spaniards, due to the imposed ignorance in which they have grown up, León still hopes that her memory will be taken up by them, even after she is gone: "Yo no quedaré, pero cuando yo no recuerde, recordad vosotros . . . Recordad nuestra pequeña alegría común, nuestra risa y las lágrimas que dolían o quemaban cuando nos sentíamos desamparados y solos" (1998, 303) [I won't remain, but when I no longer remember, you remember . . . Remember our small common happiness, our laughter and the tears that hurt or burned when we felt helpless and alone]. Memory is a responsibility that León has taken up in the name of so many others, and which she hopes others in turn will assume in her name.

Memory in León's text, as has been seen before, functions beyond the individual sphere and becomes collective. We have seen how, through the narrative strategy of "disidentification," León's recollections of her childhood underscore the manner in which her personal memory is irremediably collective, bound to the very society she is "disidentifying" from in her rememorative process. León's remembrance also embodies a collective resistance to politically imposed forgetting, a resistance shared with others and that will hopefully be passed on from one generation to the next. Loureiro underscores this collective nature of memory in León: "There is no such thing as a properly personal memory: no one owns his/her memory, because memory is always a response and a responsibility. Memory, however, is not simply marked or haunted by the other, but it is also addressed to the other, it is for the other" (2000, 97). It is this collective nature of memory as responsibility toward the past, and toward the other, that León is pointing to when, in the preface to a collection of short stories, she invents the term "transmemoria" (1950, 9) [transmemory]. León's autobiography is an example of such a "transmemoria" in that it becomes much more than the recollection of her own life story. It intentionally incorporates the lives of many other exiles to become an act of remembrance of a whole "lost generation," and further constitutes itself as a legacy for the new generations of Spaniards who, she believes, will some day be ready to inherit it.[25]

This collective "transmemoria" [transmemory] that León calls for is marked by explicit calls to include the feelings suffered by those in exile and not just the events that they have witnessed. León implores of other exiles: "Contad vuestras angustias del destierro" (1998, 402) [Recount your anguishes of exile]. In a related vein, we may recall that

Moreiras Menor describes the subversive exploration of the past in post-Franco narrative as one that explores "los afectos y efectos de la memoria" (2002, 40) [the affects and effects of memory]. These subversive explorations of the past are thus characterized by an explicit recognition of the affective dimension of memory. Memory cannot be disassociated from feeling and affect. León highlights this at every turn: "Habréis de perdonarme... la reiteración de palabras tristes. Sí, tal vez sean el síntoma de mi incapacidad como historiador. Pero no puedo disfrazarme. Ahí dejo únicamente mi participación en los hechos, lo que vi, lo que sentí, lo que oí, todo pasado por una confusión de recuerdos" (1998, 69) [You must pardon me... the reiteration of sad words. Yes, it is perhaps the symptom of my incapacity as a historian. But I cannot disguise myself. I leave there only my participation in events, what I saw, what I felt, all passed through a confusion of memories]. The theatrical language so prevalent in León's writing emerges again, as she states that she cannot "disguise" herself as a historian (interestingly, León writes the term "historian" as a masculine noun). Sadness and confusion are both affirmed by León as forces governing her rememorative venture. In this, León is holding up the affect-laden quality of memory above any supposedly objective historical account. This is one more way in which León's "act of memory" is subversive of official, patriarchal views of history, suffused as they are with a desire to present an objective view of the facts and events of the past.[26]

This acknowledgment of the affect inevitably guiding recollection is what Dominick LaCapra considers essential for an effective working through of a traumatic past. Such explorations of affect may lead to what he calls "empathic unsettlement," an emotional response that undermines cognitive certainty which victims of trauma suffer. Such "empathic unsettlement" can also productively be experienced by those responding to, or trying to understand or represent, such trauma in a manner that does not betray the horror of the experience through its representation or understanding (2001, 78). As LaCapra claims: "opening oneself to empathic unsettlement is... a desirable affective dimension of inquiry" (2001, 78). Such "empathic unsettlement," furthermore, is one of the elements that prevents a traumatic history from being repressed by a society bent on forgetting the pain of the past, for it "places in jeopardy fetishized and totalizing narratives that deny the trauma that called them into existence by prematurely (re)turning to the pleasure principle, harmonizing events, and often recuperating the past in terms of uplifting messages or optimistic, self-serving scenarios" (2001, 78). According to this view, it is in large part the affective dimension of León's recollection, the sadness and confusion that she acknowledges as guiding her memory, that will allow her autobiography to be most effective in countering the "self-serving scenario" of official discourses calling for the forgetting of the past within Francoism and then later during the transition. The multiple levels of "disidentification" in León's writing, arising from the multiple levels of exile she experienced, generate the "empathic unsettlement" that she herself suffers throughout her life. It is the "empathic unsettlement" that her writing may generate in its readers that will allow them, also, to "disidentify" from dominant discourses about forgetting the past, and find in León's writing a means for productively working through a previously repressed history.

We have seen how León's text can be understood as a *lieu de mémoire* in the form of a symbolic cemetery for all the exiles that she evokes in her writing, those poor souls who have died without being able to return to their homeland, the longed-for but forbidden place of final rest. If we recall León's depiction of her traumatic memory of exile in the epigraph to this chapter, we can now better understand the function of another *lieu de mémoire,* or place of memory, that she herself explicitly invokes: "Pero qué horrible es que los recuerdos se precipiten sobre ti y te obliguen a mirarlos y te muerdan, y se revuelquen sobre tus entrañas, que es el lugar de la memoria" (1998, 130) [How horrible it is when memories assail you, force you to look at them, bite you and wallow in our entrails, which is the place of memory]. For León, her "entrañas," her "entrails," are a place of memory, one that is very appropriate for the "affective history" that her writing embodies. Indeed, with memory placed within, and emerging from, her very entrails, it becomes clear that León's autobiography literally embodies her practice of "counter-memory."

The "empathic unsettlement" in León's writing is thus intimately connected to the various levels of "disidentification" in her text. It is also connected to the "philosophy of the phantasm" that we have seen governing León's autobiography. Her writing foregrounds the deep feelings of compassion and solidarity, of loss and emptiness, produced by the memory of the lives, and deaths, of the many ghostly exiles that haunt her writing. The term "philosophy of the phantasm" is one that Michel Foucault coined to develop his notion of a "counter-memory," or an "effective history" that emerges as a reaction to official forms of history. Unsettling multiple forms of stability and continuity is a characteristic of such "effective history" or "counter-memory." As Foucault explains: "History becomes 'effective' to the degree that it introduces discontinuity into our being.... 'Effective' history deprives the self of the reassuring stability of life and nature.... It will uproot its traditional foundations and relentlessly disrupt its pretended continuity"

(1977, 154). This is precisely what the multiple "disidentifications" and ghostly exilic presences in León's writing achieve, an "empathic unsettlement" based on the relentless undermining of reassuring stability, and an exploration of the discontinuities, in her own personal memory as much as in the collective memory of Spain, that counter official discourses. Because of the self-conscious affirmation of the role of affect in her writing (the "palabras tristes" [sad words] that León cannot and will not repress), more than an "effective history" we could call her writing an "affective history," one that truly embodies, within her very entrails, a relentless and subversive "counter-memory." León's meta-memory text is thus particularly "effective" because of it openly embraces its "affective" nature.

Such "counter-memory," or "affective history," clearly resonates with the Benjaminian view of an approach to the past that will "brush history against the grain" and "blast open the continuum of history" (1969, 257, 262). The last chapter explored the multiple images of ruins in Benet's writing as an embodiment of such a Benjaminian critique of a rhetoric of progress that is inevitably based on the forgetting of the suffering and experience of those on the losing side of History, with a capital "H." Martin Jay underscores the importance of memory in the Benjaminian critique of History and progress, as he explains that "the imperative to rescue what had been forgotten by the victors of history" is reflected in Benjamin's affirmation that the task of remembrance is "to save what has miscarried" (qtd. in Jay 1999, 230). In her autobiography, León presents an important image of ruins, reminiscent of the ruins populating Benet's Región, that can be seen to embody a Benjaminian critique of progress and an attempt "to save what has miscarried" in Spain. León imagines a time in which the exiles will finally be able to return to Spain and help the country rebuild a true democracy:

> Dejadnos las ruinas. Debemos comenzar desde las ruinas. Llegaremos. Regresaremos con la ley, os enseñaremos las palabras enterradas bajo los edificios demasiado grandes de las ciudades que ya no son nuestras. Nuestro paraíso, el que defendimos, está debajo de las apariencias actuales. También el vuestro. ¿No sentís, jóvenes sin éxodo y sin llanto, que tenemos que partir de las ruinas, de las casas volcadas y los campos ardiendo para levantar nuestra ciudad fraternal de la nueva ley? (1998, 98)

> [Leave the ruins to us. We must start from the ruins. We will return with the law, we will teach you the words buried under the excessively big buildings in cities that are no longer ours. Our paradise, the one we defended, is lying under today's façades. It is also yours. Don't you feel, young people

who have not known exile and tears, that we must start from the ruins, from the flattened houses and the burning fields in order to erect our fraternal city of the new law?]

The new democracy that León envisions some day in Spain will have to start from the ruins, because it will have to be based on "ruining" and rejecting the predominant view of history based on forgetting the suffering, the very experience, of those who lost the civil war and then spent so many years in exile. León's "transmemoria," which will help new generations recover that experience, must thus be based on ruins. The creation of a new, democratic city in Spain's future must necessarily be based on the ruins of that democratic city of the Second Republic that was devastated and ruined by the ravages of the civil war and later by the destructive effects of the long political repression under Franco.

This image of the importance of ruins in Leon's writing echoes the way Walter Benjamin envisions the work of memory, which he understands not only as the *act* that enables us to save "what has miscarried," but the very *medium* in which that act can take place. As Benjamin explains:

> Language shows clearly that memory is not an instrument for exploring the past but its theater. It is the medium of past experience as the ground is the medium in which dead cities lie interred. He who seeks to approach his own buried past must conduct himself like a man digging. This confers the tone and bearing of genuine reminiscences. He must not be afraid to return again and again to the same matter, to scatter it as one scatters earth, to turn it over as one turns over soil. For the matter itself is only a deposit, a stratum, which yields only to the most meticulous examination what constitutes the real treasure hidden within the earth: the images, severed from all earlier associations, that stand—like precious fragments or torsos in a collector's gallery—in the prosaic rooms of our later understanding. (1986, 25–26)

The theatrical reference makes Benjamin's description of the act of memory all the more relevant to León's writing, and the emphasis on the need to recover the fragments, the ruins, of what has existed, by means of an obsessive return to digging, over and over again, in the same place, is uncannily similar to León's writing, returning again and again to what has been lost, but which she refuses to forget. The "real treasure" of this relentless digging is, necessarily, fragmented and ruined, because it embodies multiple vestiges of the stories and experiences that have been been silenced and erased by official accounts of History.

The image of a new city growing from amidst the ruins of "what has miscarried" in Spain also evokes the figure of a palimpsest similar to that which we have seen at work in both Semprún and Benet's writing. Memory is what allows for the palimpsest to retain all its layers, not allowing for any of them to be simply eliminated or forgotten. This palimpsestic layering of history, which grows from the very ruins of the past without eliminating them altogether, is precisely what is at stake in the numerous projects being undertaken today with respect to the exhumation of the mass graves full of victims of the nationalist repression during, and after, the civil war. The individuals in these mass graves, like many of the individuals León mentions in her autobiography, were not allowed to have an appropriate resting place, and their exhumation and proper burial is a way to honor them and their memory. Yet the new burial grounds must, in some way, emerge out of the very ruins of those mass graves, they must, somehow, acknowledge that such mass graves have been allowed to exist for over sixty years. The resistance of some groups to the exhumations now can be understood in this context. Such groups are afraid that by exhuming the mass graves and reburying the remains found therein, the actual sites of the original mass graves may be destroyed, perhaps lost under various building or development projects, and there is a fear that such a loss would somehow betray the memory of the dead, despite the fact that the reburial of the remains would honor it. The new *lieux de mémoire* that emerge must arise from, and not allow for the total disappearance of, the ruins of the old, lest, in finally honoring the dead, we also allow for the most tragic part of their history to disappear once again.[27]

Raising the new democracy in Spain from within the ruins of what has been destroyed is also a way to heed the call of Benjamin's "angel of history," who warns us that what many call progress is, in reality, one eternal catastrophe: "His face is turned towards the past. Where we perceive a chain of events, he sees one single catastrophe which keeps piling wreckage and hurls it in front of his feet" (1969, 257–58). Like Benjamin's "Angel of history," who looks back and acknowledges the wreckage that progess has left behind, León keeps her eye on the ruins, and warns us not to allow any so-called progess to make us forget them. Of course, León recognizes that her forced exile has converted her into part of the wreckage of Spanish history, a feeling that adds a sense of personal urgency to her desire not only to call attention to the ruins left behind by progress, but to highlight that any history defined as progress is always already in ruins. The philosopher, and fellow exile, María Zambrano echoes this very sentiment when she exclaims: "Camina el refugiado entre escombros. Y en ellos, entre ellos,

los escombros de la historia" (1990, 42) [The exile walks among ruins. And in them, among them, the ruins of history].

Remembering the predominance of images from the theater in León's autobiography, we could say that not only does her text embody an example of a much-needed *lieu de mémoire,* in the form of a symbolic cemetary for the forgotten of History as well as in the form of an embodied site for memory's affect in León's very entrails, but it becomes, also, a "theatre of memory." Raphael Samuel coined this term evoking Pierre Nora's *lieux de mémoire,* but placing added stress on the fact that the memories being recollected in such "theatres of memory" are always unofficial, belonging to the underside of official narrations of national development (1997). León's autobiography does, indeed, embody a memory that is unofficial in many ways, as shown by the imbrication in her text of gender and exile. The very last image presented in her autobiography could be seen as a metaphor for how her text functions as such a "theatre of memory." This image can be read as an attempt by León to highlight the unfinished process of reconstructing a collective identity in Spain, a process that we, today, recognize as equally incomplete, one that must still strive to provide the appropriate reparation to all the ghosts haunting the present, those in the pages of León's autobiography, that were not allowed to return to Spain, as well as those in the many mass graves in Spain today still waiting to be disinterred. Memory, individual as well as collective, emerges as an ongoing performance based on the interaction of many people, including, implicitly, all of the readers/spectators of her text, as León calls on an old friend from the Guerrillas del Teatro, and fellow exile, to help her convert her memories into a play for others to attend:

> Antes de cerrar y volver la hoja me gustaría decir a Gori Muñoz: anda, Gori, hazme la escenografía de mis recuerdos. Sí, tú hubieras sido el único escenógrafo posible de mi memoria recordando. Pero, aún tengo la ilusión de que mi memoria del recuerdo no se extinga, y por eso escribo en letras grandes y esperanzadas: CONTINUARÁ. (1998, 543–44)

> [Before closing and turning the page, I would like to say to Gori Muñoz: come on, Gori, create the scenography of my memories. Yes, you would have been the only possible scenographer for my remembering memory. But, I still hold the illusion that my memory of remembrance won't be extinguished, and that is why I write in big and hopeful letters: TO BE CONTINUED.]

The awkward grammatical construction of the phrase "mi memoria recordando" [my remembering memory], with the seemingly inappropriate use of the gerund, is quite revealing. It serves to highlight the ongoing nature of the rememorative process that León's text embodies, as well as the active role of memory, since it seems that it is memory itself, here, which is remembering, and not León herself (an interpretive possibility already evoked in the ambiguous title of León's autobiography). The final announcement, with its capital letters, "CONTINUARÁ" [TO BE CONTINUED] is a dramatic call to action. It is up to the readers/public of León's text to continue her "escenografía de mis recuerdos" [scenography of my memories] scripting and performing the next "act" in this unfinished representation, this ongoing "theater of memory." The need for others to take up her unfinished rememorative process was made all the more urgent late in life for León. Tragically, León suffered from acute Alzheimer's at the end of her life, a condition that, ironically, did not allow her to enjoy fully her long-awaited return to Spain in 1977. The woman who had dedicated entire sections of her own autobiography to making sure that others were not forgotten was, at the end of her life, dependent on the remembrance of others to keep her own memory alive. The "transmemoria" that she so ardently elaborated in her writing became, in the end, her very means of survival. It is up to others in Spain today, especially those younger generations with which León so desperately wanted to connect during her life, to actively remember her and her work. In this way, the wish that her "escenografía de mis recuerdos" ["scenography of my memories"] continue after her own memory should disappear will have come true.

4
Montserrat Roig: Twilight Memory

Cal recordar i oblidar alhora. La memòria també és oblit. Algú va dir que tots tenim dues memòries: la petita memòria, que serveix per a recordar allò que és petit, i la memòria gran, que serveix per oblidar allò que és gran. Els narradors/narradores deixen, a mesura que avancen, traces dels oblits més que dels records.

[One must remember and forget at the same time. Memory is also forgetting. Someone said that we all have two memories: a small memory, to remember what is small, and a large memory, to forget what is large. As they advance, narrators leave traces of the things they forget more than of those they remember.]
—Montserrat Roig 1991a, 22[1]

As THE QUEEN, IN LEWIS CARROLL'S *THROUGH THE LOOKING-Glass,* wisely proclaims, "it's a poor sort of memory that only works backwards" (1998, 172). Indeed, the most productive kind of remembering is that whereby we are able to confront the past and then emerge from that experience ready to engage the future. Montserrat Roig (1946–1991) can be seen to have heeded Lewis Carroll's warning for, in *L'hora violeta* [*The Violet Hour*], she produced a novel in which remembering does not just work backwards, but forwards as well.[2] The main female protagonists in the text delve into their past, attempting to unearth the memory of various repressed and silenced voices of their own generation, and of the generation before them, as an attempt to redefine their situation in the present and reclaim a better future for themselves and for Spain. Whether they actually *do* manage to reclaim a better future for themselves, however, is left open at the end of the novel, for the weight of the past is strong, and the future very uncertain.

The very title of the novel, taken from a verse in T.S. Eliot's *The Waste Land* in which the mythological figure Tiresias, though blind, is able to see "at the violet hour" already hints at the novel's orientation toward both the past and the future.[3] The image of the violet hour of the title functions on several important levels in the text. The violet hour is that of twilight, a term that in English captures perfectly the double meaning of "l'hora violeta," for it is both that hour at the end of the day when nighttime begins, and the hour at the end of night when daylight commences. It is a time of uncertainty, when things are ill-defined, unclear, and caught in the midst of change. As Roig's novel was published in 1980, and set in 1979 in the Barcelona of most of her texts, the violet hour of the novel can be seen to be that of the Spanish transition to democracy, certainly a time when things were ill-defined and in the midst of change. The novel explores how all kinds of social roles and previously stable identities were being re-defined and questioned at this time, from the role and significance of political activism (just when the "desencanto" [disenchantment] is emerging and Spaniards are starting to see that political and social institutions do not change overnight) to gender roles, as women begin to realize that true liberation is a much harder thing to achieve than they had imagined.[4]

Most of the questioning of identity within the novel, at the personal and collective level, takes place through the mediation of memory. It is in relation to the very functioning of memory itself, in this metamemory text, that the image of the violet hour, of twilight, takes on an added meaning. The exploration of memory in this text echoes the concern presented by Andreas Huyssen in his book, significantly entitled *Twilight Memories*. Huyssen reflects on the paradox that, at the end of the twentieth century, many societies find themselves naturally looking back to assess their history as they enter a new century, indeed a new millennium, yet they concurrently experience a crisis of memory, a feeling that they are "terminally ill with amnesia" (1995, 1). We have already seen the concrete manifestation of this phenomenon in Spain due to the specific conditions of the transition to democracy, which Roig's novel will explore in depth. Yet Huyssen is analyzing a more generalized phenomenon, one that has to do with the necessarily unstable positioning of all memory, emerging in the present yet referring to the past, as well as with the need to "think memory and amnesia together rather than simply oppose them" (1995, 7). In both cases a double, ambivalent nature of memory emerges, one that the image of twilight, as a double, unstable, and ambivalent time, is perfectly suited to reflect. As Huyssen explains:

> The temporal status of any act of memory is always the present and not, as some naïve epistemology might have it, the past itself, even though all memory in some ineradicable sense is dependent on some past event or experience. It is this tenuous fissure between past and present that constitutes memory, making it powerfully alive and distinct from the archive or any other mere system of storage and retrieval.

The twilight of memory, then, is not just the result of a somehow natural generational forgetting that could be counteracted through some form of a more reliable representation. Rather, it is given in the very structures of representation itself. The obsessions with memory in contemporary culture must be read in terms of this double problematic. Twilight memories are both: generational memories on the wane due to the passing of time and the continuing speed of technological modernization, and memories that reflect the twilight status of memory itself. Twilight is that moment of the day that foreshadows the night of forgetting, but that seems to slow time itself, an in-between state in which the last light of day may still play out its ultimate marvels. It is memory's privileged time. (1995, 3)

L'hora violeta explicitly and self-consciously explores these issues regarding the nature of memory itself. The main characters struggle to find a way to work through memory, to work through a past of silence and repression, in a manner that acknowledges the "tenuous fissure between past and present" of memory. That is, in a manner that involves them personally, that produces the "empathic unsettlement" that was seen, in the last chapter, to be necessary for a working through of the past to appropriately deal with trauma. Without such an "empathic unsettlement," Roig's novel shows, one may remember the past, but that practice becomes the equivalent of placing recollection in an impersonal, official archive where the apparent remembering of trauma is really just a way to effectively forget and escape its unsettling and disruptive force. Memory and forgetting are ineluctably connected, and it is necessary, as Huyssen claims, to think them together. As will be seen, this is exactly what Roig does in her text.

The need for such memory work is greatly dictated, as Huyssen further makes clear, by the fact that there are whole generations of victims of historical trauma that are passing away in the late twentieth and early twenty-first century. Their twilight thus becomes the moral imperative for younger generations to deal with the inherited memory of their suffering. As we will see, this is a major issue in *L'hora violeta*, explored with regard to those who experienced the trauma of the Holocaust as well as that of the Spanish civil war and the Franco regime. In this sense, if María Teresa León evoked the possibility of a "transmemoria" where future generations would remember her traumatic experience of exile by reading her autobiography, *L'hora violeta* thematizes the process whereby those younger generations take up that challenge, attempting to work through the inherited "transmemoria" of suffering and loss experienced by their predecessors. Finally, as Huyssen mentions, twilight memories are not just attained through a "more reliable representation" of the past. This is so because such memories undermine conventional notions of representation itself, and recuperating such memories necessarily entails questioning traditional representational practices. Roig does this repeatedly throughout her novel.

There is one more way in which the double nature of the image of the "hora violeta" is significant in Roig's text. Just as twilight, that "privileged time" of memory, as Huyssen calls it, is characterized by the oscillation between looking in two directions, backwards and forwards at the same time, there is another dynamic related to memory in the novel, that of the fetish, which is likewise characterized by an oscillation between two opposite ways of seeing. As will become clear, the dynamic of the fetish in the novel will be essential for the process of working through the past, of working through the various traumatic "transmemorias" that emerge in Roig's text.

The working through of the various "transmemorias" of the novel is mostly undertaken by the two main protagonists, the two friends Natàlia and Norma, in 1979. Natàlia, a photographer, asks Norma, a novelist, to write a novel about the friendship between Natàlia's mother, Judit, and her friend Kati during the Spanish civil war. Natàlia was born in 1938 and Norma in 1946, like Roig herself. Therefore, in the process of piecing together this story they are both looking back at a history they have not lived but that has greatly determined their lives. Natàlia gives Norma a package of material that she herself has just found for the first time. This material includes Judit's diary recounting her friendship with Kati, letters from Kati to Judit and others, and notes from Natàlia's aunt, Patricia, about Judit. These texts provide Natàlia with an image of her mother as a vibrant, exciting young woman during the civil war that is completely at odds with the later image of her mother, the only one that Natàlia had known, as a self-absorbed, unhappy, sullen woman who suffered from a debilitating paralysis and an increasing detachment from reality. This disheartening image that Natàlia has of her mother culminates in the figure of Judit, at the end of her life, as a completely estranged, silent, and mentally unstable woman. All these texts that Natàlia hands over to Norma, "archeological finds that bring to light a neglected culture," as Catherine Bellver has called them, will be the basis for Norma's novelistic re-creation of the story of Judit and Kati, a re-creation that appears in the middle of Roig's novel under the title "La novel·la de l'hora violeta" (1991, 221) [The novel of the violet hour]. The mise-en-abîme technique thematizes the textual and intertextual nature of all access to the past. It underscores the mediated, and, to a certain degree, literary, nature of all constructions of history. As Akiko Tsuchiya explains, "the entire novel is a hybrid of various generic conventions, including the letter, the memoir/autobiography, and the testimony, none of which has absolute epistemological privilege. The writer figure in the text continuously undermines the historical authority of these discourses by reflecting self-critically on the process by which 'histories' are created" (1998, 164). Roig is clearly showing that to remember a past that has been repressed by official history, a past of female suffering in this case, one must necessarily question the very mechanisms through which any such recollection is enacted, a critical process that both Natàlia and Norma undertake throughout the novel. The "hybrid" nature of Roig's writing that Tsuchiya mentions reminds us, also, of the hybrid nature of the "twilight memory," as described by Huyssen, which here emerges within that ever-changing "hora violeta" of the novel's title.

At the same time that Norma writes the novel about Judit and Kati, she is interviewing Catalan ex-deportees to Nazi concentration camps during the second world war as a follow-up to a book she wrote earlier of ex-deportee testimonies. This is a book that, in real life, Roig had published in 1977 entitled *Els catalans als camps nazis* [*Night and Fog: Catalans in the Nazi Camps*].[5] Like C., the protagonist of Carmen Martín Gaite's *El cuarto de atrás* [*The Back Room*] (a novel published just two years before Roig's), who debates throughout that text whether to write a fantastic novel or a historical treatise about the postwar years, Norma, in *L'hora violeta*, engages in much disquisition about the relative merits, advantages, and disadvantages of writing a novel versus a testimonial account of the past, and about the role of veracity versus literary inventiveness in both kinds of writing. If C., in *El cuarto de atrás*, finally resolved her dilemma by combining both books into one, Norma will try to keep them separate, although it will become clear that they both influence each other, and that, as she thinks of one text while writing the other, the boundaries between testimony and novel will become increasingly blurred.

The association of Norma with Roig herself is underscored throughout the novel. Not only has Norma written the same book of testimonies of Catalan ex-deportees to the German concentration camps as Roig wrote earlier, but Norma has also recently written a novel about Natàlia's parents, Judit and Joan, which resembles Roig's own *El temps de les cireres* [*The Time of Cherries*], published three years before *L'hora violeta*. Furthermore, at a certain point, Norma tells her sons a story about the life and memory of salmon, a children's tale that is intimately connected, as will be seen, with the two stories Norma is writing about German concentration camp deportees as well as about Judit and Kati. Roig herself later published this tale as a short story, entitled "Mare, no entenc els salmons" [Mother, I don't understand salmon].[6] Fiction and history are blurred, not only *within* the novel, as Norma is unable to keep her text about Judit and Kati separate from her testimonial writing about the Catalan ex-deportees, but extratextually as well, as the line between the novel itself and other writings by Roig becomes diffuse. As Tsuchiya explains, "By inserting within a fictional framework an 'autobiographical' account of the problems that she [Roig] herself has confronted in writing testimony, Roig reveals the processes of narrativization and fictionalization to be crucial to the understanding of history" (1998, 170–71).

However, there is another important effect of this intertextual strategy by means of which Roig inserts her other writings into *L'hora violeta*. This produces a recurrent questioning of the frames within which all writing, all remembering, takes place. As the same texts, some of them historical testimonies, are found both inside and outside Roig's novel, the secure frame of the novel itself that safely defines it as fiction is undermined. The very distinction between fiction and history itself, two discourses that are usually framed in different ways, is undermined as well. In fact, the novel itself foregrounds the question of framing from the very beginning, when Natàlia, as a photographer, self-consciously reflects on photography itself, an activity in which framing a visual image is essential. Furthermore, the novel as a whole is structured around a certain framing technique. The novel that Norma finally creates about the story of Natàlia's mother, Judit, and her friend Kati during the civil war is found exactly in the middle of Roig's novel, effectively "framed" by two chapters on either side.

The first chapter, "Primavera de 1979" [Spring 1979], recounts how, in that year, Natàlia asks Norma to write a novel about the story of Judit and Kati, and the chapter includes the very letter that Natàlia sends to Norma asking for this favor. The next chapter, "L'hora perduda" [The Lost Hour], is still set in 1979 and tells the story of Natàlia's love affair with Jordi, a married man who is a devoted, if disillusioned, member of the Communist Party. This disillusionment is an important element of the novel, part of the text's reflection about the very nature of the transition to democracy in Spain. Interspersed with the story of Natàlia and Jordi's affair, which ultimately fails, is that of Jordi's wife, Agnès, who suffers as she patiently awaits his definitive return to their home. Norma's recreation of the story of Judit and Kati appears in the third chapter, entitled "La novel·la de l'hora violeta" [The Novel of the Violet Hour], and is set in the past of the civil war and the early Franco regime. The fourth chapter, "L'hora dispersa" [The Dispersed Hour], returns to 1979 and presents the story of the dissolution of Norma's marriage to Ferran, also a member of the Communist Party. As Norma finds a new lover, Alfred, she also embarks on a new round of interviews with Catalan ex-deportees to Nazi concentration camps. In this chapter, Norma finally writes the novel about Judit and Kati as she also prepares to write another testimonial account of the ex-deportees. The final chapter, "L'hora oberta" [The Open Hour], returns to the story of Natàlia, Jordi, and Agnès, as Jordi leaves Natàlia for good, only to find, at the end of the novel, that Agnès, after having endlessly waited for his return, finally refuses to take him back. The structure of the novel thus foregrounds the issue of the past being literally "framed" by the present. This narrative organization underscores the fact that the need to revisit the past is intrinsically connected to the dynamics of the Spanish transition to democracy, the time period that literally frames Roig's text.

The structure of the novel can likewise be seen to highlight that every act of remembrance emerges out of a particular context in the present, and that the present context will determine, "frame," in a literal and figurative sense, that act of recollection. Memory always reflects the present as much as it does the past, and this ultimately underscores the ways in which both are inseparable. Furthermore, just as any frame works by necessarily leaving some things out of the picture, the foregrounding of frames and framing in Roig's novel is related to the text's exploration of the way in which memory and forgetting are inextricably connected, and of how, returning to the words of Andreas Huyssen, it is necessary to learn to "think memory and amnesia together rather than simply oppose them" (1995, 7). One final implication of this self-conscious highlighting of the practice of framing in the novel is that which Iwona Irwin-Zarecka mentions in *Frames of Remembrance: The Dynamics of Collective Memory*. Frames do not just function by including certain elements while excluding others. They also implicitly evoke an evaluative process underlying this practice. Highlighting the act of framing itself is a way to call attention not just to the selective *contents* of what is framed, but the arbitrary, and very personal, *manner* in which the framing itself is done. This brings to the fore an exploration not just of *what* is remembered or forgotten, but of *why* we remember or forget, and of *how* we come to determine what is worthy of being remembered or not. Underscoring the very act of framing, as Roig does on several levels in her text, introduces a reflection of our personal engagement with the past, and of how this engagement may determine the very shape we give to any historical account. As Irwin-Zarecka explains, "Framing devices employed at this meta-level, as it were, provide the structure to both the contents of the past and the forms of remembrance. . . . [They] attend to the construction of our emotional and moral engagement with the past" (1994, 7). Roig's novel, as will be seen, explores the impact that "our emotional and moral engagement with the past" inevitably has on any project of rewriting history. Roig's work thus echoes María Teresa León's affirmation, in her autobiography, of the need to integrate feeling and affect, the "palabras tristes" [sad words] of her writing, into narrative accounts of the past.

All of the texts that are being written within Roig's novel represent efforts on Natàlia's and Norma's part to confront either their own personal past, or the collective past of Spain. They are attempts to reclaim, by giving them a voice, stories of suffering and repression, unofficial stories kept silent by the dominant views of history imposed by the Franco regime within which they have grown up. As Natàlia claims, when presenting her mother's diary to Norma: "Em semblava que calia salvar per les paraules tot allò que la història, la Història gran, o sigui la dels homes, havia fet imprecís, havia condemnat o idealitzat" (1993, 17) [I thought it was necessary to say with words all that history, grand History, that is to say, the history of men, had made imprecise, had condemned].[7] Natàlia and Norma understand the importance of rescuing stories of suffering from the margins of History with a capital H, in this case the stories of women's oppression. Yet Roig's novel will underscore the danger of thinking that these marginalized histories are somehow more "authentic" than those stories put forth by official discourses, and that all that is necessary is to somehow expand our historical perspective to include in our angle of vision previously excluded histories.[8] Like the concern raised in the previous chapter with regard to María Teresa León, Roig makes it clear that it is not enough simply to "enlarge the picture" we have of the past. This is necessary, of course, but it must be done in a way that self-consciously and critically reflects on the very manner whereby vision itself, the mechanism that either excludes or includes specific experiences and aspects of the past, is ideologically constituted.

It is important, in this respect, to pay attention to various images of seeing in the novel. Vision is evoked in the very title, as Tiresias, the "seer" (he who can foretell the future), is said to be able to "see" precisely at the violet hour. There are many images in the novel of characters "seeing" or not "seeing," descriptions of a gaze that haunts a certain character, thus pointing to the power of that gaze over her or him. As Joan Scott has explained in her article "Experience," the image of seeing, the narrative evocation of sight, is ideologically charged. Vision has been tied to knowledge, and with the Enlightenment connection of vision and rationality, sight is one of a series of binary terms gendered male that are considered superior to the corresponding terms associated with the female (rationality/irrationality, mind/body, activity/passivity, etc.).[9] Besides being thus associated with the male side of the binary system that underlies patriarchal ideology, sight is also related, according to Scott, to a metaphor of "visibility as literal transparency. . . . Knowledge is gained through vision; [and] vision is a direct, unmediated apprehension of a world of transparent objects. In this conceptualization of it, the visible is privileged; writing is then put at its service. Seeing is the origin of knowing. Writing is reproduction, transmission—the communication of knowledge gained through (visual) experience" (1992, 23).

Scott explains how appeals to this visual paradigm have been central in projects that attempt to make visible, and bring to light, previously neglected and overlooked dimensions of history in the process of creating new, alternative historical narratives. Such new "histories have provided evidence for a world of alternative values and practices whose existence gives the lie to hegemonic constructions of social worlds, whether these constructions vaunt the political superiority of white men, the coherence and unity of selves, the naturalness of heterosexual monogamy, or the inevitability of scientific progress and economic development" (1992, 24).

However, the beneficial aspects of this attempt to "enlarge the picture" of history by providing access to previously marginalized experiences are counteracted if such a project is founded on an unproblematized understanding of vision itself. The different images of seeing in Roig's novel reflect her attempt to recover the marginalized stories repressed by official constructions of Francoist history while highlighting how vision itself is always ideologically determined, and thus not a simple means of better apprehending the world, or history, or experience.

Natàlia, the photographer, is the first character to problematize vision in the text. She explains that "fa quatre anys que fotografio això que diem realitat" (1993, 13) [for four years I have been photographing that which we call reality]. She then continues to question the supposed "reality" of the world she photographs, recognizing that her vision is always conditioned by subjective recollections: "Em sembla que no som capaços de valorar la realitat fins que aquesta no es converteix en record. Com si així volguéssim tornar a viure. Per això crec que la literatura encara té un sentit. La literatura no és història. La literatura s'inventa el passat a partir d'uns quants detalls que han estat reals, encara que sigui a la nostra ment" (1993, 13) [I think we are not able to value reality until it becomes the past. As if we thus wanted to live again. That is why I think that literature still has meaning. Literature is not history. Literature invents the past based on a few details that were real, even if only in our mind].[10] In recognizing that a subjective aspect of recollection undergirds all access to reality and to the past, she decides to turn her vision, in the form of her photographic camera, inwards: "estic una mica cansada de buscar sempre l'instant fugaç d'allò que passa, retratar la realitat precisa, externa. Com si els meus ulls fossin una càmera abocada sempre cap enfora. Tinc ganes d'explorar la meva pròpia cadència" (1993, 13) [I am somewhat tired of always looking for the fleeting moment of what happens, of portraying a reality that is precise. Exterior. As if my eyes were a camera, always looking outwards. I would like to explore my own cadence].[11] This turn inwards begins a process of analyzing not only how the world around her is governed by a whole series of textual, ideological influences, but how her very way of seeing is likewise determined by such constraints.

One of the influences that has determined her identity is her mother, from whom Natàlia was completely estranged as she grew up. Thus, learning more about her mother's past, through the diary and letters she has found, becomes a way to understand herself better, too. She tells her friend Norma: "no t'ho creuràs, aquest munt de paperassa m'ha dut a pensar en mi mateixa. A mirarme cap endintre" (1993, 14) [You won't believe it, but this pile of papers has forced me to think about myself. To look at myself on the inside].[12] Natàlia turns her sight inwards, ready to understand her own identity better through a greater understanding of her mother. She further asks Norma "has provat alguna vegada de mirar-te al mirall sense analitzar si fas goig o encara ets jove? Vull dir, has provat de mirar-te al mirall i només veure-hi els teus ulls, la teva mirada?" (1993, 14) [Have you ever tried looking at yourself in the mirror without analyzing if you still look good or if you are still young? I mean, have you tried to look at yourself in the mirror and only see your eyes, your gaze?].[13] This image of trying to isolate one's gaze from all the concerns imposed on it by social conditioning (and the implicit recognition that it is impossible to do so), points to the fact that *how* we see is as problematic, as mediated by layer upon layer of ideological conditioning, as *what* we see in the world. Thus, the efforts at uncovering, bringing to light, making visible the previously invisible lives and experiences of marginalized groups (that is to say, Norma's projects of writing the story of Judit and Kati as well as of the Nazi concentration camp survivors) will have to be presented in a way that acknowledges this ideologically constrained nature of vision itself.

At a certain point, Natàlia reflects on how, long after Franco's death, her own identity, the way she sees herself and the world, is still conditioned by many of the ideological constraints prevalent during Francoism. Natàlia thought she had freed herself from such constraints by being a strong feminist, yet she exclaims: "En Franco és a dins de mi, se m'arrapa com un llimac. La vella i resseca pelleringa no se m'acaba de morir. . . . Té els ulls vermells de tanta sang que vessen. Però no té rostre. Només ulls" (1993, 92) [Franco is inside of me, he clings to me like a slug. The old and dried up rag just doesn't die. . . . He has eyes that are red and streaming with blood. But he doesn't have a face. Only eyes].[14] This image of Franco's disembodied eyes, this gaze haunting Natàlia, is an image of the power of patriarchy, of the hold that the oppressive ideology of the Franco dictatorship has on her, even after the death of the dictator. By still feeling the influence of these terrible eyes, Natàlia recognizes that her own vision is not yet free and unhampered by the past. Perhaps it never will be.[15]

This image of Franco's eyes without a face can be contrasted with an image that appears later on in the novel, that of a doll that Natàlia's mother, Judit, clings to when she goes crazy at the end of her life. This doll has a face, but no eyes, for Judit had scratched them out, leaving the doll blind. This face without eyes of Judit's doll can be seen as the reverse image of Franco's eyes without a face, the other side of patriarchy, of power. It is the side of the victim, reduced to silence, to blindness, to invisibility. If this was the image that Natàlia had of her mother, however, Judit's diaries present another, very different one.

We learn of Judit's life in the novel that Norma finally writes about her, a text entitled "La novel·la de l'hora violeta," that appears at the heart of Roig's novel. In a completely fragmentary nature, glimpses of Judit's story and of her friendship with Kati can be gleaned from Norma's novel, which is obviously based on the multiple texts that Natàlia had given her. Norma's novel presents Judit's diary entries between 1942 and 1950. These are recurrently interrupted by descriptions from an omniscient narrator's point of view of Judit's life around 1958 and by letters written by Kati, and descriptions of Kati's life in 1939 shortly before she committed suicide at the end of the civil war. Judit's diary entries are further interrupted by a section written by Patricia, Natàlia's aunt and Judit's sister-in law, in 1964. Here, Patricia describes how an undertaker makes arrangements for Judit's funeral after her death. The sections are thus not presented in chronological order at all, and the plurality of points of view and voices is not subsumed under any one dominant perspective. A fragmented, disjointed narrative is presented, a structure that reflects the fragmented and unfulfilled nature of Judit's life, one that can only be pieced together, partially, with great effort.

We learn that the only time in her life that Judit was truly happy was when she befriended Kati during the civil war. Kati dared to do as she pleased, with no regard for social conventions. She would take on and cast off lovers in a manner traditionally reserved only for men. She is described by one woman, in *El temps de les cireres,* as someone who "el que vol, és dominar el món amb els seus aires de gallimarsot" (1977a, 159) [wants to dominate the world with her manly airs].[16] Kati is thus a figure that subverts the rigid gender differentiation between traditionally feminine and masculine characteristics. This is what made her so threatening to most of the women around her, but so terribly appealing to Judit. Judit was happy to share a special intimacy with Kati, attracted precisely by her masculine power and by the possibility of sharing her unbounded sense of freedom, if only for a short while. As Judit repeatedly states, Kati was the only person who ever understood her sadness at having had to abandon a promising career as a concert pianist because of getting married. No one but her friend ever knew of Judit's desire to compose her own music and not just play that of others. Furthermore, Kati was the only person to tell Judit that, someday, when the Republicans would win the war, things would be better for women, and she would surely be able to compose and give free rein to her creativity. Kati tells Judit "algun dia també tu crearàs tot això que tens a dins, aquesta música callada que no has tingut ocasió de fer sortir. I algú t'entendrà" (1993, 134) [Some day you will also find a creative outlet for everything that you have inside, that silent music that you have not been able to produce. And someone will understand you].[17] Kati may have been a bad Tiresias, or foreseer of the future, with her belief in a Republican victory, but she was unquestionably the only person to truly see Judit and appreciate her creative potential.

During the war, Kati falls in love with Patrick, an Irish member of the International Brigades. When Patrick dies in battle, Kati asks Judit to run away with her, so that they may build a life together in a better, freer place. After Judit refuses, Kati commits suicide. Judit remains married to Joan, a devoted and faithful, if unexciting, husband. He returns a changed man after fighting for the Republic and spending almost four years in one of Franco's concentration camps after the war. Judit thus remains with Joan, but she is forever haunted by Kati's memory, the memory of the only moments of true happiness she ever had, and by the nagging question of what might have happened had they both run away together.[18]

Years later, Judit succumbs to a physical condition that leaves her progressively paralyzed, and a mental condition whereby she finally loses all touch with reality. Judit therefore dies in spirit long before she dies physically. Roig has stated, in an interview, that Judit's condition is representative of women's oppressed state in postwar Spain: "Judit era un poco paralítica porque las mujeres aquí se volvieron paralíticas" (Nichols 1989, 159) [Judit was a little paralyzed because women here became paralyzed]. Judit's spiritual death is marked when she decides to stop writing her diary. Judit's last diary entry, in 1950, years before her physical death in 1964, describes how she is haunted by the memory of Kati, in terms that suggest that Kati was the only true love of her life.

Judit's estrangement from reality at the end of her life echoes Elaine Showalter's analysis, in *The Female Malady,* that "madness is the price women artists have had to pay for the exercise of their creativity in a male-dominated culture" (1985, 4). Judit had hoped to exercise her creativity, to create her own music, but she had not been able to do so because of the stifling society in which she was forced to live after the war. Therefore her madness may be seen to emerge not so much from the exercise of her creativity in a male-dominated world, but from the *impossibility* of doing so. Roig is fully aware of the importance of the name Judit in this context, for in her essay "L'un i l'altra" [One and the Other], she evokes Virginia Woolf's invention of Judith Shakespeare. Judith, William's fictional sister, was more talented than her brother and would have been an even more brilliant poet than William Shakespeare had she been allowed to write. As Roig states, in a phrase that brings to mind the story of Natàlia's mother: "la història de la germana poeta de Shakespeare, morta sense haver escrit una sola línia, viu en totes les dones" (1991a, 75) [the story of Shakespeare's sister who was a poet, who died without having written a single line, lives in all women].[19] Silence and frustration marked Judit's life. The most appropriate way to represent her story, therefore, is to inscribe a similar silence and frustration into the very narrative that recounts her experience.

Despite the obvious love that united Judit and Kati, their story is only reproduced piecemeal in the fragmented set of disjointed texts that make up Norma's novel, which is placed at the center of Roig's work. The real nature of their relationship (a possible, maybe even realized, perhaps only dreamed of, and probably completely repressed lesbian affair) hovers over the text, haunts it, but is never entirely clarified. As Catherine Davies has pointed out, this narrative is thus spun around a "structural void" a hermeneutical gap that frustrates our attempt to *see* clearly and to understand fully (1994, 56). We are left only with a partial view of what happened, somewhat blinded, like Judit's doll, with no eyes to truly see.

This blindness at the heart of the story that Norma's novel was supposed to elucidate and clarify for us is a reminder that any vision of the past is always partial, incomplete, and fragmented. That her story is presented as a series of disparate texts not pulled together by any overarching and dominant point of view highlights the constructedness and instability of all visions of the past. We can never "see" perfectly what happened in the past, we can only catch fleeting glimpses, and then arbitrarily try to pull them together. Memory is never complete, something always remains beyond the frame. It is a necessarily "unsatisfied" memory that emereges here. Understanding the necessarily incomplete and disordered nature of memory is what allows it to become an effective strategy against the imposed order of official history. Natàlia is fully aware of this subversive potential of memory as it is explored in a creative text, such as Norma's, that does not attempt to cover up its inconsistencies or impose a semblance of order on its disarray: "tot és fet a base de retalls fraccionats que a poc a poc formen una narració íntima, la del record. L'ordre que prenen els records dins de la memòria personal no són mai ni cronològics ni coherents. Si ho encertes, de vegades les paraules t'ajuden a lligar-los per a formar-ne una 'història'" (1993, 89) [everything is done based on selected remnants, that, little by little, form an intimate narration, that of memory. And the order that these remembrances follow in memory is never chronological, nor coherent. If you succeed, words may sometimes help you to tie them together and form a "story"].[20] The "historia" that is re-created, which is neither chronological nor coherent, is thus one that resists the dominant constructions of history not only through the previously neglected content it presents, but by means of its very narrative form. This is why Natàlia claims that "el temps dins de la memòria no té res a veure amb el temps de la història" (1993, 89) [the time of interior memory has nothing to do with the time of history].[21] She further claims that "l'ordre de la imaginació s'escapa a totes les dades, a tots els fets. Aquesta és la revenja de la literatura contra la Història" (1993, 89) [the order of imagination goes beyond all facts, all events. That is literature's revenge against History].[22] Imagination, as will become increasingly clear, is necessarily allied with memory in this exploration of the past that is subversive of dominant constructions of official history.

This combination of imagination and memory will, in fact, create a "countermemory," or "effective history," in Foucault's formulation. As seen in the last chapter, such a "countermemory" is largely characterized by its introduction of discontinuity and previously marginal elements into narrative accounts of the past, something that is at the heart of Norma's re-creation of Judit and Kati's story. Using a visual metaphor that is relevant to Roig's weaving together of images of sight and recollection, Foucault claims that such a subversive "countermemory" "corresponds to the acuity of a glance that distinguishes, separates, and disperses, that is capable of liberating divergence and marginal elements—the kind of dissociating view that is capable of decomposing itself, capable of shattering the unity of man's being through which it was thought that he could extend his sovereignty to the events of the past" (1977, 153). The text that Norma has produced certainly presents such a "dissociating view" in its disordered textual presentation. By revolving around a fundamental absence, the absence of the realization of their dreams of power and happiness, the recreation of Judit and Kati's life also reflects another element of Foucault's "countermemory," namely, that it "confirms our existence among countless lost events, without a landmark or a point of reference" (1977, 155).

Judit's last diary entry is very significant, as mentioned earlier, for it presents Kati as the only true love of Judit's life, a love that haunts and torments her. In that last journal entry, about twenty years after Kati's suicide, Judit writes: "De vegades sento la seva ànima que em ronda i en diu, tornaré, Judit, tornaré, i ja no hi haurà res que en separarà, ni cap llei ni cap guerra, converteix-me en allò que vulguis . . . omple la casa del meu fantasma, Judit, . . . no em treguis de tu, Judit, amor de la meva vida, amor de la meva mort" (1993, 144) [Sometimes I feel that her soul is with me and tells me, I will return, Judit, I will return, and there will no longer be anything that will separate us, no law, no war, turn me into whatever you want, Judit. . . . Fill the house with my ghost, Judit, . . . don't take me out of you, Judit, love of my life, love of my death].[23] Judit responds to this imagined plea from Kati, "converteix-me en allò que vulguis" [turn me into whatever you want], "omple la casa del meu fantasma" [fill the house with my ghost], by adopting the doll mentioned earlier; the doll to which Judit became increasingly, obsessively attached as she progressively deteriorated; the doll that she blinded by taking out its eyes, while at the same time constantly caressing and caring for it. This doll is a fetish, an object through which Judit recognizes and at the same time denies Kati's absence, in the double and contradictory logic typical of all fetishes.

Within a psychoanalytical framework, and according to Freud, the fetish is an object that a young boy may become fixated upon when he first discovers that his mother, until then the symbol of absolute power for him, has no phallus. This perceived lack suffered by his mother triggers the fear, in the young boy, that he himself may also suffer castration. In response to such overwhelming anxiety, the boy fixates on an object, a fetish, which will substitute for the mother's phallus. This fetish is thus invested with an incompatible double logic for, as Freud explains, "both the disavowal and affirmation of the castration have found their way into the construction of the fetish itself" (1961b, 156). That is to say, a fetish involves two opposite yet simultaneous beliefs, two contrary ways of looking at the same phenomenon, one that accepts castration (that of the mother and thus, potentially of the boy himself), and the other that denies it. For Freud, of course, only a boy would usually develop such fetishism since the girl, already lacking the phallus, would not face the same fear of castration upon first perceiving her mother's "lack." As will be seen, however, in an expanded notion of fetishism, a girl may develop a similar double logic around a fetish object.

In Judit's case, the doll is only one of the many fetishes with which she decides to surround herself after the war. It is very significant that she declares her desire to accumulate all types of fetishes immediately following a passage in which she expresses how much she misses Kati, and after she has compared herself unfavorably to her friend. Judit laments that while Kati preferred to die before having to renounce the freedom, autonomy, and power as a woman that she enjoyed and which she would have lost once the Fascists gained power, she herself renounced that freedom and meekly adjusted to the submissive role she was expected to take up in Franco's Spain. Although Judit was originally from a Jewish French family, she converted to Catholicism in order to fit in. We are told, in *El temps de les cireres:* "ella [Judit] no era [valenta] com la Kati, és cert, i per això anava a missa amb en Joan i els nens i tornava dòcilment a casa quan no la deixaven entrar a l'església perquè no duia mitges" (1977a, 160) [She [Judit] was not [brave] like Kati, it is true, and that is why she went to mass with Joan and the children and returned home meekly when they did not allow her to enter the church because of not wearing stockings].[24]

Judit's docile return home contrasts sharply and painfully with the freedom to do exactly what she wanted, with no concern for what others thought, that she had experienced with Kati before and during the war. Patricia remembers how jealous she was of the sense of power and freedom that Judit and Kati felt when they were together, especially of how they experienced such a feeling in the midst of war, when she was so frightened of everything around her: "confesso que sentia molta enveja d'aquelles hores que passaven plegades, i també me'n feia que no tinguessin por" (1993, 117) [I confess that I was very envious of those hours they spent together, and also of the fact that they were not afraid].[25] Patricia further recalls how, with Kati by her side, Judit seemed like a different person: "Encara que no parlava gaire. Només l'he vista xerrar pels descosits amb la Kati. Només amb ella el seu riure era d'alegria" (1993, 113) [Although she did not speak much. I only saw her speak non-stop with Kati. Only with her was her laughter a happy one].[26]

It is this lack of freedom, power, and joy in her life that Judit misses, as much as she misses Kati herself. Judit's desire to fill her house with fetishes is thus a way to compensate for her present powerlessness. In *El temps de les cireres,* immediately after learning about Judit being turned away from church, we are told: "La Judit s'enyorava de la Kati i va decidir que volia fetitxes, objectes de tota mena que ella venerava com a petits déus.... Omplirem la casa de fetitxes!, va dir a en Joan" (1977a, 160) [Judit missed Kati and she decided that she wanted fetishes, objects of all types that she would venerate as small gods.... We will fill the house with fetishes! she told Joan].[27]

The numerous dolls that Judit collects are her most prized fetishes, and among them, the one that she cares for the most, spending hours and hours caressing, is precisely the one whose eyes she has torn out. Besides blinding her favorite dolls, Judit further maims them by cutting off their arms: "Els fetitxes més importants foren les nines. La Judit passà una temporada molt llarga comprant nines, nines de totes mides, despullades o vestides, de goma, de cel·luloide, de porcellana.... La Judit els foradava els ulls i els trencava les mans. I, com més les feia patir, més les estimava" (1977a, 161) [And the most important fetishes were the dolls. Judit spent a long time buying dolls, dolls of all sizes, nude and dressed, made of rubber, of celluloid, of porcelain.... Judit tore out their eyes and broke their hands. And the more she made them suffer, the more she loved them].[28]

This contradictory behavior of caring for and at the same time harming the dolls she collects is not surprising, but rather is at the very heart of the logic of fetishism. As Freud states: "affection and hostility in the treatment of the fetish ... run parallel to the disavowal and acknowledgment of castration [that the fetish embodies]" (1961b, 157).

However, to understand the double, contradictory, nature of Judit's treatment of her favorite fetishes we must think of the notion of castration in a broader sense than Freud used it. Among many feminist reformulations of the logic of the fetish, Elisabeth Grosz's presentation in her article "Lesbian Fetishism?" is helpful here, for it points to what is at stake in Judit's behavior. Contradicting Freud's belief that it is really not possible for a woman to be a fetishist, Grosz explains that in women, fetishism may be associated with homosexuality. In the case of the girl, the anxiety of discovering the mother's lack of the phallus may lead her to fixate on a fetish not so much to affirm her *possession* of a phallus, as in the case of the boy, but to affirm her desire to *be* the phallus, thus supposedly usurping the male position. However, what is ultimately at stake in this fetishistic negotiation is a more general anxiety about power and powerlessness, an anxiety that all women in a patriarchal society inevitably suffer. As Grosz explains: "Disavowal ... is by no means unique to men; it is a defense mechanism open and available to women. Its operations ... function as a form of protection, though not, as in the case of boys, against potential loss, but against the personal debasement and the transformation of her status from subject to object, active to passive.... It is a strategy of self-protection, even if it implies a certain mode of detachment from socio-symbolic 'reality' " (1991, 49–50).

Judit decides to start collecting fetishes precisely at the moment in which her longing for Kati, and everything that Kati represented, becomes unbearable for her. These fetishes are objects that evoke the reality of lesbian longing that remains unvoiced even in the re-creation of Judit's life, via Norma, that we read in Roig's novel. These fetishes, furthermore, allow Judit to recover a sense of power like that she experienced while being with her friend. They allow her to regain the sense of being an active subject she had felt for that short period of time. However, the very fact of *needing* a fetish to provide oneself with such a sense of power is a reminder that such power has been lost, that it is no more than an illusion. The incomplete nature of the fetishes, the lost eyes, the broken arms, symbolizes the incomplete recovery of power they offer. The very objects that serve to make Judit feel powerful and whole again are themselves partial and broken. As Emily Apter explains, what is at stake in this kind of female fetishism is an unending process of "oscillating between illusory mastery on the one hand and phantasms of lack . . . on the other" (1991, 13). It is significant, in this respect, that even within the very experience of plenitude and power that Judit experienced in her relationship with Kati, a certain lack was always present. We may recall that when Kati was encouraging Judit to write the music she so wanted to produce, she told her to create that "música callada" [silent music] that she carried inside herself. It is a music marked by lack, a "silent music," that Judit would produce if she could. Like the contradictory logic of the fetish itself, Judit's full and creative realization of her artistic talent would be one inevitably marked by lack.

It has been said that "a fetish is a story masquerading as an object" (qtd. in Gamman and Makinen 1994, 1). The fetishes with which Judit obsessively surrounds herself at the end of her life are, indeed, objects that want to tell a story. It is the story of an attempt to recover a lost love, as well as a lost sense of personal realization, power, and control over one's own destiny. At the same time, however, it is the story of the complete loss of such power and love.[29]

A fetish, therefore, always represents a double and contradictory process. It allows one to overcome a deep sense of loss and regain a sense of power through its use, but, at the same time, it underscores, by its very existence, the unreal nature of that victory. This is what leads Emily Apter to claim that the fetish functions "entirely in the realm of simulacrum" (1991, 13). It is only a simulacrum of mastery and power, of complete engagement with reality, that the fetish provides. We can only truly learn to read Judit's story masquerading as these objects, these fetishes, when we learn to unravel the contradictory threads bound together in the logic of the fetish.

This fetishism that works "entirely in the realm of simulacrum" is important to understand the very fetishistic function of the dolls, wounded as well as loved, mutilated as well as pampered, that Judit had accumulated after Kati's demise. There is yet another form of simulacrum in the text, a series of photographs, whose fetishistic double nature is likewise important to understand the way in which the oscillation of contradictory drives functions in the novel-within-the-novel that we read, the text created by Norma to tell Judit and Kati's story.

There is an interesting section of "La novel·la de l'hora violeta" [The novel of the violet hour], narrated by Patricia, Judit's sister-in-law, which is rather incongruously placed among Judit's own diary entries and the excerpts from Kati's letters. Patricia's narration, like she herself, seems to be out of place in the intimate presence of the two friends. In this section, many anecdotes of Judit's life and her friendship with Kati are told, and sometimes re-told (as some of those anecdotes are also related elsewhere in Roig's novels) from Patricia's perspective. It is a narration that takes place at the moment of Judit's death, and, more specifically, at the moment that Patricia is accompanying the undertaker as he looks over Judit's corpse while planning for her burial. Judit has been placed in her favorite room, surrounded by all her fetishes: her dolls, her knick-knacks, her many, many photographs.

As the undertaker walks around the room, looking at the photos, Patricia recounts the story of each picture: "Aquesta foto és de quan la Judit i els seus papàs vivien a Narbona" (1993, 113) [This photo is from when Judit and her parents lived in Narbonne]; "En aquest retrat, la Judit hi toca l'harpa amb la cabellera tota estesa" (1993, 114) [In this portrait Judit is playing the harp with her hair down]; "Aquí, la Judit mira cap endavant amb la mirada apagada i els cabells, que li cauen en petites onades, li fan de corona" (1993, 114) [Here Judit is looking straight ahead with her gaze extinguished, and her hair, which falls in small waves, is like a crown], and so forth.[30] All of this is not done for the benefit of the undertaker, however, for it is clear that the narration is an interior monologue, destined for no one but Patricia herself. Consistent with the double nature, the contradictory logic of the fetish, this narration is thus told and not told at the same time.

The issue of a double perspective, which, as we have seen, is at the heart of the logic of the fetish, is highlighted from the very beginning of this section. Patricia describes the undertaker's face, mentioning a scar that can be seen in two different ways: "L'enterramorts té cremada la banda esquerra de la cara. Uns grumolls de color lila sobresurten entre les arrugues. Sembla la lluna vista de prop, la lluna que jo m'imagino, tan bonica de lluny i que deu ser fastigosa si t'hi acostes" (1993, 111) [The undertaker has the left side of his face burnt. Some purple pimples stand out among the wrinkles. It looks like the moon seen from up close, the moon as I imagine it, so beautiful from afar, although it must be disgusting if you approach it].[31] Another example of something that can be seen in two different ways emerges when Patricia elaborately describes the first photograph as being of Judit and her husband, only to realize later that the picture is really of Judit's parents. These images of undecidability, of oscillation between different interpretations, are presented at the very beginning of this section, and are fundamental for understanding the importance of the photographs in this part of the novel.

For photographs themselves are bound to a double, contradictory logic themselves, one that Roland Barthes has eloquently analyzed in his meditation on photography, *Camera Lucida*. There is an unresolvable "oscillation" between presence and absence in a photograph. The photograph undeniably guarantees that the object photographed was there at some point, the deictic function of the photograph affirming such presence in what Barthes calls the "that-has-been" of the photographed object. However, as Barthes explains, "It has been there and yet immediately separated, it has been absolutely, irrefutably present and yet already deferred" (1981, 77). He further explains this double logic in words borrowed from Blanchot: "the essence of the image is to be . . . unrevealed yet manifest, having that absence-as-presence which constitutes the lure and fascination of the sirens" (1981, 106).

This absence-as-presence, this fetishistic oscillation between contradictory functions that constitutes the lure of a photograph, is strategically placed within the novel as a whole.[32] For this section is exactly in the middle of "la novel·la de l'hora violeta," which, in turn, is exactly in the middle of *L'hora violeta*. As a photograph itself, therefore, "la novela de la hora violeta," written by Norma to recount Judit's life, is "framed," as has been mentioned earlier, within Roig's novel by two chapters on either side. Norma's novel-within-the-novel, furthermore, has perfectly centered within itself, as in a visual composition, this section narrated by Patricia in which she again tells Judit's life as a series of descriptions of photographs. The presence-as-absence function of the photographs is all the more significant as this re-creation of Judit's life, this making her present, is taking place at the very moment of her disappearance, of her death. "Death is the eidos of the photograph" (1981, 15) claims Barthes and this "return of the dead" (1981, 9) that he sees underlying the illusion of presence in the photograph is clearly evidenced in this narration at the heart of "la novel·la de l'hora violeta."

The oscillation between presence and absence in this scene is enacted on yet another level of the text. The photographs themselves that Patricia describes are present to us, the readers, only in the indirect form of her verbal descriptions. They are thus simultaneously present and absent in the text. We never do see the photographs themselves, only the words that Patricia uses to describe them. We can thus never be absolutely sure of what those photographs portrayed. Presence and absence, life and death, are irreconcilably intertwined here on a number of levels, in a vertiginous oscillation which is better left unresolved, accepted in all its contradictoriness, as a way to achieve what Naomi Schor calls the "strategic appropriation of the undecidability of fetishism" (1995, 106). Undecidability, indeed, marks the recuperation of Judit's life and the very functioning of memory within the novel, reminding us that often what we most want and desire to rescue from the past remains unattainable even as we recover it. This is an important way in which Roig's novel manages to think memory and forgetting together, instead of opposing them. It is also a way in which the text produces a radically "unsatisfied" memory.

There is a final level at which such undecidability functions in this section of Roig's novel. Ultimately, we as readers never know for sure if what we are reading in "La novel·la de l'hora violeta" is an exact transcription of the texts that Norma received from Natàlia (including Judit's diary, Kati's letters, and Patricia's narration), or if it is Norma's novelistic re-creation of these documents. We are told, later in the text, that Norma has finished writing her novel about Judit and Kati, and thus we are led to assume that this central section of Roig's novel is at least a partial representation of Norma's project. Yet perhaps what we read is not Norma's novelistic re-creation but the original, unchanged documents themselves. There is a fundamental undecidability, left completely unresolved, as to who is really speaking in this section. This is one more way in which Roig's meta-memory text presents the questioning of any direct access to the past in its very narrative form. Memory is always mediated. It is inevitably based on the interpretation of texts, and it is not always clear whose mediation we are subject to when we take on the task of remembering the past.

Memory here is presented by a chorus of voices from the past which have perhaps, or perhaps not, been subsumed under one overarching voice, that of Norma in the present. This undecidability is subversive in itself. It evokes the resistance of those multiple voices, which ultimately form a fragmentary and kaleidoscopic narrative that overflows any one single perspective. However, even if the re-creation of Judit and Kati's story that we read were Norma's rewriting, it is still presented in different narrative forms from multiple people's perspectives.

The memory of the past is thus presented in a manner that recalls the de-naturalizing strategy that characterized María Teresa León's autobiography. This strategy presents the kind of dialogical, multivoiced form that Bakhtin believed created a "verbal and semantic decentering of the ideological world" (1981, 367). In "Voces y diálogos" [Voices and Dialogues], Roig claims that literature can enact such an ideological de-centering precisely through a similar dialogical presentation of multiple voices: "la literatura, a mi parecer, todavía tiene una función que nada puede sustituir: la de liberar las voces del mundo, las voces antiguas frente a la VOZ, la que brota en el altar de nuestros hogares, la que coacciona nuestra imaginación, privándonos de la libertad de soñar por cuenta propia" (1989b, 80) [literature, in my opinion, still has a role that nothing can substitute: to free the voices of the world, the old voices, in the face of the VOICE, the one that emerges from the altar of our homes, that restricts our imagination, denying us the right to dream for ourselves]. Norma, in fact, seems to refer to such a dialogical view of the world, one that accepts multiple perspectives to counter any unitary vision, when she exclaims that "tenemos la obligación de no tratar la realidad desde un solo punto de vista. Tenemos que buscar todas las piezas" (1993, 97) [We have the obligation of not treating reality from one single point of view. We have to look for all the pieces]. A narrative that produces an ideological de-centering seems to be precisely what Norma is trying to produce.

It is interesting to note that for Natàlia, the documents she finds regarding Judit and Kati (which she passes on to Norma in order for her to write her novel about the two women) become, in turn, a kind of fetish for her. They provide her with a sense of being able to create a connection with her mother, to discover the strong, vibrant, powerful young woman she once was, while at the same time underscoring how much she never really did know her mother in life. Natàlia, too, is caught in a process of endless oscillation between feeling empowered by her efforts at unearthing the story of her mother and Kati, while at the very same time feeling disempowered as she realizes that she cannot manage to make that story compatible with her own deep estrangement from the sullen, silent, and demented mother she herself knew. The documents about her mother's life trigger completely contradictory and incompatible feelings in Natàlia, as all fetishes do. This contradictory, fetishistic relation to the process of writing her mother's life becomes apparent when Natàlia recognizes "si la meva mare fos viva, escriure sobre ella podria ser un intent de reconciliació 'real'. Però, a què treu cap escriure sobre la mamà, reescriure-la més ben dit, si ja és morta?" (1993, 15) [if my mother were still living, writing about her would be an attempt at a "real" reconciliation. However, what is the point of writing about Mother, rewriting I should say, if she is already dead?].³³ Illusion and disillusion, empowerment and disenchantment, engagement and lack of engagement with her past are all inextricably intertwined for Natàlia in her endeavor.

This ambivalent logic, which has been seen to dominate the representation of the history of Judit and Kati in the novel, is also important in depicting Natàlia and Norma's story which frames the tale of the previous generation. This frame reflects the ambivalent nature of the transition to democracy that they are experiencing, a time period that likewise oscillates between hope and disenchantment.

The "desencanto" [disenchantment] experienced in Spain after the initial enthusiasm over the return of democracy was due, in part, to the way in which the political parties that emerged after Franco's death followed a strategy of pacts. These were devised in order to build an apparent consensus that would maintain political and social stability. The "Pactos de la Moncloa" were the most notable example. These pacts were often arranged behind the scenes by the party elites, leaving the rank-and-file members, indeed most of the population, on the sidelines, often feeling as mere spectators despite, of course, their obvious participation in the democratic process through participation in the various elections. For many militants who had fought clandestinely against the Franco regime this was quite demoralizing. Just when they believed they could truly participate in politics freely, the process was in part taken out of their hands, as they were made to accept compromises negotiated by the party leaders with what seemed to be insufficient input from the rank-and-file members. This was particularly hard on those who belonged to the Communist Party, for it had been the major source of political opposition against the regime within Spain. Of course, the strategy of consensus was in part necessary because many of the key players in the transition had been important figures in the regime, and many of the social forces and institutions of Francoism maintained much of their power after Franco's death. Alberto Medina Domínguez, in his cultural study of the transition, *Exorcismos de la memoria: Políticas y poéticas de la melancolía en la España de la transición* (*Exorcisms of Memory: The Politics and Poetry of Melancholia in the Spain of the Transition*), explains how the "desencanto" emerged in large part because many began to feel that with the end of Francoism they also eventually faced the end of their dreams for radical social change. As he explains, "El fin del franquismo va a ser simultáneo a la pérdida del proyecto de liberación que lo acompañó, a la esperanza misma de emancipación. Ése es el núcleo del ubicuo 'leitmotif' de la transición, el llamado 'desencanto' " (2001, 19) [The end of Francoism will be simultaneous with the end of the liberation project that had accompanied it, of the very hope of emancipation. That is the nucleus of the ubiquitous "leit-motif" of the transition, the so-called "disenchantment"].

This is the process that Roig chronicles in *L'hora violeta* within the frame of the novel set in 1979. Natàlia's lover, Jordi, and Norma's husband, Ferran, both devoted members of the Communist Party, see their faith in the party radically shaken. This causes both of them to experience major identity crises, crises that Natàlia and Norma also suffer. Jordi claims at one point: "s'ha acabat l'època de les grans revolucions, ara cal sobreviure, resistir" (1993, 57) [The time of grand revolutions is over, now it is a matter of surviving, of resisting].[34] This loss of their revolutionary ideals becomes one of the recurrent themes of their conversations. Natàlia comments on how prevalent the topic has become since the first time they started expressing such disillusionment: "Va ser una de les primeres converses en què començàrem a parlar del desengany. (Ara en parlem tant que ja sembla una llauna)" (1993, 46) [It was one of the first conversations in which we began to speak about the disenchantment (now we talk so much about it that it has become a pain)].[35] At another point, Jordi comes back from a meeting of the Communist Party and begins to cry because of what he sees as a selling out, on the part of the party leaders, of all he has believed in and worked for. Natàlia complains, "Però la crisi esclatà quan es va legalitzar el partit. De què havien servit tants anys de lluita i lliurament si la política esdevenia només un afer de professionals? Sorgiren nous militants que assetjaren com voltors els millors càrrecs" (1993, 88) [But the crisis exploded when the party was legalized. What was the point of so many years of fighting and commitment if politics now became a matter only for professionals? New militants emerged that went after the best positions like vultures].[36] Natàlia again voices her disenchantment when she imagines how younger Spaniards will judge her generation: "Potser serà l'època del fracàs, o la dels babaus.... El que estic segura és que no ens admiraran, perquè no hi veuran cap obra" (1993, 61) [Maybe it will be the era of failure, or the era of the gullible ... I am sure that they will not admire us, because they will not see any achievement].[37]

Medina Domínguez comments on the posturing maintained by political parties trying to reconcile the very different positions they held in secret toward other parties and in public toward their militants. This led eventually to a generalized view among many Spaniards that all politics is but a cynical theatrical act: "La nueva identidad nacional es caracterizada desde el principio como el teatro privado de unos pocos ocupados en encandilar a la galería, al tiempo que la mantiene bien alejada del escenario. Al público no le es dado intervenir en la trama" (2001, 56) [The new national identity is characterized from the beginning as the private theater of a few engaged in enchanting the audience, at the same time that they maintain it far from the stage. The public cannot intervene in the play]. Within this context we can better understand Natàlia's view of her own behavior as a theatrical act that has lost sight of any real belief behind the posturing: "Sóc estrangera de qualsevol paper assignat. Em sembla que m'he passat la vida observant el que succeïa al meu davant com si algun déu m'hagués col·locat en una butaca de llotja. No hi puc fer més: no sóc dalt de l'escenari, on els actors s'acoblen perfectament als papers assignats, però tampoc en trobo bé al galliner, on el públic pot esbroncar si l'obra no és del seu grat" (1993, 64) [I feel distanced from every assigned role. I feel like I have spent my life observing what was happening around me, as if some god had placed me in a box seat at the theater. I can't do anything else: I am not on stage, where the actors identify perfectly with their assigned roles, but neither do I feel comfortable in the peanut gallery where the public can create a ruckus if they do not like the play].[38]

In this process of theatrical posturing, words seem to be emptied of their meaning. Parties often say one thing and do another, and people begin to lose any belief that words really correspond to their traditional referents.[39] Natàlia again seems to voice this disenchantment with language itself, when she claims "fa temps que sento les mateixes paraules, surten de les nostres boques, descriuen cercles com en una sínia i tornen al mateix punt de partida. Les paraules neixen i moren en un sentit de circumval·lació" (1993, 47) [For a long time I have been hearing the same words: they leave our mouths, run in circles as in a Ferris wheel, and return to their point of departure. Words are born and die in an endless circumvolution].[40] Norma feels a similar disenchantment with words when she complains: "Paraules, paraules que es repetien en cercles, que es repetien i que no ajudaven a viure" (1993, 229) [words, words that were being repeated in endless circles, that were being repeated and that did not help us to live].[41] Words seem to go around in circles, losing any connection to reality. Medina Domínguez describes this loss of faith in language itself during the transition as a "corrupción del lenguaje . . . la progresiva desvalorización del lenguaje, su apartamiento de la realidad. . . . La praxis política es sostenida por un juego verbal que no le corresponde" (2001, 64) [corruption of language . . . the progressive devalorization of language, its distancing from reality. . . . Political praxis is sustained by a verbal play that does not correspond to reality].[42] And yet there is still enough of a desire on people's part to view the transition as a meaningful process so that a complete rejection of politics never takes place. After all, elections are held regularly and the results of those elections are, indeed, honored. An unresolved ambivalence thus characterizes the time period. It is significant that Medina Domínguez describes this ambivalent feeling with the image of the oscillating nature of fetishism, an image he connects to the self-awareness of politics as theatrical posturing, both elements that Roig presents in her novel:

> Todos sabemos que este maravilloso espacio de reconciliación y unidad nacional no es más que simulación de sí mismo, pero qué necesidad hay de levantar la máscara. El teatro es condición necesaria para una pacífica convivencia. . . . La política queda reducida a fetiche televisivo que oculta un lugar de falta cuyo reconocimiento resultaría demasiado traumático. La nueva actitud del ciudadano viene marcada por la cínica sentencia del fetichista: *je sais bien, mais quand même.* . . . (2001, 64, 67)

> [We all know that this marvelous space of reconciliation and national unity is nothing more than a simulacrum of itself, but why lift the mask. Theater is the necessary condition for a peaceful coexistence. . . . Politics is reduced to a television fetish that hides a lack, the recognition of which would be too traumatic. The new behavior of citizens is marked by the cynical phrase of the fetishist: I know very well, and yet. . . .]

The sentence "I know very well, and yet," the title of Octave Mannoni's study on fetishism, captures perfectly the ambivalence and contradictory logic that can be seen to run through both the depiction of the transition period in Roig's novel and the presentation of the earlier story of Judit and Kati that Natàlia and Norma are trying to re-create at that time. In fact, the disenchantment with regard to the possibility of a radical political and social change in the Spain of the transition was due not only to the growing sense that politics was becoming a cynical theatrical act, but to the realization that a real confrontation with, and compensation for, the past of repression suffered by so many during the civil war and the Franco regime were being effectively circumvented by all the theatrical political posturing. It is to combat this element of the transition's disenchantment that Norma takes on the project of writing a testimonial account of the experience of Catalan ex-deportees to German concentration camps, just like she decides to write the story of Judit and Kati.[43] Like this latter story, marked by a series of gazes that point to, without being able to present fully, the pain of a past traumatic experience (the empty gazes of Judit's blind doll and of Judit herself after the war), Norma's other project of recuperating memory through writing will emerge under the effect of a similarly haunting gaze.

Norma writes a letter asking to interview a Catalan ex-deportee to Mauthausen who, she has been told, has important information about the camp, and about the experience of Catalan prisoners there, which could help her in her project. The old man lives in Paris, where he has spent long years in exile. With the presence of these exiled concentration camp survivors that Norma interviews, it becomes clear that the recuperation of memory in Roig's text is inseparable from exile, from the various kinds of exile, in fact, that have been represented in the texts analyzed in the previous chapters. From the exile suffered by these concentration camp survivors, and that which Natàlia willingly chose for herself, to the inner exile suffered by her mother, all the memories that are being recovered here are somehow connected to one or another form of exile.[44] Exile, indeed, marks much of the repressed past that still needs to be recovered in Spain. Norma makes it clear that she believes in the necessity of making Spanish society aware of the story of these exiled concentration camp survivors: "crec que la història de la deportació dels nostres compatriotes ha de ser explicada, no la podem bandejar de la memòria col·lectiva" (1993, 187) [I believe the story of the deportation of our compatriots must be told, we cannot banish it from our collective memory].[45]

Despite her good intentions, however, Norma will discover that this story is much more difficult and painful to appropriately recover than she thought. She will struggle to find a way to remember and transmit such a story without being destroyed by it herself, and without betraying the unspeakable pain that it contains. Norma will have to work through a strong sense of ambivalence, an ambivalence similar to that which we have seen within other parts of Roig's novel, in which the attempt to recover a painful memory coexists with a desire to forget it and be freed from its grip. It is only by means of self-consciously working through the contradictory elements of this ambivalence that Norma will ultimately find a way to effectively recover the memory of the traumatic history she is exploring. Only then will she find the appropriate way to write about it.

The difficulties arise when Norma sees a memory much more painful than anything she imagined in the eyes of the ex-deportee. Underscoring the interrelated nature of the two projects she is writing, Norma thinks of her interview with the ex-deportees as she is writing her novel about Judit and Kati:

> Mentre intentava d'escriure la novel·la sobre la Judit i la Kati, la Norma pensava en el vell ex-deportat. . . . En aquelles converses, la Norma havia comprès que hi ha coses pitjors que la deportació, un camp d'extermini o les cambres de gas, i una d'elles és la vida que ha de dur un ex-deportat després d'haver estat alliberat. Els mires als ulls i t'adones que no hi ha res a fer. Res contra les nits d'insomni, les al·lucinacions, les escenes que es

repeteixen cada matinada, quan els altres no hi són, quan el cos i l'ànima d'un ex-deportat es concentren dins el punt indefugible i intransferible de la memòria. Els mires als ulls i veus què vol dir haver iniciat un camí sense retorn. Quan pensava en el vell amic ex-deportat, sobretot ara, en escriure la novel·la de la Judit i la Kati, la Norma es negava a fer literatura. (1993, 189)

[While she tried to write the novel about Judit and Kati, Norma thought of the old ex-deportee. . . . In those conversations, Norma understood that there are worse things than deportation, than an extermination camp, or than the gas chambers. And one of those things is the life that ex-deportees must lead after they have been liberated. You look at their eyes and you realize that there is nothing that can be done. Nothing against the nights of insomnia, the hallucinations, the scenes that repeat themselves at dawn, when no one else is around, when the body and soul of the ex deportee focus on an inescapable and intransferable memory. . . . When she thought about her old friend, the ex-deportee, especially now, while writing the novel about Judit and Kati, Norma refused to create literature.][46]

Norma discovers in the survivor's eyes one of the harshest realities about a traumatic experience. As Cathy Caruth explains about the aftermath of trauma: "it is not only the moment of the event, but of the passing out of it that is traumatic, . . . survival itself, in other words, can be a crisis" (1995, 9). Confronted with the eyes of the old Catalan ex-deportee, Norma thinks that she cannot afford to be literary in her account of the trauma that he, like so many others, has lived. Yet she soon realizes, also, that she cannot afford *not* to use some measure of inventiveness, because the real, historical experience of such a trauma will forever remain beyond her reach. As the old man repeats obsessively to her every time they meet, even as he hands her sheet after sheet of painstakingly recorded names, dates, and facts about the camps: "La veritat, no la sabreu mai" (1993, 193) [You will never know the truth].[47] Norma wants to be true to the historical experience of deportation while recognizing that the reality of what it meant will remain forever beyond her capacity to represent. Like Semprún writing about his experiences in Buchenwald, Norma discovers that she will have to find some form of artifice to make that reality comprehensible and representable.

The testimonial text that Norma will write, therefore, must be woven around a "structural void," somewhat like the structural void at the heart of Judit and Kati's story. This becomes the only way to reflect the nature of trauma, where oftentimes "a history can be grasped only in the very inaccessibility of its occurrence" (Caruth 1995, 8). Structuring the narrative of a traumatic experience around such a void, a lack of knowledge, is a way to further recognize the "fundamental dislocation implied by all traumatic experience that is both its testimony to the event and to the impossibility of its direct access" (Caruth 1995, 9). As Norma tries to find a way to present this "fundamental dislocation" in her writing, she discovers that she will also have to suffer a parallel kind of "dislocation" herself. Not until she becomes personally affected, and invested in, the story she is trying to tell will she be able to adequately address it. Not until she realizes that, although she may not have lived it directly, this story also affects her, will Norma be able to appropriately recover it, inasmuch as such a task is ever possible.

In the text that Roig herself had written about the camps three years before *L'hora violeta*, she underscores this fundamental limit in the capacity to understand the Holocaust that Norma is discovering. In *Els catalans als camps nazis* [*Night and fog: Catalans in the Nazi Camps*], Roig openly affirms "Val a dir que després d'haver treballat durant tres anys en aquest llibre, no sé què és un camp d'extermini nazi. És impossible de fer-se'n una idea" (1977b, 20) [I want to make it very clear that, after having worked on this book for three years, I do not know what a Nazi extermination camp is. It is impossible to have any idea of what it was].[48] Again echoing Norma's experience, Roig declares that it was the eyes of one of the real-life survivors whom she interviewed that made her become aware of everything she would never be able to learn nor transmit effectively: "foren els ulls terriblement cansats de l'Amat-Piniella allò que més coses em van saber dir del què havia significat l'infern nazi" (1977b, 13) [it was the terribly tired eyes of Amat-Piniella that were able to tell me the most about what the Nazi hell had meant].[49] In fact, it is this real-life survivor of a German concentration camp that first tells Roig what the ex-deportee in the novel will later tell Norma: "la veritat, la veritat, no la sabria mai" (1977b, 13) [the truth, the truth, you will never know it].[50] As has been mentioned earlier, Roig's extraliterary writing and her novelistic creations blend into each other, generating a productive "dislocation" of the fine line between historical and fictional writing.

The fine line between life and death is also effectively "dislocated" in the experience of trauma, as survival becomes a form of crisis and life after the traumatic event becomes a form of death. This is something that Semprún repeatedly expresses in his writing about Buchenwald, and it is reflected in the story of another one of the Mauthausen survivors that Norma interviews in *L'hora violeta*. Many years after his liberation, this survivor commits suicide. It is clear that the memory of his experience in the camp has haunted him incessantly since his liberation, for he dies while listening to the story of his deportation that he himself had recorded years before: "Havia deixat el magnetòfon engegat i va morir mentre sentia el seu propi relat: 'Quan vaig entrar a Mauthausen, vaig comprendre l'infern del Dante...'" (1993, 191) [He had left the tape recorder on and he died listening to his own tale: 'when I entered Mauthausen, I understood Dante's inferno...'"].[51] Life and death are inextricably connected at this moment, and the fact that the survivor is effectively "re-living" his deportation at the very moment of his death implies that the experience never did become a part of his past, that it remained perpetually present for him. This, in fact, is one of the terrible realities of trauma: "Trauma survivors live not with memories of the past, but with an event that could not and did not proceed through to its completion, has no ending, attained no closure, and, therefore, as far as its survivors are concerned, continues into the present and is current in every respect" (Felman and Laub 1992, 69).

This is another form of "dislocation" that Norma will have to suffer in her search for the appropriate way to present the stories of the ex-deportees she is interviewing. Not until she truly realizes the extent to which their story is, indeed, "current in every respect," current and relevant for her even though she may not have lived it, will she be able to produce the testimonial writing of their experience. Recovering the memory of their experience cannot be a form of attaining "closure" with regard to the past, as Norma at first hopes, for their story is one that, by its traumatic nature, "has no ending." How to recover a traumatic and previously repressed historical experience without attaining such a false sense of closure is the great challenge Norma faces here, and the challenge that Roig herself takes up in much of her writing. In *Els catalans als camps nazis,* Roig explicitly states the importance of this lack of closure, while acknowledging, as she has done elsewhere, the importance of recognizing that such projects are the products of many voices, never of a single, unitary voice: "aquest llibre no és més que la coordinació de totes aquestes veus: totes elles formen una con-vincent presència col·lectiva. De tota manera, cal dir que és un llibre obert, una obra que haurà de ser continuada, revisada i ampliada" (1977b, 13) [this book is only the coordination of all these voices, they all form a convincing collective presence. In any case, I have to say that it is an open book, a text that must be continued, revised, and expanded].[52] Like Semprún imagining the endless layers of writing he will need to add to the first blank Spanish copy of *Le grand voyage,* or León ending her autobiography with the capitalized announcement "CONTINUARÁ" [TO BE CONTINUED], or Benet claiming, in *Volverás a Región,* that "la memoria mantiene abierta la cuenta," Roig recognizes that a project such as hers cannot reach any final point of completion. Such a project will necessarily be a palimpsest, always open to new layers of inscription as new perspectives of a previously repressed past are uncovered.

If Norma, like Roig herself had done before, wants to communicate something of the suffering of these victims of History with a capital H, if she wants to "enlarge the picture of history" as Joan Scott expressed it, to include the experiences of such marginalized and victimized people, she will have to recognize that a definitive, completely true and accurate account is simply not possible. She will have to accept that she cannot simply rescue their experience from oblivion and make it finally and completely visible for all. This acknowledgment is all the more significant since, in *L'hora violeta,* the survivor who tells her that she will never know "the truth" about the camp is the same person who gives her countless lists he has compiled with endless facts concerning his fellow deportees to Mauthausen. He keeps these lists religiously, a deluge of historical information that is nevertheless unable to present the "truth" of the experience:

> No hi faltava ningú: el nom, data d'entrada al camp, data de trasllat al camp annex, número de matrícula, data de la mort. Nom darrera nom, desenes, centenars, milers de noms. . . . Noms desconeguts que no existien per a la història. Ningú no els reclamaria. No tenien cos, no tenien cadàver. No tindrien un nínxol on serien enterrats, ni làpida individual. Ni flors. Res. (1993, 192)

> [No one was missing: the name, the date of entry into the camp, the date of transfer to the next camp, the identity number, the date of death. Name after name, tens, hundreds, thousands of names. . . . Unknown names that did not exist for history. No one would reclaim them. They did not have a body, they did not have a corpse. They did not have a niche in which to be buried, nor a personal tombstone. Nor flowers. Nothing.][53]

We find here an image that has appeared in all the texts analyzed in previous chapters: the ghostly presence of the victims of traumatic historical experiences that have been denied proper burial. Granting some form of a proper burial becomes one of the main functions of texts such as Roig's. Labanyi claims, in discussing texts such as Roig's which attempt to recover previously repressed and marginalized histories, that "ghosts, as the traces of those who have not been allowed to leave a trace . . . are by definition the victims of history who return to demand reparation; that is, that their name, instead of being erased, be honored" (2000, 66). Norma's writing, like María Teresa León's autobiography, will serve as a symbolic cemetery, a place to provide some form of "reparation" through remembrance. By providing a place to remember all these unmarked deaths, Norma's text will necessarily embody a form of what Foucault calls "countermemory" which, as seen earlier with respect to Norma's novel about Judit and Kati, is a way of recalling the past that "confirms our existence among countless lost events, without a landmark or a point of reference" (1977, 155).

Norma will also visit a real cemetery that serves a similar function. The ex-deportee she has been interviewing invites her to go with him to the inauguration of a cemetery in the south of France for the Republican Spaniards who died in exile. Built originally on the site of one of the French concentration camps for Spanish Republican soldiers leaving Spain at the end of the civil war, the cemetery had been abandoned and ruined for many years. It had been invaded by weeds and wild shrubs until the tombs had effectively disappeared and the small buildings around it had been destroyed. This cemetery thus evokes an image of ruin similar to that of the old tombstones dotting the landscape, ruined embodiments of a vision of history as catastrophe, in Benet's *Volverás a Región*. The clearing and reconstruction of the Republican cemetery Norma visits, allowing for the names on each tomb to become visible once again, serve as a symbolic form of remembrance not only for the exiles physically buried there, but for all those other exiles, named in the lists of the ex-deportee whom Norma is interviewing, who did not even have the chance to have an engraved tomb to mark their death in Mauthausen. These names may be absent in the real Republican cemetery, but they are present in the memory of the ex-deportee. Again, as in so many aspects of Roig's text, presence and absence are intertwined, and the recovery of a previously forgotten past is made possible only by acknowledging an inevitable absence and lack at the heart of this very process.

This is why, in the middle of the inauguration ceremony, a powerful silence suddenly emerges: "les paraules ja no servien i ara el silenci ho cobria tot. Només la remor del vent més enllà de les vinyes, una remor suau que baixava de les muntanyes. Potser era el murmuri dels morts, que retornavan ara per a sentir-se acompanyats" (1993, 212) [words were of no more use and then silence surrounded everything. Only the rumor of the wind beyond the vines, a soft murmur that descended from the mountains. Maybe it was the murmur of the dead, who returned now in order to feel that they were accompanied by others].[54] Norma imagines that the ghosts of the people buried in the cemetery have returned now that they feel that others remember them, and she likewise sees the exiles who have come to honor their fallen comrades as living ghosts themselves: "Els fantasmes acompanyaven la remor dels morts que no tenien nom. Els fantasmes avançaven i reculaven, feien la roda. No deien res, només uns ulls esbatanats que no es podien cloure. Nosaltres no oblidem, feien els ulls, deia la remor" (1993, 212)

[The ghosts accompanied the rumor of the dead that had no name. The ghosts advanced and receded around her in unison. Without saying a word, only their bulging eyes that could not be closed. We do not forget, said the eyes, repeated the rumor].[55] The eyes of these living ghosts have a deep silence and emptiness within them, like the eyes of the ex-deportee Norma is interviewing, or the eyes of Judit's blinded doll and of Judit herself after the war. This is perhaps why Norma cannot separate both projects, and why they both require a similar strategy of inscribing this silence and emptiness into her very writing. In so doing, Norma will have to acknowledge the way in which these gazes address her directly, changing her position from impartial observer of their story to its addressee. Norma's writing process will effectively transform her into a secondary witness to trauma herself, not just a reporter, and this change will be difficult for her to accept. This change implies a greater sense of responsibility in the face of the past than she was at first willing to accept.

Norma begins to feel how the story of the ex-deportees she is writing affects her own life when she returns home from the visit to the cemetery and cannot forget the images of the ghostly exiles walking among the tombs. She acknowledges that "les penes dels ex-deportats havien quedat ben endintre de [ella]" (1993, 199) [the sadness of the ex-deportees remained deep inside [her]].[56] One night, she tells her two sons the story of salmon. Her sons are fascinated by the way in which these fish have such a strong sense of memory that, at the end of their life, they swim miles and miles upstream to reach the place where they were born. Only there will they lay their eggs. One of Norma's sons asks her what it means to swim upstream: "què vol dir 'neden contracorrent'?" (1993, 211) [what does it mean, "they swim upstream"?]. When Norma explains how difficult the task is, and that many salmon die along the way, crushed against the rocks, he responds "quina pena, aquests salmons" (1993, 213) [I feel very sad for those salmon].[57]

As Norma tells her sons the story, she cannot help remembering the exiles with whom she has just been, and the names of so many others in the lists provided to her by the ex-deportee, all of them ghosts "que s'han estavellat contra la historia" (1993, 210) [that had crashed against history].[58] Norma is beginning to sense that the tragedy of these exiles, crushed against the rocks of history, is more intimately connected to her own life than she had wanted to acknowledge. This is partly reflected by the very way in which the story of her visit to the cemetery is presented in the text. This story is interrupted several times by the image of Norma telling her sons the children's story about salmon. Or maybe it is the other way around. Perhaps the story of her visit to the cemetery repeatedly interrupts the anecdote of the scene with her children. There is an unresolvable undecidability surrounding both stories, as it becomes less and less clear which story interrupts, and which is interrupted. What is clearly reflected, however, is that both stories cannot be held separate. Norma is starting to understand what it means for such a traumatic experience like that of the ex-deportees to be a story that "has no ending, . . . [that] continues into the present and is current in every respect" (Felman and Laub 1992, 69).

The image Norma remembers of the exiles who had "crashed against history" evokes Benjamin's image of the "angel of History." This angel, instead of looking back and seeing what people call "progress," sees "one single catastrophe which keeps piling wreckage and hurls it in front of his feet" (1969, 257–58). A view of the past that focuses on the wreckage produced by progress is one that manages, according to Benjamin, to "brush history against the grain" (1969, 257). Following the image of the salmon in Norma's children's story, we could say that it is also a history that swims "contra-corrent" (1993, 211) [upstream]. This is the history that Norma is trying to write. Cristina Moreiras Menor, in her study of texts like Roig's that, during the transition, reject the predominant and triumphant denial of the past, has made this connection to the Benjaminian view of history explicit. This kind of novel, according to Moreiras Menor, "se asienta bajo la premisa benjaminiana de pensar no el progreso, no la linealidad de la historia, sino los destrozos que la estela del progreso, o de la historia, va acumulando a sus pies. Recoger la mirada oblicua del Ángel, su mirada dirigida hacia atrás mientras avanza hacia delante, es hacerse cargo del olvido, de lo residual dejado afuera, poseerlo y erigirlo en la crisis del momento actual y por tanto en el lugar del pensamiento" (2002, 125–26) [is based on the Benjaminian premise of thinking not progress, not the lineality of history, but the wreckage that the path of progress, or of history, accumulates at its feet. To gather the oblique gaze of the angel, its gaze directed backwards as he advances forwards, is to recognize what has been forgotten, what is residual and has been excluded, to possess it and convert it into the crisis of the present moment and therefore into the very place of thinking]. This view of history attempts to think from the place of the ruins of history, not despite them, ruins like those of the old Cemetery for Republican exiles. Such a view of history, furthermore, must necessarily destabilize the present, just like the memory of Norma's visit to the cemetery interrupts her later interaction with her sons.

It is significant that Moreiras calls attention to the oblique gaze of Benjamin's "Angel of History," a gaze that looks backwards, with a sideways glance, to the catastrophe of history while he is being pushed forward by the winds of progress. Roig herself has theorized the need for a similarly oblique gaze in her writing. In her essay "Del 'ja no' a l' 'encara no' " [From "no longer" to "not yet"], Roig recalls a critic's call for a feminist practice of seeing obliquely, "mirar de cua d'ull" (1991a, 80), and claims that she would like to imagine a way of looking that would embody "la mirada bòrnia" (1991a, 80) [a one-eyed gaze].[59] This gaze would allow one to look in two directions at once, despite the fact that one eye is supposedly blind. That eye, covered by a patch, would look inwards, while the other would look outwards, as normal. Roig explains of these two simultaneous gazes, "Podriem dir que la primera mirada pertany al 'ja no', mentre que l'altra és l' 'encara no', i l'unica manera de no tornar-nos boges és aprendre a mirar en dues direccions divergents al mateix temps" (1991a, 80) [We could say that the first gaze belongs to the "no longer" while the other is the "not yet," and the only way of not going crazy is to learn to look in diverging directions at the same time].[60] Roig imagines this kind of double vision as a strategy that would be able to see how much a feminist practice has improved gender relations and made certain forms of oppression obsolete (the "ja no" [no longer]), while acknowledging at the same time how much is still needed to be done (the "encara no" [not yet]). Such a double vision, therefore, embodies the acceptance that social change is an ongoing process, never fully achieved, always somehow temporary, never attaining "closure" nor "resolution." It further implies that to effectively see the world and work to change it, one must simultaneously look inside oneself and accept change in that realm as well.

We are reminded of Natàlia's comment, when she had asked Norma to write the story of Judit and Kati based on their documents that she had found, that "aquest munt de paperassa m'ha dut a pensar en mi mateixa. A mirar-me cap endintre" (1993, 14) [that pile of papers has forced me to think about myself. To look at myself on the inside].[61] For Natàlia, recovering the forgotten story of her mother necessarily involved looking inside herself too, acknowledging her own implication in her mother's unhappy life. For the photographer, such an inwards glance, part of her taking up the "mirada tuerta" that Roig advocates, leads to a recognition that she is not as strong nor as whole as she had wanted to believe. We have already seen how this inwards vision leads her to recognize that she has inside herself vestiges of the ideology against which she had fought so hard: "En Franco és a dins de mi, se m'arrapa com un llimac" (1993, 92) [Franco is inside of me, he clings to me like a slug].[62] On another occasion, while making love to Jordi, such an inwards glance will force Natàlia to recognize her own vulnerability and fragmentation: "tot el meu cos es va dividir en trossos, les mans anaven per un cantó, la vagina per un altre, l'esquena s'escampava en diverses partícules, el ventre s'estavellava, res no es recomponia" (1993, 66) [my whole body broke up in pieces, my hands on one side, my vagina on another, my back fell apart into thousands of particles, my womb exploded, nothing could be reconstituted].[63]

For Norma, it is only when she returns from the visit to the Cemetery for the Republican exiles that she begins to focus part of her gaze inwards. As she looks in a mirror, trying to isolate her gaze from all the social conditioning and external influences, as Natàlia had once asked her to do, she also recognizes her own vulnerability and fragmentation: "la visió se li feia insuportable. No hi havia comèdia, en aquella mirada.... Era ella mateixa que volia entendre's, copsar com era, sense la mirada dels altres.... Tenia por d'entrar dins d'ella, terror a trobar-se buida" (1993, 218) [her own gaze became insufferable. In that gaze there was no pretending.... It was just she trying to understand herself, to comprehend what she was like without the gaze of others.... She was afraid to go inside herself, terrified to find herself empty].[64] When Norma looks inside herself, she sees a fragmented and vulnerable image, much like Natàlia had experienced: "Una Norma petita i dèbil, incapaç d'unificar els contraris.... Era com si s'estigués estripant, com si trossos d'ella mateixa s'aguantessin de manera fràgil, enganxats amb goma, recompostos feixugament. Com l'arqueòleg, que no sap si reconstruirà la peça tot retornant-la a la forma primitiva" (1993, 219) [A small and fragile Norma, incapable of unifying contraries.... It was as if she was coming apart, as if the pieces of herself were only held together precariously, glued together, awkwardly reconstituted. Just like the archaeologist, who never knows if he will be able to reconstitute the object to its original form].[65] This sense of fragmentation emerges in part because she is starting to see the past that she chronicles, the story of Judit and Kati as well as that of the Republican exiles and ex-deportees, as something that truly affects her, and not merely as a story she is telling from a detached point of view.

Before this moment in which she looks at herself in the mirror and recognizes her own vulnerability, Norma struggles against being overly affected by the memories of suffering and repression that she is documenting in her writings. Even after she has finished writing the story of Judit and Kati, for example, she recognizes that she has not really confronted the full implications of that past, that she has maintained an emotional distance in order to defend herself: "Damunt de la taula, amb els fulls col·locats de manera simètrica, sense que cap en sobresortis, hi deixà el manuscrit de la Judit i la Kati. S'adonava que només era un esbós de novel·la, que no hi havia anat fins al fons. El present li feia mal, la burxava, l'allunyava del projecte-Judit i el projecte-Kati. Eren passat i prou" (1993, 230) [On the table, with all the sheets symmetrically aligned, with none of them protruding, she left the manuscript about Judit and Kati. She realized that it was only a first draft of a novel, that she had not managed to get to the bottom of it. The present hurt her, persecuted her, distanced her from the Judit-project and the Kati-project. They were past and nothing more].⁶⁶ Norma acknowledges that she did not "get to the bottom" of the story she presented, for she had kept an emotional distance from the material. The fact that she labels it a "project" implies such a distance, as does the affirmation that what she has written is "past, and nothing more." This statement defensively underscores the distance between her life in the present and that past. Even the perfectly aligned manuscript pages, with no single sheet out of place, reflect the emotional distance with which the project has been written, for it is a project that has not been allowed to create any "disorder" in her life. The perfectly aligned and ordered pages, furthermore, present an image of a fully completed project, an image far removed from the fragmented, irreparably shattered archaeological object that Norma sees in the mirror when she looks inside herself. Norma's manuscript, comprising of perfectly aligned pages, also contrasts sharply with the image María Teresa León presents in her autobiography of a manuscript strewn in disarray all around her. This difference may imply that Norma, unlike León, has, up to this point, carefully protected herself from using the "palabras tristes" with which León had filled her own writing.

At first, Norma tries to impose the same kind of distance on her project of recovering the story of the Republican ex-deportees and exiles. During her visits to the ex-deportee who gives her the lists of information about his fellow Mauthausen inmates, and throughout the visit to the Cemetery for Republican Exiles, Norma is constantly tempted to forget all the pain she is witnessing. In fact, in many of these visits, she is more worried about how to get in contact with her new lover, Alfred, than with what is happening around her. She is devoted to her testimonial task, but she does not want it to interfere too much with her own life. At one point, she confesses that she "volia oblidar tots els ex-deportats, els camps d'extermini, les xemeneies del crematori, les cambres de gas. Esborrar les imatges espectrals, les piles i piles de cadàvers arrenglerats com ninots de goma. Esborrar-ho tot" (1993, 201) [she wanted to forget all of the ex-deportees, the extermination camps, the crematorium chimneys, the gas chambers. Erase the spectral images, the mountains and mountains of cadavers piled like rubber dolls. Erase everything].⁶⁷ She envisions that she can give this story the same kind of distanced narrative treatment that she imposed on the ordered manuscript of Judit and Kati's life, creating a testimonial account that in effect will permit her to free herself of the haunting memories she wants to erase: "La Norma s'asserenà. Aviat oblidaria la història dels deportats, dels fantasmes que li exigien, des del passat, sobreviure dins de la memòria. La historia havia quedat arxivada al seu llibre, aquest n'era l'homenatge, què més 'i volien?" (1993, 220) [Norma calmed down. She would soon forget the story of the ex-deportees, of the ghosts that demanded, from the past, to survive in her memory. The story was archived in her book, that was her homage, what more did they want?].[68] This text-as-archive that she wants to produce allows her to neatly contain the memory that she has recovered in an impersonal account. This narrative will perhaps help integrate that past into the collective memory of Spain, as she had promised the ex-deportee, but it will do so in a manner that will not affect or disrupt her own personal life.

This desire on Norma's part to recover memory as some kind of an impersonal archive is thwarted when she receives a phone call and is told that the ex-deportee that she had been interviewing, who had invited her to go to the inauguration of the Cemetery for Exiled Republicans, has just died. He had left a series of pictures from the inauguration ceremony of the Cemetery for her, because, as she is told, he claimed that "vostè era amiga seva i que no oblidava segons quines coses" (1993, 230) [you were a friend of his and there are certain things that you would not forget].[69] Norma is changed by this direct address from beyond the grave, this confidence placed on her by someone who had nobody else to whom he could offer his legacy. She feels, at this moment, the full weight of, and responsibility for, this gift with which she is being entrusted. At this moment, she remembers the pain in the eyes of the ex-deportee, and she recognizes that she cannot be simply an impersonal transmitter of his story, for his story truly concerns her. Jacques Derrida uses this term, in fact, to describe how a ghost always implicates us directly into its unfinished story, for the ghost is the being "that looks at us, that concerns us" (1994, 6). The expression that Derrida uses to express that the ghost "looks at us" and "concerns us" is the same in French, (*qui nous regarde*), and this double meaning perfectly captures Norma's reaction to the ex-deportee's death (1993, 26). His eyes had looked at her and, as she finally realizes, the story of pain and suffering in those eyes directly concerns her. She now acknowledges that all these stories that she is recovering in order to integrate them into the "collective memory of Spain" are also, in some sense, her own stories. She has to assume them, assuming with them all the unsettling pain and emotional vulnerability this implies.

As she remembers the ex-deportee who has just died, leaving her the legacy of his story in the pictures that will be sent to her, Norma remembers all the figures she has been writing about: "No sentia pena pel deportat, sinó també per l'amic escriptor, per en Villapalacios, per la Marie, la dona que assumí per amor la traïció del seu home. I per la Patricia . . . Eren cosa seva. I la Judit, i la Kati. Ella també hi era, dins de la Història. I mai no s'en podria deseixir. Encara que la Història fos un malson, encara que fos plena de fantasmes . . ." (1993, 231) [She didn't feel sorry only for the ex-deportee, but also for his friend, the writer, and Villapalacios, and Marie, the woman who assumed for love the betrayal of her husband. And Patricia. . . . They were a part of her. And Judit, and Kati. Also herself, she was also there, within History. And she would never be able to separate herself. Even if History were a nightmare, even if it were full of ghosts].[70] She is part of the history of suffering and oppression that she is narrating, no longer just a distanced chronicler. It is at this moment that Norma accepts her role as a secondary witness to the trauma that she has been recording. Dori Laub explains how this emotional involvement is necessarily part of becoming such a secondary witness to trauma: "The relation of the victim to the event of the trauma, therefore, impacts on the relation of the listener to it. And the latter comes to feel the bewilderment, injury, confusion, dread and conflict that the trauma victim feels. He has to address all of these, if he is to carry out his function as a listener. . . . The listener, therefore, by definition, partakes of the struggle of the victim with the memories and residues of his or her traumatic past. The listener has to feel the victim's victories, defeats and silences, know them from within, so that they can assume the form of testimony" (Felman and Laub 1992, 58).

It is only when Norma allows herself to be unsettled by the pain of the stories that she is reporting that she can truly present their testimony. She has to accept the "empathic unsettlement" that, as was seen in the last chapter, Dominick LaCapra claims is an inescapable part of the process of working through a traumatic past. According to LaCapra, such a process of working through the past that is open to an appropriate empathic unsettlement involves a "reconstruction of the past . . . wherein knowledge involves not only the process of information but also affect, empathy, and questions of value" (2001, 35). All of these affective and value elements necessary for such memory to be effective are underscored by Roig herself when she quotes exiled poet Joseph Brodsky: "Si hi ha un acte d'amor, aquest és la memòria" (1991a, 19) [if there is an act of love, memory is it].[71] Memory as an act of love, not as a mere recovery of past events; this is what Norma finally realizes she must produce.

We may recall how María Teresa León claimed that, for her, the place of memory for her recollections was to be located in her entrails, "las entrañas." With this image, she seemed to acknowledge that any place of memory that will allow one to remember a traumatic past must be somehow embodied, located in a site that allows for the pain of that past to be felt. Norma presents a similar image of an embodied memory, implying that the most appropriate place of memory she can provide for these marginalized stories of the past is one that involves her directly, even physically: "Els records es barrejaven amb les penes dels altres, li queien damunt com les fulles d'un ametller. En aparença eren fràgils, a punt de volar per la força del vent—o sigui, l'oblit—, però el cert és que les penes dels altres i els records s'amuntegaven fins a formar una segona pell" (1993, 175) [The memories melded with the pain of others, they fell over her like leaves of an almond tree. In appearance they were fragile, about to be blown away by the wind—that is to say, by oblivion-, but the truth is that the pain of others and the memories continued to accumulate until they formed a second skin].[72] Memory is like a second skin. This is the most effective place of memory that Norma can produce, one that is grafted onto her own body, and thus implicates her directly and physically. It is only when her writing becomes like this second skin that it, too, will become an appropriate place of memory for the stories she wants to tell. It is only when Norma accepts that she cannot easily shake off other people's pain that she is ready to rewrite the tale of Judit and Kati and "get to the bottom" of their story. Norma recognizes this, and accepts that the neat pile of manuscript pages she has produced will have to be rewritten, for she recognizes at the end that "potser ara podria escriure fins al fons la història de la Judit i de la Kati. Potser" (1993, 231) [perhaps now she would be able to write and get to the bottom of Judit and Kati's story. Perhaps].[73] Norma is recognizing that both of the stories she is trying to tell are connected, and that her writing will, in fact, become a palimpsest in which the layers of each story will inevitably blend into one other, and intrude into her own life, as well.

Norma has learned that to give testimony to other people's trauma, to recover traumatic histories like the ones she is pursuing, she has to open herself to what Kaja Silverman, in *The Threshold of the Visible World,* calls "heteropathic recollection" (1996, 185). This kind of memory, according to Silverman, allows one to integrate into one's self the pain of others, without trying to take their place. As Silverman explains, "if to remember is to provide the disembodied 'wound' with a psychic residence, then to remember other people's memories is to be wounded by their wounds. More precisely, it is to let their struggles, their passions, their pasts, resonate within one's own past and present, and destabilize them" (1996, 185). "Heteropathic recollection" necessarily opens the present up to the destabilizing forces of the past, something that Norma had tried at all costs to avoid. She finally realizes, however, that such a process is the only way to integrate appropriately the stories of suffering that she is investigating into the collective memory of Spanish society.[74]

It is important to note that Norma had used the term "collective memory" when she had written to the ex-deportee for the first time: "crec que la història de la deportació dels nostres compatriotes ha de ser explicada, no la podem bandejar de la memòria col·lectiva" (1993, 187) [I believe that the story of the deportation of our compatriots must be told, we cannot exile it from our collective memory].[75] In his article explaining Maurice Halbwachs's conception of collective memory, Ramón Ramos clarifies the difference between this kind of memory and historical memory: "el pasado histórico subraya las diferencias entre pasado y presente, mientras que el pasado de la memoria busca y recrea la continuidad entre el entonces y el ahora" (1989, 78) [the historical past underlines the differences between past and present, whereas the past of memory looks for and re-creates the continuity between then and now]. Whereas historical memory implies a distance between the past and the present, collective memory underscores their connection. Ramos goes on to explain that "la memoria colectiva desaparece allí donde el pasado se historifica.... Vivimos en un mundo que tiende, de manera incontenible, a historificar el pasado, incluso a historificarlo apresuradamente, cuando todavía está el pasado vivo—como ha ocurrido recientemente con el franquismo" (1989, 79) [the collective memory disappears where the past becomes historified.... We live in a world that tends, in an uncontainable manner, to historify the past, even to historify it prematurely, when that past is still alive—as has happened recently with Francoism]. We can now better understand what is at stake when Norma realizes that her original version of Judit and Kati's story is not appropriate, recognizing that "només era un esbós de lovel·la, que no hi havia anat fins al fons" [it was only a first draft of a novel, that she had not managed to get to the bottom of it], and that the stories she recounted therein "eren passat i prou" (1993, 230) [were past and nothing more].[76] Norma had treated their story as if it belonged to historical memory, distanced from her present situation. In the end, however, she realizes that to truly tell their story and "get to the bottom" of it, as well as of the story of the Republican exiles and ex-deportees, she needs to acknowledge that they are part of collective memory, that they are connected to her present.

By presenting this struggle that Norma undergoes in her attempt to work through the past, and work through her very attitudes toward that past, Roig is implying that this is the very process that all of post-Franco Spanish society must undertake. As Ramos explains, Spain, during the transition, has tried to relegate the Franco era to the realm of historical memory (when not attempting to forget it altogether) in order to hide the very real connections between the transition itself and that previous time period. Roig's meta-memory text makes it clear that what is needed is not just to recover previously marginalized histories, but to do so in a way that underscores how they are intimately connected to the present. We may recall Andreas Huyssen's explanation of one the defining characteristics of twilight memories: "It is this tenuous fissure between past and present that constitutes memory, making it powerfully alive and distinct from the archive or any other mere system of storage and retrieval" (1995, 3). At the violet hour of twilight that is the Spanish transition to democracy, therefore, Norma is learning that what she needs to produce is not a series of texts that will function as impersonal historical documents. She need to create texts that, through the presentation of a "heteropathic recollection," will recover the histories of those who had "crashed against history" in a manner that underscores how these histories of trauma are "current in every respect."

It must be remembered that Huyssen further explained that such twilight memories emerge from a process that manages to "think memory and amnesia together rather than simply oppose them" (1995, 7). Roig, too, has said "Cal recordar i oblidar alhora. La memòria també és oblit" (1991a, 22) [We have to remember and forget at the same time. Memory is also forgetting].[77] Norma's texts manage to do this by being woven around a "structural void," a gap that acknowledges that no matter how accurate a vision of the past you may produce, there are always things that remain beyond your reach, especially when dealing with stories of trauma and loss such as the ones she is recovering through her writing. These texts will thus necessarily embody a form of "unsatisfied" memory. In this process, Norma may not have to invent anything, but in order to imagine what remains beyond reach she will surely need to produce something more than a supposedly historical account. As she claims: "No, no cal inventar res, només imaginar.... Calia imaginar, la imaginació és una bona aliada del record" (1993, 217) [No, there is no need to invent, only to imagine.... It is necessary to imagine, imagination is a good ally of memory].[78] This echoes what Natàlia had stated earlier, that "l'ordre de la imaginació s'escapa a totes les dades, a tots els fets. Aquesta és la revenja de la literatura contra la Història" (1993, 89) [the order of imagination goes beyond all facts, all events. That is literature's revenge against history].[79] Ultimately, Roig's novel demonstrates that literature can, indeed, have its vengeance on history, as long as that literature is composed, as Norma reminds us, of imagination allied with memory. Imagination allied with memory, perhaps that is the best way to truly recover such histories of oppression. Perhaps that is the best way to tell the story that lies deep within the absent gaze of the ex-deportee, haunted by memories of the camp and of his survival of the camp. Perhaps that is the best way to tell the story that hides deep within the blinded eyes of Judit's doll, and the blank stare of Judit herself, all haunted by the memory of so much unfulfilled promise. Imagination allied with memory, perhaps that is the best way to guarantee, finally, that memory does not just "work backwards" but opens up to the future as well.

5
Antonio Muñoz Molina: Memory and Postmemory

Yo desde años estoy intentando eso, contar la memoria y el deseo.

[That is what I have been trying to do for years, to tell the story of memory and desire.]
—Antonio Muñoz Molina, qtd. in E.F.S. 1991

IN HIS SPEECH ACCEPTING THE PRESTIGIOUS PLANETA PRIZE FOR his novel *El jinete polaco* [*The Polish Rider*] in 1991, Antonio Muñoz Molina (1956–) recalled the verse from T. S. Eliot's poem "The Waste Land" ("mixing memory and desire") which he had used as an epigraph to his first novel, *Beatus Ille*, published five years earlier.[1] His statement, which appears as an epigraph to this chapter, clearly connects both novels, and points to the fact that Muñoz Molina sees both works as part of a larger project characterized, precisely, by his attempt at "mixing memory and desire" in his texts. Both *Beatus Ille* and *El jinete polaco* revolve around the efforts of young protagonists trying to re-create or remember part of their family past. In both cases, this inevitably implies confronting the memory of the Spanish civil war and the postwar years. Although the protagonists are too young to have lived through these experiences themselves, these historical events have had an immense impact on their lives, as they have greatly determined their family histories.

In *Beatus Ille*, the protagonist, Minaya, is a young college student studying literature in Madrid in 1969. He decides to escape the police surveillance he is suffering, due to his involvement in illegal political activities, by visiting Mágina, the small town in the south where his uncle Manuel lives. Minaya is researching the life and work of Jacinto Solana, a poet of the generation of 1927 whom he admires greatly, and who had been his uncle Manuel's friend before and during the civil war. Solana supposedly died in 1947, after having spent several years in prison due to his membership in the Communist Party. *Beatus Ille* is, in fact, the title of an unfinished novel that Solana had been writing for years.

In Mágina, Minaya's research on Solana slowly unearths the hidden truth about the death of Mariana, his uncle Manuel's bride, who died on their wedding night in 1937. Mariana had supposedly been mistakenly shot by soldiers as they pursued an escaping prisoner. However, Minaya discovers that she was actually shot by the town sculptor, Utrera, at the command of Manuel's mother. She had wanted Mariana dead because the young woman was having an affair with Solana.

By the end of the novel, the reader discovers that all the evidence and material that Minaya has been unearthing about the two mysteries with which he has become increasingly obsessed (Solana's life and work, as well as Mariana's death) have been planted for him by Solana himself, who is alive and well, although in hiding, and orchestrating Minaya's every move. Solana's plan even includes making sure that Minaya falls in love with his own young girlfriend, Inés, whom the old and cynical Solana convinces in the end to leave Mágina with the young and still idealistic Minaya.

In Muñoz Molina's first novel, therefore, desire and memory are inexorably intertwined. Minaya's research is spurred as much by his love and desire for Inés as by his need to uncover the truth about the past. Muñoz Molina's invention of a fictitious poet who, in turn, invents a false myth about his life and then manipulates a young researcher into tracing his real life story becomes a tale in which not only memory and desire are mixed, but history and fiction are as well. This novel is thus a paradigmatic example of what Linda Hutcheon has called historiographic metafiction, as the exploration of the past, presented as a narrative re-creation, is explicitly thematized in the text.[2]

Many of these elements reappear in *El jinete polaco,* in which past stories of the same town, Mágina, are re-created by two young protagonists, this time in 1991. Just as Montserrat Roig had the same characters and settings populate her novels, Muñoz Molina returns to Mágina in many of his writings. In fact, characters tied to that town reappear in several of his texts. Memory and desire do not just mix within any single one of Muñoz Molina's novels, but between them as well, as memory overflows from one text to another, unable to be contained, like desire itself. In this creation of a fictional geographical setting that metonymically represents Spain, and that reappears in many of his novels, Muñoz Molina's work is also similar to that of Benet, with the latter's development of the fictional realm of "Región" throughout so many of his texts. The literary styles of both authors are radically different, however, as Muñoz Molina is part of a generation that has consciously returned to a narrative style that is less taxing on the reader, in contrast to the highly demanding, esoteric, experimental prose of Benet's novels.

The connection between Muñoz Molina's work and Montserrat Roig's *L'hora violeta*, in turn, goes beyond the fact that she, too, had used a verse from "The Waste Land" as an epigraph to her novel. The task of "mixing memory and desire" is one that looks in two directions at once, toward the past, through memory, and toward the future, in a process that, like desire itself, is forever under way, never reaching a final point of rest. In fact, in this project (which Muñoz Molina sees as underlying much of his writing) looking backwards, to the past, is a necessary first step to be taken before attempting to construct a better, more desirable, future. As seen in the last chapter, this double vision characterized the function of memory in Roig's text, and it will likewise govern the exploration of remembering in much of Muñoz Molina's work.

In an article entitled "La invención de un pasado" [The Invention of a Past], Muñoz Molina explains his use of Eliot's verse as an epigraph to his first novel. In *Beatus Ille*, the exploration of an invented literary history, in the form of the fictitious life of the likewise imaginary poet Jacinto Solana, is a re-creation of an imaginary past that Muñoz Molina presents not merely as a postmodern literary game. It becomes a strategy of moral survival and rebellion against the deformed view of the past that Muñoz Molina received in his Francoist education: "Se trataba, entre otras cosas, de la búsqueda de una tradición, de un heroísmo literario y político sepultados bajo varias décadas de tiranía, bajo el silencio del olvido, pero no de una búsqueda con intereses arqueológicos, sino puramente prácticos, de supervivencia moral, de afirmación de la vida en el deseo" (1998c, 210) [It was a matter, among other things, of the search for a tradition, of a literary and political heroism buried under various decades of tyranny, under the silence of oblivion; not a search based on an archaeological interest, but one based on a purely practical one, of moral survival, of an affirmation of life through desire].

Muñoz Molina further explains, in the same article, that the first step his generation needed to take before creating a better future was to investigate, uncover, even *invent* a past that was different from the one the Franco regime presented as they were growing up. Although Muñoz Molina belongs to a generation of writers that began publishing after Franco's death, these authors' view of their literary work is much determined by their deficient education under the regime.[3] The mixing of memory and desire is thus an explosive political combination that recognizes the need to look back and reclaim a past that has been repressed before one can look forward and create a different Spain:

> Los españoles, al menos los que nacimos y nos formamos después de la guerra civil, hemos vivido la paradoja de no poder o no saber vincularnos a nuestro propio pasado intelectual y político en un país regido por la preponderancia fósil del pasado. Para nosotros la palabra tradición sólo podía significar oscurantismo e ignorancia, del mismo modo que las palabras patria o patriotismo significaban exclusivamente dictadura. El pasado era embustero, desconocido o repugnante: algunos de nosotros hemos dedicado una parte de las mejores energías de nuestra vida adulta a reconstruir otro pasado, a inventarlo, del mismo modo que a falta de una tradición literaria hemos tenido que inventárnosla, y en los mismos tiempos en que todos nosotros estamos intentando inventar un país. (1998c, 202)

> [Spaniards, at least those of us born and educated after the civil war, have lived the paradox of not being able, or not knowing how, to connect with our own intellectual and political past in a country dominated by the fossilized preponderance of the past. For us, the word tradition could only mean obscurantism and ignorance, in the same way that the words homeland or patriotism exclusively meant dictatorship. The past was a lie, unknown or repugnant: some of us have dedicated a great part of our energy as adults to reconstructing another past, to inventing it, in the same way that, due to the lack of a literary tradition, we have had to invent it, and all this at the same time as we are all trying to invent a new country.]

Regarding this confession on Muñoz Molina's part, Jo Labanyi has commented on the fact that "this need to 'invent the past' is perhaps more than anything else what gives contemporary Spanish culture its affinity with postmodernism, while at the same time giving it a particular historical urgency" (1995, 403). Again, the strategy of exploring the past, and in so doing, realizing that one must inevitably invent it, is not just a postmodern literary game in Muñoz Molina's work, but an ethical stand, one that clearly rejects the version of history he grew up with, and that explicitly sides with all those who were forgotten, silenced, and excluded from that official view of the past.[4]

Muñoz Molina further made this attitude toward history clear in his speech accepting the Planeta Prize for *El jinete polaco* in 1991, as he highlighted the influence of William Faulkner on his own work and claimed, of the frequent exploration of memory they both undertake, that "la memoria, si no es un arma útil, se convierte en vehículo del sentimentalismo y... sin memoria no habrá piedad para los desdichados" (qtd. in E.F.S. 1991) [Memory, if it is not a useful weapon, becomes the vehicle of sentimentalism and... without memory there will be no pity for the downtrodden]. For Muñoz Molina, therefore, the narrative exploration of remembering is not meant to be a reassuring trip down nostalgia lane. It is to be taken up as a useful tool for the vindication of the less fortunate who cannot take up memory themselves. To paraphrase the famous verse by Gabriel Celaya about poetry, for Muñoz Molina memory is "un arma cargada de futuro" [a weapon charged with future]. A Benjaminian view of history clearly undergirds Muñoz Molina's exploration of memory in *El jinete polaco,* and it is no coincidence that the title under which he submitted his novel to the Planeta Prize was, precisely, *El porvenir de los vencidos* [*The Future of the Vanquished*].[5]

Again, the future and the past are connected in the alternative title of Muñoz Molina's novel, *El porvenir de los vencidos,* as they are throughout the text. As has been the case in all the works analyzed previously in this study, in Muñoz Molina's novel the future of the vanquished will depend on the capacity of subsequent generations to remember their plight, and, more importantly, to recognize that their own present and future are inescapably linked to the past suffering of those who have come before them. The image of what León called her "transmemoria" [transmemory], which is what she hoped her own writing would become when read by subsequent generations within Spain, reappears here. Likewise, a form of "heteropathic recollection" emerges in Muñoz Molina's novel, just as it did in Roig's text. There, Natàlia and Norma struggled with the responsibility to make their own the pain of those who had suffered exile, internal or external, in the generation preceding theirs. Roig's novel explored how the development of such "heteropathic recollection" was especially necessary during the transition to democracy, based as it was on the illusion of creating a clean break with the past. Muñoz Molina's novel will explore a similar concern, from the vantage point of the end of the twentieth century. *El jinete polaco* explores the dynamic of "postmemory," a concept that has been compared to Kaja Silverman's "heteropathic recollection" but which, appropriately for Muñoz Molina's novel, emphasizes the generational transmission of a traumatic past within primarily, but not exclusively, a family history.[6]

Marianne Hirsch has coined the term "postmemory" to describe the experience of children of Holocaust survivors, and survivors of other traumatic historical events, who are indelibly marked by the past of their parents and grandparents, a past they did not live but whose traumatic weight they must bear. It is a past that is both present and absent in their memories, echoing throughout their life like a hauntingly familiar yet completely alien ghost. Hirsch explains: "Postmemory characterizes the experience of those who . . . have grown up dominated by narratives that preceded their birth, whose own belated stories are displaced by the powerful stories of the previous generation, shaped by monumental traumatic events that resist understanding and integration. It describes as well the relationship of the second generation to the experiences of the first—their curiosity and desire, as well as their ambivalences about wanting to own their parents' knowledge" (2001, 12).

The "mixing [of] memory and desire" in *El jinete polaco* takes place precisely as the text explores this dynamic of postmemory. In the novel, Manuel, the son of poor peasants from Mágina (the same town to which Minaya returned in *Beatus Ille*), is tormented by his parents' memories of growing up during and after the Spanish civil war, even though those are not experiences he himself lived, having been born in 1956. Despite trying to escape these memories by finally leaving his hometown, becoming a simultaneous translator for an international nongovernmental organization and traveling all over the world, he remains forever haunted by these memories inherited from his parents. Just like his own voice as a simultaneous translator is but the echo of the voices of others, his own memory becomes the echo of those voices from his parents' and grandparents' past.[7]

When Manuel meets Nadia, the daughter of Comandante Galaz [Commander Galaz], an officer of the Spanish Republican army in Mágina who was exiled to the United States after the civil war, he is able to share and piece together his own postmemory with hers. She was born and grew up far from Mágina, in New York City, born to an American woman her father married there, yet always bearing the weight of her father's memories of his pre-exile past in Spain. Together, Manuel and Nadia, with the help of a series of photographs, will be able to assume the voices of their past, the voices of the postmemories that have haunted each of them. As Manuel defines this process: "oigo las voces que cuentan, las palabras que invocan y nombran no en mi conciencia sino en una memoria que ni siquiera es mía" (1991, 27) [I hear the voices that speak, the words that invoke and name not in my conscience but in a memory that is not even mine]. This feeling of bearing the burden of a memory that is not even one's own is at the heart of postmemory. What is more, this memory that is not one's own has irremediably determined, from the beginning, one's life and behavior. As the text elsewhere claims about Manuel and Nadia's process of exploring their past: "las voces que llevaban años sin oír usurpan las suyas y les devuelven palabras y circunstancias olvidadas, anteriores a ellos pero cimentadoras de sus gestos" (1991, 495) [the voices that they had not heard for years usurp their own and give them back forgotten words and circumstances that pre-date them, yet which have laid the foundation for their gestures].

El jinete polaco is thus not only an exploration of memory itself, but, just as importantly, of the dynamics of memory transmission over several generations. As Hirsch explains, "the work of postmemory defines the familial inheritance and transmission of cultural trauma" (2001, 9). Furthermore, as James Young states, in *At Memory's Edge, After-Images of the Holocaust in Contemporary Art and Architecture,* second-generational accounts of traumatic historic events become "double-stranded narratives" that explore a "vicarious past" (2000, 3) because they present both the recalling of the events themselves, and, necessarily, the *transmission* of the memories of those events from the previous generation who suffered them to their offspring. This approach "sees history itself as a composite record of both events and these events' transmission to the next generation" (2000, 2). *El jinete polaco* does, indeed, present such a "double-stranded narrative," much like Roig's *L'hora violeta* does. In fact, *El jinete polaco* is made up of the intertwining of two such "double-stranded narratives," as the reminiscences of Manuel and Nadia are interwoven throughout the text. Memory, even one's most personal and individual recollection, is thus inherently an interpersonal and collective phenomenon, not only because it is always partly inherited from others, but also because its articulation is always, in some sense, directed toward others as well.

It is highly significant that photographs are the main instruments of this process. Hirsch has analyzed "the privileged status of photography as a medium of postmemory" (2001, 13). Such visual *aides mémoire* can be seen to re-create a dynamic similar to that of postmemory: they allow one generation to inherit, assume as if they were their own, the images, even the experiences of a previous generation, thus often collapsing distinctions between self and other, present and past, absence and presence.

The effort presented in this novel by the two protagonists can be seen as emblematic of the long journey that post-Franco Spanish society has undertaken. New generations of Spaniards have had to come to terms with such experiences of postmemory, of inheriting a devastating memory of a civil war, postwar repression, and long dictatorship that they have not necessarily lived, but that haunt their lives in the voices and echoes, in the fears and recollections of their parents' and grandparents' generations. It is a characteristic of postmemory, in fact, that its haunting power is often strongest when least recognized. It is thus perhaps just when new generations, at the end of the twentieth and beginning of the twenty-first century, feel that they have broken with the past and that they can reject the weight of that past, that their very rebellion can be seen to be a manifestation of the enduring power of postmemory.[8]

* * * *

El jinete polaco is divided into three sections, each one a recollection of a different part of the two protagonists' past. The frame of the novel, the present in which their recollective process takes place, is 1991, when Manuel and Nadia spend a few days in her New York apartment after having met and had a one-night stand at an international conference in Madrid one month earlier. Love and storytelling are intertwined, in a veritable sexual/textual frenzy, as they tell each other the stories of their families' past, exploring each other's memory as much as they do each other's body. Memory and body are, indeed, inseparable here in a process that is, once again, "mixing memory and desire." A chest full of old photographs that Mágina's town photographer, Ramiro Retratista, had given to Nadia's father, and that she has inherited after his death a few days before finding Manuel, serves the function of a Proustian madeleine, sparking the rememorative process for both protagonists. Memory as inheritance, or postmemory, is thus symbolized in the very history of the chest full of photographs that will be the basis for both Manuel and Nadia's recollections. Two other objects that Nadia has inherited from her father will also serve as particularly significant sites for recollection. One is an old Protestant Bible, which belonged to the character that, as is only discovered late in the novel, can be identified as Manuel's great-great-grandfather. The other is a copy of a painting, supposedly by Rembrandt, called "The Polish Rider" ("El jinete polaco" of the novel's title), which Nadia's father had bought the day he arrived in Mágina to take up his new post in the army station in the early 1930s, and which he had always carried with him ever since. A painting, a Bible, and multiple photographs will all serve as textual and visual traces of the past that highlight not only the mediated access to history, but also the interrelation of visual and narrative aspects of memory formation. To this we can add one more strand, an auditory one, as the metaphor of the voice is added to the previous two, visual image and written text, to show the multidimensional nature of memory itself.

The first section, is, in fact, called "El reino de las voces" [The Kingdom of Voices] and in it we discover much of the story of Manuel's family history. The second section, "Jinete en la tormenta" [Rider on the Storm], focuses primarily on the summer of 1973, and the adolescent Manuel's rebellion against everything his family represents, especially the fear and poverty that still govern their lives in what seems like an endless extension of the postwar years. Manuel's rebellion is largely enacted through his identification with the American rock songs that have begun to be heard in Spain, one of which, Jim Morrison's "Riders on the Storm," provides the title for this part of the novel. This section also recalls Nadia and her father's first, and only, visit to Spain in 1973, after his long years of exile. The text recalls how Nadia and her father rented a house in Mágina for a few months, during which time Nadia met Manuel one night, a night he cannot remember because he was drunk and desperately depressed because Marina, the girl of his dreams at the time, showed absolutely no romantic interest in him. It is during this visit to Mágina that Commander Galaz receives the chest of photographs from Ramiro Retratista.

The last section, entitled, like the novel as a whole, "El jinete polaco" [The Polish Rider], mostly brings us closer to the present, to the time immediately preceding Manuel and Nadia's chance encounter in a Madrid international conference in 1991, and then to their re-encounter in New York a month later, just days after Nadia's father has died, and shortly before Manuel, at the end of the novel, returns to Mágina after receiving the news of his grandmother's death. At the end of the novel, in circular fashion, Nadia arrives in Mágina, the place of origin of both of their postmemories. For both Manuel and Nadia, therefore, the deaths of their family members presage the beginning of a new relationship with their past in the city that is at the heart of both their family histories.[9]

In the first section of *El jinete polaco* we learn about Don Mercurio, Manuel's great-great-grandfather, a doctor who arrived in Mágina from Madrid shortly after the assassination of General Prim, in 1870. This section tells of Don Mercurio's adulterous relation with a wealthy young married woman in town. Upon his discovering the affair, the woman's husband kills her, and then encases her in a basement wall of their house, where she will remain, in mummified form, for over thirty years. This mummy is one of the metaphors in the novel of the past coming back to haunt the present, literally haunt, in this case, since Manuel as a child is always frightened by the many ghost stories told around town about the mysterious "mujer emparedada" [mummified woman]. The Protestant Bible that Manuel and Nadia find with the photographs is the Bible that Don Mercurio and his young lover used to read together, focusing especially on the erotically charged Song of Songs. The son of their illegitimate affair, Pedro Expósito Expósito, was abandoned in an orphanage upon birth, and later fought in the Cuban war of independence. His son, or Manuel's grandfather,

Manuel, fought in the civil war and suffered internment in one of Franco's concentration camps after the fighting. Manuel's grandmother, Leonor, never forgot the fear produced by not knowing if her husband would ever return alive from the camp. Manuel's parents, who experienced the civil war as children, live forever governed by fear, too, and by the experience of lack and sense of impending doom that characterized their childhood. As Manuel later explains to Nadia, this unending sense of fear was one of the elements of the postmemory inherited early by him and his friends, for they were all "habitados hasta la médula de su conciencia por las voces de sus mayores, herederos de un valor fracasado mucho antes de que ellos nacieran y modelados sin saberlo por hechos memorables o atroces de los que nada sabían, herederos involuntarios de la soledad, del sufrimiento y del amor de quienes los habían engendrado" (1991, 12) [inhabited to the core of their conscience by the voices of their elders, inheritors of a courage that had failed long before they were even born and unknowingly molded by memorable or atrocious events of which they knew nothing, involuntary inheritors of the loneliness, of the suffering, and of the love of those that had engendered them]. This image of the voices of the elders that inhabit their children and grandchildren's conscience is a constant presence throughout the text. The Bakhtinian notion of the multivoicedness of reality comes to mind. These voices from the past that return to haunt the voices of Manuel and Nadia in the present reflect Bakhtin's notion that any words we use inevitably carry with them the voices of all the people who previously used those words: "there are no words that belong to no one . . . and those whose voices are heard in the word before the author comes upon it also have their rights" (1986, 124). In this respect, according to Bakhtin, in any act of communication between two people, "the word is a drama in which three characters participate (it is not a duet, but a trio)" (1986, 122). Manuel and Nadia's dialogue is, in fact, a drama in which not just two voices participate, but three or more. Theirs, as well as all those other voices from the past that haunt their voices, take part in this exchange. Their voices, as well as their memories, do not fully belong to them, for just as they have inherited their genetic makeup from their parents, they have inherited their fears and memories as well. As Manuel remarks: "igual que la memoria y que las palabras que nos decimos, tampoco nuestras caras nos pertenecen del todo" (1991, 142) [just like the memory and the words that we tell each other, our own faces do not completely belong to us].

These voices from a past that Manuel did not live but that determines his whole life (this "memoria que ni siquiera es mía" [memory that is not even mine]), creep up on him not only when he is reminiscing with

Nadia, but when he makes his own voice, as simultaneous translator, become, yet again, the echo of other people's voices: "Y mientras escucho palabras que no me importan y busco equivalencias con un automatismo instantáneo oigo detrás de esas voces y de la mía propia otras voces que vuelven y que parecen hablarme al oído como si fueran ellas las que suenan en el interior de los auriculares acolchados, monótonas, escondidas, tan fieles como los latidos de mi sangre" (1991, 80) [And while I listen to words that don't interest me and I look for equivalences with an instant automatism, I hear behind these voices as well as my own, voices that return and seem to whisper in my ear as if they were echoing inside the padded headphones, monotonous, hidden, as faithful as the beating of my own blood]. This is reminiscent of León's recognition in her autobiography that her own recollection is made up of the voices of so many of her precursors when León states "estamos llenos de frases ajenas" (1998, 185–86) [we are full of other people's phrases] and that, furthermore, "nos traemos adentro una carga inquietante de gustos y de gestos ajenos que se nos van quedando enganchados" (1998, 146) [We have inside ourselves a disquieting burden of other people's tastes and gestures that cling to us].

Fear is the experience that most characterizes these voices that return to haunt Manuel's conscience, a fear that almost seems to take over his own life, substituting itself for his own experience, as often happens in the realm of postmemory. Manuel explains: "Así he vivido, enfermo y muerto de miedo, vivo de miedo ..., auscultando el miedo en mi piel y en los tejidos secretos de mi corazón y mis pulmones.... Se me había olvidado la mayor parte de mi vida y solo me quedaba su osamenta de miedo" (1991, 398) [This is how I have lived, sick and dying of fear, living of fear ..., auscultating the fear on my skin and on the secret tissue of my heart and lungs.... I had forgotten most of my life and only its skeleton of fear remained]. Manuel feels that he is made up of a skeleton of fear, a fear that permeated all of his home town growing up, a town haunted by "los fantasmas nacidos del miedo de varias generaciones sucesivas ... en la memoria acobardada de Mágina y en las palabras siempre clandestinas o ambiguas de nuestros mayores, escoria del miedo y de las desgracias de la guerra" (1991, 77–78) [the ghosts born of the fear of various successive generations ... in the cowardly memory of Mágina and in the always clandestine or ambiguous words of our elders, dross of the fear and of the tragedies of the war].

The psychological weight of this sense of fear is reflected, among other things, in the long list of prohibitions with which Manuel grows up, lists that go on for entire pages at a time in the novel, highlighting a childhood governed by an oppressive sense of limitation and intimidation (see, for example, 1991, 43 and 173). Along with these long lists of prohibitions, the text recurrently presents the songs that Manuel and other children used to sing, songs that unfailingly evoked some menacing terror to which they would be subjected if they did not behave (see, for example, 1991, 53). Such songs include riddles about the old doctor Don Mercurio, whose presence always signaled someone's illness, or about the nightly raids on the town supposedly undertaken by hordes of people infected with consumption and looking to kidnap young children for their fresh blood. Along with these songs, the children endlessly repeated a number of ghost stories telling, for example, of their fear of the house haunted by the mummified woman, or of the cart that would go through town whenever someone had died to take the body away, and which the children always feared was coming to take them away, too.

The recurring presence of these songs and ghost stories not only highlights the fear with which Manuel grew up, but enlarges the scope of the memory that is being presented in the text. As the oral historian Alessandro Portelli has shown, highlighting such " 'formalised materials' like proverbs, songs, formulaic language, stereotypes, can be a measure of the presence of a 'collective viewpoint' " in a text (qtd. in Kuhn 2000, 192). The endless repetition of these songs and stories is one more indication, therefore, that the memory that is being presented and worked through in this novel is collective, even though it is being presented through the perspective of two individuals. Manuel feels trapped by this collective memory, or postmemory, for "no solo repetíamos las canciones y los juegos de nuestros mayores y estábamos condenados a repetir sus vidas: nuestras imaginaciones y nuestras palabras repetían el miedo que fue suyo y que sin premeditación nos transmitieron desde que nacimos" (1991, 46) [we not only repeated the songs and the games of our elders and were condemned to repeat their lives: our imaginations and words repeated the fear that had been theirs and which, without premeditation, they transmitted to us from the moment of our birth].

The fact that Manuel exclaims that he, like his home town, has been haunted by "los fantasmas nacidos del miedo" [the ghosts born of fear] emerging from "las palabras siempre clandestinas o ambiguas de nuestros mayores" [the always clandestine or ambiguous words of our elders] is significant. We can identify here the dynamic of a process similar to that of postmemory, a process that Nicolas Abraham and Maria Torok have called the "transgenerational phantom." This concept also reflects how sometimes, after a traumatic historical event, one generation may be haunted not so much by the loss of loved ones, but by the secrets and unspeakable fears that governed the lives of those loved ones. As Abraham explains, "All the departed may return, but some are destined to haunt: the dead who have been shamed during their lifetime or those who took unspeakable secrets to the grave" (1994, 171). In the workings of the "transgenerational phantom," therefore, "what haunts are not the dead, but the gaps left within us by the secrets of others" (1994, 171). Manuel's family history is made up of secrets, from the illegitimate origin of his great-grandfather, to the secret suffering that Manuel's grandfather had undergone in the Francoist concentration camp, which he never shares with his family. Manuel's grandfather, in fact, grows silent any time the topic comes up, "como si le agobiara la posesión de un secreto que a pesar suyo le era imposible revelar y que en cualquier caso no merecían los testigos incrédulos de su narración" (1991, 118) [as if he were overwhelmed by the possession of a secret that, despite himself, he was unable to reveal, and of which, in any case, the incredulous witnesses of his narration would not have been worthy].[10]

The past of Nadia's father is also based on a secret, one which he only discloses to her on his deathbed. He already had a wife and child in Spain before leaving for exile. He had abandoned them, just like he had abandoned his homeland, after the war, and had never revealed their existence to his new family in the United States. It is no wonder, then, that Nadia, at a certain point, thinks that even the Polish rider in the copy of Rembrandt's painting that she has inherited from her father holds some secret: "[Nadia] mira el grabado del jinete y piensa por primera vez que él también tiene cara de guardar un secreto" (1991, 313) [[Nadia] looks at the painting of the rider and thinks for the first time that he also seems to be keeping a secret]. These family stories of traumatic experiences are thus made up of secrets, and it is those secrets, that "unspeakable" nature of the trauma experienced, that the new generations inherit in a process that is extremely difficult to work through. This is so precisely because it is an inherited history that is not really *there*, and is not really *theirs*, although its effects are everywhere. As Abraham explains: "the phantom represents the interpersonal and transgenerational consequences of silence" (1994, 168). This is similar to Hirsch's description of postmemory as "an intersubjective transgenerational space of remembrance, linked specifically to cultural or collective trauma" (2001, 10). Both of these concepts, therefore, understand the working of memory within a collective, rather than individual framework.

Here lies the difference between the experience of the "transgenerational phantom," or postmemory, and either mourning or melancholia, for example. Whereas in the latter two experiences one is working through a loss that one has suffered, however difficult this may be, in the previous two cases one is working through someone else's loss, which one has inherited as one's own, even though it is not one's own experience. It is because of this that Abraham claims that the "transgenerational phantom . . . works like a ventriloquist, like a stranger within the subject's own mental topography" (1994, 173). It is not surprising, then, that Manuel's best friend, Félix, likens him, precisely, to a ventriloquist: "Félix dice que podría haberme ganado la vida de ventrílocuo, es como viajar a otro país sin moverse, como cambiar de alma y de memoria, hasta de identidad, y a mí la mía se me escapa en cuanto me descuido, no sé quedarme en la primera persona del singular" (1991, 391) [Félix says that I could have made a living as a ventriloquist, it is like traveling to another country without even moving, like changing your soul or your memory, even your identity, and as for me, my own identity constantly escapes me, I don't know how to remain in the first person singular]. In claiming that he doesn't know how to remain within the first person singular pronoun, Manuel acknowledges that the boundaries of the self are blurred. He feels, in a way, exiled from his own identity, and, as Hirsch explains, "this condition of exile from the space of identity, this diasporic experience, is characteristic of postmemory" (1996, 421). Manuel further evokes the experience of postmemory when he explains, while sharing his past with Nadia, how the feeling that his voice cannot be contained by the first person singular pronoun emerges from the fact that he is telling a story that precedes his own life:

> Entonces mi voz repite para ella lo que me contaron otras voces y me parece que le estoy hablando no de mi propia vida, sino de otro tiempo mucho más lejano al que no es posible que yo haya sido testigo, a no ser que ese pronombre esconda más de una identidad o se dilate más hondo y más lejos que mi conciencia y que mi torpe memoria igual que mi cuerpo algunas veces se pierde y se confunde en el suyo. (1991, 87)

> [Then my voice repeats for her what other voices have told me, and it seems to me that I am talking not of my own life, but of another time much more distant, which I cannot possibly have witnessed, unless that pronoun hides more than one identity or expands deeper and further than my conscience and my awkward memory, just like my body sometimes loses and confuses itself with hers.]

El jinete polaco, therefore, through an exploration of postmemory and the "transgenerational phantom," enacts a process of working through memory. Memory here, however, is irremediably collective. It is the product of an "I" that is not singular but represents a plurality of voices.[11] This explains the endless oscillation of point of view throughout the novel, shifting back and forth between the first and third person, mostly focalized through the perspective of Manuel. The third person point of view could be seen as a textual manifestation of the expanded first person pronoun which, as Manuel states, "hides more than one identity" and encompasses the story of his family from long before his own birth.[12] Just as Manuel's body becomes lost in Nadia's, so does her perspective arise at times in the text, as she also takes up the first person narration when presenting her story.

Nadia, too, had grown up inheriting from her father a homeland that was not her own, but that he carefully created for her through the music, stories, and children's toys from Spain that he would find for her in second-hand stores in New York City. These constant reminders of a homeland she never even knew "le dieron un país irreal y un idioma arbitrario y un pasado al que eligió pertenecer aunque lo desconociera" (1991, 206) [gave her an unreal country and an arbitrary language, and an unfamiliar past to which she chose to belong although it was unfamiliar to her]. Nadia thus also lives in the realm of postmemory, and, like Manuel, inherits the "transgenerational phantom." Her postmemory is also made up of silences, for she inherits "un país inventado por el desarraigo perpetuo y el dolor sin palabras ni queja de su padre" (1991, 154) [a country invented by the perpetual uprootedness and the silent pain of her father].

The fact that the Spanish toys that Nadia's father gives her are found in second-hand stores is significant. This symbolizes that the "patria irreal" [unreal country] which her father had tried to give her is, indeed, a second-hand one, a perfect image for the "postmemorial" space it inhabits. The fact that many of these second-hand items are storybooks, such as the popular adventures of the young Republican girl "Celia," or the Calleja stories (1991, 154), highlights the narrative transmission of this postmemory. This underscores the fact that the images Nadia will have of this inherited homeland will never quite be her own, both because they are based on her father's experience, of which she knows almost nothing, and because they are based on these narratives obtained second-hand.

This highlighting of the narrative texts by means of which Nadia conjured an image of the "invented country" that her father wanted to pass on to her is, of course, fundamental for the "double-stranded narrative" that this postmemory text presents. *El jinete polaco* thus not only underscores the weight of a past on those who have not lived the traumatic experiences that haunt their parents, it also highlights the varied means of *narrative transmission* of that past over generations. The songs and ghost stories that Manuel remembers from his childhood, just like the written tales that Nadia received from her father, point to the textual mediation of any and all access to the past. They likewise highlight the fact that both Manuel and Nadia have grown up overshadowed by experiences they have not lived and that they cannot understand except through the mediation of certain texts that are available to them.

This understanding of the inevitable textual mediation of any access to the past is underscored time and again throughout the novel. Manuel, growing up, is often told of events from the war or postwar period, which he can only imagine as stories from the comic books or adventure novels he loves to read. Thus, for example, when people talk about the civil war, Manuel can only imagine the wars he has seen in films and comic books: "una guerra, esa de la que se acuerdan siempre los mayores y que yo asocio oscuramente a las guerras de las películas y a las de los tebeos" (1991, 82) [a war, the one which older people are always remembering and that I associate obscurely with the wars in movies and comic books]. The concentration camp in which his grandfather was detained after the war becomes, for Manuel, "aquel lugar que yo imaginaba como los campos de concentración de las películas" (1991, 107) [that place which I imagined like the concentration camps in movies].[13] When his father and uncles admiringly recall Comandante Galaz's heroic deed of remaining faithful to the Republic even though his soldiers wanted to join Franco's insurgency at the outset of the civil war, Manuel thinks about the larger-than-life image that Galaz's name evokes, and ponders "ese nombre tan rotundo y tan raro que sólo era posible atribuir a un hombre imaginario, a un héroe tan inexistente como el Cosaco verde o Miguel Strogoff" (1991, 24) [that name so rotund and strange that it was only possible to attribute to an imaginary man, to a hero as inexistent as the Green Cossack or Miguel Strogoff].

The image of Miguel Strogoff, the hero of the adventure novel by Jules Verne which Manuel read as a child, reappears throughout *El jinete polaco*. Manuel sometimes imagines his father on his horse as being Miguel Strogoff on his steed. More often than not, however, it is his grandfather who takes on the image of the literary hero. Manuel creates this image based on his grandfather's tales of the war, of the concentration camp in which he was interred, and, especially, of the solitary, exhausting, seemingly never-ending walk home from the camp. Manuel compares this voyage on foot to Miguel Strogoff's heroic journey across Russia to deliver a message from the czar to his brother, a message that would save the country from a ruthless enemy invasion (see, for example, 1991, 188–89).[14]

The intertextual reference to Miguel Strogoff is especially important, for Muñoz Molina has confessed that his novel is partly modeled on that of Jules Verne: "en mi novela más aventurada o más temeraria,

El jinete polaco, la protagonista se llama Nadia, como la heroína de *Miguel Strogoff,* y es además la hija de un militar exiliado" (1998c, 206) [in my most adventurous and daring novel, *El jinete polaco,* the protagonist is called Nadia, like the heroine of *Miguel Strogoff,* and she is also the daughter of an exiled military officer]. Several elements of Verne's adventure story are important in understanding the function of postmemory in Muñoz Molina's novel. First of all, as he himself highlights, Nadia is the name of the female protagonist in both stories, and in both cases she is the daughter of an exiled military commander. Just as Nadia's father in Verne's tale is finally vindicated and brought back from exile, *El jinete polaco* also implicitly becomes a tale of the vindication of the exiled figure Comandante Galaz. In fact, the whole novel is made possible because Galaz is the person who received the chest of photographs from Ramiro Retratista, and it is he who has kept it faithfully and bequeathed it to Nadia. The past of Mágina, which Nadia and Manuel piece together throughout the novel, is thus inherited from the exiled commander. Symbolically, therefore, Muñoz Molina is showing not only that the forgotten story of exile must be incorporated into the contemporary history of Spain, but, even more radically, that the history of Spain will only be fully re-created after it has passed through the story of exile. The privileged bearers of history, and of history's remains, in the novel are he who had been exiled from history in the first place and his daughter.[15]

It is also important to remember that Miguel Strogoff had been captured by his enemies during his journey and, supposedly, was blinded with a red-hot sword. Only at the end of the tale do the readers discover that he had not, in fact, lost his sight. Immediately before having the sword lifted to his eyes, he had thought of his mother. The sadness he felt upon thinking of her, imagining her suffering, filled his eyes with tears, and those tears had protected his eyes from the sword's blinding heat. In a similar manner, Manuel is metaphorically blind throughout much of his life, blind to the true suffering of his parents and grandparents, from whom he only wishes to distance himself as he is growing up. It is only when he can look at their faces, in the photographs he shares with Nadia, and imagine the suffering with which they have lived, that his vision is restored, so to speak. It is only when he can engage in the process of "heteropathic recollection," as Norma and Nàtalia had managed to do in *L'hora violeta* with regard to the stories they were recalling, that he can begin to establish a new relationship with his own past, one of acceptance and connection instead of resistance and fear.

David Herzberger has commented on the symbolic meaning of the scene, early in the novel, in which Manuel awakens in Nadia's apartment, after they have spent hours looking at the photographs, sharing with each other their respective memories. Manuel imagines what time it must be back in Mágina. He thus awakens to a renewed sense of connection with Mágina after years of running away from his hometown, and, as Herzberger explains, "Manuel's literal and symbolic awakening stems from his conscious decision to reinvest his identity in the past when for nearly two decades he had attempted precisely the opposite" (2000, 128). Manuel's symbolic awakening can also be understood as his gaining back his sight, a sight with which he can truly see the past of his family and experience it now not only as a burden, as he has throughout his life, but as a positive legacy. This connection between awakening and remembering is not coincidental. Muñoz Molina himself has commented that in old Castilian the same word refers to both verbs, as is clear from the first verse of Jorge Manrique's poem "Coplas por la muerte de su padre" [The *Coplas* on the death of his father]: "en el castellano antiguo recordar también significa despertarse: 'Recuerde el alma dormida' " (1998d, 176) [in old Castilian, to remember also means to awaken: "Let from its dream the soul awaken"].

To awaken is to remember, and, in turn, remembering is equated with seeing. Manuel, at a certain moment in Nadia's apartment, again awakens, and upon seeing the copy of Rembrandt's painting feels a sense of calm as he hears himself telling his story to Nadia. Significantly, the memory those words evoke is described as a "mirada" [a gaze], and this act of seeing that Manuel assumes turns him into a new incarnation of the Polish rider, or of Miguel Strogoff himself, who only now is able to embark on the long journey of reconciliation with a past that has haunted him his whole life:

Oigo mi voz lenta y oscurecida por el sueño, y aunque he vuelto a despertarme del todo las palabras me traen poderosas sensaciones visuales que fluyen delante de mis ojos tan detalladamente como la figura del jinete colgada enfrente de nosotros, las palabras no cuentan, invocan, la memoria es una mirada pura y arcaica que me convierte en un testigo inmóvil de lo que estoy diciendo, y me oigo hablar igual que me oye Nadia, abrazado a ella en la serenidad de un viaje que sólo ahora he sabido o me he atrevido a emprender" (1991, 171–72)[16]

[I hear my voice, slow and darkened by sleep, and although I have fully woken up again, the words create powerful visual sensations that float before my eyes as realistically as the figure of the rider hanging in front of us, words do not tell, they invoke, memory is a pure and archaic gaze that transforms me into an immobile witness of what I am saying, and I hear myself speak just like Nadia hears me, embracing her in the serenity of a voyage that I only now know how to, or dare to, begin.]

Memory emerges as a "mirada" [gaze] that the previously blinded Manuel can now take up. Like the valiant Strogoff or the enigmatic Polish rider, Manuel feels that now, for the first time, he is able to embark on a journey that brings him "serenity." This journey into the future on which he is embarking is at the same time a journey into the past. It is no coincidence that such a double movement, forwards and backwards, characterizes the painting of the Polish rider. The painting is mysterious, no indication given of where and when the action is happening. Nadia had, in fact, interpreted this mystery as an indication that the rider was keeping a secret. As his horse strides forward, the unknown rider faces backwards, or at least sideways, as if glancing at whoever is looking at the painting and inviting him or her to participate in his secret which, of course, remains forever elusive.

One description of the painting mentions the ambiguous time of day it evokes, highlighting "la figura del jinete que cabalga por un paisaje donde muy pronto amanecerá o acaba de hacerse de noche" (1991, 18) [the figure of the rider galloping through a landscape where the day will soon dawn or night has just fallen]. The time reflected in the painting is thus that of "la hora violeta," the violet hour of twilight. Just as in Roig's novel, it is a time that is connected both to something that is ending and something about to begin. Caught between the past and the future, between memory and desire, Manuel, like the Polish rider of the painting or Miguel Strogoff from his childhood readings, is now embarking for the fist time on an adventurous journey. In this journey, it is an "act of memory" that transforms Manuel into a hero, similar to all the supposedly heroic figures that he has earlier associated with the Polish rider and Miguel Strogoff (his father, his grandfather, Commander Galaz, etc.). For Mieke Bal, such "acts of memory" are the various ways in which one manages to make a traumatic event "narratable" and, therefore, communicable and able to be shared (1999, x). By means of integrating the traumatic event into a story one can tell and share with others, one begins to be freed from the haunting power of the past. It is thus important that it is precisely this act of storytelling, of narrating the tale of his past, that gives Manuel his sense of "serenity": "me oigo hablar igual que me oye Nadia, abrazado a ella en la serenidad de un viaje que sólo ahora he sabido o me he atrevido a emprender" (1991, 172) [I hear myself speak just like Nadia hears me, embracing her in the serenity of a voyage that I only now know how to, or dare to, begin]. In this meta-memory text, therefore, the past is being re-created in the endless stories that Nadia and Manuel share with each other. We may recall that for Semprún, also, narrating his memories of Buchenwald in *El largo viaje* was equated with a journey, a therapeutic narrative journey into his past which retraced his boxcar journey to the camp, and which the author was finally able to undertake only after many years of forgetting.

Mieke Bal further explains that for an "act of memory" to be truly effective, it must be directed toward someone who can receive the narration, and that other "can be whoever functions as the 'second person' before or to whom the traumatized subject can bear witness, and thus integrate narratively what was until then an assailing specter" (1999, x–xi). Nicolas Abraham, in "Notes on the Phantom," also emphasizes the need to share with others the traumatic past one has inherited, converting all the secret words underlying the haunting power of that past into "staged words" (1994, 176). As he explains, "to stage a word ... constitutes an attempt at exorcism, an attempt, that is, to relieve the unconscious by placing the effects of the phantom in the social realm" (1994, 176). This is exactly what Manuel does with Nadia, and what she does with him, in a shared process of storytelling which becomes one prolonged and sustained "act of memory," an act in which they both manage to "stage" all the secret words, all the fears and burdens they have inherited from their elders by exteriorizing them through the art of narration. For both of them, this becomes the first time in which they are able to work through the postmemory they have inherited. Manuel acknowledges the therapeutic value of this "act of memory" he is undertaking when he states, shortly after the moment in which he feels memory arising for him like a "mirada" [gaze], that he can finally assume: "y entonces me doy cuenta de que por primera vez en mi vida soy yo quien cuenta y no quien escucha ... yo soy, a través de Nadia, el testigo de mi propia narración" (1991, 180) [and then I realize that for the first time in my life, it is I who speaks and not who listens ... I am, through Nadia, the witness of my own narration]. For the first time, Manuel is telling his story, not inheriting or rebelling against it, and this "act of memory" is his truly heroic, and liberating, deed. It is all the more heroic and liberating because it involves becoming the recipient of Nadia's own "act of memory" as well. Taking up the active role of storyteller of his past finally manages to free Manuel of the fear that has characterized the experience of postmemory which has governed most of his life. It is only once he begins telling his tale to Nadia, therefore, that Manuel "no sentía angustia, ni premura, ni miedo, como tantas veces, como casi siempre en su vida, ni el remordimiento sin motivo que lo había trastornado desde que tuvo uso de razón" (1991, 17) [did not feel anguish, nor worry, nor fear, like so many other times, like almost always in his life, nor the unfounded guilt that had besieged him since he could remember]. Of course, the novel places the reader in a position similar to that of Manuel or Nadia, for he or she is also a "second person," or "secondary witness," who receives Manuel and Nadia's narration throughout the text. The reader thus becomes part of the process of working through postmemory in the novel. The dialogic experience thematized in the novel, the process of exorcism that Abraham likens to "placing the effects of the phantom in the social realm," is thus extended beyond the textual frame of the novel, as it effectively incorporates the reader (Abraham, 1994, 176).

It is significant that these "acts of memory" in which both protagonists are "exorcising" the "phantoms" they have inherited arise from the act of looking at Ramiro Retratista's photographs. Marianne Hirsch explains: "Photographs offer a prism through which to study the postmodern space of cultural memory composed of leftovers, debris, single items that are left to be collected and assembled in many ways, to tell a variety of stories, from a variety of often competing perspectives" (1997, 13). The fact that different perspectives can be elicited from the photos is underscored by the manner in which Manuel and Nadia each provide different accounts of what they see in a photograph, as it relates differently to each of their lives. The photographs are thus one more level of textual mediation through which Manuel and Nadia have access to their family past. The disordered photographs in the old chest, as well as the partial and incomplete nature of the collection, inevitably lead to a likewise disordered, incomplete, and partial reconstruction of history. Memory is thus highlighted as a necessary, yet necessarily incomplete, recuperation of the past. As Jo Labanyi states, the novel presents an "ambivalent attitude to history as something to be recuperated but also something unknowable except in mediated form" (1995, 402).

The impossibility of a direct access to the past that such mediation imposes is further underscored by the fact that many of the photographs of people are studio pictures, presenting unrealistic poses with false props and backdrops. Furthermore, Manuel and Nadia realize that the images they are seeing are only copies, the originals having been given by Ramiro Retratista to the photographed individuals (1991, 495).[17] The text often mentions that the photographs are scattered in a disorganized fashion, as they are "desordenadas en el suelo" (1991, 15) [disarrayed on the floor]. They are described as "las caras en blanco y negro, las fotografías desplegadas como una población de fantasmas, en desorden caudaloso de cronologías y de vidas" (1991, 494) [the faces in black and white, the photographs displayed like a population of ghosts, in a copious disarray of chronologies and lives]. That the photos are described as a population of ghosts is highly significant, but it is also important to note that the disorder of the photos themselves extends to Manuel's very memory, as he finds himself incapable of ordering his recollection. He feels that it is as fragmentary as many of the images he has before him: "no es que no se acuerde, es que no sabe o no quiere regir la disposición de su memoria: ve imágenes detalladas y absurdas como fragmentos de sueños" (1991, 112) [it is not that he doesn't remember, it is that he doesn't know how to, or want to, control the disposition of his memory: he sees detailed and absurd images like fragments of dreams]. The past re-created through memory is not only inevitably fragmentary, it is also not easily distinguishable from a dream. Realizing that memory involves a creative process whereby dream and reality, truth and falsehood coexist, Manuel thinks of how difficult it is to separate these opposing qualities in the recollective process:

> Puedo inventar ahora, impunemente, para mi propia ternura y nostalgia, uno o dos recuerdos falsos pero no inverosímiles, no más arbitrarios, solo ahora lo sé, que los que de verdad me pertenecen. . . . Hasta ahora supuse que en la conservación de un recuerdo intervenían a medias el azar y una especie de conciencia biográfica. Poco a poco, desde que vi las fotografías innumerables de Ramiro Retratista y fui impregnándome del rostro y de la voz y de la piel y la memoria de Nadia igual que una cartulina blanca y vacía se impregna de sombras grises y luces sumergida en la cubeta del revelado, empiezo a entender que en casi todos los recuerdos comunes hay escondida una estrategia de mentira, que no eran más que arbitrarios despojos lo que yo tomé por trofeos o reliquias, que casi nada ha sido como yo creía que fue, como alguien, dentro de mí, un archivero deshonesto, un narrador paciente y oculto, embustero, asiduo, me contaba que era. (1991, 193)

> [I can invent now, with impunity, for my own fondness and nostalgia, one or two false, but not implausible, memories, no more arbitrary, only now do I know this, than those that really belonged to me. . . . Until now I assumed that both chance and a kind of biographical conscience contributed in equal measure to the conservation of a particular memory. Little by little, since I saw the countless photographs of Ramiro Retratista, and since I began to become infused with Nadia's face and voice and skin and memory, just like an empty white paper becomes infused with gray shadows and lights when it is submerged in the developing liquid, I begin to understand that in almost all common memories lies hidden a strategy of lying, that what I took for trophies or relics were nothing but arbitrary debris, that almost nothing has been like I thought it was, like someone, inside me, a dishonest archivist, a patient, hidden, relentless and mendacious narrator, told me it was.]

Manuel is awakening to a realization that the past may not have been as he has always seen it, that there may be another way to engage with it.[18] This new way to work through the past involves not only accepting that truth and falsehood are inexorably interrelated in any rememorative process, but that this process is never purely an individual one. Both of these realizations are greatly liberating for Manuel. Paradoxically, Manuel's freedom to invent, as much as remember his past emerges only when he abandons the isolated existence he has led, while trying to escape his childhood memories, and allows himself to lose his independence by becoming as one with Nadia: "impregnándome del rostro y de la voz y de la piel y la memoria de Nadia" (1991, 193) [impregnated by Nadia's face and voice and skin and memory]. The isolation of his previous existence is perfectly symbolized by his work as a simultaneous translator, a profession he carries out from the physical confinement of the translating booth, and in which he simply echoes the words of others, never truly engaging with those words in any real, personal manner. That distance has now disappeared, for Manuel does not just repeat Nadia's words and memories, but becomes "infused" with them.

We also have here an image for the *lieu de mémoire* that emerges in *El jinete polaco* as the most appropriate place for the working through of the postmemory with which both protagonists struggle. It is by becoming "infused" with the face, voice, memory, and, especially, the skin of the other that each one of the protagonists is able to deal with his or her own "postmemorial" legacy. We may recall that, in *L'hora violeta*, Norma had to allow the memory of the pain that others had suffered to become like a second skin before she could adequately write their stories: "Los recuerdos se mezclaban con las penas de los demás, caían sobre ella como las hojas de un almendro. En apariencia eran frágiles, estaban a punto de ser llevados por la fuerza del viento— es decir, del olvido—, pero lo cierto era que las penas de los demás y los recuerdos se iban acumulando hasta formar una segunda piel" (Roig 1991, 200) [The memories melded with the pain of others, they fell over her like leaves of an almond tree. In appearance they were fragile, about to be blown away by the wind—that is to say, by oblivion—, but the truth is that the pain of others and the memories continued to accumulate until they formed a second skin]. In a similar manner, Manuel here becomes enveloped by Nadia's face and voice, and her own skin becomes as his as they share their memories. He, too, like Norma, needs to assume the suffering of the other as his own "segunda piel" [second skin], and this skin, which is literally grafted on the body, becomes the *lieu de mémoire* in which he can, with her, work through his postmemory.

Of course, this place of memory is intimately connected with the other important *lieu de mémoire* in the text, the chest full of photographs. In fact, Manuel, in the last quote examined, equates the process of his becoming "infused" with Nadia's face, voice, memory, and skin with the process of a photograph being developed, an image in which photography becomes not only the medium for memory work, but a metaphor for that very process: "fui impregnándome del rostro y de la voz y de la piel y la memoria de Nadia igual que una cartulina blanca y vacía se impregna de sombras grises y luces sumergida en la cubeta del revelado" (1991, 193) [I began to become infused with Nadia's face and voice and skin and memory, just like an empty white paper becomes infused with gray shadows and lights when it is submerged in the developing liquid]. We may recall that Hirsch had described how "photographs offer a prism through which to study the postmodern space of cultural memory composed of leftovers, debris" (1997, 13). It is significant, therefore, that Manuel, after equating memory work itself with the process of photographic development, mentions that such a process allows him to acknowledge that what he earlier held in his memory as trophies are really nothing but "despojos" (1991, 193), that is, precisely, "leftovers, debris." There is thus a radical inversion of values connected with this new manner of working through the past that Manuel and Nadia are discovering, an inversion that will be seen to be very important for the value of memory itself in the novel. That photographs of the past function as "leftovers" and "debris" is, of course, connected to the fact that the past that Manuel and Nadia are working through is really their postmemory, and this experience is inexorably connected, as has been examined earlier, with all kinds of things that are passed down, that they receive, necessarily, secondhand. These debris function much like the ruins that have been explored in the previous chapters, partial remnants of a past that is beginnig to be seen in a different light.

Furthermore, there are other reasons why photographs are, according to Hirsch, "the medium connecting memory and postmemory" (1996, 429). Photographs combine presence and absence in the same way that postmemory does. As discussed in the last chapter, with regard to the photos of Judit described in *L'hora violeta*, photographs of people guarantee that a person was there, in front of the camera, at a certain moment (at least at the time those photos were taken, for now the possibility of digitally altering a photograph and creating a virtual reality has shaken such confidence). And yet that very moment in which the photo was taken is irrecoverably gone once one is looking at the final print. The photograph stops time and simultaneously reminds us that time marches inevitably forward. Because of this, there is an inexorable connection between photographs of people and death.

As Susan Sontag exclaims, "photographs state the innocence, the vulnerability of lives heading toward their own destruction and this link between photography and death haunts all photos of people" (1990, 70). Roland Barthes, likewise, sees that "death is the eidos of the photograph" (1981, 15) and claims that all photographs embody the "return of the dead" under their illusion of presence and life (1981, 9). Photographs are thus the perfect medium for Manuel and Nadia to exorcise the "transgenerational phantoms" that haunt them, for photographs are inevitably connected to the experience of haunting. Hirsch makes this explicit when she explains that "the referent haunts the picture like a ghost: it is a revenant, a return of the lost and dead other" (1997, 5).

The connection between photography and ghosts, between photography and death, is made recurrently throughout *El jinete polaco*. Upon seeing a photograph of his parents as children, Manuel feels that he can already see their future suffering in their faces: "llevaban escrito en la inocencia de sus caras todo el desamparo de su porvenir" (1991, 105) [they had written, on the innocence of their faces, all of their future helplessness]. Different time periods coexist in the photograph Manuel examines: the moment in which it was taken, the future that Manuel knows his parents will later face, and the present in which Manuel is regarding the photograph. Photography can thus collapse linear time. One time period overflows onto another, as inevitably happens in any experience of haunting, where something from the past overflows into the present.

It is Ramiro Retratista, however, who establishes the most significant connections between photography and death, between photography and ghosts. Ramiro had, in fact, inherited a series of supposed photographs of ghosts from his teacher of photography, the German expatriate Otto Zenner. Ramiro's obsession with the inevitable connection between photography and death partly grew out of the hold these images had on his imagination. He is also haunted by the image of the photograph that he once took of a beautiful young bride who was shot and killed the day after her wedding. This image, of course, is of Mariana, whose death is one of the mysteries deciphered in Muñoz Molina's first novel, *Beatus Ille,* and whose presence in *El jinete polaco* is one of many elements connecting both texts. Ramiro's work as a morgue photographer for the police further heightens his awareness of the similarities between the images of the dead and of the living, as he eventually finds that he cannot tell them apart. In his work, therefore, Ramiro inverts the relation between life and death, as photographs of the living make him imagine people's inevitable death, and photos of the dead seem to bring them back to life before his eyes. The town photographer reflects that "cuando examinaba una foto recién hecha pensaba que a la larga sería, como todas, el retrato de un muerto" (1991, 93) [when he examined a newly taken photograph, he thought that, in the long run, it would be, like all of them, the portrait of a dead person]. This makes him feel, inevitably, like an "enterrador prematuro" (1991, 93) [premature undertaker]. If Ramiro's photographs seem to anticipate the death of his subjects, thus integrating death into life, those same photographs later seem to bring the people photographed back to life after death. Ramiro is, in fact, described as "el único testigo y depositario de aquellas vidas que luego no quiso nadie recordar y que surgen ahora como en una clandestina y universal resurrección de los muertos" (1991, 495) [the only witness and custodian of those lives that no one wanted to remember and that now emerge as if in a clandestine and universal resurrection of the dead].

Such inversions ultimately have a powerfully subversive effect. Ramiro eventually develops a complete inability to accept and respect the authority of any of the powerful figures he photographs. The inversion of life and death in the photograph that Ramiro establishes is reinforced by the visual inversion that a photographic image creates within the camera:

> Veía a alguien posando en su estudio y antes de esconder la cabeza bajo la cortinilla ya se imaginaba la cara que tendría en la foto cuando estuviera muerto, y solo se olvidaba de este vaticinio lúgubre cuando miraba a través de la lente la figura invertida: entonces el caballero solemne o la dama vanidosa o el jerarca mutilado con boina y condecoraciones se convertían en equilibristas absurdos que intentaran mantener cabeza abajo toda su irrisoria dignidad. De tanto ver a la gente del revés tras el objetivo de su cámara acabó perdiendo el respeto por toda autoridad y adquirió una secreta irreverencia. (1991, 92–93)

> [He would see someone posing in his study and before hiding his head under the little curtain, he already imagined the face that would appear on the photo once that person were dead, and he only forgot this somber premonition when he saw, through the lens, the inverted figure: then the solemn gentleman or vain lady or the mutilated officer with a beret and medals became an absurd acrobat, trying to maintain all of his or her laughable dignity while upside down. From seeing people upside down so often through the lens of his camera, he ended up losing all respect for authority, and acquired a secret irreverence.]

Photography, through the undermining it entails of clear differences between life and death, between up and down, is thus seen to radically subvert established order. Inasmuch as, in the novel, photography becomes an image for memory itself, remembering will likewise be shown to have a similarly subversive power.

In fact, photography does not just serve as a *catalyst for* memory in the text, but becomes a *metaphor for* the very process of memory formation, as was the case with the quote in which Manuel explicitly compared his becoming infused with Nadia's memory with the image of a photograph being developed. This comparison emerges again in the scene in which Ramiro is developing a photograph that will change him forever. This is the photograph of the mummified woman that he took as a police photographer when she was discovered interred in a wall. The photograph he took made Ramiro fall madly in love with the woman who had died many years before he was able to capture her incorrupt beauty with his camera. This photo spurred him on a quest to discover her story, a story that Don Mercurio eventually told him only in partial and falsified form. The way her image emerges in the developing process is described in detail, as Ramiro "vería la cara formándose delante de sus ojos . . . vio surgir la figura cada segundo más precisa de la muchacha emparedada . . . miraba fijamente, lo miraba desde el fondo del lavabo que usaba para revelar como si respirara bajo el agua y en el interior de la muerte" (1991, 91) [would see her face developing before his eyes . . . he saw the figure of the mummified woman emerge ever more clearly . . . she gazed fixedly, she looked at him from the bottom of the basin that he used for developing, as if she were breathing under the water and within death]. The mummified woman, the protagonist of many of the ghost stories that haunted Manuel as a child, here emerges to haunt Ramiro Retratista as well. She, of course, is one of the most powerful images of haunting in the novel, as her power is felt long after her death. She seems to be breathing inside the liquid within which her photograph is being developed, and appears to be looking intently at Ramiro Retratista from beyond the grave.[19]

The ghostly life-after-death that the mummified woman represents is a perfect image of the "transgenerational phantom" in the novel, also a ghostly force that lives on over several generations. The scene in which she slowly appears from within the developing liquid is a perfect image for memory itself, emerging out of oblivion and gaining a hold on someone. That the mummified woman seems to be looking intently at Ramiro Retratista brings to mind Jacques Derrida's explanation, in *Specters of Marx,* that a ghost always implicates us directly into its unfinished story, for it is the being "that looks at us, that concerns us" (1994, 6). The expression that Derrida uses for something that looks at us and concerns us is the same in French, *qui nous regarde* (1993, 26). In Roig's *L'hora violeta,* Norma felt this power of a ghostly being when she remembered the ex-deportee's eyes while trying to write his story after his demise. In *El jinete polaco*, remembering is also presented as something that engages us, and makes us become engaged with, the past. Memory functions like the alluring image of the mummified woman that emerges from within the developing fluid, looks directly at Ramiro Retratista, and seduces him into wanting to know everything about her. Walter Benjamin claims that "every image of the past that is not recognized by the present as one of its own concerns threatens to disappear irretrievably" (1969, 255). In presenting various images of a ghost "that looks at us, that concerns us," *El jinete polaco* is heeding this warning, making sure that the past these ghosts represent does not, in fact, "disappear irretrievably."

Manuel also feels the power of similar gazes from the past calling his attention, drawing him into their world. When he visits the Frick collection in New York (where he will encounter the original version of the painting "The Polish Rider"), he realizes uncomfortably that all the people in the portraits he admires are long dead. However, he still feels the power of their eyes looking at him: "es como si el silencio viniera hacia él desde el interior de los cuadros y fuera el espacio desde donde lo miran esas pupilas sosegadas de muertos" (1991, 439) [it is as if the silence came towards him from the interior of the paintings, and as if it were from within that silence that those calm and dead pupils regarded him]. Significantly, also, when he is in Nadia's apartment and he scrutinizes one of his parents' wedding photographs, he realizes that his father is looking at him directly from within the photo, in a way he never does in real life: "Mira los ojos de su padre en la foto: cuando están juntos, las pocas veces que él ha ido a Mágina en los últimos años, los dos eluden mirarse abiertamente" (1991, 160) [He looks at his father's eyes in the photo: when they are together, the few times he has gone to Mágina in the last few years, they both avoid looking at each other directly]. If Manuel has averted his father's direct gaze in real life, he cannot do so when confronted with these photographs. The direct stare coming from his father's image in the photo does not allow Manuel to escape the weight of the past, as he has done throughout his life. That gaze draws him in, just like Ramiro Retratista had been drawn in, wanting to discover the real story of the mummified woman.

The gaze of Manuel's father, which seems to emerge out of the photograph to strike his son, can be understood as that element of the photograph that Barthes calls the *punctum*. Barthes compares the *punctum* to the *studium* of a photograph. Whereas the latter is based on the social codes that make an image comprehensible to most people of a given culture, the *punctum* is any marginal element in the photograph, any detail, that evokes something to a particular viewer based on his/her personal past and individual reaction to the image. That is why, explains Barthes, "the *studium* is ultimately always coded, the *punctum* is not" (1981, 51). The *punctum*, furthermore, emerges from the photograph with a wounding force: "It shoots out of it [the photograph] like an arrow, and pierces me.... A photograph's *punctum* is that accident which pricks me (but also bruises me, is poignant to me)" (1981, 26–27). In this sense, Barthes's *punctum* functions somewhat like Derrida's concept of the ghost, an image related to the past "that looks at us, that concerns us" (Derrida, 1994, 6), which is to say, that it "is poignant" in a particularly striking manner. Manuel is, indeed, struck and pierced by his father's direct gaze emerging from the photograph, and that gaze initiates a new relation between Manuel and his past.

There is a fundamental dialectic in the novel, therefore, in which memory connects past and present, and photographs are the mediators of this dialectic. On the one hand, photographs permit Ramiro, Nadia, and Manuel to re-create the past from the vantage point of the present. The past is the object of a narrative process that the protagonists of the novel undertake at different times. As discussed earlier, the novel presents a postmodern highlighting of the fact that there is no access to the past except through various forms of textual and visual mediation, and that this process inevitably combines truthful recall with creative invention. On the other hand, however, it is the past that seems to come back to the present, to affect the present, just like the image of the mummified woman looks directly at Ramiro Retratista, and later the people in Ramiro's photos stare directly at Manuel. In this sense, the past affects that narrative process in the present whereby it is being re-created, it is not solely the object of that endeavor. It is here that the Benjaminian nature of the novel's exploration of memory and post-memory becomes most evident.

In *The Arcades Project*, Benjamin explains his concept of the dialectical relation between past and present that memory establishes. He sees this new way of understanding the past as a "Copernican revolution," for it implies an inversion of previous conceptions of the relation between past and present: "The Copernican revolution in historical perception is as follows. Formerly it was thought that a fixed point had been found in 'what has been,' and one saw the present engaged in tentatively concentrating the forces of knowledge on this ground.

Now this relation is to be overturned, and what has been is to become the dialectical reversal—the flash of awakened consciousness. Politics attains primacy over history. The facts become something that just now first happened to us, first struck us: to establish them is the affair of memory. Indeed, awakening is the great exemplar of memory" (1999, 388–89).

In this dialectical relation between past and present, the past is no longer just there, passively waiting to be explained from the vantage point of the present. The past "strikes us," somewhat like Barthes's *punctum* arising from a photograph. It has an agency that can affect the very process by means of which it is re-created in the present. For Benjamin, of course, the past that "strikes us" is that which has been omitted from dominant views of history. Its power to "strike us" derives from the fact that it shatters the illusion of continuity and progress on which such dominant views of history are based as it embodies, precisely, all that was left out and repressed from those constructions. For Benjamin, "awakening is the great exemplar of memory" because remembering such a past that "strikes us" is something that inevitably shakes us, awakens us from the blind acceptance of such dominant views of the past. In this sense, indeed, "politics attains primacy over history." As if he had been aware of the equivalence that Muñoz Molina points out between the old Castilian terms for remembering and awakening, Benjamin elsewhere states: "Remembering and awakening are most intimately related. Awakening is namely the dialectical, Copernican turn of remembrance" (1999, 389). The Spanish philosopher Manuel Reyes Mate summarizes this "Copernican turn of remembrance" that Benjamin proposes: "poco a poco va haciéndose diáfano el cambio copernicano en la consideración de la historia que aquí se maneja: si antes el pasado era un punto fijo y muerto que había que animar desde el presente, ahora ese pasado está llamado a incidir directamente en el despertar de la conciencia del presente" (1991, 211) [little by little the Copernican change in the consideration of history that is presented here becomes clear: if before, the past was a fixed and dead point that had to be animated from the present, now that past is called to spark the awakening of conscience in the present].

We have already seen how, in *El jinete polaco,* memory is, in fact, compared to an awakening. It now becomes clear that such an awakening recognizes the need to remember those that had been forgotten, omitted from official views of history. It is thus important that most of the photographs by Ramiro Retratista that Manuel and Nadia study are those of "aquellas vidas que luego no quiso nadie recordar y que surgen ahora como en una clandestina y universal resurrección de los muertos" (1991, 495) [those lives that no one wanted to remember and that now emerge as if in a clandestine and universal resurrection of the dead]. The ghostly resurrection of forgotten lives in these images is thus a reflection not only of the inversions between life and death that photography establishes, but of the radically subversive force of photography as a medium for the emergence of a memory that enables the past to "strike us," thus undermining a blind faith in progress. The remembrance that emerges from viewing these photographs is certainly a "vigilant" memory, as it brings to life the stories of so many "lives that no one wanted to remember."

In this context, it is important to note that when the adolescent Manuel begins to prepare for his long-awaited escape from Mágina in 1973, as he is about to go study in Madrid after his last year of high school, he fantasizes that he and his friends "viviríamos otras vidas en ciudades lejanas, y el tiempo habría perdido su tediosa eternidad circular, la rotación de los cursos, de las cosechas, de los trabajos en el campo.... Desde ahora el tiempo era una línea recta que se prolongaba en dirección al porvenir y al vacío" (1991, 344) [we would live other lives in distant cities, and time would lose its tedious circular eternity, the rotation of school years, of harvests, of the work in the fields.... From now on, time was a straight line projecting itself in the direction of the future and the void]. The circularity of time that had governed his life until then will be replaced with the supposedly freeing sense of a time that marches forward like a straight line. This archetypal image of progress, however, which Manuel hopes will characterize his life after he escapes the burden of the past, the eternal return of classes and work in the fields of Mágina, is already associated with a "vacío" [void]. Manuel's future life will, indeed, be empty. His profession as a simultaneous translator is a perfect metaphor for the fast-paced new lifestyle that the post-Franco world will usher in, as he runs around from country to country, from conference to conference, endlessly translating words that mean nothing to him with perfect, split-second timing. It is this fast-paced, yet empty, lifestyle that is interrupted when he meets Nadia and allows himself to again enter that circular time of the past by remaining in her apartment in New York for over a week, immersed in the history that "strikes him" as it emerges from Ramiro's photographs.

One moment in which the past emerges to "strike him" is when Manuel is looking at a photograph of his family that includes several generations, from his great-grandfather to his parents. A change takes place in Manuel, for now he realizes that, although his life has been overwhelmingly determined by the traumatic experiences they have suffered, he does not know very much about what their lives were really like. He has, in fact, grown up rejecting the effect that those lives had on his own. Manuel here is beginning to work through his postmemory, something that is only possible because he has stopped trying to escape it. As he looks at the image, Manuel thinks:

> Miro sus caras y tengo la sensación de que nunca los he conocido verdaderamente, de que nunca he sabido cómo eran, quiénes son fuera y lejos de mí, de qué se acuerdan, qué saben, cómo vivían en las edades oscuras del hambre y del terror, no hace siglos, sino años, no muchos, un poco antes de que yo naciera. . . . Ya casi no puedo acordarme de sus palabras y es posible que no tenga ocasión de pedirles que me sigan contando, cómo era el campo de concentración donde te llevaron, le preguntaba a mi abuelo, qué sentía uno al saber que era fácil que lo condenaran a muerte, cómo es tener entre las manos un fusil y tenderse en una trinchera. (1991, 105–6)

> [I look at their faces and I have the feeling that I have never really known them, that I have never really understood what they were like, who they were aside from and far from me, what they remember, what they know, how they lived in the dark times of hunger and terror, not centuries but years ago, not too many, just shortly before I was born. . . . Now I can hardly remember their words, and it is possible that I will not be able to ask them to continue telling me, what was the concentration camp where they took you like, I asked my grandfather, what did one feel when one knew it was easy to be condemned to death, what is it like to have a rifle in your hands and to lie down in the trenches.]

The "act of memory" that Manuel engages in throughout the novel is liberating for him because it is the first time he is telling his story instead of inheriting it. It now becomes clear that this "act of memory" also emerges from a desire to learn about his family past in a new way, one that does not solely react against it. That straight line of progress with which he had fantasized as he was preparing to escape from Mágina has been interrupted. Through the stories he tells Nadia, Manuel returns to that past he has repressed for so long, recognizing that there is much that he still needs to discover about it. At the end of the novel, Manuel will physically return to Mágina only after his grandmother has died. Thus, although he will be able to find out many things about his family past, his fear that there are certain questions he will no longer be able to ask is realized, for he will no longer have access to his grandmother's personal perspective of history.

It is, again, not coincidental that Ramiro's photographs are the mechanisms that trigger this experience in Manuel amounting to a

"Copernican turn of remembrance." Benjamin has likened the new approach to the past that he advocates to the process of photographic development. The inversion in the visual image that such a process entails is what makes photography a perfect model for an approach to history that highlights what dominant versions of the past have repressed, that manages to "brush history against the grain" and "blast open the continuum of history" (1969, 257, 262). David Frisby explains that for Benjamin the historian is like "someone operating a camera who is interested not merely in the inverted reality of the actual photographic image of bourgeois society—that is as that society wishes to see itself—but in what the camera actually produces, namely negatives in which what is light is dark and vice-versa" (1986, 237). *El jinete polaco* explicitly underscores this subversive function of photography when Ramiro Retratista loses all respect for authority because of constantly seeing the powerful social figures he photographs standing on their head in the image within his camera.

Furthermore, the very way in which Manuel and Nadia study Ramiro's photographs, with the photos spread out in a disordered manner on the floor, evokes another image that Benjamin often used to represent the approach to history that the "Copernican turn of remembrance" generated: that of the montage. The disordered grouping of images that a montage presents resists a unitary linear reading. It resists, also, being subsumed under dominant versions of history as progress. Max Pensky explains the subversive nature of the montage, for in such an arrangement of images "the formerly insignificant fragments, rescued and redeployed in a critical text, would shatter the 'philosophy of history' that determined them as insignificant" (2004, 187). As has been mentioned before, the disordered photos that are strewn about Nadia's apartment represent "aquellas vidas que luego no quiso nadie recordar" (1991, 495) [those lives that no one wanted to remember]. Thus, Manuel and Nadia's effort to identify and remember the people in these images is a way to give renewed meaning to what society has relegated as supposedly insignificant. The montage principle, in which the photographs are presented not in a linear, ordered form but in a manner that can be read in various directions simultaneously, also helps to "blast open the continuum of history" (Benjamin 1969, 262) because it forces a recognition of the spaces between images instead of trying to present them in a seamless evolution. Manuel, in fact, is very aware of the discontinuity between images and experiences that are supposed to be connected by a seamless flow. As Jo Labanyi explains, "In *El jinete polaco*, the protagonist compares his experience of history to that of watching a film lacking in continuity editing ... or where the images succeed each other so fast that one loses the thread and cannot make out the connections ...; his reconstruction of the past, as he attempts to fill in the gaps between Ramiro Retratista's photographs, highlights these discontinuities rather than ironing them out" (2000, 73). Manuel further "highlights the discontinuities" in experience "rather than ironing them out" when he explains his growing disillusionment with his fast-paced lifestyle. He complains that his jet-setting life is based on "no detenerse nunca, no perder ni una de las palabras escuchadas en el auricular, no quedarse solo a una cierta hora de la noche, no llegar tarde al trabajo ni al mostrador de facturación del aeropuerto, añadir cada minuto al próximo sin mirar la delgada fisura de vacío que hay entre los dos" (1991, 400) [never stopping, never losing a single one of the words coming through the headphones, not remaining alone at a certain hour of the night, not arriving late to work nor to the check-in counter of the airport, adding one minute to the next without ever looking at the thin fissure of emptiness that exists between them]. His experience with Nadia becomes an opportunity to stop the tiring rush forward and concentrate on the narrow fissure of emptiness that exists between one moment and the next.

The notion of an interruption in the flow of time is essential for the Benjaminian view of memory, and of the past, in the novel. Reyes Mate further describes the Benjaminian "Copernican turn of remembrance" as a relation between the present and the past in which "el pasado olvidado y despreciado está ahí dispuesto a asaltar el presente" and where "el pasado es una interrupción del tiempo presente" (1993, 162, 164) [the forgotten and spurned past is there, ready to assault the present], [the past is an interruption of present time]. The image of the past that "interrupts" the present is crucial for understanding Manuel and Nadia's encounter. Manuel first meets Nadia, as an adult, in a conference in Madrid only after he has almost died in a car accident driving up from Mágina overnight. His whole life is metaphorically interrupted, as Manuel arrives at the conference feeling that he had, in a sense, died in that car incident and that "ya estaba muerto" (1991, 449) [he was already dead]. Significantly, it is this experience of being almost literally engulfed by death, by that "thin fissure of emptiness" between two consecutive moments, that antecedes his encounter with Nadia. Benjamin has described his approach to history as one that manages "to seize hold of a memory as it flashes up at a moment of danger" (1969, 255), and this is exactly what happens in the novel. The danger of death is precisely what shakes Manuel from being subsumed in his fast-paced forward-looking life, and makes him stop and face his past.

5: ANTONIO MUÑOZ MOLINA: MEMORY AND POSTMEMORY

His subsequent encounter with Nadia in New York, and the experience of being isolated from the present as they allow the past to be resurrected and envelop them in her apartment, is a perfect image of the past "assaulting" and "interrupting" the present. In fact, their stay in Nadia's apartment is recurrently described as an interruption of normal time. The apartment is often described as an island, a space in the present where time stands still, or flows in many directions simultaneously except in the narrowly straight, forward-moving line that Manuel's life has become since he left Mágina. Time in the apartment cannot be measured by normal markers of chronology, such as calendars and clocks, for Manuel and Nadia are "fuera del día y de la noche, del calendario y del reloj, como supervivientes en una isla desierta" (1991, 18) [outside of the day and the night, of the calendar and the clock, like survivors on a deserted island]. At a certain moment, Manuel is thinking of the past of Nadia's father, and imagines a nightfall that could be similar to the time outside Nadia's abode, except that

> el tiempo de este anochecer no se parece al de mi vida de ahora, no fluye y se escapa como las horas y las semanas y los días de los relojes digitales y de los calendarios automáticos, gira huyendo y regresa en una tenue perennidad de linterna de sombras en la que algunas veces el pasado ocurre mucho después que el porvenir y todas las voces, los rostros, las canciones, los sueños, los nombres, sobre todo las canciones y los nombres, relumbran sin confusión en un presente simultáneo. (1991, 25–26)

> [the time of this nightfall does not resemble that of my current life, it doesn't flow and escape like the hours and the weeks and the days of the digital clocks and the automatic calendars, it escapes, it turns and returns tenuously and perennially like a shadow lantern in which sometimes the past occurs long after the future, and all the voices, the faces, the songs, the dreams, the names, especially the songs and the names, shine without confusion in a simultaneous present.]

Manuel and Nadia's stay in her apartment clearly represents an interruption of normal time. Not only do they inhabit a space where the past has emerged to "interrupt" and destabilize the present, but the past is seen as not being past at all, for it and the future coexist in a "presente simultáneo" [simultaneous present].[20] In fact, in this inversion of normal chronology, the past is yet to come, perhaps because its effect on the present as it "strikes" both Manuel and Nadia is still to be fully assimilated by both protagonists. If these temporal inversions are important in reflecting a Benjaminian view of the past as having the ability to interrupt and change the present, the image of the "linterna de sombras" [shadow lantern] evokes the inversions of optical images, where "what is light is dark and vice-versa" (Frisby 1986, 237), whose subversive potential Benjamin much appreciated.

It is also significant that the past that emerges to interrupt the present in Manuel's memory is populated by the songs of his childhood. We have already seen how references to those songs, and to adventure novels, radio programs, "folletines" [serial novels], comic books, the rock songs of Manuel's adolescent rebellion as well as the photographs in Ramiro's chest, are all part of the "double-stranded narrative" of postmemory that Manuel and Nadia are producing. In this "double-stranded narrative," the textual modes of transmission of the past are at the heart of the narrative re-creations of history presented. The constant presence of such popular mass-cultural forms, moreover, is also essential for the Benjaminian approach to the past that the novel presents, and which Jo Labanyi sees as predominant in much post-transition Spanish narrative: "It seems significant that the shadow figures of history's losers and *desaparecidos* which insist on returning in so much Spanish fiction and film of the transition and since . . . do so via reference to a variety of popular or mass-cultural forms: cinema, the thriller, family photographs. For the return to demand reparation of the victims of modern Spanish history is also the demand for recognition of the popular and mass-cultural forms whose modes of consumption constitute the lifestyle of the 'ghosts of history'; that is, modernity's losers" (2002, 8). If all the references to popular and mass-cultural forms of art in the novel are part and parcel of the text's vindication of the memory of the losers of history, it is interesting to note that the maximum example of high art in the novel, the copy of "The Polish Rider," can also be seen to serve a similar function. One could see in the double movement of the rider in the painting, a movement whereby he is riding forwards while looking mysteriously backwards or sideways, a double orientation somewhat similar to that of Benjamin's "angel of history." The "angel," also, is being swept forward by the winds of progress, while he, looking back, sees only a growing heap of wreckage. Perhaps this is the true secret that the Polish rider seems to keep, when Nadia observes him, a secret of which both she and Manuel are starting to become aware. This secret involves a recognition that the straight line of progress which had held so much promise for them as they hoped to be freed of the burden of their family past was, in fact, not only "empty," but inevitably built upon, and thus inseparable from, the suffering of the victims of history that now look at them from Ramiro's photographs.

It is important to remember that Manuel's fantasy of leaving Mágina and experiencing a new sense of time as progress instead of

5: ANTONIO MUÑOZ MOLINA: MEMORY AND POSTMEMORY

stagnation, of time as "una línea recta que se prolongaba en dirección al porvenir y al vacío" (1991, 344) [a straight line projecting itself in the direction of the future and the void], occurred in 1973, just as he is about to move to Madrid to continue his studies. Manuel's new experience of time as progress, which he hopes will leave the past behind, thus coincides with the very end of Francoism, and will continue with the transition to democracy. As has been amply discussed in previous chapters, the transition to democracy was as eager as Manuel was to leave the past behind. The new paradigm of time as the straight line of progress that Manuel evokes can be interpreted in several ways. In a more general sense, it refers to the change that Spanish society underwent, from the 1960s on, evolving from a traditional, predominantly rural society, to an industrialized one. In the words of historian Raymond Carr, in Spain "an agrarian society with a rachitic industrial appendage had become, by 1975, an industrial society—ranked tenth in the world—with an agrarian appendage" (1987, 1). The fact that the cyclical nature of time that Manuel is trying to escape is characterized by the "tediosa eternidad circular ... de las cosechas, de los trabajos en el campo" (1991, 344) [tedious circular eternity ... of the harvests, of the work in the fields] surely points to this interpretation. Manuel thus represents a generation of Spaniards who grew up at the time of this striking social change, and his apparent success in escaping the hardship of his parents' life, especially his father's endless and exhausting work in the fields, is emblematic of how things had changed within one generation. Of course, his all-consuming guilt over the emotional distance he feels with this father because of their very different lives, and his inability to stay for long periods of time with his family in Mágina due to a general sense of unease when he returns, both indicate that such success may come at a high personal price. Another perspective, however, could also understand the new linear time that Manuel dreams of in 1973 as more specifically representing that which would govern the Spanish transition, a time period in which so many were obsessed with proving that Spain was finally becoming fully modern and European. The interruption of this time line that occurs with Manuel's accident, and with his enclosure with Nadia in her apartment, thus also represents the interruption of the dominant view of the transition as a *tabula rasa* that supposedly had laid the past to rest. Manuel and Nadia's "acts of memory" embody the inevitable "return of the repressed" that emerges once that straight line of progress and development is interrupted.

The Benjaminian critique of progress is taken one step further in this novel, however. It is highly significant that Manuel and Nadia's isolation in her apartment during more than a week in early 1991 occurs exactly at the time that the first Gulf War is initiated. In their brief encounters with the outside world, through newspapers and television, Nadia and Manuel become aware that the war is beginning, although they turn away from the present as they are summoned by the past: "encienden la televisión y la apagan rápidamente, ha empezado una guerra muy lejos y cunde en los noticiarios y hasta en los anuncios una histeria de banderas, un patriotismo de exterminio que ellos pueden ilusoriamente abolir con el mando a distancia" (1991, 493) [they turn the television on and quickly switch it off, a war has begun far away and the news programs and even the commercials are full of a hysteria of flags, a patriotism of extermination that they can illusorily abolish with the remote control]. By turning the television off, Manuel and Nadia are also rejecting a whole rhetoric of nationalism and belligerence that has greatly sustained the Western discourse of historical progress. The Gulf War, of course, was supposed to represent a great milestone in that discourse, based as it was on an unquestionable faith in technological and mass-media advancements, the very same advancements that allowed the war to be won so quickly and to be televised and supposedly made available for mass consumption in real time. By becoming an "island" outside of normal time, Nadia's apartment becomes a refuge from this dominant, and dominating, rhetoric. The past that comes back to "interrupt" the present in Nadia's apartment thus "interrupts" not only the ideology of progress that has characterized the Spanish transition to democracy, but also this late twentieth-century ideology of progress that goes far beyond the Spanish context. In this sense, Muñoz Molina's novel explores the effects of postmemory, of the enduring weight of the past of Spain's civil war and postwar repression on the younger generations of Spaniards who have not lived those events, but it does so within a broader international framework.[21] In fact, the exploration of memory and postmemory in the novel may be understood in the context of a wider manifestation of a series of memory practices, which Andreas Huyssen has called a "memory culture" at the end of the twentieth and beginning of the twenty-first century, that have emerged in part as a response to the most pernicious effects of the dominant Western ideology of progress:

> The current transformations of the temporal imaginary brought on by virtual space and time may highlight the enabling dimension of memory culture. Whatever their specific occasion, cause, or context, the intense memory practices we witness in so many different parts of the world articulate a fundamental crisis of an earlier structure of temporality that marked the age of high modernity with its trust in progress and development.... Polit-

ically, many memory practices today counteract the triumphalism of modernization theory in its latest guise of the discourse of "globalization." Culturally, they express the growing need for spatial and temporal anchoring in a world of increasing flux in ever denser networks of compressed time and space. (2003, 27)

The Gulf War of 1991 is, indeed, a paradigmatic example of those "ever denser networks of compressed time and space" that Huyssen mentions. Muñoz Molina's novel thus explicitly thematizes the problematics that Huyssen analyzes. The novel presents a practice of memory that grows out of, and articulates, a crisis in predominant paradigms of progress and development, both those that characterized the Spanish transition to democracy, and those on a global scale that later are embodied in the first Gulf War.

Furthermore, the exploration of the past that Manuel and Nadia undertake also represents a certain "spatial and temporal anchoring." This exploration is based on an interruption of a way of life that had attempted to escape the effects of history, and reflects a new desire and ability to face and work through that past. At a certain point, the text explains that the rememorative process that Manuel is sharing with Nadia is liberating, as has been seen before, because it is the first time that he is the one telling the story of the past instead of being haunted and possessed by it. The text also specifies that this new narrative agency makes Manuel feel like he has finally found a certain "anchoring" and stability: "Pero ahora no está siendo poseído por los recuerdos de otros: como si se acercara nadando a una orilla y extendiera cobardemente el pie hacia el fondo del agua y tocara la arena, pisa la primera tierra firme que de verdad le pertenece" (1991, 156) [But now he is not being possessed by the memories of others: as if he were swimming and approached a shore, cravenly extending his foot to the bottom of the water and touching sand, stepping on the first solid land that truly belongs to him]. From the island that Nadia's apartment has become, Manuel feels, for the first time, that he is finally stepping onto secure ground. He has only been able to do this by means of working through his memory and postmemory with Nadia. This process that the protagonists have undergone together is a perfect example of the kind of "productive remembering" that Huyssen calls for, a rememorative practice that must, in a Benjaminian sense, "interrupt the present" to make space for all that had been previously repressed and forgotten (2003, 27).

Such "productive remembering" is necessary for the working through of the postmemory of both protagonists. The "anchoring" that this process provides entails an acceptance of, instead of resistance to, the past. It is based on a recognition that the past is part of one's life, of one's identity, and that one must be responsive to it. Just like Spanish society needs to accept that the effects of the past are ever-present, Manuel must come to terms with the fact that his family past, from which he has been running away for so long, is a part of him. As David Herzberger expresses it, "Manuel had sought to maintain his life as a blank page but now realizes that it is an unavoidable palimpsest" (2000, 137). The image of the palimpsest again reappears, as in the previous chapters. It is an image that embodies the persistence of the past in the present, a persistence that is continually renegotiated, in all the meta-memory texts studied here, in an ongoing process of "productive remembering."

It should not be forgotten, moreover, that this new identity as palimpsest, which is being narratively re-created throughout the novel, is based on references to and interpretations of a whole array of visual and literary texts. These levels of mediation of memory are more layers that inevitably become part of that new palimpsest of identity. The narrative process whereby this new identity is being forged, furthermore, combines recollection and imagination in a manner that re-creates the past not in its official versions, but in new constructions that give a voice to those who previously had been silenced and forgotten. When accommodating these voices from the past, Manuel explains that they "congregaban con la imaginación y la memoria" (1991, 18) [congregated with imagination and memory]. He elsewhere states that in his process of remembering, "se me confunden los hilos de la imaginación y la memoria" (1991, 508) [I confuse the threads of imagination and memory]. Imagination and memory are allied in a process that leads to the emergence of a "vigilant" memory that interrupts and subverts dominant constructions of the past. In *L'hora violeta*, we may recall, Natàlia also claims that "la imaginació es una buena aliada del recuerdo" (Roig 1980a, 250) [imagination is a good ally of memory] and that "el orden de la imaginación se sale de todos los datos, de todos los hechos. Ésta es la venganza de la literatura contra la historia" (1980a, 103) [the order of imagination goes beyond all facts, all events. That is literature's revenge against history]. The mixture of imagination and memory, in *El jinete polaco* as in *L'hora violeta*, allows for a new view of history to emerge, one that may change the present, and the future, for the better.

At the end of the novel, when Manuel finally leaves Nadia's apartment and reenters normal time, he returns to Mágina after learning of his grandmother's death. As Manuel wanders around Mágina, waiting for Nadia's arrival, he finds, in an antiques store, the mummified woman he had seen in Ramiro's photographs. However, he is surprised to discover that she is only a wax copy of the real mummy. One more level of mediation is thus added to his ability to access the story of her life, which is central to his own, as the son of that woman's affair with Don Mercurio had been Pedro Expósito Expósito, Manuel's great-grandfather. Truth and falsehood, original and copy are again intermingled in Manuel's process of accessing the past. This knowledge of his past, however, would have been forever lost to Manuel had he waited much longer to return to Mágina. Manuel is only able to discover the truth about the wax copy of the mummy, and about Don Mercurio's affair with the beautiful woman, because he manages to interview Don Mercurio's chauffeur, Julián, who is very old and living in a retirement home. Manuel's act of interviewing Julián is a manifestation of his newly discovered interest in his past, of the change he has experienced with Nadia. He is now aware of all the questions he must ask about his family past while there is still time. With this newly found interest in uncovering his family past, Manuel here becomes a representative of the new generation in Spain, that of "la generación de los nietos de los vencidos" (Rojo 2004) [the generation of the grandchildren of the vanquished], which looks to the past with a healthy curiosity and desire to discover all that had previously been repressed.

From Julián, Manuel discovers that shortly after the mummified woman was discovered and Ramiro Retratista took her picture, Don Mercurio ordered Julián to steal her so that he could live the rest of his days in the company of the incorrupt remains of the woman who had been the love of his life. When the mummy began to decompose, however, Don Mercurio asked the town sculptor secretly to make a copy of the mummy. It was the sculptor who made the wax copy that Manuel found in the antiques store years later.

A copy of a mummified woman, who was, in turn, but the ghostly echo of the real woman who had been Manuel's great-great-grandmother, is thus the key to much of Manuel's past. Just as Ramiro's photos and the image of "The Polish Rider" are copies, the past in the novel can only be re-created based on such simulacra, in a process that ultimately makes it hard to distinguish what was true and what was not. The wax copy of the mummified woman, which the antiques dealer tries to convince Manuel to buy, is partly a metaphor for the commodification of memory in contemporary society. Yet it also signals the power of a memory that persists, irrespective of so many efforts to repress, falsify, or forget it. As Jo Labanyi claims: "The postmodern stress on the impossibility of direct access to the past may be a response to the ubiquitousness of the media, advertising and heritage industries, which convert history into a consumer commodity; but it can also be seen as a recognition of the spectral quality of the traces left by past on the present, and of the moral imperative that requires us to bear witness to 'the traces of those who were not allowed to leave a trace'; namely, ghosts" (2000, 80). The return of the mummified woman, in all her forms, shows that, as Faulkner claimed, "the past is not dead, it is not even past" (qtd. in Muñoz Molina 1998b, 146), and that an accurate historical account of history may be less important, if it is ever possible to attain, than a responsible acceptance of the effects of that past in the present. As Muñoz Molina explains in one of his articles, "Pasado y presente se superponen en la conciencia, se invaden y falsifican entre sí, y lo nunca ocurrido cobra tanta o tan poca importancia como lo que de verdad ocurrió, y la memoria y el deseo acaban entrelazados en una misma irrealidad que... se transmuta... en una deslumbradora alegoría moral" (1998b, 145) [Past and present are superimposed in consciousness, they invade and falsify each other, and what has never happened gains as much or as little importance as what really occurred, as memory and desire become intertwined in the same unreality which . . . is transformed into . . . a dazzling moral allegory]. Again, the mixing of memory and desire appears as one of Muñoz Molina's literary preoccupations. This mixture can become "una deslumbradora alegoría moral" [a dazzling moral allegory], for it points to the debt that we in the present have to all those who were on the underside of history. By the end of the novel, Manuel and Nadia have developed a keen understanding of this debt. The experience of "mixing memory and desire" that they had undergone in Nadia's apartment in New York continues now in Mágina, with a small, significant change. The very last words of the novel, which have shifted imperceptibly from Manuel's first person perspective to a third person narration, state, of Manuel and Nadia, that "no sienten más que gratitud y deseo" (1991, 577) [they feel only gratitude and desire]. Memory has been transformed into gratitude, and gratitude and desire come together in a true "alegoría moral" [moral allegory] that makes a sense of responsibility and appreciation for the past a necessary condition for any possibility of a better future.

Like the mysterious horseman in the painting "The Polish Rider," therefore, Muñoz Molina's novel presents characters that are riding forward into the future, but who must face backwards as they do so and pay attention to the calls from the past. The voices from the past heard throughout the novel are clearly those of the victims of history, the losers of the Spanish civil war and of the postwar repression, those suffering internal as well as external exile long after the war. Theirs are ghostly voices that, as the concept of postmemory makes clear, do not just belong to the past, even when they are apparently no longer heard by the new generations growing up in a newly democratic Spain. These voices reverberate throughout the present. Meta-memory texts like *El jinete polaco*, which explicitly explore the workings of postmemory, help us understand how such traumatic events affect subsequent generations in ways that are similar, but also significantly different, from how they affected those that suffered the events directly. Texts such as this one are invaluable, therefore, for helping to create not only an effective "culture of memory" in Spain, but a much-needed "culture of postmemory" as well.

Conclusion

WORKING THROUGH MEMORY IS NO EASY TASK. HOWEVER, IT IS necessary if one is to come to terms with the past. All the meta-memory texts analyzed here explore the process by means of which a traumatic past is written and rewritten, recounted or repressed, transmitted or forgotten. Each, therefore, presents a reflection about the nature and function of remembering itself. Pierre Janet, Freud's colleague at the Paris hospital *La Salpêtrière,* claimed that "memory is an action: essentially, it is the action of telling a story" (qtd. in Bal 1999, ix). If this is true, then all the texts analyzed here must of necessity be self-reflexive, as they are stories about the very process of telling a story that all recollection embodies. The self-reflexivity of these meta-memory texts has been shown to be at the heart of their politically transformative potential, as it provides an explicit reflection on the possibility of telling and retelling the past in ways that run counter to dominant versions of history. From autobiographies to novels, from texts in which the protagonists struggle with their own recollections of past trauma to works in which such traumatic memories are transmitted from one generation to the next, these works become models for a process of working through memory which Spanish society as a whole must adequately learn to undertake.

As Jo Labanyi claims, "in a country that has emerged from forty years of cultural repression, the task of making reparation to the ghosts from the past—that is, to those relegated to the status of living dead, denied voices and memory—is considerable" (2000, 80). *Working through Memory: Writing and Remembrance in Contemporary Spanish Narrative* studies texts in which such "reparation to the ghosts from the past" takes place on a symbolic level. All of these works are populated by specters of one kind or another. These figures are the victims of a history of war and repression, a history that has left its scars throughout Spain in the form of numerous mass graves. This same history has likewise left its mark on the texts studied here in the form of a recurrent preoccupation with those who have not received proper burial, those whose memory has not been properly honored and who thus inevitably haunt the living. This is the case with the Republican deportees to German concentration camps whose memory triggers the need to write on the part of Jorge Semprún and Norma, of *Le grand voyage* [*El largo viaje*] and *L'hora violeta* [*La hora violeta*], respectively. In this latter novel, the memory of these deportees becomes inseparable from that of the other ghostly beings in the text, Judit and Kati, who seem to call out, from beyond the grave, for their story to be told. The fellow exiles, unable to die in their homeland, whom María Teresa León dutifully remembers in *Memoria de la melancolía,* find their counterparts in the exiled Republicans that populate Nadia's childhood memories in *El jinete polaco.* The civil war dead, whose spirits are believed to haunt the landscape in *Volverás a Región,* are like the mummified woman haunting Mágina in Antonio Muñoz Molina's novel. They are also not unlike Manuel's grandfather, who did not die in the civil war, but whose existence since then is presented as a form of living death in *El jinete polaco.* It is important to note that all the ghostly figures in these texts have suffered some form of exile, either internal exile or the forced abandonment of the homeland. One of the main insights provided by the present study is that any "reparation to the ghosts from the past" that may take place in Spain must necessarily include an acknowledgment of the central role that various forms of exile have played in contemporary Spanish history.

Clearly, some of the ghosts populating these texts belong to the realm of history and others to the realm of fiction, although the distinction may sometimes be diffuse. Fiction, here, is always intimately tied to history. The texts analyzed in this study range from autobiographies to novels, including literary works that are autobiographical to a greater or lesser degree. Memory itself is a practice that emerges out of a constant interplay between fact and fiction, and this is highlighted by the spectrum of texts represented in this study. Indeed, as each work shows, only by accepting and fully exploring the imbrication of fact and fiction out of which all recollection emerges, as well as the various forms of distortion that necessarily characterize all remembrance, can one effectively confront the traumatic memory that is embodied by ghosts in these texts.

The process of working through memory exemplified in these narratives is what allows for the "reparation to the ghosts from the past" to be fulfilled. As mentioned in the introduction, Manuel Reyes Mate has observed that post-Franco Spanish society has been notoriously deficient in creating effective "lugares de la memoria" [places of memory] to work through the traumatic memory of the civil war and the Franco regime. In contrast, every one of the texts analyzed here presents concrete places of memory that become sites for the working through of this traumatic past. More specifically, these *lieux de mémoire* become sites for the exploration and recovery of the stories of the victims of that history. In fact, each of these places of memory can also be seen as paradigmatic examples of the "lugares de reconocimiento" [places of recognition] which Ulrich Winter claims are needed in Spain, places that are not stable and unitary, but "escabrosos y dislocados, pero que posibilitan un proceso social de reconocimento entre memorias confictivas" (2005, 23) [scabrous and dislocated, but that allow for a social process of recognition of conflicting memories]. Each of the places of memory in these texts becomes a "place of recognition" inasmuch as it emerges out of a struggle between different voices from the past, and thus embodies an ongoing process of negotiation rather than a final resting place.

The tales presented by the protagonists of *Le grand voyage* and *L'hora violeta,* for example, are places of memory in which the experiences of those who suffered the trauma of exile and deportation are transmitted to others. Each novel, however, makes it clear that the process of recounting such tales of suffering cannot be neatly contained within the pages of the text. León also presents frequent reflections about her own process of writing as she creates her autobiography. Her text, in turn, becomes a place of memory where fellow exiles are rescued from oblivion, a most terrible form of banishment. *Memoria de la melancolía* further evokes the image of the author's very entrails as the site where the process of working through memory must take place if it is to become something other than a supposedly objective recollection of past events. These entrails are, indeed, a place of recognition, inasmuch as multiple voices from the author's past are found therein, many of them held in an unresolved tension through the process of "disidentification" that characterizes her writing. The long conversations in which two individuals re-create the past, central elements within the plots of *Volverás a Región* and *El jinete polaco,* become *lieux de mémoire* themselves, rituals in which individual memory is made collective in the process of being shared, and in which the recognition of different accounts of the past is enacted through dialogue. The photographs, thanks to which the protagonists of *L'hora violeta* and *El jinete polaco* re-create the stories of their families, are other places of memory, or "places of recognition," explored here. In the case of the latter novel, the painting of the Polish rider that reappears throughout the text becomes yet another object that not only serves to spark a rememorative process, but becomes a metaphor for the interminable meanderings and transformations of memory itself. The endless nature of this process is highlighted by the fact that any final and conclusive interpretation of the painting ultimately remains elusive, as if it were the very secret guarded by the Polish rider himself, held at bay in that point, eternally beyond the frame of the painting, at which the rider is forever staring.

Within all these texts, furthermore, a recurring image emerges: that of improper burial sites. These include, among others, cemeteries and tombstones in ruin, a wall in which a woman becomes mummified, and a crematorium intended to destroy any trace of the existence of the prisoners of a concentration camp. These images all become places of memory whose very emergence in a narrative allows for a symbolic burial process to take place within the confines of the texts themselves. This is one of the ways in which the practice of working through memory in these texts reflects symbolically what needs to be undertaken in Spain, where only in the past few years has the pressure from nongovernmental organizations created a general awareness of the need to seriously address the issue of the mass graves of the civil war and postwar repression.

These texts further illustrate other important dimensions of an effective practice of working through memory. Each text underscores how this process must forcefully and consistently reject narratives of the past that provide a comforting, and false, sense of closure. Examples of such narratives are the various discourses of "peace," "order," and "progress" that emerged during the late Franco regime, and later in post-Franco Spain, and which effectively swept the stories of the victims of the civil war and postwar repression under various ever-more-appealing rugs. All of the texts studied here present a process of working through memory in which the stories of the victims are recovered at the same time as these dominant discourses, which sought to silence them in the first place, are systematically undermined. In every text, therefore, working through memory is shown to be an ongoing process in which an "unsatisfied" and "vigilant" memory must continually shatter dominant narratives of the past in order to rescue that which previously had been repressed. Since such a process of working through memory rejects any form of closure, the past that it recovers will always remain fragmentary and incomplete, much like the multiple ruins that emerge throughout the narratives studied in the previous chapters. The need to return to such ruins over and over again underscores that the process of working through the past enacted in these texts is, indeed, a form of remembrance, in the Benjaminian sense, as well as an example of the practice described, in the introduction, as emerging from the Spanish verbs "rememorar" and "remembrar." As part of this process, every text, in one way or another, illustrates how the practice of working through memory is only effective if it unsettles the present, and if it fully allows for the pain and suffering of the victims of a traumatic past to emerge within the very narrative in which it is presented. The various forms of narrative disruption and fragmentation present in all the texts studied are shown to embody the "empathic unsettlement" that characterizes any effective practice of working through memory.

Finally, all of the texts analyzed here underscore that the process of working through memory must focus not only on ways to recover previously silenced stories from the past, but also on how to transmit that recovered remembrance from one generation to the next. This is the only way in which a society will adequately address the burdens and repercussions, over time, of a traumatic past. This is especially true since many of the effects of collective trauma often appear belatedly, leaving later generations to face the implications of a previously repressed history. As the generation that lived through a historical trauma passes on, younger generations find themselves having to work through their postmemory; that is, facing the inherited memory of a trauma that they may not have experienced, but that has greatly determined their life. Such is the case in Spain with respect to the experience of the civil war. Natàlia and Norma, in *L'hora violeta*, as well as Manuel and Nadia, in *El jinete polaco*, can be seen as representatives of these younger generations in Spain. The renewed interest they show in recovering their family history, after they have spent most of their lives running away from that past, is an encouraging sign. The fact that they do so only after the deaths of important members of their family who had lived through the war (such as both of Natàlia's parents, Nadia's father, and Manuel's grandmother), underscores that the urgency to work through the memory, and postmemory, of the civil war in Spain is related to the disappearance of the generations that directly experienced the bitter conflict.

As explained in the introduction, a certain sector of these younger generations has been christened "la generación de los nietos de los vencidos" (Rojo 2004) [the generation of the grandchildren of the vanquished]. It is perhaps the new, freer perspective that this generation can provide, with respect to the memory of the civil war and Francoism, that may allow it to help society as a whole to finally undertake a process of working through memory similar to that analyzed in this study. Unfortunately, there are many obstacles to be overcome if this is to be the case, not the least of which is a disheartening ignorance that many young Spaniards demonstrate with regard to contemporary Spanish history. It is interesting, however, to note that Jordi Gracia uses the image of the "grandchildren of the vanquished" as a metaphor for the role that writers can take up if they produce texts, such as those studied here, that work through Spain's traumatic memory of war and repression:

> El escritor tiene mucho a su favor para no resignarse y ser valiente: hacer el papel, real o figurado, del nieto que pregunta y no se conforma con respuestas evasivas y sigue preguntando hasta que quizá encuentra la cuña—la carpeta, la foto, el cuaderno, el lápiz del carpintero—que abre la brecha cerrada de la memoria y regresa a cuando todo empezó a gangrenarse moralmente. (2004)

> [A writer has much in his favor to prevent him from giving up, and to help him be brave: he can take on the role, real or figurative, of the grandson who asks questions and is not content with evasive answers and who continues to ask until he finds the wedge—the folder, the photo, the notebook, the carpenter's pencil—that opens the closed gap of memory and returns to when everything began to morally deteriorate.]

Jordi Gracia is alluding here to a number of novels that have appeared in Spain within the last few years, and which, were it not for limitations of space, could have been included in this study. Many of them are meta-memory texts, like those analyzed in the previous chapters. They enact the process of working through memory, a process that necessarily functions, as Gracia claims, like a wedge, opening up spaces of memory within dominant discourses bent on closing them. These texts, furthermore, enact this process by creating specific *lieux de mémoire,* some of which Gracia enumerates. These notebooks and writing utensils, photos and folders, not only serve to rescue stories of past suffering and repression from oblivion, but also allow for those recollections to be passed from one generation to the next.

Among the novels to which Gracia alludes, one could include *El lápiz del carpintero* [*The Carpenter's Pencil*] (2000), by Manuel Rivas and *Soldados de Salamina* [*Soldiers of Salamina*] (2001), by Javier Cercas.[1] Both of these novels were made into popular movies, the first by Antón Reixa in 2001 and the latter by David Trueba in 2003. Dulce Chacón's *La voz dormida* [*The Sleeping Voice*] (2002) went through five editions in the four months after it first appeared, and has continued to sell exceedingly well. *Veinte años y un día* [*Twenty Years and a Day*] (2003), by Jorge Semprún, and *El hijo del acordeonista* [*The Accordion Player's Son*] (2004), by Bernardo Atxaga, are further examples of recent texts that wrestle with the issue of the recovery and transmission of the traumatic memory of the civil war.[2]

There are, of course, many more names that could be added to the list. The continued publication of such meta-memory texts that return, again and again, to the memory of the civil war and the Franco era is a clear sign that the process of working through Spain's traumatic past of war and repression is still ongoing. These texts continue to present many of the elements analyzed in the works studied here, but there may also be new issues and questions relevant for understanding their function within the process of working through Spain's past from the vantage point of the twenty-first century. In what follows, I briefly present a few of these questions, within an open-ended reflection on the directions that a study of these new, and more recent, meta-memory texts might take.

One such question is related to an observation by Andreas Huyssen, presented in the introduction. Huyssen claims that one factor that explains the growing concern with memory at the end of the twentieth, and beginning of the twenty-first, centuries is a general anxiety in many cultures with changing experiences of time and space. He describes this as "a slow but palpable transformation of temporality in our lives, brought on by the complex intersections of technological change, mass media, and new patterns of consumption, work, and global mobility" (2003, 21). Huyssen further explains that the new information and technological revolutions of the last few decades have created a need for some kind of "temporal anchoring" which has been filled, in various ways, by a turn to the past (2003, 28). Therefore, while recognizing that local, regional, and national specificities determine the particular shape that memory practices may take in different contexts, he wonders whether "contemporary memory cultures in general can be read as reaction formations to economic globalization" and claims that "such is the terrain on which new comparative work on the mechanisms and tropes of historical trauma and national memory practices could be pursued" (2003, 16). This is, indeed, a fruitful question to ponder as one attempts to understand the role of new meta-memory texts as they continue to appear in Spain. The overwhelming influence of such new technologies and the effects of globalization as a background to the process of working through the past is already present in *El jinete polaco*. Manuel and Nadia's entire process of jointly reconstructing their past takes place in her apartment in New York City, and is recurrently interrupted by images on the television of the first Gulf War. This war, of course, was supposed to represent a great milestone in a discourse of progress based on an unquestionable faith in technological and mass-media advancements, the very same advancements that allowed the war to be won so quickly and to be televised and supposedly made available for mass consumption in real time. That this is the backdrop to Manuel and Nadia's collective reconstruction of their past is thus quite significant. As the effects of globalization become ever greater, and new information and technological revolutions continue to affect our experiences of time and space, it will be interesting to see whether the new meta-memory texts in Spain that work through the past of the civil war and the Franco era will increasingly reflect such developments.

Of course, it must be recognized that not all narrative texts that turn to the past as a way to achieve some kind of "temporal anchoring" in the face of rapidly changing experiences of time and space, due partly to ever-expanding information and technological revolutions, will embody a process of critical working through of the past as has been studied here. In fact, many such texts effectively do quite the opposite. Far from producing the "empathic unsettlement" that is so vital to the process of working through memory, such texts may turn to the past as a form of escapism, with a desire to generate a nostalgic, ultimately comforting, view of history. In fact, there is an entire "heritage industry" bent on selling such products. The popular television program *Cuéntame como pasó* can be seen as one such enterprise, whose view of the late Franco era, despite acknowledging certain hardships, ultimately presents quite a whitewashed version of those years. Far from generating a critical engagement with the most repressive and difficult aspects of that past, the series encourages a nostalgic longing, which can then be conveniently satisfied by purchasing one of the many commercial products associated with the show, such as, for example, one of several CDs with music from the 1960s and '70s that are heard on the program. Other texts may present an overly romanticized and idealized view of the Second Republic as a kind of lost paradise, a perspective that does not acknowledge its historical and political complexity, and, ultimately, inhibits any critical analysis of that time period.

Within this context, it is important to recognize, as many critics have done, that, since the 1980s, many novels in Spain that deal with the civil war and postwar era demonstrate a marked tendency to present a mythical, apolitical, and increasingly de-ideologized view of the war and postwar. As Maryse Bertrand de Muñoz claims, such texts increasingly present the war and postwar as "simplemente un telón de fondo sobre el cual actúan pasiones eternas" (1996, 34) [simply a backdrop against which eternal passions are played out].[3] Myth has taken the place of history in these texts. Rather that encouraging a process of working through the concrete past of war and repression in Spain, many such novels present the war and postwar era as a mere background and setting for stories exploring universal themes of love, hate, the eternal battle of good versus evil, and so on, in a predominantly ahistorical manner. This approach to, and use of, the past effectively curtails any real critical engagement with the history of war and repression in Spain, and certainly discourages any exploration or recognition of the legacy of that past as it continues to affect Spanish society long after the war. Both of these critical practices are, of course, important elements of the meta-memory texts studied here. It is thus of vital importance to be aware that the process of remembering embodied in recent, and future, texts that are set during the civil war or postwar era can have very different ideological and political implications, and can, in cases, produce an effect that is completely at odds with the kind of politically transformative function characterizing the meta-memory texts analyzed in the previous chapters.

It has been stated recurrently throughout this study that one of the reasons the memory of the civil war and the Francoist repression of the postwar era has emerged with increasing force in the recent past in Spain has, in part, to do with the fact that the generations that lived through those events are inevitably disappearing. As this continues, and the civil war and postwar repression increasingly become a matter *solely* of postmemory, rather than personal memory, it will be interesting to see how new meta-memory texts continue to reflect, and be affected by, this historical development. The inevitable disappearance of older generations, and the effect this will have on the possibility of studying, recalling, and representing the traumatic experiences they have lived, is a major concern felt, for example, by Jorge Semprún, with respect to one of the experiences that most marked his life: deportation to Buchenwald. In an interview, when Semprún is asked what worries him most about the future, he replies:

> La memoria. Están desapareciendo los testigos del exterminio. Bueno, cada generación tiene un crepúsculo de esas características. Los testigos desaparecen. Pero ahora me está tocando vivirlo a mí. Aún hay más viejos que yo que han pasado por la experiencia de los campos. Pero no todos son escritores, claro. En el crepúsculo la memoria se hace más tensa, pero también está más sujeta a las deformaciones. Luego hay algo.... ¿Sabe usted qué es lo más importante de haber pasado por un campo? ¿Sabe usted qué es exactamente? ¿Sabe usted que eso, que es lo más importante y lo más terrible, es lo único que no se puede explicar? El olor a carne quemada. ¿Qué haces con el recuerdo del olor a carne quemada? Para esas circunstancias está, precisamente, la literatura.... Yo tengo dentro de mi cabeza, vivo, el olor más importante de un campo de concentración. Y no puedo explicado. Y ese olor se va a ir conmigo como ya se ha ido con otros. (Qtd. in Espada, 2000)

> Memory. The witnesses of the extermination are disappearing. Well, every generation has a twilight of this kind. But now it is my turn to live through it. There are still people older than I who experienced the camps. But they are not all writers, of course. At twilight, memory becomes more tense, but

it is also more subject to various kinds of deformations. Then there is something. . . . Do you know what is the most important thing of having been in a camp? Do you know what it is, exactly? The smell of burning flesh. What do you do with the memory of the smell of burning flesh? For these kinds of circumstances, there is literature. . . . I have inside my head, alive, the most important smell of a concentration camp. And I cannot explain it. And that smell will disappear with me, as it has already disappeared with others.[4]

How new accounts of the Holocaust will deal with the fact that soon nobody will have that "smell of burning flesh" available to them as a real, personal memory is surely an important concern. With respect to the same issue as it relates to the Spanish civil war, Semprún makes a similar observation: "Es preciso recuperar la memoria histórica a través de la ficción, porque pronto no quedarán testigos de lo sucedido" (qtd. in Vilá 2003) [It is necessary to recover historical memory through fiction, because soon there will be no direct witnesses of what happened]. Semprún here explicitly claims that fiction has a particularly important role in exploring postmemory, and surely future meta-memory texts will continue to assume that role. One danger is that the inevitable shift from memory to postmemory may eventually contribute to the emergence of more representations of the civil war and postwar era characterized by the mythologized, ahistorical perspectives that have been increasingly present since the 1980s. However, this generational shift may also contribute to a greater critical engagement with the past such as the one present in the texts studied here. It will certainly be interesting to see how individual texts that arise in the future negotiate the possibility of adopting such politically and ideologically different perspectives toward the past.

One of the reasons fiction can be particularly effective in presenting stories of past repression and suffering, once those who have experienced them have passed, is that literary language can often convey the feeling of such painful experiences with a richness and texture not available to other discourses. This is precisely why literature, in its many forms, is particularly well suited to incite the empathic unsettlement necessary for an effective process of working through memory to emerge, as evidenced in all the texts analyzed in the previous chapters. Fiction is thus a necessary companion and complement to historical research, and both will continue to be essential elements in Spain's ongoing process of confronting the legacy of historical periods that fewer and fewer Spaniards will have experienced directly. Thinking back to Semprún's concern about the Holocaust, historical research may continue to bring to light new aspects of the camps, but it is fiction that will most be able to explore, without being able to re-create it completely, that element that Semprún is so concerned about: what it feels like to be surrounded by the smell of burning flesh. Along these lines, Paul Ricoeur has stated: "You have to accurately *count* the corpses in the death camps as well as offering vivid narrative *accounts* that people will remember" (1999, 15). History and literature join hands in providing both of these important elements, a body *count* as well as multiple life *accounts,* needed to effectively confront a traumatic past. It remains to be seen how these two kinds of discourse will influence each other as new novels, as well as historical research, about Spain's past of civil war and Francoist repression continue to be published in the future.

Along these lines, Manuel Vázquez Montalbán presents an important reflection in his 1992 novel, *Autobiografía del general Franco.* In this text, Marcial Pombo, an old, left-wing, second-rate writer of pseudoautobiographies of famous cultural figures and author of abridged history books for children, is commissioned by a young editor, Ernesto Amescua, to write an autobiography of Franco. The book Amescua asks him to write is scheduled to appear in 1992, the anniversary of Franco's birth, as the first of a new collection of autobiographies of important political figures from Spanish history. The idea for the book arose when Amescua's young son asked him who Franco was, and the editor realized the importance of narrating the life of the dictator to all the Spanish children who had not experienced the dictatorship and who were growing up not even knowing who the Caudillo had been.

Most of the novel comprises the pseudoautobiography of Franco that Pombo writes, with the supposed voice of the dictator telling his life in minute historical detail. As Franco's autobiography progresses, however, Pombo begins to interject his own and his family's story, thus incorporating into the discourse of the victor the voices of the defeated (his family had suffered political persecution under Franco's Regime). All these interjections, however, are finally eliminated by the editor, who considers them unnecessary noise and therefore, once again, represses the voice of the defeated from the representation of history in the text. Just like his own text has been thus sanitized, Pombo imagines a completely sanitized version of the civil war and the Franco regime, reduced to a few lines, which could be found in a hypothetical future audiovisual encyclopedia of Spanish history and culture. He likewise imagines the books that will be written by certain historians, following the supposedly objective view of their work which his editor praises. These will perhaps extend the length of the description of the Franco regime beyond that of the encyclopedia, but they will still not allow for the pain and suffering of so many to emerge within their schematized views of history. After leaving his carefully whitewashed manuscript with the editor, Pombo continues to hold an imaginary conversation with Franco that he has maintained throughout the writing of his text:

> Los historiadores insistirán algo más pero le objetivarán y nos objetivarán: guerra de crueldades equivalentes, posguerra de autoritarismo a cambio de desarrollo... en fin, la historia es biplana y en ella no caben los ruidos, sean gemidos o gritos de rabia y terror. Y cada vez que un ciudadano del futuro lea la historia objetivada o presencie esos videos, será como si usted emergiera del horizonte conduciendo un fantasmal bulldozer negro dispuesto a cubrir con una capa más de tierra a todas sus víctimas de pensamiento, palabra, obra y omisión. (Vázquez Montalbán 1992, 663)

> [Historians will insist a bit more, but they will objectify you and objectify us: war of equivalent cruelties, postwar of authoritarianism in exchange for development... in the end, history is flat and in it there is no place for the noises, be they moans or cries of rage and terror. And every time that a citizen of the future will read that objectified history, or see one of those videos, it will be as if you emerged from the horizon driving a ghostly black bulldozer intent on covering with one more layer of earth all of your victims, those of thought, word, deed, or omission.]

It is up to the new meta-memory texts appearing in the twenty-first century to ensure that the "noises" of history, the "moans or cries of rage and terror," are not silenced once more. It remains to be seen exactly how these new texts will do so.

Marcial Pombo imagines the sanitized historical descriptions of the war and Franco era that may emerge in the future as exercises that will throw a new layer of dirt on the graves of the victims of the civil war and Francoist repression. This image is, of course, uncannily relevant today. The exhumations in Spain that have begun to take place in the past few years, led by various civic and nongovernmental organizations, have certainly allowed for that "noise" of pain and suffering to be heard, as the stories of the victims found in the mass graves are brought to light along with their remains, and as the oral testimonies of relatives and other witnesses are collected. The exhumations have certainly had the impact in Spain that Katherine Verdery has analyzed, within the context of former Communist countries, of "enlivening" politics, and making a society confront its past of repression as it is faced with the material traces of that past in the form of bones and skeletons requiring proper burial (1999, 27). It still remains to be seen, however, how this process of exhumations will develop in Spain, especially as it becomes more institutionalized. How will the tensions be resolved among various organizations with very different ideas as to how the exhumations should be carried out? Will the central government, perhaps with the long awaited "Ley de memoria histórica" [Law of historical memory], take up more responsibility for the entire enterprise? How will this affect that very process? Helen Graham in fact ponders this question when she exclaims that "even the lack of funds hampering the work of the Association for the Recuperation of Historical Memory may be a price worth paying for its independence. For when governments and states—even if they are liberal democratic ones—promote public remembrance, this changes the meaning and value of such remembrance" (2005, 146). It will certainly be interesting to see how the "meaning and value" of the practice of remembrance embodied in the exhumations change as the entire process becomes increasingly institutionalized, as it inevitably will. It remains to be seen, likewise, how such changes may ultimately be reflected in future meta-memory texts that appear in Spain. It will be interesting, in fact, to see if the very process of exhumations becomes increasingly thematized within these texts, and how it is presented, if it does.

It is to be hoped that, ultimately, as expressed in the introduction, the process of remembrance that emerges from the practice of exhumations, and other related legislation that might emerge in the future, will go beyond the proper burial of the human remains found in the mass graves, despite the enormous importance of this task. We may recall that Manuel Reyes Mate hoped that the members of the generation of the grandchildren of the vanquished who have been instrumental in organizing the exhumations "no se van a contentar con llevar los restos a un cementerio, sino que acabarán preguntándose por una civilización que ha montado el progreso sobre una tierra con tantos cadáveres" (2003c) [will not be content with taking the remains to a cemetery, they will eventually question a whole civilization that progress has built upon a land full of corpses]. It is this form of questioning, which goes beyond the process of an appropriate mourning for disappeared loved ones, that is ultimately sought in the process of working through memory as it is analyzed here. *Working through Memory: Writing and Remembrance in Contemporary Spanish Narrative* shows how meta-memory texts can be effective models for understanding this process. Narratives such as the ones analyzed in the previous chapters are, as Paul Ricoeur has claimed, "the place where a certain healing of memory may begin" (1999, 9). The present study explores the healing of memory embodied in these texts in the hope that this understanding may guide us in achieving a similar healing of memory within Spanish society at large.

Appendix

ANTEPROYECTO DE LEY POR LA QUE SE RECONOCEN Y AMPLIAN DERECHOS Y SE ESTABLECEN MEDIDAS EN FAVOR DE QUIENES PADECIERON PERSECUCIÓN O VIOLENCIA DURANTE LA GUERRA CIVIL Y LA DICTADURA EXPOSICIÓN DE MOTIVOS

El espíritu de reconciliación y concordia, y de respeto al pluralismo y a la defensa pacífica de todas las ideas, que guió la Transición, nos permitió dotarnos de una Constitución, la de 1978, que tradujo jurídicamente esa voluntad de reencuentro de los españoles articulando un Estado social y democrático de derecho con clara vocación integradora.

El espíritu de la Transición da sentido, de este modo, al modelo constitucional de convivencia más fecundo que los españoles hayamos disfrutado nunca. Y es ese mismo espíritu el que explica también las diversas medidas y derechos que se han ido reconociendo, desde el origen mismo de todo el período democrático, en favor de las personas que, durante los decenios anteriores a la Constitución, sufrieron las consecuencias de nuestra devastadora guerra civil y del régimen dictatorial que la sucedió.

Pese a ese esfuerzo legislativo, quedan aún iniciativas por adoptar para dar cumplida y definitiva respuesta a las demandas de esos ciudadanos, planteadas tanto en el ámbito parlamentario como por distintas asociaciones cívicas. Se trata de peticiones legítimas y justas, que nuestra democracia, apelando de nuevo a su espíritu fundacional de concordia, y en el marco de la Constitución, no puede dejar de atender.

Es la hora, así, de que la democracia española, y las generaciones vivas que hoy disfrutan de ella, honren y recuperen para siempre a todos los que directamente padecieron las injusticias y agravios producidos, por unos u otros motivos políticos o ideológicos, en aquellos dolorosos períodos de nuestra historia. Desde luego, a quienes perdieron la vida. Con ellos, a sus familias. También a quienes perdieron su libertad, al padecer prisión, trabajos forzosos o internamientos en campos de concentración dentro o fuera de nuestras fronteras. También, en fin, a quienes perdieron la patria al ser empujados a un largo, desgarrador y, en tantos casos, irreversible, exilio. La presente Ley parte de la consideración de que los diversos aspectos relacionados con la memoria personal y familiar, especialmente cuando se han visto afectados por conflictos de carácter público, forman parte del estatuto jurídico de la ciudadanía democrática, y como tales son abordados en el texto. Se reconoce, en este sentido, un derecho individual a la memoria personal y familiar de cada ciudadano, que encuentra su primera manifestación en la Ley en el reconocimiento general que en la misma se proclama en su artículo 2.

En efecto, en dicho precepto se hace una proclamación general del carácter injusto de todas las condenas, sanciones y expresiones de violencia personal producidas, por motivos inequívocamente políticos o ideológicos, durante la Guerra Civil, así como las que, por las mismas razones, tuvieron lugar en la Dictadura posterior.

Esta declaración general, contenida en el artículo 2, se complementa con la previsión de un procedimiento específico para obtener una Declaración personal, de contenido rehabilitador y reparador, que se abre como un derecho a todos los perjudicados, y que podrán ejercer ellos mismos o sus familiares.

Se ha considerado conveniente, dado su importante valor simbólico, atribuir la emisión de estas Declaraciones, que serán publicadas en el Boletín Oficial del Estado, a un Consejo de designación parlamentaria, creado *ad hoc*, e integrado por personalidades de reconocido prestigio cuya elección se vea respaldada, además, por una mayoría cualificada del Congreso de los Diputados (arts. 3 a 7).

En los artículos 8 a 12 se establece el reconocimiento de diversas mejoras de derechos económicos ya recogidos en nuestro Ordenamiento. Y en la Disposición adicional segunda se prevé, en esta misma dirección, el derecho a una indemnización en favor de todas aquellas personas que perdieron la vida en defensa de la democracia, de la democracia que hoy todos disfrutamos, y que no habían recibido hasta ahora la compensación debida. A continuación, se recogen diversos preceptos (arts. 13 a 16) que, atendiendo también en este ámbito una muy legítima demanda de no pocos ciudadanos, que ignoran aún el paradero de sus familiares, prevén medidas e instrumentos para que las Administraciones públicas faciliten, a los interesados que lo soliciten, las tareas de localización, y, en su caso, identificación de los desaparecidos, como una última prueba de respeto hacia ellos. Y ello se hace tratando de atender, con sentido de la ponderación y del equilibrio, los diferentes derechos, intereses, y respetables opciones morales que resultan potencialmente concurrentes al respecto.

Se establecen, asimismo, una serie de medidas (arts. 17 y 18) en relación con los símbolos y monumentos conmemorativos de la Guerra Civil o de la

Dictadura que sean de titularidad estatal, sustentadas en el principio de evitar toda exaltación del conflicto entre españoles, y en el convencimiento de que los ciudadanos tienen derecho a que así sea, a que los símbolos públicos sean ocasión de encuentro y no de enfrentamiento, ofensa o agravio.

El legislador considera de justicia hacer un doble reconocimiento singularizado. En primer lugar, a los voluntarios integrantes de las Brigadas internacionales, a los que se les permitirá acceder a la nacionalidad española sin necesidad de que renuncien a la que ostenten hasta este momento (art. 20); y, también, a las Asociaciones ciudadanas que se hayan significado en la defensa de la dignidad de las víctimas de la violencia política a que se refiere esta Ley, a las que podrá concederse la Gran Cruz del Mérito Civil de tipo colectivo como testimonio de este reconocimiento (art. 21).

Con el fin de facilitar la recopilación y el derecho de acceso a la información histórica sobre la Guerra Civil, la Ley refuerza el papel del actual Archivo General de la Guerra Civil Española, con sede en Salamanca, estableciendo que se le dé traslado de toda la documentación existente en otros centros estatales (arts. 22 a 25).

En definitiva, la presente Ley quiere contribuir a cerrar heridas todavía abiertas en los españoles y a dar satisfacción a los ciudadanos que sufrieron, directamente o en la persona de sus familiares, las consecuencias de la tragedia de la Guerra Civil o de la represión de la Dictadura. Quiere contribuir a ello desde el pleno convencimiento de que, profundizando de este modo en el espíritu del reencuentro y de la concordia de la Transición, no son sólo esos ciudadanos los que resultan reconocidos y honrados sino también la Democracia española en su conjunto. Y quiere contribuir a ello, por último, con la convicción de que no es tarea de la ley, o de las normas jurídicas en general, fijarse el objetivo de implantar una determinada "memoria histórica", de que no le corresponde al legislador construir o reconstruir una supuesta "memoria colectiva". Pero sí es deber del legislador, y cometido de la ley, consagrar y proteger, con el máximo vigor normativo, el derecho a la memoria personal y familiar como expresión de plena ciudadanía democrática. Este es el compromiso al que el texto legal responde.

Artículo 1. Objeto de la Ley.

La presente Ley tiene por objeto reconocer y ampliar derechos en favor de quienes padecieron persecución o violencia, por razones políticas o ideológicas, durante la Guerra Civil y la Dictadura, promover su reparación moral y la recuperación de su memoria personal y familiar, y adoptar medidas complementarias destinadas a suprimir elementos de división entre los ciudadanos, todo ello con el fin de fomentar la cohesión y solidaridad entre las diversas generaciones de españoles en torno a los principios, valores y libertades constitucionales.

Artículo 2. Reconocimiento general.

1. Como expresión del derecho de todos los ciudadanos a la reparación de su memoria personal y familiar, se reconoce y declara el carácter injusto de las condenas, sanciones y cualquier forma de violencia personal producidas, por razones políticas o ideológicas, durante la Guerra Civil, cualquiera que fuera el bando o la zona en la que se encontraran quienes las padecieron, así como las sufridas por las mismas causas durante la dictadura que, a su término, se prolongó hasta 1975.

2. Las razones políticas o ideológicas a que se refiere el apartado anterior incluyen la pertenencia o colaboración con partidos políticos, sindicatos, organizaciones religiosas o militares, minorías étnicas, sociedades secretas, logias masónicas y grupos de resistencia, así como el ejercicio de conductas vinculadas con opciones culturales, lingüísticas o de orientación sexual.

Artículo 3. Declaración de reparación y reconocimiento personal.

1. Se reconoce el derecho a obtener una Declaración de reparación y reconocimiento personal a quienes durante la Guerra Civil y la Dictadura padecieron los efectos a que se refiere el artículo anterior.

2. Esta Declaración será de aplicación respecto de las penas y sanciones de carácter personal impuestas durante la Guerra Civil por Juzgados, Tribunales u órganos administrativos de cualquier naturaleza y respecto de todas las ejecuciones llevadas a cabo por cualquier organización o grupo durante el mismo período, siempre que, en uno y otro supuesto, se vinculen, directa o indirectamente, con motivaciones políticas o ideológicas, en los términos del artículo 2.2 de esta Ley.

3. También será de aplicación en relación con las ejecuciones, penas y sanciones de carácter personal que se hubiesen producido tras el fin de la Guerra Civil, cuando hubiesen tenido como objeto la represión o persecución de quienes defendieron la legalidad institucional anterior al 18 de julio de 1936, pretendieron el restablecimiento en España de un régimen democrático o intentaron vivir conforme a opciones amparadas por derechos y libertades hoy reconocidos por la Constitución. En todos los casos, será necesario que los comportamientos en su día enjuiciados o sancionados resulten conformes a los principios y valores constitucionales hoy vigentes.

Artículo 4. Tramitación de la solicitud.

1. Tendrán derecho a solicitar la Declaración las personas afectadas y, en su defecto, su cónyuge o persona ligada por análoga relación de afectividad, sus ascendientes, sus descendientes y sus colaterales hasta el segundo grado.

2. Asimismo podrán solicitar la Declaración las instituciones públicas, previo acuerdo de su órgano colegiado de gobierno, respecto de quienes, careciendo de cónyuge o de los familiares mencionados en el apartado anterior, hubiesen desempeñado cargo o actividad relevante en las mismas.

3. Las personas o instituciones previstas en los apartados anteriores dirigirán su solicitud a la Comisión Interministerial a que se refiere la Disposición adicional primera de la presente Ley, en el plazo máximo de un año a partir de la entrada en vigor de esta Ley.

4. La solicitud se acompañará de la documentación que, sobre los hechos y sobre el proceso o procedimiento originario, obre en poder de los solicitantes, así como de todos los antecedentes que se consideren oportunos.

5. La Comisión podrá inadmitir la solicitud por no encontrarse el peticionario en alguno de los supuestos de los apartados 1 y 2 del presente artículo o por haberla formulado fuera de plazo.

6. La Comisión, de oficio o a instancia de parte, podrá recabar de las distintas Administraciones públicas y de los órganos judiciales, de acuerdo con la legislación vigente, los documentos o la información que resulten procedentes para resolver. A estos efectos, podrá suspender la tramitación durante un plazo no superior a seis meses. Una vez recibida la documentación o información, la Comisión la pondrá en conocimiento del solicitante para que, en el plazo de veinte días, manifieste lo que considere oportuno.

7. A la vista de la documentación e información aportada, la Comisión, en el plazo máximo de un año a contar desde la presentación de la solicitud, elevará su propuesta al Consejo previsto en el artículo siguiente.

Artículo 5. Órgano de resolución.

1. Al objeto de resolver sobre las solicitudes de Declaración a que se refieren los artículos precedentes, se constituye un Consejo integrado por cinco personalidades de reconocido prestigio en el ámbito de las ciencias sociales, elegidas por mayoría de tres quintos del Congreso de los Diputados.

2. Sus miembros no estarán sujetos a mandato imperativo, ni recibirán instrucciones de ninguna autoridad. Desempeñarán sus funciones con autonomía y libertad de criterio, conforme a lo previsto en la presente Ley, y guardarán reserva sobre cuanto conozcan en el ejercicio de aquéllas. No podrán ejercer ningún otro cargo de representación o designación políticas.

3. Cesarán por alguna de las siguientes causas:

    a) Renuncia
    b) Finalización de sus funciones
    c) Fallecimiento o incapacitación sobrevenida
    d) Haber sido condenado mediante sentencia firme por delito doloso

4. Los miembros del Consejo elegirán de entre ellos a su Presidente. Será Secretario del Consejo, con voz pero sin voto, el que lo sea de la Comisión Interministerial a que se refiere la Disposición adicional primera de esta Ley.

5. El Ministerio de la Presidencia facilitará al Consejo los medios personales y materiales necesarios para su adecuado funcionamiento.

Artículo 6. Funciones del Consejo.

Corresponden al Consejo las siguientes funciones:

   a) Resolver, en el plazo máximo de seis meses, las propuestas elevadas por la Comisión Interministerial, emitiendo Declaración favorable o denegándola, en los términos previstos en el artículo siguiente.
   b) Reclamar de la Comisión Interministerial que complete la información necesaria para pronunciarse antes de emitir la Declaración, y con suspensión del plazo para emitirla.
   c) Elaborar un informe anual sobre su actividad, que remitirá al Congreso de los Diputados

Artículo 7. Contenido de la Declaración.

1. Las Declaraciones de reparación y reconocimiento personal tendrán por único objeto la constatación de que las ejecuciones, condenas o sanciones sufridas son manifiestamente injustas por contrarias a los derechos y libertades que constituyen el fundamento del orden constitucional hoy vigente y son la base de la convivencia de la sociedad.

2. En ningún caso la Declaración a que se refiere este artículo constituirá título para el reconocimiento de responsabilidad patrimonial del Estado ni

de cualquier Administración Pública, ni dará lugar a efecto, reparación o indemnización de índole económica o profesional.

3. La Declaración omitirá toda referencia a la identidad de cuantas personas hubiesen intervenido en los hechos o en las actuaciones jurídicas que dieron lugar a las sanciones o condenas.

4. La fórmula de reparación regulada en esta Sección será compatible con cualquier otra ya instada por el interesado y prevista en el ordenamiento jurídico.

5. Las Declaraciones de reparación y reconocimiento personal se publicarán en el Boletín Oficial del Estado para su general conocimiento.

Artículo 8. Mejora de las prestaciones reconocidas por la Ley 5/1979, de 18 de septiembre, de reconocimiento de pensiones, asistencia medicofarmacéutica y asistencia social a favor de las viudas, hijos y demás familiares de los españoles fallecidos como consecuencia o con ocasión de la pasada Guerra Civil.

1. Con el fin de completar la acción protectora establecida por la Ley 5/1979, de 18 de septiembre, de reconocimiento de pensiones, asistencia medico-farmacéutica y asistencia social a favor de las viudas, hijos y demás familiares de los españoles fallecidos como consecuencia o con ocasión de la pasada Guerra Civil, se modifican las letras a) y c) del número 2 de su artículo primero, que quedan redactadas como sigue:

   "a) Por heridas, enfermedad o lesión accidental originadas como consecuencia de la guerra.
   c) Como consecuencia de actuaciones u opiniones políticas y sindicales, cuando pueda establecerse asimismo una relación de causalidad personal y directa entre la guerra civil y el fallecimiento."

2. Las pensiones que se reconozcan al amparo de lo dispuesto en el apartado anterior tendrán efectos económicos desde el primer día del mes siguiente a la fecha de entrada en vigor de la presente Ley, siendo de aplicación, en su caso, las normas que regulan la caducidad de efectos en el Régimen de Clases Pasivas del Estado.

Artículo 9. Importe de determinadas pensiones de orfandad.

1. La cuantía de las pensiones de orfandad en favor de huérfanos no incapacitados mayores de veintiún años causadas por personal no funcionario al amparo de las Leyes 5/1979, de 18 de septiembre, y 35/1980, de 26 de junio, se establece en 132,86 euros mensuales.

2. A las pensiones de orfandad a que se refiere el presente artículo les será de aplicación el sistema de complementos económicos vigentes y experimentarán las revalorizaciones que establezcan las Leyes de Presupuestos Generales del Estado para cada año.

3. Lo dispuesto en los dos apartados anteriores tendrá efectividad económica desde el primer día del mes siguiente a la fecha de entrada en vigor de la presente Ley, sin perjuicio de las normas que sobre caducidad de efectos rigen en el Régimen de Clases Pasivas del Estado.

Artículo 10. Modificación del ámbito de aplicación de las indemnizaciones a favor de quienes sufrieron prisión como consecuencia de los supuestos contemplados en la Ley 46/1977, de 15 de octubre, de amnistía.

1. Con el fin de incorporar supuestos en su día excluidos de la concesión de indemnizaciones por tiempos de estancia en prisión durante la Dictadura, se modifican los apartados uno y dos de la Disposición adicional decimoctava de la Ley 4/1990, de 29 de junio, de Presupuestos Generales del Estado para el año 1990, que quedan redactados como sigue:

"Uno. Quienes acrediten haber sufrido privación de libertad en establecimientos penitenciarios o en Batallones Disciplinarios, en cualquiera de sus modalidades, durante tres o más años, como consecuencia de los supuestos contemplados en la Ley 46/1977, de 15 de octubre, y tuvieran cumplida la edad de sesenta años en 31 de diciembre de 1990, tendrán derecho a percibir por una sola vez una indemnización de acuerdo con la siguiente escala:

Euros
Tres o más años de prisión 6.010,12
Por cada tres años completos adicionales 1.202,02

Dos. Si el causante del derecho a esta indemnización hubiese fallecido, y en 31 de diciembre de 1990 hubiera podido tener cumplidos sesenta años de edad tendrá derecho a la misma el cónyuge supérstite, que sea pensionista de viudedad por tal causa o que, aun no teniendo esta condición, acredite ser cónyuge viudo del causante."

2. Se añade un apartado siete a la Disposición adicional decimoctava de la Ley 4/1990, de 29 de junio de Presupuestos del Estado con la siguiente redacción:

"Siete. Quienes se consideren con derecho a los beneficios establecidos en los apartados uno y dos anteriores, ya sean los propios causantes o sus cónyuges supérstites o pensionistas de viudedad por tal causa, deberán solicitarlos expresamente ante la citada Dirección General de Costes de Personal y Pensiones Públicas."

Artículo 11. Tributación en el Impuesto sobre la Renta de las Personas Físicas de las indemnizaciones a favor de quienes sufrieron privación de libertad como consecuencia de los supuestos contemplados en la Ley 46/1977, de 15 de octubre, de Amnistía.

Con efectos desde el 1 de enero de 2005, se añade una nueva letra u) al artículo 7 del texto refundido de la Ley del Impuesto sobre la Renta de las Personas Físicas, aprobado por el Real Decreto Legislativo 3/2004, de 5 de marzo, que quedará redactada de la siguiente manera:

"u) Las indemnizaciones previstas en la legislación del Estado y de las Comunidades Autónomas para compensar la privación de libertad en establecimientos penitenciarios como consecuencia de los supuestos contemplados en la Ley 46/1977, de 15 de octubre, de Amnistía".

Artículo 12. Ayudas para compensar la carga tributaria de las indemnizaciones percibidas desde el 1 de enero de 1999 por privación de libertad como consecuencia de los supuestos contemplados en la Ley 46/1977, de 15 de octubre, de Amnistía.

1. Las personas que hubieran percibido desde el 1 de enero de 1999 hasta el 31 de diciembre de 2004 las indemnizaciones previstas en la legislación del Estado y de las Comunidades Autónomas para compensar la privación de libertad en establecimientos penitenciarios como consecuencia de los supuestos contemplados en la Ley 46/1977, de 15 de octubre, de Amnistía, podrán solicitar, en la forma y plazos que se determinen, el abono de una

ayuda cuantificada en el 15 por ciento de las cantidades que, por tal concepto, hubieran consignado en la declaración del Impuesto sobre la Renta de las Personas Físicas de cada uno de dichos períodos impositivos.

2. Si las personas a que se refiere el apartado 1 anterior hubieran fallecido, el derecho a la ayuda corresponderá a sus herederos, quienes podrán solicitarla.

3. Las ayudas percibidas en virtud de lo dispuesto en el presente artículo estarán exentas del Impuesto sobre la Renta de las Personas Físicas.

4. Por Orden del Ministro de Economía y Hacienda se determinará el procedimiento, las condiciones para su obtención y el órgano competente para el reconocimiento y abono de esta ayuda.

Artículo 13. Colaboración de las Administraciones Públicas con los particulares para la localización e identificación de víctimas.

1. Las Administraciones públicas, en el marco de sus competencias, facilitarán a los descendientes directos de las víctimas que así lo soliciten las actividades de indagación, localización e identificación de las personas desaparecidas violentamente durante la guerra civil o la represión política posterior y cuyo paradero se ignore.

   Lo previsto en el párrafo anterior podrá aplicarse respecto de las entidades que, constituidas antes de 1 de junio de 2004, incluyan el desarrollo de tales actividades entre sus fines.

2. Conforme a su normativa reguladora, podrán arbitrarse subvenciones para contribuir a sufragar los gastos derivados de las actividades contempladas en este artículo.

Artículo 14. Mapas de localización.

1. Las Administraciones públicas competentes elaborarán y pondrán a disposición de los interesados a que se refiere el artículo 13, dentro de su respectivo ámbito territorial de actuación, mapas en que consten los terrenos en que se localicen los restos de las personas a las que se refiere el artículo anterior incluyendo la información complementaria disponible sobre los mismos.

2. El Gobierno determinará el procedimiento de elaboración de un mapa integrado que comprenda todo el territorio español, que será igualmente accesible para los interesados y al que se incorporarán los datos que, en los términos que se establezcan, deberán ser remitidos por las distintas Administraciones públicas competentes.

3. Las áreas incluidas en los mapas serán objeto de especial preservación por parte de sus titulares, en los términos que reglamentariamente se establezca.

Artículo 15. Autorizaciones administrativas para actividades de localización e identificación.

1. Las Administraciones públicas competentes autorizarán las tareas de prospección encaminadas a la localización de restos de las víctimas referidas en el apartado 1 del artículo 13, de acuerdo con la normativa sobre patrimonio histórico.

2. Las Administraciones públicas, en el ejercicio de sus competencias, establecerán el procedimiento y las condiciones en que los descendientes directos de las víctimas referidas en el apartado 1 del artículo 13, o las entidades que actúen en su nombre, puedan recuperar los restos enterrados en las fosas correspondientes, para su identificación y eventual traslado a otro lugar.

3. En cualquier caso, la exhumación se someterá a autorización administrativa por parte de la autoridad competente, en la que deberá ponderarse especialmente la existencia de oposición por cualquiera de los descendientes directos de las personas cuyos restos deban ser trasladados. A tales efectos, y con carácter previo a la correspondiente resolución, la administración competente deberá dar adecuada publicidad a las solicitudes presentadas, comunicando en todo caso su existencia a la Administración General del Estado para su inclusión en el mapa referido en el apartado primero del artículo anterior.

4. Los restos que hayan sido objeto de traslado y no fuesen reclamados serán inhumados en el cementerio correspondiente al término municipal en que se encontraran, a cargo de los solicitantes de la exhumación.

Artículo 16. Acceso a los terrenos afectados por trabajos de localización e identificación.

1. La realización de las actividades de localización y eventual identificación o traslado de los restos de las personas referidas en el apartado 1 del artículo 13 se constituye en fin de utilidad pública e interés social, a los efectos de permitir, en su caso y de acuerdo con los artículos 108 a 119 de la Ley de Expropiación Forzosa, la ocupación temporal de los terrenos donde deban realizarse.

2. Para las actividades determinadas en los apartados anteriores, las administraciones autorizarán, salvo causa justificada de interés público, la ocupación temporal de los terrenos de su titularidad por parte de los descendientes directos de las víctimas o de las organizaciones que asuman su realización.

3. En el caso de terrenos de titularidad privada, los descendientes, o las organizaciones legitimadas de acuerdo con el apartado anterior, deberán solicitar el consentimiento de los titulares de derechos afectados sobre los terrenos en que se hallen los restos. Si no se obtuviere dicho consentimiento, las Administraciones públicas podrán autorizar la ocupación temporal, siempre tras audiencia de los titulares de derechos afectados, con consideración de sus alegaciones, y fijando la correspondiente indemnización a cargo de los ocupantes.

Artículo 17. Símbolos y monumentos públicos.

Los órganos que tengan atribuida la titularidad o conservación de los monumentos, edificios y lugares de titularidad estatal, tomarán las medidas oportunas para la retirada de los escudos, insignias, placas y otras menciones conmemorativas de la Guerra Civil, existentes en los mismos, cuando exalten a uno sólo de los bandos enfrentados en ella o se identifiquen con el régimen instaurado en España a su término. Lo previsto en el párrafo anterior no será de aplicación cuando concurran razones artísticas, arquitectónicas u otras de interés general que lo hagan improcedente. En estos casos, podrá considerarse, de acuerdo con las circunstancias, la forma de dar testimonio de homenaje y recuerdo a todas las víctimas de la Guerra Civil.

Artículo 18. Valle de los Caídos.

1. El Valle de los Caídos se regirá estrictamente por las normas aplicables con carácter general a los lugares de culto y a los cementerios públicos.

2. En ningún lugar del recinto podrán llevarse a cabo actos de naturaleza política ni exaltadores de la Guerra Civil, de sus protagonistas, o del franquismo.

3. La Fundación gestora del Valle de los Caídos incluirá entre sus objetivos honrar la memoria de todas las personas fallecidas a consecuencia de la Guerra Civil de 1936–1939 y de la represión política que la siguió, con el objeto de profundizar en el conocimiento de ese período histórico y en la exaltación de la paz y de los valores democráticos.

Artículo 19. Edificaciones y obras públicas realizadas mediante trabajos forzosos.

Conforme a su normativa reguladora, las Administraciones públicas podrán prever subvenciones para la confección de censos de edificaciones y obras públicas realizadas por miembros de los Batallones Disciplinarios de Soldados Trabajadores, así como por prisioneros en campos de concentración, Batallones de Trabajadores y prisioneros en Colonias Penitenciarias Militarizadas.

Artículo 20. Concesión de la nacionalidad española a los voluntarios integrantes de las Brigadas Internacionales.

1. Con el fin de hacer efectivo el derecho que reconoció el Real Decreto 39/1996, de 19 de enero, a los voluntarios integrantes de las Brigadas Internacionales que participaron en la guerra civil de 1936 a 1939, no les será de aplicación la exigencia de renuncia a su anterior nacionalidad requerida en el artículo 23, letra b, del Código civil, en lo que se refiere a la adquisición por carta de naturaleza de la nacionalidad española.

2. Mediante Real Decreto aprobado por el Consejo de Ministros, se determinarán los requisitos y el procedimiento a seguir para la adquisición de la nacionalidad española por parte de las personas mencionadas en el apartado anterior.

Artículo 21. Reconocimiento a las Asociaciones de víctimas.

El Gobierno, mediante Real Decreto acordado en Consejo de Ministros, podrá conceder la Gran Cruz del Mérito Civil de tipo colectivo a las Asociaciones, Fundaciones y Organizaciones que se hayan destacado en la defensa de la dignidad de las víctimas de la violencia política a que se refiere esta Ley y en la contribución a la recuperación de la memoria histórica.

Artículo 22. Creación del Centro Documental de la Memoria Histórica.

1. De conformidad con lo previsto en la Ley 21/2005, de 17 de noviembre, se constituye el Centro Documental de la Memoria Histórica, con sede en la ciudad de Salamanca.

2. Son funciones del Centro Documental de la Memoria Histórica:

   a) Mantener y desarrollar el Archivo General de la Guerra Civil Española, y proceder a la actualización de las técnicas para su uso y conservación.
   b) Recuperar, reunir, organizar y poner a disposición de los interesados, los fondos documentales y las fuentes secundarias que puedan resultar de interés para el estudio de la Guerra civil, la dictadura franquista, la resistencia guerrillera contra ella, el exilio, el internamiento de españoles en campos de concentración durante la Segunda Guerra Mundial y la transición.
   c) Fomentar la investigación histórica sobre la Guerra civil, el franquismo, el exilio y la transición, y contribuir a la difusión de sus resultados.
   d) Impulsar la difusión de los fondos del Centro, y facilitar la participación activa de los usuarios y de sus organizaciones representativas.

3. La estructura y funcionamiento del Centro Documental de la Memoria Histórica se establecerá mediante Real Decreto acordado en Consejo de Ministros.

Artículo 23. Archivo General de la Guerra Civil Española.

1. Los documentos originales, o copias fidedignas de los mismos, referidos a la Guerra Civil de 1936–1939 y a la represión política subsiguiente sitos en Archivos, Museos o Bibliotecas de titularidad estatal, se integrarán en el Archivo General de la Guerra Civil Española, de titularidad estatal y con sede en la ciudad de Salamanca, creado por Real Decreto 426/1999, de 12 de marzo, en la forma y mediante el procedimiento que reglamentariamente se determinen.

2. Se arbitrarán los medios necesarios para que la Administración General del Estado proceda a la recopilación de los testimonios orales relevantes sobre

la Guerra Civil española y la represión política subsiguiente y a su integración en el Archivo General de la Guerra Civil Española.

Artículo 24. Adquisición y protección de documentos sobre la Guerra Civil y la Dictadura.

1. La Administración General del Estado aprobará, con carácter anual y con la dotación que en cada caso se establezca en los Presupuestos Generales del Estado, un programa de convenios para la adquisición de documentos referidos a la Guerra Civil o a la represión política subsiguiente que obren en archivos públicos o privados, nacionales o extranjeros, ya sean en versión original o a través de cualquier instrumento que permita archivar, conocer o reproducir palabras, datos o cifras con fidelidad al original. Los mencionados fondos documentales se incorporarán al Archivo General de la Guerra Civil Española.

2. De conformidad con lo dispuesto en la Ley 16/1985, de 25 de junio, de Patrimonio Histórico Español, los documentos obrantes en archivos privados y públicos relativos a la Guerra Civil y la Dictadura se declaran, a todos los efectos, constitutivos del Patrimonio Documental y Bibliográfico.

Artículo 25. Derecho de acceso a los fondos de los Archivos públicos y privados.

1. A los efectos de lo previsto en esta Ley, se garantizará a los interesados y a sus herederos el derecho de acceso a los fondos documentales depositados en los archivos públicos y la obtención de la copia que soliciten de los documentos que les conciernan.

2. Lo previsto en el apartado anterior será de aplicación, en sus propios términos, a los Archivos privados sostenidos, total o parcialmente, con fondos públicos.

3. El acceso a los documentos contenidos en los Archivos a que se refieren los apartados anteriores se regirá por lo previsto en el artículo 57 de la Ley 16/1985, de 25 de junio, del Patrimonio Histórico Español. Lo dispuesto en el apartado 3 del citado artículo 57 será de especial aplicación cuando los documentos identifiquen a los autores o a otras personas intervinientes en los hechos o en las actuaciones jurídicas sobre los mismos, en cuyo caso los responsables de los archivos públicos sustituirán la entrega de una copia de los mismos por un certificado sobre su contenido, con el fin de preservar la identidad de aquellos.

DISPOSICIÓN ADICIONAL PRIMERA.—COMISIÓN INTERMINISTERIAL PARA LA ATENCIÓN A QUIENES PADECIERON LAS CONSECUENCIAS DE LA GUERRA CIVIL Y DE LA DICTADURA.

1. Se crea una Comisión Interministerial para la atención a quienes padecieron las consecuencias de la Guerra Civil y de la Dictadura, con la composición, organización y funciones que se determinen reglamentariamente.

2. La norma reglamentaria a que se refiere el apartado anterior dispondrá la disolución y el cese en sus funciones de la Comisión Interministerial para el estudio de la situación de las víctimas de la guerra civil y del franquismo, creada por Real Decreto 1891/2004, de 10 de septiembre.

3. Antes de comenzar sus trabajos, la Comisión Interministerial para la atención a quienes padecieron las consecuencias de la Guerra Civil y de la Dictadura dictará una resolución organizativa por la que se crearán las subcomisiones de apoyo que considere oportunas, integradas por personal al servicio de las Administraciones públicas. La existencia y composición de las mismas se reflejará en la correspondiente relación de puestos de trabajo del Ministerio de la Presidencia.

DISPOSICIÓN ADICIONAL SEGUNDA.—RECONOCIMIENTO EN FAVOR DE PERSONAS FALLECIDAS EN DEFENSA DE LA DEMOCRACIA DURANTE EL PERÍODO COMPRENDIDO ENTRE 1 DE ENERO DE 1968 Y 6 DE OCTUBRE DE 1977.

1. En atención a las circunstancias excepcionales que concurrieron en su muerte, se reconoce el derecho a una indemnización, por una cuantía de 135.000 €, a los beneficiarios de quienes fallecieron durante el período comprendido entre el 1 de enero de 1968 y el 6 de octubre de 1977, en defensa y reivindicación de las libertades y derechos democráticos.

2. Serán beneficiarios de la indemnización a que se refiere el apartado primero de esta disposición los hijos y el cónyuge de la persona fallecida, si no estuviere separado legalmente ni en proceso de separación o nulidad matrimonial, o la persona que hubiere venido conviviendo con ella de forma permanente con análoga relación de afectividad a la del cónyuge durante, al menos, los dos años inmediatamente anteriores al momento del fallecimiento, salvo que hubieren tenido descendencia en común, en cuyo caso bastará la mera convivencia. Subsidiariamente, si no existieran los anteriores, serán beneficiarios, por orden sucesivo y excluyente, los padres, nietos, los hermanos de la persona fallecida y los hijos de la persona conviviente, cuando dependieren económicamente del fallecido.

Cuando se produzca la concurrencia de diversas personas que pertenezcan a un grupo de los que tienen derecho a la indemnización, la cuantía total máxima se repartirá por partes iguales entre todos los que tengan derecho por la misma condición, excepto cuando concurran el cónyuge o persona con análoga relación afectiva y los hijos del fallecido, en cuyo caso la ayuda se distribuirá al 50 por ciento entre el cónyuge o la persona con análoga relación de afectividad y el conjunto de los hijos.

3. Procederá el abono de la indemnización siempre que por los mismos hechos no se haya recibido indemnización o compensación económica alguna o, habiéndose recibido, sea de cuantía inferior a la determinada en esta disposición.

4. El Gobierno, mediante Real Decreto, determinará las condiciones y el procedimiento para la concesión de la indemnización prevista en esta disposición. Corresponderá la tramitación de este procedimiento a la Comisión prevista en la Disposición adicional primera de esta Ley y al Consejo de Ministros su resolución definitiva.

5. Los beneficiarios de la indemnización establecida en esta disposición dispondrán del plazo de un año, a contar desde la entrada en vigor del Real Decreto a que se refiere el apartado anterior, para presentar su solicitud ante la Comisión en él mencionada.

Disposición adicional tercera.— Protección de datos.

1. La recogida, cesión y tratamiento de datos de carácter personal de las personas implicadas en los expedientes contemplados en la presente Ley sólo podrán realizarse en ficheros informáticos de titularidad pública y se regirá por lo dispuesto en la Ley Orgánica 15/1999, de 13 de diciembre, de Protección de Datos de Carácter Personal.

2. El acceso a los documentos obrantes en los archivos públicos referidos a víctimas de la Guerra Civil y de la Dictadura estará sometido a los plazos y condiciones establecidos en el artículo 37 de la Ley 30/1992, de 26 de noviembre, de Régimen Jurídico de las Administraciones Públicas y del Procedimiento Administrativo Común, y en el artículo 37 de la Ley 16/1985, de 25 de junio, del Patrimonio Histórico Español.

Disposición adicional cuarta.— Adecuación del Archivo General de la Guerra Civil Española.

Se autoriza al Gobierno a que lleve a cabo las acciones necesarias en orden a organizar y reestructurar el Archivo General de la Guerra Civil Española.

Disposición final primera.—Aplicación supletoria.

Será aplicable supletoriamente al procedimiento regulado en los artículos 3 a 7 de la presente Ley lo previsto en la Ley 30/1992, de Régimen Jurídico de las Administraciones Públicas y del Procedimiento Administrativo Común.

Disposición final segunda.—Habilitación para el desarrollo.

Se habilita al Gobierno y a sus miembros, en el ámbito de sus respectivas competencias, para dictar cuantas disposiciones sean necesarias para el desarrollo y aplicación de lo establecido en esta Ley.

Disposición final tercera.—Entrada en vigor.

La presente Ley entrará en vigor al día siguiente de su publicación en el Boletín Oficial del Estado.

Notes

Introduction

1. It should be noted that, although the original, spontaneously generated "place of memory" was taken down about a month after the terrorist attack, a more permanent "virtual" memorial was established in Atocha. Screens connected to an Internet site (http://www.mascercanos.com) were installed in the station. People could type in a message on the screens, or through the Internet site, attaching it to the image of a white hand (the symbol that has arisen in Spain as a condemnation of terrorist violence). Thus, although Reyes Mate's general observations about the problem of memory in contemporary Spain are still valid, it is important to note that an effort was made to maintain a more permanent "place of memory" in Atocha. On the first anniversary of the bombings, furthermore, a permanent memorial was also inaugurated in the Parque del Retiro [Retiro Park]. This memorial, first called the Bosque de los Ausentes [Forest of the Absent] and later the Bosque del Recuerdo [Forest of Remembrance], comprises 192 olive and cypress trees in memory of those who died in the terrorist bombings. Such acts of remembrance and commemoration cannot be separated from apparently unrelated political struggles. As an article in *El País* explains, when describing the inauguration ceremony, different people and political groups arrive at the victim count of 192 in different ways: whereas right-wing groups within the local government in Madrid count among the victims the fetus of a pregnant woman who died in the bombings, the Socialist government counts, instead, a special forces agent who died while trying to apprehend several suspected terrorists a few weeks after the attacks (*El País* 2005b).

2. The ever-increasing number of scholarly monographs and collections of essays exploring various issues related to memory has in fact led to the emergence of the new interdisciplinary field of memory studies, which is slowly but surely being institutionalized within academic circles. The creation of the Masters Degree Program in Cultural Memory in the Institute of Cultural Studies at the University of London, the founding of the journal *History and Memory*, as well as the emergence of the new Routledge book series "Memory and Narrative," among many other such projects, attest to the recent wide-ranging interest in memory studies within different academic contexts.

3. For more information on the mass graves of the Spanish civil war and postwar repression, see Silva and Macías 2003, as well as the Web site of the organization they founded, "Asociación para la Recuperación de la Memoria Histórica" ["Association for the Recovery of Historical Memory"] (http://www.memoriahistorica.org). See also the Web site of another important organization, associated with the Spanish Communist Party, "Foro por la Memoria" (http://www.nodo50.org/foroporlamemoria/inicio.htm), which has likewise been organizing exhumations. More information

can be found in Armengou and Belis 2004, Ferrándiz 2005a and 2005b, and Fernández de Mata 2005 and 2006.

4. The term "desaparecido" was also used by Silva to counter a long-standing problem in Spain, whereby the true extent of Francoist repression, during and after the civil war, has been systematically downplayed during the transition and is only recently being adequately recognized, as in, for example, the volume, coordinated by Santos Juliá, *Víctimas de la guerra civil* [*Victims of the Civil War*]. One of the historians who contributed to this book, Julián Casanova, explains the fallacy underlying the predominant view during the transition that claimed that both sides of the civil war had committed comparable violence. This perspective was sustained only by means of a systematic under-representation of Francoist repression both during and after the war. As he explains, recent investigations show that between 50,000 and 60,000 people were killed by the Republican forces during the war, while Nationalist forces killed more than 100,000 during the war and another 50,000 afterwards. These figures, however, only count the executions for which official documentation has been found. The real numbers of Nationalist killings are undoubtedly higher, but cannot be adequately documented because much of the evidence of Francoist repression was systematically destroyed at the end of the war as well as at the beginning of the transition. Another researcher, for example, has stated that the number of people killed by Nationalist forces after the war reached 100,000 (see Ximénez de Sandoval 2004). According to another estimate, it is believed that between 1939 and 1944 Franco's forces summarily executed 192,684 people (see Amalio Blanco 2003). Whatever the real number may be, as Casanova exclaims, "si uno hace la fotografía completa, ve un plan premeditado, un exterminio llevado a sus últimas consecuencias incluso después de la guerra, y nos damos cuenta que hay una desproporción clarísima entre la violencia exterminadora del franquismo y la republicana.... creo que, por el bien de la democracia y de la civilización, hay que empezar a denunciar este tipo de cosas de verdad" (Armengou and Belis 2004, 112) ["if one looks at the complete picture, one sees a premeditated plan, an extermination taken to its final consequences even after the war, and we realize that there is a clear disproportion between the exterminating violence of Francoism and that of the Republicans.... I think that, for the good of democracy and civilization, we have to start denouncing this type of thing"].

The very terminology used to describe the Francoist repression is thus part and parcel of a recent effort by many historians and others to shatter a long-standing practice of downplaying its magnitude and scope in order to recognize the full implications of its effect on Spanish society. Other similar efforts are Armengou and Belis's argument for the appropriateness of using the term "genocidio" [genocide] to describe Francoist repression (see 2004, 138–39), and Paul Preston's claim that it would not be inappropriate to use the term "holocaust" (2005). It is not altogether unexpected that others have reverted to old conservative arguments that minimize, and, indeed, justify such repression. Pío Moa's revisionist accounts of the war are a case in point (2003). What is most striking, and worrisome, about such a backlash of right-wing revisionism is the great commercial success of such texts, despite their blatant lack of historical rigor.

5. Some exhumations of mass graves had been informally undertaken during the early years of the transition. Most of these efforts were abandoned, out of fear of reprisals, after the failed military coup in 1981. Not until the early twenty-first century did an official organization with a national scope such as the ARMH emerge.

6. The article in *El País*, "La tierra devuelve a sus muertos" [The earth returns its dead], by Carlos Cué, appeared on July 1, 2002.

It is important to note that the ARMH is not the only association that has emerged whose mandate is related to the problem of the mass graves in Spain, although it is the one that has gained the most public recognition. Among others, there is an association affiliated with the Spanish Communist Party, "Foro por la Memoria" (http://www.nodo50.org/foroporlamemoria/inicio.htm). Its objective is also to recover the memory of the victims of Francoist repression, with a special emphasis on recognizing and celebrating the leftist politics and ideology of many of them. Like the ARMH, the "Foro por la Memoria" is an advocate for the exhumation of mass graves, although many disputes have arisen between them regarding how to organize and enact the exhumations. In fact, both organizations disagree about what the ultimate objective of the entire process should be, whether to provide proper re-burial for the bodies, or to recover and extol the leftist ideology of many of the victims.

Other organizations, however, claim that the best way to honor the memory of those who are interred in such graves is not to exhume them, but to maintain the graves as they are, marking them appropriately. One such organization is the "Asociación de Familiares y Amigos de la Fosa Común de Oviedo" [Association of Relatives and Friends of the Mass Grave of Oviedo] (http://humano.ya.com/fosaoviedo/). Organizations such as this one are not opposed to commemorating and honoring those interred in the graves, but believe that the process of exhumation will destroy the very site, the mass grave itself, which is the most valuable "place of memory" to remember the history of violence it represents. The most famous dispute over this issue involves the mass grave in which the remains of Federico García Lorca are believed to be located, along with those of three other men. The family of the poet has strongly argued against the exhumation of the grave, claiming that Lorca's memory is more appropriately honored by not engendering the inevitable media and publicity nightmare that they believe the exhumation would create. Their position may soon change, however, as more and more exhumations are undertaken and the process is perceived to be more institutionalized. For more on the polemic surrounding Lorca's grave, see Soria Olmedo 2004 and Kolbert 2003. For an analysis of the disputes among the various groups, and the different approaches to the process of exhumations, see Ferrándiz 2005a and 2005b.

That there are associations espousing such different positions regarding the mass graves clearly demonstrates that the problem of recovering, or not, the memory of the past, and of how to do so, is always tied to the interests in the present that are served by such a task.

7. This is precisely something that the 2005 Amnesty International special report on Spain warns against (2005, 12).

8. This dynamic adds an interesting twist to the debate during the transition of whether the political process should be characterized by reform or rupture with regard to the Franco regime. As Teresa Vilarós observes: "la ruptura psíquica con la historia reciente junto a la reforma política que tal proceso exigió es lo que está en el corazón de la transición. Aunque 'reforma', y no 'ruptura', fuera el estribillo político de la transición española, tal reforma se construyó con la eliminación súbita de toda referencia al pasado inmediato franquista, con un 'Pacto del Olvido' al que fervorosamente se aferró el imaginario colectivo español" (1998, 16) [the psychological rupture with the recent past, together with the political reform demanded by that process, are at the heart of the transition. Even though "reform," and not "rupture," became the political slogan of the transition, that reform was constructed with the sudden elimination of any reference to the immediate Francoist past, with a "pact of forgetting" to which the Spanish collective imaginary ardently clung].

9. See Moreno-Nuño 2006 for another analysis of this "schizophrenic" condition, defined as the dialectic between two modes of representing the civil war: myth (the desire to forget) and trauma (the desire to remember) (13).

10. During the early transition, many of the efforts by right-wing forces to lay a veil of forgetting over the past were in fact not so subtle, although they were definitely intended to go unnoticed by society at large. In *Las fosas de Franco* [*Franco's Mass Graves*], Silva explains how, in 1976, an order of the then Minister of the Interior, Rodolfo Martín Villa, was presented to all the Offices of the Guardia Civil [Civil Guard] in Spain commanding them to send to Madrid all the information in their archives related to the repression of individuals considered dangerous to the Nationalist cause during the war and later to the Franco regime. From 1976 to 1978, mountains of documents were secretly destroyed in Madrid (2003).

In *Las fosas del silencio* [*The Graves of Silence*], Armengou and Belis record a similar order that Martín Villa sent to all provincial headquarters of the Movimiento [the Movement, the official name for the Francoist national political organization], soon after Adolfo Suarez formally abolished the Movimiento in 1977. The order also called for the destruction of all documents pertaining to Francoist repression during the war and throughout the regime. A worker who was put in charge of destroying such documents in Barcelona presents a graphic description of the secret and systematic elimination of this information:

> La orden era clara y venía del Gobierno Civil: había que destruir todos los archivos. Con la orden nos prometieron algunos medios para ejecutarla. Prometieron que nos enviarían una máquina trituradora. Ni que decir tiene la risa que nos cogió. ¡Una maquinita trituradora para cientos de miles de documentos! ... Un policía amigo, ... se encargó de buscar el horno. Yo busqué los camiones. ... La fábrica llevaba tiempo sin funcionar. Costó poner en marcha el horno. ... Ese horno quemó ocho horas durante cuatro días. (2004, 90)

> The order was clear and it came from the Civil Government: we had to destroy all the archives. With the order, they promised us some means to execute it. They promised they would send us a shredding machine. You can't imagine the way we laughed, a little shredding machine for hundreds and thousands of documents! ... A policeman friend of mine, ... was in charge of finding the oven. I looked for the trucks. ... The factory had been closed for a while. It was hard to start up the oven. ... That oven burnt for eight hours during four days.

Obviously, the well-planned, and well-hidden, destruction of such documents just when Spanish society was supposedly establishing a free and open democracy has made the search by organizations such as the ARMH for individuals "disappeared" by Francoist repression during the civil war and postwar years very difficult. It has likewise hindered the efforts of post-Franco Spain to confront the true implications and legacy of Francoism.

11. In 1990, Eduardo Subirats criticized the obsession of the Socialist government with creating the image of a modern Spain at the expense of dealing with many of the real problems the country faced, such as that of confronting its Fascist past:

> Diríase que España ha sido política y mediáticamente modernizada en la misma medida en que los conceptos de modernización y modernidad se han vaciado de cualquier otro contenido que no sea el formalismo inherente a los valores de la producción mediática de la realidad. ... Somos modernos. Y lo somos porque un día ya fuimos o debimos de ser lo bastante antifranquistas, luego demócratas en demasía, por fin socialistas hasta la saciedad. ... Somos modernos porque hemos superado definitivamente la historia de España: en la medida en que la hemos suprimido de nuestras modernizadas cabezas. (1990)

> One would say that Spain has become modernized, politically and media-wise, in the measure that the concepts of modernization and modernity have become emptied of any content that is not the formalism inherent in the values of a media-created reality. ... We are modern. And we are so because once upon a time, we must have been anti-Francoist enough, then all too

democratic, and finally, socialists to satiety.... We are modern because we have definitely overcome the history of Spain: in the measure that we have eliminated it from our modernized heads.

12. Felipe González continues to defend the decision of the various Socialist governments he led, in the 1980s and '90s, to forego any real confrontation with the recent Spanish past of war and repression in the name of a peaceful reconciliation. See, for example, the article he published in *El País* in 2001 (González 2001). For one response to that article, among others, see Navarro 2001.

13. For more on the 1992 celebrations, see Richards 2000, as well as Graham and Sánchez 1995 and Gabilondo 2003.

14. Another example of an element within an important commemoration that could be seen as ultimately contributing to a significant act of forgetting is a comment included in the catalogue of the enormously popular exhibit "Exilio" held in Madrid in 2002, at the Palacio de Cristal del Retiro, and organized by the Fundación Pablo Iglesias with the cooperation of the Reina Sofía art museum. As José María Naharro-Calderón explains, the exhibit was framed with the Republican flag and the current national Spanish flag placed in a manner that seemed to imply that there was a natural, unquestionable progression from one to the other. In the exhibit catalogue this transition was further naturalized in a problematic comment by Alfonso Guerra, exclaiming that "entre la pobreza, la indigencia, el desarraigo y la humillación, los españoles del destierro concebían una España reconciliada, en Paz: soñaban lo que mucho más tarde sería la Constitución de 1978" (Naharro-Calderón 2005, 113) [Amidst poverty, indigence, displacement, and humiliation, the Spaniards in exile conceived of a Spain reconciled and peaceful: they dreamed of what, much later, would become the Constitution of 1978]. This statement, within the context of an exhibit that was massively attended by Spaniards, many of whom were learning for the first time about many aspects of the Spanish exile(s) of 1939, is especially problematic. This is so not only because it obviates the many ideological differences among various groups and political parties in exile, attributing to them one supposed belief held by all, and not only because it naturalizes the Constitution of 1978, presenting it as an inevitable end of a process that supposedly could not have been otherwise, but because it is ultimately false. The comment, in fact, completely obviates something that was quite central to the ideological beliefs of many exiled Spaniards: that they had fought for a Republic that defined itself, among other things, against a monarchical system of government. For more on this and other such commemorations related to the experience of exile, see Naharro-Calderón 2005.

15. The debate in *El País* was entitled "Olvidar o asumir nuestro pasado inmediato?" [To forget or assume our immediate past?] (see, among other contributions to this open debate, those by Santos Juliá 1999a, and Fernando Vallespín 1999. From the outset, the question posed by the newspaper established a dichotomy not between forgetting and *remembering* Spain's recent past, but between forgetting and *assuming* that past. The very manner of framing the question reveals that the memory of the past to be discussed is not a matter of merely *recalling* events, but of exploring the *responsibility* that contemporary Spanish society might have toward those events. It was the acceptance of this responsibility for the past that had been effectively barred from discussion in the earlier stages of the transition.

It is important to note that *El País* acknowledged two recent events as having made the newspaper realize the need for such a public debate. One was the unexpected success of a documentary aired earlier that year on Spanish television, "Los campos de concentración de Franco" [Franco's concentration camps]. Many people were shocked to hear for the first time of the system of over 50 concentration camps that Franco created throughout Spain after the civil war, and in which over half a million people were detained. The last of these camps to close, in Los Merinales (Sevilla), did not do so until 1962. The strong response of viewers to this documentary made it clear that a generalized debate within society at large about Spain's recent Francoist past was long overdue.

The other event took place in the pages of *El País*. An article written by novelist Javier Marías ("El artículo más iluso") in June 1999 generated a heated exchange over the next few months between the author and various people responding to his views. Javier Marías criticized several well-known Spanish intellectuals (although he did not name them explicitly, the subsequent exchange made it clear that he was referring to philosopher José Luis Aranguren, novelist Camilo José Cela, and author and journalist Eduardo Haro Tecglen) for not taking full responsibility, later in their life, for early pro-Fascist actions or writings. This exchange thus signaled a growing need in society at large to deal more openly with such issues.

For the exchange of letters by Marías and others in *El País*, see Marías 1999a, 1999b, 1999c; Eduardo López-Aranguren 1999a, 1999b; Javier Muguerza 1999a, 1999b; Elías Díaz 1999, and Javier Tusell 1999.

16. That such a reckoning with the past is becoming more present within society at large at this time in Spain partly reflects expected historical patterns in the working of collective memory. In his book on the mass graves of the civil war and postwar era, Silva mentions a conversation he had with French sociologist Alain Touraine about the growing popular interest and support for the work of his organization in the last few years. Touraine explained that, in both Germany and France, twenty-five years had to pass before those societies were able to deal in any meaningful way with their Nazi and collaborative past, respectively. Darío Paez et al., likewise highlight sociological theories claiming that societies often follow a regular cycle of remembering and forgetting the past. They explain that every twenty to thirty years a process of remembering and critically confronting the past often emerges in societies, due in part to the coming of age, as well as the attainment of positions of political and social power, of a new generation within that time span (1998, 126). This partly explains why it is only now, twenty to thirty years after Franco's death, that Spanish society is beginning to critically review the way in which the transition failed to appropriately confront Spain's past. What is significant about this process in Spain, however, is that this critical revision of the transition, which is occurring within the expected cycle of twenty-five to thirty years, is also the first time that a real critical revision of the legacy of the civil war is occurring in a way that engages society beyond academic circles. This cycle of critical revision and remembering of the civil war, therefore, is long overdue, and shows that Spain has not been able to neatly follow expected cyclical patterns in the development of collective memory.

17. For accounts of this process, see J.V. 2004 as well as Vitzthum and Carreyrou 2004.

18. As part of this ongoing process of dealing with such Francoist places of memory, the past two years have seen the removal of major statues of Franco in Madrid, Guadalajara, and Pobla de Vallbona (Valencia). It is significant that the first two removals were enacted without a public announcement, at nighttime, in order to minimize any protests. Such protests, from conservative institutions and citizens alike, did, however, emerge in the days following the removal. Equally significant is the fact that a statue of Franco removed in Melilla had to be returned to its pedestal within a week, due to the number of complaints that emerged, and that a similar statue in Salamanca is still standing. Although local governments and townships throughout the country have changed many street names related to the Franco regime since the dictator's death, many more still remain untouched.

The concern with the removal of such places of memory does not reflect solely conservative arguments that are more or less pro-Franco. Many who condemn the regime are nevertheless concerned that a radical policy of eliminating all such places of memory is not the best plan of action, as it would erase the traces of that past, and thus possibly contribute to the process of forgetting it. These arguments call for a way to maintain some of these markers, but recontextualize them so that they no longer signify an attitude of honoring and commemorating that past, but of critical engagement with it. These proposals would like to see some of these places of memory incorporated into a broader policy of learning about that past, as well as about its continued influence on the present. The historian Paul Preston, for example, has presented an argument along these lines (*El País* 2006c). Ray Loriga has suggested that instead of removing the equestrian Franco statue in Madrid one could have surrounded it with prison bars in order to make a powerful statement. This proposal, despite its apparent lighthearted tone, engages crucial aspects of this dilemma. For more on this issue, see *El País* 2006c; Cué 2005b, 2005d; Galaz 2005; and Loriga 2005.

19. There are other encouraging signs that point to a commitment on the government's part to assume a real responsibility for Spain's past of repression. In January 2005, the government passed a resolution to pay the equivalent of a pension as compensation to citizens who were forced to flee Spain, as children, during the civil war (*El País* 2005a). Although this will only affect a relatively small number of individuals, it is hopefully a first step toward what the government is claiming will be a broader system of compensations to victims of Francoism. It is important to point out that there have been measures, however insufficient, implemented at various moments during the transition to provide some form or other of compensation to victims of Francoist repression. For information on some of these measures, see Aguilar 2001 and Aguilar and Humlebaek 2002.

In early 2005, also, the government declared that it would return to Cataluña the documents that had been taken from the region by Nationalist forces during the civil war. These documents, used mainly for Franco's political repression, have been in the Archivo de la Guerra Civil [Civil War Archive] in Salamanca for many years, and the Catalan government has long demanded, to no avail, that they be returned to Cataluña.

Other initiatives at the level of regional autonomous governments are also encouraging. Within Cataluña, in 2004, the Generalitat, the Catalan autonomous government, has stated that it will create a new institution, the "Memorial Democrático," to recover the historical memory of Francoist repression and to acknowledge the significance for today's democracy of anti-Franco resistance forces of all kinds. This institution, scheduled to open in 2007, will possibly be built on the grounds of the "Camp de la Bota," the site in Barcelona where some 1,466 people were shot by Nationalist forces between 1939 and 1952. Among other projects, the institution plans to create an audiovisual archive of life testimonies during the Franco regime, a documentation and research center, and a complete register of all Spaniards who were deported to Nazi concentration camps. The institution will house all kinds of exhibits and cultural events destined to inform the public about Francoist repression and the various forces that fought against the Franco regime. This institution may very well become one of the first official "places of memory" where the past of the civil war and Francoism are effectively confronted. For more information on the "Memorial Democrático," see Corcuera 2004 and Preston 2005.

In 2002, the Basque autonomous government created an interministerial commission to help finance and coordinate all exhumations in the Basque country as well as develop a policy of reparations to the victims, within the Basque country, of Francoist repression. In 2005 a similar commission was established in Andalucía by the Junta de Andalucía, the Andalucian autonomous government. This commission is expected to fulfill functions similar to those of the Basque country commission, as well as establish a document and research center on the Franco era and Francoist repression.

20. See Aguilar 2001, as well as Aguilar and Humlebaek 2002 and Amnesty International 2005, for more on the unequal opportunities for redress and acknowledgment of human rights abuses experienced by the victims of both sides of the civil war. In this context, the existence of the *Causa general*, an official report published in 1945 documenting (although the legitimacy of the very documentation process used is highly questionable) all the crimes committed by the Republican forces during the civil war, contrasts sharply with the nonexistence of any such official report for the crimes committed, during and after the war, by Nationalist forces. No such official report has been created after Franco's death, and this is precisely one of the tasks that Amnesty International, in its 2005 report, urges the Spanish government to take up.

21. On July 28, 2006, after the manuscript of this book was completed, the interministerial commission finally presented its proposal for the law. Because there is no space here for a detailed account of the proposal, and for the reader's easy reference, the entire proposal, entitled "Anteproyecto de ley por la que se reconocen y amplían derechos y se establecen medidas en favor de quienes padecieron persecución o violencia durante la guerra civil y la dictadura," is presented in the appendix, at the end of this book, as it appears on the Web site of the ARMH: http://www.memoria historica.org/modules.php?name=News&file=article&sid=304. The proposal will only become law after it has been debated in the Spanish Congress, where political parties of various persuasions are sure to demand amendments that may modify it significantly. The president of the Partido Popular, Mariano Rajoy, for example, has denigrated the proposal, stating: "Yo creo que ocuparse ahora de la memoria histórica, generar tensiones y crear problemas es un enorme error.... La inmensa mayoría de los españoles ni quieren revisión histórica, ni quieren volver a hablar de la República, ni quieren volver a hablar de Franco, ni creo que eso sirva absolutamente para nada" (*El País*, 2006b) [I believe that dealing now with historical memory, generating tensions, and creating problems is an enormous error ... The vast majority of Spaniards neither want historical revisionism, nor do they want to talk again about the Republic, or Franco, nor do I think that any of this serves absolutely any purpose]. Political parties on the left, as well as many associations representing the interests of victims of Francoism, consider that it is an important step on the part of the government, but that it is insufficient, and does not fully address many of their needs and concerns.

In fact, the proposal clearly shows that the interministerial commission ultimately made serious concessions to the political right. Among the most polemical of these is the fact that it dropped a measure, originally intended for inclusion, which would annul the sentences passed by the "consejos de guerra" [war tribunals] under the Franco regime, whereby individuals considered to de dangerous to the regime were summarily tried and sentenced to death, incarceration, or forced labor. Instead, the proposal will create a measure by means of which individuals who suffered any kind of sanctions, sentences, or personal violence because of ideological reasons on either side of the civil war, or individuals who did so for similar reasons under the Franco regime, can appeal to be morally rehabilitated. These individuals, or their family members, will have to present their case before a council comprised of five members chosen by a majority of three-fifths of the Spanish Congress. This council will then review the case and decide weather or not to provide an official declaration stating that the execution, sentence, or sanction suffered was unjust, and an infringement of the rights and liberties currently upheld by the Spanish constitution. Furthermore, it is stated that the final declaration of moral rehabilitation presented by the five-member council must omit any reference to any individuals who were responsible for creating those unjust sentences or sanctions, for example, any members of war tribunals, or Francoist courts of law. Many political parties on the Left will surely fight against this proposal. Not only does it stop short of presenting what many feel is necessary (a strong condemnation of the illegality characterizing much of the Francoist repressive legal system through the revocation of all the sentences suffered by those summarily tried by Francoist "consejos de Guerra"), but it puts the burden of proof on the individuals who suffered persecution, ultimately protects those responsible for the repression, and, finally, by not allowing the names of those responsible to be known, does not guarantee the right of the victims, and their descendants, to full knowledge of the crimes committed.

Another concession made at the last minute by the interministerial commission is related to the removal of Francoist monuments and symbols. Although the proposal states that any such items under the regulation of the central government must be removed, at the last minute a section of the proposal was eliminated. The section called for local and regional governments to do the same. For many, the elimination of this provision at the local and regional level is highly problematic, especially because it is at those levels that many such symbols, plaques, street names, and so on, commemorating the Franco regime are found. In fact, even at the level of symbols and monuments under the regulation of the central government, the proposal calls for the elimination not only of those that refer to, or commemorate, the Franco regime, but of any such items that commemorate only one side of the civil war. Furthermore, the proposal contains a provision allowing for any such symbol or monument to be maintained if there is an overriding artistic or architectural interest at stake. For more on these and other polemical aspects of the proposal, as well as reactions from different political parties, see Cué 2006b, 2006c, 2006d, 2006e; *El País* 2006a, 2006b, 2006d, 2006e.

22. See Aguilar 2001 and Colomer 1998 for other analyses along the same lines. Within this context, Aguilar cites a revealing phrase by Colomer: "The virtues of the transition have become the vices of democracy" (qtd. in Aguilar 2001, 117).

23. Another positive sign is the fact that on March 17, 2006, the European Council unanimously passed a resolution officially condemning Francoism. This is the very first such official international condemnation of the regime, and it puts more pressure on the Spanish government to follow through appropriately with the long-awaited "law of historical memory." As a spokesman explained: "La resolución se ha hecho sin voluntad de reabrir heridas, pero sí de decir con autoridad, y por primera vez, que el franquismo fue una dictadura que conculcó todos los valores de la convención europea de derechos humanos. El Consejo de Europa no puede dar lecciones de cómo alcanzar la democracia en algunos países y callarse ante el franquismo" (Cué 2006a) [The resolution has been made without wanting to reopen old wounds, but to say with authority, and for the first time, that Franco's was a dictatorship that violated all the values of the European convention on human rights. The Council of Europe cannot give lessons to some countries on how to achieve democracy, and remain silent about Francoism].

24. It is important not to forget that the transition to democracy was characterized by much more economic hardship, and political instability, than is often recognized in hindsight. In this light, Silva's comments may be somewhat problematic if they lead to a vision of the transition that underestimates these difficult aspects of the transition years. Aguilar, for example, reminds us that despite the predominant view of the transition today, which tends to overemphasize its peaceful nature, "more than 460 violent deaths for political purposes were registered between 1975 and 1980 and about 400 people died in right and left-wing terrorist acts," while "63 people died in street demonstrations" (2001, 96). Monedero, among others, highlights various international

factors that imposed serious limits, including economic ones, on the transition. These include, among others, the international oil crisis of 1973, and the cold war, so important in determining the limitations of what was possible for any political transition process at the time.

25. See Zoë Crossland 2000 and 2002 for analyses of similar debates within the context of the exhumations of the disappeared in post-dictatorship Argentina.

26. Cristina Moreiras Menor also highlights the role that the improper burial of the victims of the civil war and Francoist repression plays in the spectral reemergence of that traumatic past in post-Franco Spain, despite official attempts to keep that history buried: "matar la historia a golpe de olvido es, así, paradójicamente, el mecanismo que impide que los muertos sean enterrados debidamente y que su aparición se prolongue en la historia actual a modo de presencias espectrales, de heridas sin suturar que emergen desde los márgenes de la historia" (2002, 57) [the killing of history by means of forgetting is thus, paradoxically, the mechanism that prevents the dead from being properly buried and that forces their reappearance in contemporary history as spectral presences, un-sutured wounds that emerge from the margins of history].

27. See Ricoeur 2004, 452–56, for some examples of the historical treaties and decrees that Juliá uses as models for the process of "echar en el olvido." These include the decree promulgated in Athens, in 403 b.c., after the victory of the democracy over the oligarchy of the Thirty Tyrants. The official decree proclaimed: "it is forbidden to recall the evils (the misfortunes)." The decree was accompanied by an oath that had to be taken by every citizen, stating: "I shall not recall the evils (misfortunes)" (Ricoeur 2004, 453). Another example is that of the Edict of Nantes issued by Henry IV in France after much brutal fighting. The first article of the treaty states: "let the memory of all things that have taken place on both sides . . . remain extinguished and dormant as something that has not occurred," while the second article proclaimed: "we forbid any of our subjects regardless of their state or quality to retain any memory thereof, to attack, resent, insult, or provoke one another as a reproach for what has occurred for any reason or pretext whatsoever, to dispute, challenge, or quarrel, nor to be outraged or offended by any act or word; but to be content to live peacefully together as brothers, friends, and fellow citizens, under penalty, for those who contravene this decree, of being punished as violators of the peace and disturbers of the public tranquility" (Ricoeur 2004, 454). Santos Juliá agrees with Ricoeur's analysis that such decrees are interesting for their paradoxical nature. At the very moment that one is being told, or that one is promising, to forget a past atrocity, the memory of that event is necessarily invoked, and thus the desire to forget ultimately ensures a certain level of remembrance of that very thing one is trying to forget by decree.

28. See Katherine Verdery's book *The Political Lives of Dead Bodies: Reburial and Postsocialist Change* (1999) for a discussion of these processes in the context of countries transitioning from Communist regimes. Her analysis of the political use and manipulation of dead bodies and statues in such moments of transition is highly relevant to the current debates in Spain regarding the mass graves as well as to the debates over the many Francoist monuments throughout the country.

29. For discussions of the development of such a "heritage industry," see, among others, Shaw and Chase 1989, as well as Hobsbawm and Ranger 1983. For more on politically conservative memory practices, see Todorov 2000.

30. For more on the way these factors have led to an unprecedented interest in the study of memory, see works by LaCapra, as well as Andreas Huyssen.

31. One area of study reflecting this increasingly prevalent concern is that which focuses on the function of various kinds of art and museums in the process of mem-

ory transmission. For examples, among others, of such analyses, see works by James Young, Barbie Zelizer, and Marianne Hirsch.

32. See Susannah Radstone's introduction to the collection of essays entitled *Memory and Methodology* (2000) for a compelling argument along these lines.

33. For a discussion of the connection between memory and the heart in classical conceptions of remembering, see Draaisma 1995.

34. This is a central concern in many discussions regarding the possibility or impossibility of representing the Holocaust, and is explored in depth in chapter 1. For a representative collection of essays, see Friedlander 1992.

35. Michael Schudson makes this a crucial tenet of his view of memory: "Memory is distortion since memory is invariably and inevitably selective. A way of seeing is a way of not seeing, a way of remembering is a way of forgetting, too. If memory were only a kind of registration, a 'true' memory might be possible. But memory is a process of encoding information, storing information, and strategically retrieving information, and there are social, psychological, and historical influences at each point" (1995, 348). The book to which Schudson's essay belongs, *Memory Distortion: How Minds, Brains, and Societies Reconstruct the Past*, presents fascinating discussions, from disciplines as varied as cognitive psychology, psychiatry, neurobiology, sociology, history, and religious studies, of the role of distortion in many forms of memory.

36. See, for example, the introduction by Robert O'Meally and Geneviève Fabre to *History and Memory in African-American Culture* for an example of a perspective in which Nora's concept of *lieux de mémoire* is no longer understood as tied to dominant national forms of history, but is explicitly transformed into a useful "form of counterhistory that challenges the false generalizations in exclusionary 'History'" (1994, 8).

37. This is, in part, what Nora means when he exclaims that "we speak so much of memory because there is so little of it left.... There are *lieux de mémoire*, sites of memory, because there are no longer *milieux de mémoire*, real environments of memory" (1989, 7).

38. For more on the collective nature of all memory, see Maurice Halbwachs (1980, 1992). His work has had an enormous influence on the recent boom in memory studies, especially on the growing interest in theories of collective memory.

1. Jorge Semprún

1. The emphasis on the importance of *loci* for remembering is the reading recurrently extracted from this anecdote, which appears in numerous memory treatises. Frances Yates begins her study of memory with the anecdote.

2. Michael Perlman, in *Imaginal Memory and the Place of Hiroshima*, does emphasize this aspect of the anecdote in an interesting discussion of memory and trauma within the framework of archetypal psychology (1988 see esp. 47–48).

3. These novels are: *Le grand voyage* (1963) [*El largo viaje; The Long Voyage*], which won the prestigious Formentor European literary prize in 1964; *L'Évanouissement* (1967) [*El desvanecimiento; The Fainting*]; *Quel beau dimanche!* (1980) [*Aquel domingo; What a Beautiful Sunday!*]; *La montagne blanche* (1986a) [*La montaña blanca; The White Mountain*]; *L'écriture ou la vie* (1994a) [*La escritura o la vida; Literature or Life*]; and *Le mort qu'il faut* (2001a) [*Viviré con su nombre, morirá con el mío; I Will Live With His Name, He Will Die With Mine*]. *Mal et modernité suivi de*

"... *Vous avez une tombe au creux des nuages*..." (1995c) [*Evil and Modernity followed by "You have a tomb in the clouds"*] is not a novel but the transcription of two of Semprún's lectures dealing with his concentration camp experience: the first delivered at the Sorbonne on June 19, 1990, as part of the Marc Bloch Conferences and the second given in Frankfurt on October 9, 1994, upon Semprún's receiving the German Book Guild Freedom Prize. I focus here on *Le grand voyage*, although other texts are brought to bear on the discussion. All of these works were originally written in French, due to Semprún's exile in France. I cite from the French editions of the books appearing in Works Cited. Because Semprún often plays with words in a way that may come across in a Spanish translation, but is sometimes lost in an English one, I am providing both the Spanish and English translations of original quotations. These are taken from the translations of Semprún's texts appearing in Works Cited. The English translations appear, within the body of the text, immediately following the French original, and the Spanish translations are provided in endnotes.

4. Two of Semprún's texts are centered on his political activity. In 1977, *Autobiografía de Federico Sánchez* [*The Autobiography of Federico Sánchez*], originally written in Spanish, won the prestigious Planeta Prize in Spain. Under the *nom de guerre* that he used most frequently during his clandestine activity against the Franco regime, he narrates his work within, and final expulsion from, the Spanish Communist Party. For a study exploring the impact of this text on the politics of memory during the Spanish transition to democracy, see Ferrán 2000. *Federico Sánchez se despide de ustedes* [*Federico Sánchez Says Good-Bye*] (1993a), also written originally in Spanish, tells of his work as minister of culture from 1988 to 1991. Two other texts are especially important for understanding Semprún's work within a Spanish context. *Adieu, vive clarté*... (1998) [*Adiós, luz de veranos; Good-Bye, Light of Summers*], originally written in French, complements Semprún's autobiographical project with an account centered mostly on his life before deportation, although, as in most of his texts, the narration inevitably refers to that central experience in his life. In 2003, Semprún published his first fictional novel written originally in Spanish. *Veinte años y un día* [*Twenty Years and a Day*], which explores the lingering effects of the Spanish civil war in 1956 Spain, was awarded the José Manuel Lara prize for novel in 2004.

5. In 2004, for example, he wrote the play "Gurs: una tragedia europea" [Gurs: A European Tragedy] under the aegis of the European Theater Convention. The play, produced collaboratively by two French and one Spanish theater companies, was represented first in Nova Gorica, Slovania, and then in Sevilla, Spain, and timed to coincide with the official entry into the European Union in 2004 of ten new Eastern European countries. The play is set in the French concentration camp of Gurs in the early 1940s, where the Vichy government interned some 23,000 Spanish Republican soldiers after the Spanish civil war along with members of the International Brigades, the French Resistance, and numerous Jews who had emigrated from Germany, all totaling over 60,000 prisoners. Many were deported from Gurs to the concentration camp of Drancy and then to Auschwitz. This multinational production, at the time of the biggest enlargement of the European Union to date, is a reminder of a collective history of horror that must be addressed collectively if a new Europe is to be built.

6. For representative studies that contextualize Semprún's work within the French literary tradition, or within that of Holocaust testimonies, see Davis 1991 Egri 1969, Gartland 1983, Langer 2001, and Mertens 2003. Most major book-length studies devoted to Semprún have appeared in French, including the critical studies by Nicoladzé and Cortanze. Until recently, most of the book-length studies that included an analysis of Semprún's work in the context of Spanish literature focused on his novel *Autobiografía de Federico Sánchez*. For examples of such studies see Soto-Fernández

1996, and Sinnigen 1982. Angel Loureiro's excellent book *The Ethics of Autobiography: Replacing the Subject in Modern Spain* (2000), is one of the first to study Semprún's novels dealing with his concentration camp recollections within the Spanish narrative tradition, in particular, that of autobiographical writing.

7. "Desde el punto de vista del idioma literario, o soy apátrida—por bilingüe empedernido, por esquizofrenia lingüística definitiva—, o tengo dos patrias. Cosa, esta última, a todas luces imposible.... A fin de cuentas, mi patria no es la lengua, ni la española ni la francesa: mi patria es el lenguaje. O sea, un espacio de comunicación social, de invención lingüística; una posibilidad de representación del universo, de modificarlo también, aunque sea mínima o marginalmente, por el lenguaje mismo" (Semprún 1994b, 15–16).

8. This problematized relation of language and referentiality also points to what Susannah Radstone and Katharine Hodgkin, in *Regimes of Memory* (2003), see as "the opacity, the non-transparency, and the arbitrariness of language as a medium for remembrance" (6). Semprún recurrently explores this opacity of language as a medium of remembrance.

9. Cathy Caruth's work has a central place in current debates about trauma. In the introduction to her book *Unclaimed Experience, Trauma, Narrative and History*, she studies the relationship between trauma and wound, underscoring why literature is an appropriate place to explore such a connection. In the introductions to the two sections of her book *Trauma: Explorations in Memory* (1995), she explores the repercussions of the "belatedness" of trauma, which, as the work of Felman and Laub (1992) also indicate, subverts any traditional sense of chronology when dealing with the recounting of traumatic events. As will become evident, this is a crucial element in Semprún's writing.

10. "la realidad suele precisar de la invención para tornarse verdadera. Es decir verosímil" (Semprún, 1995b, 280).

11. Berel Lang, in *Writing and the Holocaust,* echoes this notion when he explains that the literature that might best deal with the problematic relationship of the Holocaust and its representation is not "writing *about* the Holocaust . . . but *writing-the-Holocaust*" (1988, 250; emphasis added).

12. "A mí, en cambio, cada página escrita, arrancada al sufrimiento, me hundía en una memoria irremediable y mortífera, me asfixiaba en las angustias de aquel pasado Tenía que elegir entre la escritura o la vida y opté por la vida.... Tuve que optar por ser otro, por no ser yo mismo, para seguir siendo algo: alguien" (Semprún, 1994b, 9).

13. Loureiro provides an illuminating discussion of this meta-narrative reflection of the text's very origin within *L'écriture ou la vie.* Loureiro highlights Semprún's recurrent thematization of a real or symbolic dialogue with another author throughout his text. The relationship of his own work with that of Primo Levi is one example. This is seen as part of a larger question, recurrent in all of Semprun's work, of the need to find, even to invent, an adequate addressee for one's narration of trauma. For this discussion, see esp. Loureiro, 2000, 177–80.

14. "De todas formas, cuando describo esta sensación de estar dentro, que me atrapó en el valle del Mosela, ante la gente que paseaba por la carretera, ya no estoy en el valle del Mosela. Han pasado dieciséis años. Ya no puedo detenerme en aquel instante. Otros instantes vinieron a añadirse a él, formando un todo con esta sensación violenta de tristeza física que me acometió en el valle del Mosela" (Semprún, 1976, 27).

15. "Quizá no debiera hablar más que de esta gente que pasea y de esta sensación, tal como ha sido en este momento, en el valle del Mosela, para no trastornar el orden del relato. Pero esta historia la escribo yo, y hago lo que quiero" (Semprún, 1976, 26).

16. "Este hacinamiento de cuerpos en el vagón, este punzante dolor en la rodilla

derecha. Días, noches. Hago un esfuerzo e intento contar los días, contar las noches. Tal vez esto me ayude a ver claro. Cuatro días, cinco noches. Pero habré contado mal, o es que hay días que se han convertido en noches. Me sobran noches; noches de saldo. Una mañana, claro está, fue una mañana cuando comenzó este viaje. Aquel día entero. Después una noche. Levanto el dedo pulgar en la penumbra del vagón. Mi pulgar por aquella noche. Otra jornada después.... Olvídate de aquel día, fue una desesperación. Otra noche. Yergo en la penumbra un segundo dedo. Tercer día. Otra noche. Tres dedos en mi mano izquierda. Y el día en el que estamos. Cuatro días, pues, y tres noches. Avanzamos hacia la cuarta noche, el quinto día. Hacia la quinta noche, el sexto día. Pero ¿avanzamos nosotros? Estamos inmóviles, hacinados unos encima de otros, la noche es quien avanza, la cuarta noche, hacia nuestros inmóviles cadáveres futuros" (Semprún, 1976, 11).

17. "llevamos cuatro días y tres noches encajados el uno en el otro..." (Semprún, 1976, 12); "La cuarta noche de este viaje" (65); "Es la cuarta noche, no lo olviden, la cuarta noche de este viaje" (80); "Por ahí llegamos, en el corazón de la quinta noche de aquel viaje" (190).

18. "esta historia la escribo yo, y hago lo que quiero" (Semprún, 1976, 26).

19. "Pero ¿avanzamos nosotros? Estamos inmóviles, hacinados unos encima de otros, la noche es quien avanza, la cuarta noche, hacia nuestros inmóviles cadáveres futuros" (Semprún, 1976, 11).

20. "tengo la impresión de que mi cuerpo se va a quebrar en mil pedazos. Siento cada pedazo por separado, como si mi cuerpo ya no fuera un todo" (Semprún, 1976, 143).

21. "Hay otra solución también. Es aprovechar este viaje para seleccionar.... Tengo veinte años, puedo todavía permitirme el lujo de escoger en mi vida lo que asumiré y lo que rechazo.... Dentro de quince años, cuando escriba este viaje, ya no será posible. Por lo menos, lo imagino. Las cosas no sólo tendrán un peso en tu vida, sino también en sí mismas" (Semprún, 1976, 34).

22. Another strategy that the narrator of *Le grand voyage* uses to make the time of the boxcar ride more "livable" is to try to remember literary texts that he likes, word for word. One of these texts is Proust's *Remembrance of Things Past,* the beginning of which he recites to himself during the trip. This recourse to Proust is not only an example of how literature comes to the aid of the narrator when trying to live through, and later retell, his experience, but performs a mise en abîme in which the unstable relation between control and lack of control inherent in the narrator's discursive strategies is reproduced in the play of voluntary and involuntary memory within Proust's text. For further discussion of Semprún's use of Proust in this novel, see Kaplan 2003.

23. "He tenido una idea, de golpe,... la sensación, en cualquier caso repentina, muy fuerte, no de haberme librado de la muerte, sino de haberla atravesado. De haber sido, mejor dicho, atravesado por ella. De haberla vivido, de cierto modo" (Semprún, 1995b, 27).

24. "Había decidido contar esta historia en su orden cronológico. No porque me guste la simplicidad, no hay nada tan complicado como el orden cronológico. Ni porque me preocupe el realismo, no hay nada tan irreal como el orden cronológico. Es una abstracción, una convención cultural, una conquista del espíritu geométrico.... El orden cronológico es una forma para el que escribe de demostrar su dominio sobre el desorden del mundo, de marcarlo con su sello. Actúa como si fuera Dios" (Semprún, 1981, 109).

25. "Era mi memoria la que me arraigaba en la irrealidad de un sueño. La vida no era un sueño, ¡ni mucho menos! lo era yo. Y lo que es más: el sueño de alguien muerto tiempo atrás. Ya he mencionado, a pesar de su innombrable indecencia, esa sensación

que me ha asaltado en el transcurso de los años. Esa certeza serena y totalmente desesperada de no ser sino el fantasma soñador de un joven muerto tiempo ha" (Semprún, 1981, 133).

26. "La memoria es el mejor recurso, aunque ello pueda parecer paradójico a primera vista. El mejor recurso contra la angustia del recuerdo, contra el desamparo, contra la locura familiar y sorda. La criminal locura de vivir la locura de un muerto" (Semprún, 1981, 94).

27. One of the ways in which the repetition compulsion characteristic of trauma can be seen to operate in Semprún's work is in his narration of many of the same anecdotes over and over again in different texts, sometimes in exactly the same manner, sometimes with slight variations. This story of his fall onto the train tracks shortly after his liberation from Buchenwald, for example, is presented in detail again in *L'écriture ou la vie,* this time recounted in the first person. Loureiro sees this image of Semprún's "awakening" after a fall in that book as one metaphor, among many, of how his autobiographical text presents not so much a referential account of the historical events of his life, but a performative act of "self-reconstruction" (2000, 164). As this act of "self-reconstruction," based on a traumatic experience, is forced to incorporate death into the self, any knowledge upon which that self is built is forever traversed by a radical insecurity, or, as Loureiro claims, a complete "epistemological uncertainty" (2000, 155). I would add that the narrative strategy of compulsively repeating the same anecdotes in different texts, sometimes with slight variations, not only reflects the traumatic dimension of Semprún's writing, but transfers that "epistemological uncertainty" onto the readers, who are thus faced with a task similar to that of the narrators of Semprún's texts, trying to piece together disjointed, oftentimes incompatible, memories. For an enlightening study of another anecdote that Semprún repeatedly narrates in his texts, that of his entrance into and first registration in Buchenwald, see Susan Rubin Suleiman's 2004 article, "Historical Trauma and Literary Testimony." A similar sense of "epistemological uncertainty" is central to Juan Benet's narrative elaboration of memory, as will be analyzed in the next chapter.

28. "El chico de Semur contempla el rostro del anciano y no responde. El cuerpo del anciano se contrae de repente. Sus ojos recobran vida y mira fijamente la noche ante sí.—¿Os dais cuenta?—dice en voz baja pero clara. Luego, su mirada se le apaga otra vez y su cuerpo se desploma en nuestros brazos" (Semprún, 1976, 73).

29. "¿Os dais cuenta?" (Semprún, 1976, 73).

30. "Sí que me doy cuenta. No hago otra cosa, darme cuenta y dar cuenta de ello.... Claro que me doy cuenta, no hago otra cosa. Me doy cuenta e intento dar cuenta de ello, ése es mi propósito" (Semprún, 1976, 77–78).

31. "darse cuenta," and "dar cuenta de ello."

32. The acknowledgment of a personal responsibility freely and consciously assumed by the individual evoked by the expression "por su cuenta y riesgo" could also be seen to be at the heart of the philosophical problem of "Radical Evil" that the experience of the camps embodies and that Semprún analyzes in his texts. For a discussion of this concept in Semprún, see Loureiro (2000, 146–52).

33. "el artificio de un relato dominado" (Semprún, 1995b, 25).

34. For more on the scandal of Enric Marco, see Cué and Rahola 2005.

35. "He decidido hablar de este chico de Semur, a causa de Semur y a causa de este viaje. Murió a mi lado, al final de este viaje, acabé este viaje con su cadáver contra mí, de pie. He decidido hablar de él, y eso no interesa a nadie, nadie tiene nada que decir. Es una historia entre este chico de Semur y yo" (Semprún, 1976, 26).

36. "El chico de Semur ha muerto y estoy solo. Pienso que había dicho 'No me dejes, viejo,' y ando hacia la puerta, para saltar al andén. Ya no me acuerdo si había

dicho eso: 'No me dejes, viejo,' o si me había llamado por mi nombre, es decir, por el nombre por el que me conocía.... Tal vez había dicho: 'No me dejes, Gérard,' y Gérard salta al andén, en medio de la luz cegadora" (Semprún, 1976, 256).

37. "optar por ser otro, por no ser yo mismo, para seguir siendo algo: alguien" (1994b, 9).

38. Ibid.

39. "Me gusta el augurio y el símbolo: que este libro esté todavía por escribir, que esta tarea sea infinita, esta palabra inagotable" (Semprún, 1995b, 295).

40. Montserrat Roig is one of the few exceptions, as her book *Els catalans als camps nazis* (1977b) [*Night and Fog: Catalans in the Nazi Camps; Noche y niebla: los catalanes en los campos nazis* (1978)] records the testimonies of Catalan survivors of the German concentration camps. This text plays an important role in my discussion of Montserrat Roig in chapter 4. José Luis Abellán's multivolume study *El exilio español de 1939* [*The Spanish Exile of 1939*] also includes a section on the experience of Spanish prisoners in the German concentration camps. Within that collection, see Alfaya's "Españoles en los campos de concentración nazis" (1976)[Spaniards in the Nazi Concentration Camps]. More recently, Manuel Reyes Mate has edited *La filosofía después del Holocausto* (2002a)[*Philosophy after the Holocaust*] and written *Memoria de Auschwitz, Actualidad moral y política* (2003a) as well as *Por los campos de exterminio* (2003b), all of which try to redress the fact that there is relatively little reflection on the Holocaust, and on its effects on later culture and thought, within the Spanish context.

41. "Estos muertos horribles y fraternales no necesitaban ninguna explicación. Necesitaban que viviéramos, sencillamente, que viviéramos con todas nuestras fuerzas con la memoria de su muerte: cualquier otra forma de vida nos separaría del arraigo en este exilio de cenizas" (Semprún, 1995b, 138).

42. In the later documentary for French television that Semprún made in 1995, the same scene is presented, as Semprún again takes up the role of Simonides in evoking the correct placement of all the disappeared buildings of the camp.

43. "El resultado tenía una fuerza dramática increíble. El espacio vacío creado de este modo, rodeado por la alambrada, dominado por la chimenea del crematorio, barrido por el viento del Ettersberg, era un lugar de memoria estremecedor" (Semprún, 1995b, 315).

44. "un lugar de memoria y de cultura internacional de la Razón democrática" (Semprún, 1995b, 326).

45. A similar dialectic between "identification" and "disidentification" is a fundamental characteristic of María Teresa León's autobiographical project, studied in chapter 3.

46. "Apoyé una mano sobre el hombro de Thomas Landman, que estaba junto a mí. Le había dedicado *Quel beau dimanche!* para que pudiera, más tarde, después de mi muerte, recordar mi recuerdo de Buchenwald.... Apoyé la mano en el hombre de Thomas, como si le pasara el testigo" (Semprún, 1995b, 311).

47. The concern for the transmission of a traumatic memory to younger generations is also a central theme in the autobiographical writing of María Teresa León, studied in chapter 3.

48. A new edition of *Le grand voyage* was published in 2004 by Tusquets, an indication of its perceived relevance in Spain today. The fact that Semprún's latest novel, his first fully fictional novel written directly in Spanish, *Veinte años y un día* (2003), is about the Spanish civil war, and the fact that it presents many of the same narrative strategies that Semprún has developed in his texts about Buchenwald, shows that there is an important connection between Semprún's exploration of his memory of Buchenwald and his remembrance of the Spanish civil war.

49. "una mano ligera como la ternura que le profesaba, pesada como la memoria que le transmitía" (Semprún, 1995b, 312).

2. Juan Benet

1. Although many critics have studied the theme of memory and, more broadly, of time in Benet's work, none, to my knowledge, has sufficiently analyzed the dynamic of the *pharmakon* in his texts. For representative studies, among others, that investigate, to a greater or lesser degree, the importance of memory and the representation of time in Benet, see esp. Aranguren 1976; Benson 2000–2001 and 2004; Bravo 1985; Chamorro 1976; Cibreiro 1993; J. Díaz 1976a and 1976b; Gimferrer 1986; Gullón 1973, 1985, and 1986; Herzberger 1976, 1995, and 1999; Manteiga 1984; Nelson 1984; Ortega 1986; Pérez Magallón 1991; Pope 1984; Rivkin 1984; Sobejano 1970; Vásquez 1984; and Vernon 1989.

2. After a brief review of Benet's relevant critical writings, I will limit my study to an analysis of *Volverás a Región* [*Return to Región*], although many of the observations about memory in this text are applicable to the rest of his Región novels. Translations of quotations from *Volverás a Región* are from the English translation in the list of Works Cited. All translations of quotations from Benet's critical articles are my own.

3. See esp. his contribution to the round table on the novel in *Cuadernos para el Diálogo* [*Notebooks for Dialogue*] ("A treinta años" 1970) and the fiery exchange between Benet and Isaac Montero in the same volume. For an illuminating discussion of Benet's tense relationship with social realism, see Epps 2000 and 2003.

4. For studies analyzing the influence of the French *nouveau roman* in Benet, see esp. Castellet et al. 1973; Corrales Egea 1971; J. Díaz 1976a and 1976b; Durán 1986; Gimferrer 1986; and Herzberger 1980.

5. For studies analyzing the influence of Bergson on Benet's treatment of memory, see: Cibreiro 1993; Manteiga et al. 1984; and Pope 1984.

6. Benet states: "A eso se refería tal vez Bergson cuando hablaba de la 'desarticulación de lo real que realiza el lenguaje' queriendo dar a entender sin duda esa selección de piezas y puntos aislados entresacados del continuo que el lenguaje—todo lenguaje—precisa hacer para comunicar la impresión más simple... parece un todo y no son más que detalles" (1976a, 60) [This is perhaps what Bergson was referring to when he spoke of the "disarticulation of reality undertaken by language" trying to imply, certainly, that the selection of isolated pieces and points taken out of the continuum that language—any language-has to make in order to communicate the simplest idea... seems to be a complete whole, but is nothing but details].

7. It is, precisely, the understanding of memory as a *pharmakon,* a double-natured entity, that makes Benet's memory ultimately differ from Bergson's. The wholly redemptive value it had for Bergson is impossible in Benet's novelistic world. David Herzberger notices that Benet's characters lack the "process of continual renewal in which the ever-present past plays an active role" (1976, 69), which Bergson's positive approach to memory typically entails.

8. As Benet claims: "guardo mi mayor desconfianza para toda literatura elaborada mediante un elaboración ideológica" [I retain the greatest distrust toward a literature based on an ideological elaboration.] and "la literatura, por tener un 'status' propio, tiene su propia moral que no tiene por qué coincidir con el deber social, más general o más específico, impuesto por el momento histórico" [Literature, because it has its own

"status," has its own morality that need not coincide with a more generalized or more specific social duty imposed by the historical moment.] (1970c, 75).

9. Gonzalo Sobejano humorously alludes to the collapsing of the distinctions between the different narrative voices by calling the two interlocutors "yuxtalocutores" (1983, 18) [yuxtalocutors]. This conflation of narrative voices highlights the problematic relation between simultaneity and temporal linearity in the text, a problematic that will have everything to do with the workings of memory in the novel.

10. The presentation of plot is so convoluted and confusing that many critics' affirmations are contradictory among themselves and sometimes completely at odds with what a careful reading of the text yields. For examples of such mistaken assertions, see Costa 1979, 10.

11. Jo Labanyi has commented on this oxymoronic nature of a limited omniscience: "A disconcertingly inconsistent blend of omniscience and fallibility characterizes the whole narrative, mixing insights into the characters' repressed or unconscious thoughts with hypothetical alternative versions of events introduced by the qualifications `perhaps' or `no doubt'" (1989, 122). She claims that this narrative strategy creates in the reader "the illusion that [the text] will gradually fill in all the missing details ... but the more information we accumulate, the less certain we become of what `really happened'" (1989, 122). This is another procedure by means of which the text creates the reader's "hesitancy," to use Herzberger's expression. Such "hesitancy" is similar in many ways to the "epistemological uncertainty" that was seen to govern Semprún's novels about Buchenwald in the previous chapter.

12. Benet himself has acknowledged the influence of Frazer's study in his creation of Numa. See Benet 1976b, 160.

13. The conflict between instinct and social order has, of course, been analyzed by Freud. For studies highlighting the Freudian dimension of Benet's work see esp. Summerhill 1984 as well as Herzberger 1976. Summerhill points out that both Freud (especially in *Totem and Taboo*) and Benet were highly influenced by Frazer's *The Golden Bough* (1984, 58).

14. This liminal time between day and nighttime will be an important image governing Montserrat Roig's novel *La hora violeta,* analyzed in chapter 4.

15. The use of third person narration when talking about her past and her moral upbringing, from which Marré wants to distance herself in the present, is a strategy that governs much of the writing of the autobiography of María Teresa León, as will be studied in the next chapter.

16. See Paul Preston (1993, 173–84) for an explanation of how this anecdote is in all probability apocryphal, as well as for an understanding of how the Nationalist forces started creating a mythology of valor and sacrifice around this invented anecdote as soon as they saved the Alcazar from Republican attacks. This mythologizing process already began during the war, when, for propaganda purposes, the liberation of the Alcazar was re-staged and filmed two days after it ended, with Franco himself triumphantly walking among the ruins beside a tired and haggard Moscardó.

17. One is reminded here of Semprún taking up the danger of recounting his traumatic memories "por su cuenta y riesgo" [assuming personal responsibility and even risk for the project], as discussed in the previous chapter.

18. Although talking specifically about *Una meditación,* Summerhill makes an observation about this dynamic of the sacrifice in the novel that is apposite to *Volverás a Región:* "In this context, the entire novel can be seen as representing a highly stylized and mythical *sacrifice* in which each person is immolated on the altar of society" (1984, 60).

19. It is interesting to note that when Marré tries to adjust to the dominant social order after the war, she presents an infantilized image of herself in her room "rodeada de inocentes fetiches y muñecos de trapo" (1967, 163) [surrounded by innocent fetishes and rag dolls (1985, 146)]. This same image will be central to the argument of Roig's *La hora violeta*, as I explore in chapter 4. There, the ideological function of the fetish, as related to the working of memory, will be analyzed.

20. Brad Epps has explicitly made this connection, although without developing it: "I will only note in passing that the reference to the child's game bears a delicious resemblance to the Freudian *fort/da*, whereby the child attempts (unsuccessfully) to control the comings and goings, the presence and absence, of the mother" (1997, 81). He further adds in a note on the same page that Freud's *Beyond the Pleasure Principle* "bears a considerable affinity to Benet's [text]." The relation of the *Fort/Da!* game to trauma is explained in depth in my chapter on Semprún.

21. The Franco regime's view of the relationship between history and progress is a complex one. On the one hand, as Herzberger argues, the regime's desire to anchor the identity of Spain, and its future development, in its mythic past develops a conception of time where the future and the past are equated, and thus where any concept of linear historical progress as a straight line, the concept of progress predominant in modernity, is undermined. As Herzberger explains, from the regime's perspective, "time (history) is perceived not as a progression or a becoming, but rather as a static entity anchored in all that is permanent and eternal" (1995, 33). However, Jo Labanyi has explained that in a very important sense, the regime's view of history can be seen as compatible with modernity's idea of progress: "While history has, of course, always been written (and rewritten) by the winners, modernity has specifically meant the implantation—even in countries where Catholicism has remained dominant—of a Protestant-based work ethic whereby success is equated with moral strength and failure with moral weakness.... In this sense Francoism, which historians are now starting to rethink not as a rejection of modernity but rather as a form of conservative modernity ... subscribed just as much as its liberal and socialist antagonists to the modern capitalist ethos of progress—that is, put crudely, a view of history based on the notion that those who triumph are by definition the best" (2002, 7). As will be seen, this notion of progress based on ascribing moral superiority to those who triumph is relentlessly undermined in Benet's writing.

22. One is reminded of Benedict Anderson's discussion of the role of newspapers in the creation of nations as "imagined communities." See *Imagined Communities* (1983), esp. Chapter 2.

23. Randolph Pope, in his discussion of memory in Benet's novels, also highlights this image of the palimpsest: "At a deeper level, every sentence is haunted by disquieting ghosts that give to Benet's texts the density of a palimpsest" (1984, 114).

3. María Teresa León

1. The Web site is http://www.Portaldelexilio.org. The groupings of images on the Web site are divided into the following stages: "la retirada" [the retreat], "la diáspora" [the diaspora]," "la segunda derrota" [the second defeat], "el gobierno en el exilio" [the government in exile], "trasterrados" [the displaced], "la Numancia errante" [the errant Numancia], and "los retornos" [the returns]. These are the same stages, and images, used in the popular exhibit entitled "Exilio" that was held in Madrid, at the Palacio de

Cristal del Parque del Retiro, in the fall of 2002. The exhibit was organized by the Fundación Pablo Iglesias, with the cooperation of the Museo Nacional Centro de Arte Reina Sofía.

2. For two examples, among others, of recent studies that explore the development and repercussions, with respect to diverse cultural practices, of the "pact of amnesia" during the transition, see Joan Ramon Resina 2000a and 2000b, and Cristina Moreiras Menor 2002.

3. The problem of speaking about a homogeneous and unitary category of exile, instead of a multiplicity of exiles, is one of a series of fallacies that, according to José María Naharro-Calderón, in "Falacias de exilios," have dominated much of the study of this topic. Among these fallacies are such notions as treating the experience of exile as a disruption, a breakdown of the process of nation formation, instead of recognizing that exile is inherent in the very emergence of a nation. The narration of a national identity, in fact, is based precisely on the exclusions that such an identity is defined against. Studying many narratives of exiles as predominantly oriented toward the past, as nostalgic expressions of longing for the homeland, is another fallacy. This perspective has often prevented scholars from understanding what such texts can contribute to a forward-looking project in which these texts are seen as having much to contribute to our understanding of issues of the present, such as, among others, the tense relationship among different nationalist narratives and projects today in Spain, or the difficult integration of the new waves of exile and inmigration of which Spain is now on the receiving end.

4. Much of *Memoria de la melancolía* seems to have been written in the 1960s during León's exile in Rome, and the text was published in 1970 in Argentina. As Loureiro mentions, however, sections of León's autobiography incorporate parts of texts she had written in the '40s and '50s. For example, some material from León's 1944 booklet *La historia tiene la palabra: noticia sobre el salvamento del tesoro artístico de españa*, recounting how she helped transport many valuable works of art from the Prado museum to Valencia during the Spanish civil war, is reproduced in her autobiography. Likewise, various anecdotes she recalls in her autobiography regarding her theatrical activities during the civil war are told in almost exactly the same way in her 1959 novel *Juego Limpio*, where a character, sometimes called "la secretaria" and at other times identified as "María Teresa," is clearly a fictionalized version of León herself. This narrative overlap not only points to an extended period of writing underlying her autobiography, but also hints at an interesting convergence of texts belonging to supposedly different genres, such as autobiography, fictional novel, and historical account. For more on this topic, see Loureiro 2000.

5. The task of the Grup d'Estudis de l'Exili Literari (Grupo de Estudios del Exilio Literario: GEXEL), headed by Professor Manuel Aznar Soler at the Autonomous University of Barcelona, is to be commended in this context. The international conferences organized by the GEXEL, as well as the various publication series it directs, are recovering a wealth of material from/about the Republican exile(s) of 1939. This is the foremost such project in Spain today.

6. For overviews of all of León's publications, see Estébanez Gil 1995 and Torres Nebrera 1996.

7. León had written one play before the civil war (*Huelga en el puerto*, 1933) [*Strike in the Port*] and two more in exile, *La libertad en el tejado* [*Liberty on the Roof*] and *Sueño y verdad de Francisco de Goya* [*Dream and Reality of Francisco de Goya*], both first published posthumously in 1989 and 2003, respectively. She also wrote theater adaptations of literary works, among them Galdos's *Misericordia* [*Compassion*],

and various essays on theater. León's most important novel, *Juego limpio* [*Fair Play*], presents the experiences of the theater troupe that León organized during the civil war, the Guerrillas del teatro [Theater Guerrillas]. In this novel, León appears as a secondary character, the secretary of the Alianza de Intelectuales Antifascistas [Alliance for Anti-Fascist Intellectuals] where the theater troupe is housed. For more detailed information on León's work in theater and theatrical writings, see especially León 2003a and 2003b and Aznar Soler 1993. In recognition of León's legacy in theater and feminism, in 1993 the Asociación de Directores de Escena de España [Association of Theater Directors of Spain] created the annual Premio María Teresa León para Autoras Dramáticas [María Teresa León Prize for Female Playwrights].

8. Other studies that have analyzed the relationship of gender and exile in León's text include those by López 2004, Alda Blanco 1991, Ridell 2000, and Ugarte 1998. My analysis builds on these, adding a greater emphasis on the way theater works in her text as metaphor and narrative strategy highlighting the interrelatedness of representations of gender and exile within her rememorative project.

9. The shifting use of pronouns in an autobiography, which may reflect the process of gender "disidentification" mentioned here, is not the preserve of female authors. Male writers have used such a technique to create autobiographical accounts in which they likewise highlight the way in which their identity has developed, in many ways, *against* a series of stifling and restrictive gender norms. Within the Spanish context, Juan Goytisolo's autobiographical texts *Coto vedado* [*Forbidden Territory*] and *En los reinos de taifa* [*Realms of Strife*] are powerful examples.

10. In "El teatro internacional" [International Theater], one of the articles that León wrote after her travels in 1932 studying European theater, she shows a keen understanding of how power functions through theatrical stagings and spectacles. In the section "Teatro de masas" [Mass Theater] of the aforementioned article, León mentions, among other examples, the Nazi spectacles of power that she and Alberti witnessed in Germany: "Cabalgatas, procesiones, torneos, triunfos: todo lo que era acción y espectáculo al mismo tiempo es arte de masas, teatro de masas. La Iglesia, los emperadores, la Revolución francesa: todos los Poderes que necesitaron exteriorizar su poderío han usado esa sugestión colectiva de las grandes fiestas al aire libre. Hitler paseó antorchas, encendió hogueras, hizo desfilar (a) los 'nazis' entre músicas, dándole a todo un valor de espectáculo y de rito" (2003a, 375) [Cavalcades, processions, tournaments, triumphs: everything that was action and spectacle was also popular art, popular theater. The Church, emperors, the French Revolution: all the Powers that have needed to exteriorize their strength have used this collective suggestion of grand open-air feasts. Hitler paraded torches, lit fires, made the "Nazis" parade to music, giving it all the value of a spectacle and a rite]. León clearly understands the way power is "staged" in society, and thus it is no surprise that her own writing will also be self-consciously "staged," presenting memory as a theatrical endeavor.

11. Alda Blanco reflects on the gender implications of this dialogical nature of León's narrative: "Establece así María Teresa León una dinámica textual en la cual la presencia constante de voces autoritarias se contrasta con el silencio de los personajes interpelados anunciando, de esta manera, una de las vertientes del importante tema del silencio, la de la otredad de la mujer" (1991, 46) [María Teresa León thus establishes a textual dynamic in which the constant presence of authoritarian voices contrasts with the silence of the interpellated character announcing, in this manner, one of the variants of the important theme of silence, that of the otherness of woman]. For more information on the gender dynamics of the early twentieth-century Spanish patriarchal society that León is reacting to in this section of her autobiography, see, among

other sources: López 2004, Alda Blanco 1991, Mangini (1995 and 2001), and Vosburg 2001 for texts that talk about León specifically, as well as Nash (1983 and 1999b) and Scanlon 1976 for more general discussions.

12. If León "disidentifies" with many elements of the patriarchal society in which she grew up, she also underscores that there was another, alternative tradition, one made up of strong women, with which she chooses to identify more closely. This tradition includes, among others, her aunt, María Goyri, the first woman to obtain a doctorate in Philosophy and Letters in Spain, and her daughter, Jimena, as well as María de Maeztu and Emilia Pardo Bazán. For more on this "female genealogy" that León creates, see López 2004.

13. This deconstruction of "home," through a conscious highlighting of the legacies of colonialism within the family history, echoes a similar project that Juan Goytisolo undertakes in his autobiography, *Coto vedado* [*Forbidden Territory*], as well as in his novel *Señas de identidad* (1980) [*Marks of Identity*]. There are, in fact, many interesting points of contact between León and Goytisolo. Among them are similar strategies of gender "disidentification" from prevalent cultural norms expressed through the shifting use of pronouns within their autobiographies. Another example is the continuation of the autobiographical project through the writing of novels in which the autobiographical self of the memoirs is basically disguised as a character (in the case of León this is clear with the overlap of her novel *Juego limpio* and her autobiography, as is the case with the intimate relation of Goytisolo's *Coto vedado* and *Señas de identidad*). Finally, both autobiographical projects share the same purpose of using their personal memory to vindicate histories that were repressed and silenced by official versions of Spanish history. Goytisolo clearly states this objective in his autobiography, in a manner that echoes the underlying purpose of León's own writing, as a "resolución de luchar con uñas y dientes contra el olvido, esa sima negra de fauces abiertas que acecha, lo sabes, a la vuelta de cualquier camino" (1999, 29) [resolution to fight tooth and nail against forgetting, that black abyss with open jaws that lurks, you know it, at every turn]. For more information of Goytisolo's autobiography, see Loureiro 2000 and Moreiras Menor 2002.

14. See Halbwachs's important works *On Collective Memory* (1992) and *The Collective Memory* (1980) for more on his theory of the collective nature of memory.

15. I disagree, here, with Ridell, who seems to propose that there is such a progression: "María Teresa León narra en tercera persona cuando representa el pasado en el que se le adjudicó una identidad femenina y esencial, y en primera persona a partir del momento en que ella elabora una identidad propia, basada en su actividad, resultado de sus experiencias, de sus vivencias existenciales (2000, 45) [María Teresa León narrates in the third person when she is representing the past in which an essential feminine identity was adjudicated to her, and in the first person from the moment in which she elaborates her own identity, based on her activity, the result of her experiences, of her existential experiences].

16. This sense of "disidentification" with Spain and people living in Spain is the recurring theme of a text that resonates deeply with *Memoria de la melancolía*: Max Aub's *La gallina ciega: diario español* (1995) [*The Blind Chicken: Spanish Diary*]. Here, Aub recounts his visit to Spain in 1969 after years of exile, and expresses the extreme sense of "homelessness" he feels precisely when he returns to his supposed "home." For more on this aspect of Aub's text, see Ferrán, forthcoming.

17. Such an ambivalent relationship to memory is already present in the fundamental ambiguity of the title of León's autobiography, as Loureiro appropriately underscores. At first glance, *Memoria de la melancolía* evokes a textual process in which León herself is remembering her life in a melancholy manner. However, another

interpretation of the title would seem to suggest that it is not León, but melancholia itself, that is doing the remembering. In this case, as Loureiro explains, melancholia "is the subject of a memory that is then no longer ascribable to María Teresa León" (2000, 66). This ambiguity thus puts into play the issue of control so central to trauma, which León continues to evoke throughout the text in her various comments about her autobiography being composed of loose papers that are dispersed about her, escaping her control. This ambiguity also suggests the importance of the concept of melancholia in León's autobiography, a melancholia so strong that it may be the true subject of the act of remembering in her text. For two different, yet equally enlightening, explorations of the dynamics of melancholia in the text, see Loureiro 2000 and López 2004.

18. In *Memoria de la melancolía,* León explains how she and Alberti knew the German playwright Bertolt Brecht, and how he was, in fact, scheduled to direct a production of one of Alberti's plays, *Noche de Guerra en el Prado* [*A Night of War at the Prado*], when he died (1998, 444–52).

19. Although here, as elsewhere, León makes important connections between different historical experiences of oppression, connections that allow for more powerful strategies of resistance, in some cases, she falls into the trap of silencing certain repressive practices that may have been a little too close to home for her, given her membership in the Spanish Communist Party. She thus all-too-easily glosses over any account of the repressive practices of Stalinism in the Soviet Union, even when describing the time that she and Alberti visited Stalin in 1937, an account she is writing when that repression is well known. She does the same thing when describing a visit to Communist China in 1957, and is curiously silent about any ideological divisions and fighting among the various Spanish political parties in exile, preferring to generally uphold an unwavering rhetoric of solidarity and fraternity. This is an undeniable contradiction in her work. Loureiro has analized this contradiction, and sees it, in part, as a reflection of the fact that León often confuses an ethical discourse with a political one. As he explains: "Her self-interested ideological beliefs derive from, and display, an overwhelming affect of the other: her affliction is her affection, stemming as it does from the inordinate ascendancy the ethical has over her, which leads her to conflate it with the political.... *Ethical* is then the word that best explains Leon's condition: she is obsessed by her debt toward the other, she is consumed with guilt and obligation, and thus her ideological distortions originate in the unwarranted infringement of the ethical on the political, in the error of understanding the latter in the former's terms" (2000, 77).

20. María Zambrano points to a similar consciousness of exile as an experience that not only disrupts life, but also death, defining exile as an "imposibilidad de vivir que, cuando se cae en la cuenta, es imposibilidad de morir. El filo entre vida y muerte que igualmente se rechazan. Sostenerse en ese vilo es la primera exigencia que al exiliado se le presenta como ineludible" (1990, 32) [impossibility of living that, ultimately, is an impossibility of dying. The razor's edge between life and death that equally reject each other. To live on that edge is the first inescapable exigency that an exile faces].

21. For more information on the mass graves of the Spanish civil war, see Silva and Macías 2003, as well as the work of the association they co-founded: La Asociación para la Recuperación de la Memoria Histórica. See also the Web site of the association Foro por la memoria (http://www.nodo50.org/foroporlamemoria/inicio.htm), as well as Kolbert 2003, Armengou and Belis 2004, and Ferrándiz 2005b.

22. It is symptomatic in this respect, as Kolbert mantains, that, in a ceremony in 2003 honoring Franco's victims held in the Congreso de Diputados in Spain, the Partido Popular, under the leadership of José María Aznar, refused to participate, "arguing, in the words of a party spokesman, that the ceremony represented a 'return to the

past' which 'contributed nothing positive' " (2003, 70). It is encouraging, however, as explained in the introduction, that, in September 2004, the Spanish government, under the leadership of Socialist president José Luis Rodríguez Zapatero, created an interministerial commission to study the ways in which the government may provide a "moral and judicial rehabilitation" to victims of the civil war and of Francoism (Cué 2004). The results of this commission will eventually lead to what has come to be called the "ley de recuperación de la memoria histórica" [law for the recuperation of historical memory]. Furthermore, the government, for the first time, has stated that it will financially support and promote the process of exhuming the numerous mass graves from the civil war. These are very important steps in Spain's long-overdue confrontation with its traumatic past. It still remains to be seen, however, how effectively these policies will be put into practice. As explained in the introduction, it is already troubling that the government has had to repeatedly postpone the deadline for the presentation of its "ley de recuperación de la memoria histórica." Most significantly, in the last such postponement, the vice president of the government, María Teresa Fernández de la Vega, explained that the implementation of the new law had been postponed, again, because the government had decided to change the law's mandate. No longer considering that the law should provide various means of redress solely for the victims of Francoism, it will now become a law that seeks to provide some form of compensation to victims of both sides (Cué 2005a). This, of course, dilutes the power and meaning of the law, and demonstrates how hard it is, still today, to officially acknowledge the uneven level of repression suffered by each side of the war, as well as the uneven recourse to recognition and compensation for that suffering that each side had enjoyed since the war. In this, the law may, unfortunately, ultimately continue, instead of finally rupture, the predominant narratives of the transition.

23. The Web page mentioned at the beginning of this chapter presented precisely this view of contemporary Spanish history. León's absence from the picture that mentioned only Alberti's return to Spain in 1977 not only converted her into a kind of ghost, but can now be seen precisely as an example of a "grieta" [fissure] that undermines the entirely positive picture the Web page is implicitly presenting of how the exiled community was adequately incorporated into the new, fully democratic Spain that is celebrated at the end of the series of pictures.

24. See Balibrea (2003), for a similar positive valuation of melancholia versus mourning in reading Spanish exile literature.

25. Semprún provides an image of such a "transmemoria" when he hopes that the young boy accompanying him on his trip back to Buchenwald after almost forty years will remember his experience after he no longer can. Also, the novels of Montserrat Roig and Antonio Muñoz Molina, analyzed in the next two chapters, explicitly revolve around the problem of memory transmission over generations.

26. Helena López and Michael Ugarte have both commented on the feminist implication of León's acknowledgment of sadness and confusion, and rejection of objectivity, as guiding forces in her writing. López explains: "La memoria de León, como la de tantas exiliadas y exiliados, entra así en conflicto con las directrices políticas hegemónicas y con el archivo oficial de los recuerdos colectivos. Por eso declara . . . 'Pero no puedo disfrazarme.' No disfrazarse significa no ceder al deseo del padre, a la compulsión patriarcal por domesticar y conformar el cuerpo femenino" (2004, 152) [León's memory, like that of so many exiles, thus enters into conflict with hegemonic political precepts and with the official archive of collective memory. That is why she declares . . . "But I cannot disguise myself." To not disguise herself means not giving in to the desire of the father, to the patriarchal compulsion to domesticate and conform the feminine body]. Ugarte claims: "Contrary to both male historical discourse

of the civil war and to the revisionist history put forth by those who are responsible for having exiled her, she willingly accepts confusion as the guiding force of her life story" (1998, 211). Such views resonate deeply with the perspective presented in this chapter of the many ways in which León "disidentifies" with social precepts of all kinds. In this case, she is "disidentifying" with the view of history as an objective account of the past.

27. One organization resisting the exhumation of mass graves in Spain for such reasons is the "Asociación de Familiares y Amigos de la Fosa Común de Oviedo" [Association of Relatives and Friends of the Mass Grave of Oviedo]. For information on this group, see their Web site: http://humano.ya.com/fosaoviedo/. Zoë Crossland has explored a similar controversy in Argentina, in the 1980s and 1990s, where certain human rights groups, including a splinter group from the famous Madres de la Plaza de Mayo [Mothers of the Plaza de Mayo], have also publicly resisted the exhumations of mass graves from the time of the military dictatorship. Such groups claim that the exhumation process in Argentina has developed in such a way as to only focus on identifying and giving proper burial to the dead, certainly an important task, but that what is being left out of the process is bringing those responsible for the creation of the mass graves to justice in an appropriate manner. Similarly, Frazier explains how in Chile, even after an official commemorative mausoleum was built, in 1993, to contain the remains fround in a mass grave from the time of the military dictatorship, many relatives of the dead, and political activists, continued to visit the site of the then-empty original mass grave. These relatives and activists clearly felt that, in the ruins of that original site, there was something important to be remembered that was not contained in the new mausoleum. What Frazier calls "countermourning" in the context of Chilean politics bears a resemblance to the politically resistant dynamics of melancholia in León's text. For more on these controversies, see Crossland 2000 and 2002, as well as Frazier 1999.

4. MONTSERRAT ROIG

1. "Hay que recordar y olvidar al mismo tiempo. La memoria también es olvido. Alguien dijo que todos tenemos dos memorias: la pequeña memoria, que sirve para recordar lo pequeño, y la memoria grande, que sirve para olvidar lo grande. A medida que avanzan, los narradores/narradoras dejan pistas de los olvidos más que de los recuerdos" (Roig 2001, 31).

2. Roig wrote in her native Catalan. I quote from the original Catalan editions of her texts appearing in Works Cited. English translations immediately follow the original quotes in the body of the text, and Spanish translations are provided in endnotes. Wherever numbers follow the translations, they refer to the editions of the translated text appearing in Works Cited. If no number follows a translation, it is my own.

3. The following verses from Eliot's poem appear as an epigraph to the novel: "At the violet hour, when the eyes and back / Turn upwards from the desk, when the human engine waits / Like a taxi throbbing waiting, / I, Tiresias, though blind, throbbing between two lives, / Old man with wrinkled female breast can see / At the violet hour..." (1991, 31). The double nature of the mythological figure of Tiresias himself, who experienced life as both a man and a woman, and thus is an "old man with wrinkled breasts," points to a gender duality that is being questioned in the novel. This duality is intimately connected with the double temporal orientation of the text.

4. *L'hora violeta* is the third of a trilogy of Roig's novels in which the interrelated stories of two families in Barcelona, the setting for most of her writing, are traced throughout most of the twentieth century. In all three the double orientation of memory, toward the past as well as the future, is present. In the first novel of the trilogy, *Ramona adeu* (1972) [*Ramona, Goodbye; Ramona adiós*], the stories of three generations of women from the Ventura-Claret family, all called Ramona, are traced. Each story is related to a significant time period of Spanish history: the grandmother's story takes place mainly after the 1898 disaster period, the mother's story is focused mostly on the pre-civil war years, and the granddaughter's tale is focused on the post-1968 period of student rebellion and social upheaval. The novel is open ended, as the youngest Ramona seems to be able to break with the pattern of submissive behavior that her predecessors were made to uphold.

The second novel, *El temps de les cireres* (1977a) [*The Time of Cherries; Tiempo de cerezas*], mostly tells the story of the Miralpeix family, which is also one of the narrative axes of *L'hora violeta*. *El temps de les cireres* begins with the return to Barcelona of Natàlia Miralpeix in 1974, after living for twelve years in England in self-imposed exile. Natàlia belongs to the same generation as the youngest Ramona of the previous novel, and is one of the protagonists of *L'hora violeta*. The plot is again tied significantly to Spanish politics. Natàlia left Spain in 1962, the year the Communist leader Julián Grimau was detained, and one year before he was killed after being thrown out of the window of a police building while being interrogated and tortured. Natàlia returns in 1974, two days after the Franco regime has executed the young anarchist activist Salvador Puig Antich, a militant in the Movimiento Ibérico de Liberación (MIL). Political repression is thus an integral part of the stories recounted in Roig's novels. Besides presenting Natàlia's return to Spain, in anticipation of the political prospects inherent in Franco's anticipated death, *El temps de les cireres* recalls Natàlia's political activism and rebellion in the years before her self-imposed exile as well as the estrangement she felt with regard to her family while growing up. The novel also presents anecdotes of her parent's life before, during, and after the civil war, a narrative taken up again in *L'hora violeta*. Natàlia's brother, Lluís, marries Silvia Claret, the sister of the youngest Ramona of the previous novel, and thus the two family histories intersect. After *L'hora violeta*, Roig published two more novels, *L'opera quotidiana* (1982) [*The Cotidian Opera; La ópera cotidiana*] and *La veu melodiosa* (1987) [*The Melodious Voice; La voz melodiosa*]. Both combine an analysis of gender relations with reflections on the necessity, as well as the dangers, of Catalan nationalism. Many of the characters from Roig's novels appear in her short stories. Furthermore, many of the ideas she presents in her novels also appear in her essays. This gives her work a strong sense of coherence, as the same issues are explored over and over again from different angles. The role of memory in unearthing stories marginalized by official versions of history is one of the recurrent themes in her work. It is related to her other main literary concerns: a feminist critique of traditional gender relations, a defense of Catalan culture (one that recognizes the dangers of extreme versions of nationalism), and a vindication of political activism that counters oppression of all kinds. For more on the interrelatedness of these concerns in Roig's work, see Davies 1994 and Dupláa 1996.

5. *Noche y niebla: los catalanes en los campos nazis.*
6. "Madre, no entiendo a los salmones."
7. "Me parecía que era necesario salvar con palabras todo lo que la historia, la Historia grande, es decir, la de los hombres, había hecho impreciso, había condenado" (Roig 1980a, 17).
8. This is the somewhat problematic assertion made by Christina Dupláa when she affirms that Natàlia and Norma are rescuing a woman's history from oblivion, a his-

tory that she characterizes as "la que no es oficial ni pública, pero real, auténtica y cotidiana" (1996, 118) [that which is not official nor public, but real, authentic and quotidian].

9. Roig is fully aware of the way in which this binary logic is a cornerstone of the patriarchal oppression of women. In her essay entitled "L'un i l'altra" [One and the other; El uno y la otra] from her last collection of essays, *Digues que m'estimes encara que sigui mentida* (1991a) [*Tell me that you love me, even if it is a lie; Dime que me quieres aunque sea mentira*], she presents various examples of such logic, among them the Pythagorean saying she sees as paradigmatic of this binary logic: "Hi ha un principi bo, creador de l'ordre, la llum i l'home; i un principi dolent que ha creat el caos, les tenebres i les dones" (Roig 1991a, 62) [There is a good principle, creator of order, light and man; and a bad principle that has created chaos, darkness, and women] (Hay un principio bueno, creador del orden, la luz y el hombre; y un principio malo que ha creado el caos, las tinieblas, y las mujeres (Roig 2001, 84)).

10. "hace cuatro años que fotografío eso que llamamos realidad"; "Creo que no somos capaces de valorar la realidad hasta que ésta no se convierte en pasado. Como si quisieramos así volver a vivir. Por eso creo que la literatura todavía tiene un sentido. La literatura no es historia. La literatura inventa el pasado basándose en unos cuantos detalles que fueron reales, anque sólo lo fueran en nuestra mente" (Roig 1980a, 13).

11. "estoy algo cansada de buscar siempre el instante fugaz de lo que pasa, de retratar la realidad precisa. Exterior. Como si mis ojos fuesen una cámara siempre asomada hacia fuera. Tengo ganas de explorar mi propia cadencia" (Roig 1980a, 13).

12. "No te lo vas a creer, pero ese montón de papelotes me ha obligado a pensar en mí misma. A mirarme por dentro" (Roig 1980a, 14).

13. "¿Has intentado alguna vez mirarte al espejo sin analizar si todavía luces o bien si eres aún joven? Quiero decir, ¿has intentado mirarte al espejo y sólo ver en él tus ojos, tu mirada?" (Roig 1980a, 14).

14. "Franco está dentro de mí, se me aferra como una babosa. La vieja y reseca piltrafa no se acaba de morir. . . . Tiene los ojos rojos de la sangre que vierten. Pero no tiene rostro. Sólo ojos" (Roig 1980a, 106).

15. Roig often expressed this concern that the ideology of the Franco regime continued to permeate Spanish society, even the thinking of those who had fought hard to undermine the regime, well into the transition. In an interview with Geraldine Cleary Nichols, Roig expresses something reminiscent of Natàlia's frightening vision in *L'hora violeta*: "Había una cosa muy clara: todos llevamos un Franco en el corazón, todos hemos sido educados en el fascismo y esto no te lo quitas nunca. Puedes luchar contra ello si eres consciente, pero el Franco lo tienes dentro" (Nichols 1989, 165) [There is one thing that is very clear: we all carry a Franco in our heart, we have all been educated within fascism and you never get rid of that. You can fight against it if you are conscious, but Franco is inside you]. It is precisely because many elements of Francoism endure during the transition to democracy that Roig feels the need to write novels in which the main characters self-consciously explore their personal past and their memory in a critical, even self-critical, manner.

16. "lo que quiere es dominar el mundo con sus aires de marimacho" (Roig 1996, 165).

17. "algún día tú también crearás todo eso que tienes dentro, esa música callada que no has tenido ocasión de hacer salir. Y alguien te entenderá" (Roig 1980a, 152).

18. There is an interesting parallelism here between Roig's text and both María Teresa León's autobiography and Benet's novel. In all three cases, the civil war becomes, quite paradoxically, one of the happiest times of a woman's life, despite the surrounding death and destruction. This is evident in León's depiction of the war as a time when she felt a great sense of participation in a common cause, as well as a feel-

ing that her active role as a woman was encouraged and respected. Judit and Kati likewise enjoyed the jubilant sense of new possibilities for self-realization and agency that emerged during the war. Marré also found, during the war, a way to rebel against constraining social mores. Catherine Bellver has commented on the fact that this is a common paradox in women's lives, as moments of political crisis, or war, often destabilize rigid gender roles, creating a new space for women's agency (1991, 222). For an analysis of the changing roles of women during the civil war, see Nash 1999a.

19. "la historia de la hermana poeta de Shakespeare, muerta sin haber escrito una sola línea, vive en todas las mujeres" (Roig 2001, 101).

20. "todo está hecho a base de recortes seleccionados, que poco a poco van formando una narración íntima, la del recuerdo. Y el orden que siguen los recuerdos dentro de la memoria no es nunca cronológico ni coherente. Si aciertas, las palabras a veces te ayudan a enlazarlos para formar con ellos una 'historia' " (Roig 1980a, 102).

21. "el tiempo de la memoria interior no tiene nada que ver con el tiempo de la historia" (Roig 1980a, 102).

22. "el orden de la imaginación se sale de todos los datos, de todos los hechos. Ésta es la venganza de la literatura contra la historia" (Roig 1980a, 103).

23. "A veces siento que su alma me ronda y me dice, volveré, Judit, volveré, y ya no habrá nada que nos separe, ninguna ley, ninguna guerra, conviérteme en lo que quieras, Judit. . . . Llena la casa con mi fantasma, Judit, . . . no me saques de ti, Judit, amor de mi vida, amor de mi muerte" (Roig 1980a, 163).

24. "Ella [Judit] no era [valiente] como Kati, es verdad, y por eso iba a misa con Joan y los niños y se volvía dócilmente a casa cuando no la dejaban entrar en la iglesia porque no llevaba medias" (Roig 1996, 167).

25. "confieso que sentía mucha envidia de aquellas horas que pasaban juntas, y también de que no tuvieran miedo" (Roig 1980a, 133).

26. "Aunque no hablaba mucho. Sólo la vi charlar por los codos con Kati. Sólo con ella su risa era de alegría" (Roig 1980a, 128).

27. "Judit añoraba a Kati y decidió que quería fetiches, objetos de todas clases que ella veneraba como a pequeños dioses. . . . Llenaremos la casa de fetiches! le dijo a Joan" (Roig 1996, 167).

28. "Y los fetiches más importantes fueron las muñecas. Judit pasó una temporada muy larga comprando muñecas, muñecas de todas las medidas, desnudas o vestidas, de goma, de celuloide, de porcelana. . . . Judit les agujereaba los ojos y les rompía las manos. Y cuanto más las hacía sufrir, más las quería" (Roig 1996, 168).

29. It is now possible to understand the full implications of the fact that when Marré, in Benet's *Volverás a Región,* tries to adjust to the dominant social order after the war, she locks herself in her room "rodeada de inocentes fetiches y muñecos de trapo" (Benet 1967, 163) [surrounded by innocent fetishes and rag dolls (Benet 1985, 146)]. The fetishes here function according to the same double logic as in *L'hora violeta,* reflecting Marré's desire to affirm the plenitude and power she felt during her wartime love affairs, while at the same time recognizing the loss of all such power after the war. As in the dynamics of trauma and the *pharmakon* prevalent in Benet's novel, the fetish is an object that simultaneously puts into play contradictory experiences of mastery and powerlessness, remedy and illness.

30. "Esta foto es de cuando Judit y sus padres vivían en Narbonna" (Roig 1980a, 128); "En este retrato Judit está tocando el arpa con la cabellera suelta" (Roig 1980a, 129); "Aquí Judit mira hacia el frente con la Mirada apagada, y los cabellos, que le caen en pequeñas ondas, le hacen de corona" (Roig 1980a, 129).

31. "El enterrador tiene quemado el lado izquierdo de la cara. Unos grumos de color lila sobresalen entre las arrugas. Parece la luna vista de cerca, la luna como yo me

imagino, tan bonita de lejos y que debe ser asquerosa si te acercas a ella" (Roig 1980a, 126).

32. Catherine Davies has noted the connection between the fetish and the photograph in Roig's novel: "closely associated with the theme of fetishism is photography: like the novel itself, both sustain the illusion that something absent is present" (1994, 49). Both, of course, are also intimately related to the dynamics of memory, also a process that "sustain[s] the illusion that something absent is present."

33. "si mi madre todavía viviese, escribir sobre ella podría convertirse en un intento de reconciliación 'real.' Sin embargo, ¿a qué santo venía escribir sobre mamá, reescribir mejor dicho, si ya estaba muerta?" (Roig 1980a, 15–16).

34. "Se acabó la época de las grandes revoluciones, ahora hay que sobrevivir, que resistir" (Roig 1980a, 64).

35. "Fue una de las primeras conversaciones en que comenzamos a hablar del desencato (ahora hablamos tanto de él, que ya resulta una lata)" (Roig 1980a, 52).

36. "Pero la crisis estalló cuando se legalizó el partido. ¿De qué sirvieron tantos años de lucha y de entrega si la política se convirtió en un asunto sólo para profesionales? Surgieron nuevos militantes que asediaron como buitres los mejores cargos" (Roig 1980a, 101).

37. "Tal vez será la época del fracaso, o la época de los cándidos. . . . Y de lo que estoy segura es de que no nos admirarán, porque no verán ninguna obra realizada" (Roig 1980a, 69).

38. "Soy ajena a cualquier papel asignado. Me parece que he pasado la vida observando lo que sucedía ante mí, como si algún dios me hubiera colocado en una butaca de palco. No puedo hacer más: no estoy sobre el escenario, en donde los actores se acoplan perfectamente a los papeles asignados, pero tampoco me encuentro bien en el gallinero, donde el público puede armar una bronca si la obra no es de su agrado" (Roig 1980a, 73).

39. Medina Domínguez presents a quote from Juan Luis Cebrián's account of the transition years in which the celebrated journalist describes the transactions within the newly constituted Parliament in theatrical terms that are similar to the image that Roig presents in her novel:

> Ha llegado el momento en el que casi nadie de los que suben a la tribuna de las Cortes dice verdaderamente lo que piensa, sino lo que es obligado a decir. Para mayor irritación ni aun eso ha de ser una sorpresa, pues el método de la junta de portavoces seguido en las cámaras ha hecho posible que gran parte de lo que va a suceder en los plenos sea conocido de antemano, incluso en sus aspectos de confabulación o pacto, otorgándo a la cámara una faz teatral y de farsa que en nada contribuye al fortalecimiento de las escasas creencias democráticas de nuestra población.
>
> La repetición del espectáculo . . . supuso ya un nuevo desentendimiento popular: los líderes hablaban para la galería, buscando votos. La galería se dio cuenta de ello y comenzó a aburrirse. (qtd. in Medina Domínguez 2001, 66)

> [The moment has arrived in which hardly anybody who steps up to the tribune in Congress really says what he thinks, but only what he is obliged to say. What is even more irritating is that even this has stopped being a surprise, for the method followed in the two houses of Congress has made it possible for a large part of what is going to happen in the plenary sessions to be known ahead of time, even in its aspects of confabulation or pact, giving the houses of Congress an appearance of theater and farce that does nothing to strengthen the already weak democratic beliefs of the general population.
>
> The repetition of this spectacle . . . has created yet another popular disenchantment: the leaders were talking to the public, looking for votes. The public realized this and started to become bored.]

40. "hace tiempo que oigo las mismas palabras: salen de nuestras bocas, describen círculos como en una noria y vuelven al mismo punto de partida. Las palabras nacen y mueren en un sentido de circunvalación" (Roig 1980a, 54).

41. "palabras, palabras que se repetían circularmente, que se repetían y que no ayudaban a vivir" (Roig 1980a, 264).

42. In an interview, Roig expresses her concern that younger generations will inherit from the generation that underwent the transition this sense of a cynical suspicion of all political language and a lack of hope in the possibility for change. She fears that the legacy these younger generations will inherit is "el de la zafiedad y de un cierto cinismo... el legado de que lo que hoy es verdadero mañara será mentira" (Nichols 1989, 176) [that of boorishness and of a certain cynicism... the legacy of believing that what today is true will tomorrow be a lie].

43. In an interview, Roig explicitly repeats this idea, making it clear, as she does in *L'hora violeta,* that the only way in which post-Franco Spain will be able to build a better future is by recovering the memory of oppression: "Un altre error molt greu que estem cometent és la pèrdua de la memòria. No ens podem vantar ara que estem començant de nou, que estem 'instituint' alguna cosa.... Som fills del franquisme, de les coses bones i de les coses dolentes de l'època franquista. Fins que no assumim la totalitat—les parts tèrboles i les parts extraordinàries de la nostra història passada—, no podrem reconstruir res" (Roig 1985, 75) [Another very serious error that we are committing is that of the loss of memory. We cannot boast that we are starting from scratch, that we are "creating" something new.... We are sons and daughters of Francoism, of the good things as well as the bad things of the Franco era. Until we assume that totality—the shady as well as the extraordinary things of our past-, we will not be able to construct anything] (Otro error muy serio que estamos cometiendo es la pérdida de la memoria. No podemos jactarnos de estar comenzando de nuevo, de que estamos "instituyendo" algo nuevo.... Somos hijos e hijas del franquismo, de las cosas buenas y malas de la época franquista. Hasta que no asumamos la totalidad—las partes oscuras y las partes extraordinarias de nuestra historia pasada—no podremos reconstruir nada).

44. For further explorations of the relation between exile and gender in the novel, see Cornejo-Parriego 1999 and Zatlin 1988.

45. "creo que la historia de la deportación de nuestros compatriotas tiene que ser contada, no la podemos desterrar de la memoria colectiva" (Roig 1980a, 214).

46. "mientras trataba de escribir la novela sobre Judit y Kati, Norma pensaba en el viejo ex deportado.... En aquellas conversaciones, Norma comprendió que hay cosas peores que la deportación, que un campo de exterminio o que las cámaras de gas. Y una de esas cosas es la vida que tienen que llevar los ex deportados después que les liberan. Les miras a los ojos y te das cuenta de que ya no hay nada que hacer. Nada contra las noches de insominio, las alucinaciones, las escenas que se repiten todas las madrugadas cuando los demás no están, cuando el cuerpo y el alma de un ex deportado se concentran en un punto inesquivable e intransferible de la memoria.... Cuando pensaba en su viejo amigo ex deportado, sobre todo ahora, al escribir la novela de Judit y Kati, Norma se negaba a hacer literatura" (Roig 1980a, 216).

47. "La verdad no la sabrá nunca" (Roig 1980a, 221).

48. "Pero quiero hacer constar que, después de haber trabajado tres años en este libro, no sé lo que es un campo de exterminio nazi. Es imposible hacerse una idea de ello" (Roig 1978, 37).

49. "fueron los ojos terriblemente cansados de Amat-Piniella los que más cosas supieron decirme sobre lo que había significado el infierno nazi" (Roig 1978, 21).

50. "la verdad, la verdad, no la sabrá nunca" (Roig 1978, 22).

51. "Había dejado el magnetófono en marcha y murió escuchando su propio relato: 'cuando entré en Mauthausen, comprendí el infierno de Dante...' " (Roig 1980a, 219).
52. "este libro no es más que la coordinación de todas estas voces, todas ellas forman una convincente presencia colectiva. De todas maneras, hay que decir que es un libro abierto, una obra que deberá ser continuada, revisada y ampliada" (Roig 1978, 23).
53. "no faltaba nadie: el nombre, la fecha de entrada en el campo, la fecha de traslado al campo anexo, el número de matrícula, la fecha de la muerte. Nombre tras nombre, decenas, centenares, millares de nombres.... Nombres desconocidos que no existían para la historia. Nadie les reclamaría. No tenían cuerpo, no tenían cadaver. No tenían un nicho donde ser enterrados, ni una lápida individual. Ni flores. Nada." (Roig 1980a, 220).
54. "las palabras ya no servían y entonces el silencio lo envolvió todo. Sólo el rumor del viento más allá de las viñas, un suave murmullo que bajaba de las montañas. Tal vez era el murmullo de los muertos, que regresaban para sentirse acompañados" (Roig 1980a, 244).
55. "Los fantasmas acompañaban el rumor de los muertos que no tenían nombre. Los fantasmas avanzaban y retrocedían a su alrededor, en corro. Sin decir nada, sólo unos ojos desorbitados que no podían cerrarse. Nosotros no olvidamos, decían los ojos, repetía el rumor" (Roig 1980a, 245).
56. "las penas de los ex deportados se le quedaron muy adentro" (Roig 1980a, 228).
57. "qué quiere decir, 'nadar contra-corriente'?" (Roig 1980a, 243); "qué pena me dan esos salmones" (Roig 1980a, 246).
58. "que se habían estrellado contra la historia" (Roig 1980a, 242).
59. "mirar de reojo" (Roig 2001, 109); "la mirada tuerta" (Roig 2001, 110).
60. "Podríamos decir que la primera mirada pertenece al 'ya no' mientras que la otra es el 'todavía no', y la única manera de no volvernos locas es aprender a mirar en dos direcciones divergentes al mismo tiempo" (Roig 2001, 109–10).
61. "ese montón de papelotes me ha obligado a pensar en mí misma. A mirarme por dentro" (Roig 1980a, 14).
62. "Franco está dentro de mí, se me aferra como una babosa" (Roig 1980a, 107).
63. "todo mi cuerpo se dividió en trozos, las manos por un lado, la vagina por otro, la espalda se desparramaba en miles de partículas, el vientre estallaba, nada se recomponía" (Roig 1980a, 76).
64. "la mirada se le hacía insoportable. En aquella mirada no había fingimiento.... Era ella misma que pretendía entenderse, comprender cómo era sin la mirada de los demás.... Tenía miedo a entrar dentro de sí misma, terror a encontrarse vacía" (Roig 1980a, 251).
65. "Una Norma pequeña y frágil, incapaz de unificar los contrarios.... Era como si se estuviese desgarrando, como si los pedazos de sí misma se sostuvieran precariamente, pegados con goma, recompuestos torpemente. Igual que el arqueólogo, que no sabe si podrá reconstruir la pieza devolviéndole su forma primitiva" (Roig 1980a, 253).
66. "Sobre la mesa, con las hojas colocadas simétricamente, sin que sobresaliese ninguna, dejó el manuscrito de Judit y de Kati. Se daba cuenta de que sólo era un esbozo de novela, que no había ido hasta el fondo. Le dolía el presente, la perseguía, la distanciaba del proyecto-Judit y el proyecto-Kati. Eran pasado y nada más" (Roig 1980a, 265).
67. "quería olvidar a todos los ex deportados, los campos de exterminio, las chimeneas del crematorio, las cámaras de gas. Borrar las imágenes espectrales, los montones y montones de cadáveres alineados como monigotes de goma. Borrarlo todo" (Roig 1980a, 231).

68. "Norma se tranquilizó. Pronto olvidaría la historia de los deportados, de los fantasmas que exigían, desde el pasado, sobrevivir en su memoria. La historia había quedado archivada en su libro, éste era su homenaje, ¿qué más querían?" (Roig 1980a, 254).

69. "usted era amiga suya y que había cosas que usted no iba a olvidar" (Roig 1980a, 266).

70. "no sólo le daba pena el deportado, sino también su amigo el escritor, y Villa-palacios, y Marie, la mujer que asumió por amor la traición de su marido. Y Patricia.... Eran cosa suya. Y Judit, y Kati. También ella estaba allí, dentro de la Historia. Y nunca podría apartarse. Aunque la Historia fuese una pesadilla, aunque estuviese llena de fantasmas" (Roig 1980a, 266).

71. "si existe un acto de amor éste es la memoria" (Roig 2001, 27).

72. "Los recuerdos se mezclaban con las penas de los demás, caían sobre ella como las hojas de un almendro. En aparienca eran frágiles, estaban a punto de ser llevados por la fuerza del vientos—es decir, del olvido-, pero lo cierto era que las penas de los demás y los recuerdos se iban acumulando hasta formar una segunda piel" (Roig 1980a, 200).

73. "quizás ahora podría escribir hasta el fondo la historia de Judit y Kati. Quizás" (Roig 1980a, 267).

74. Marianne Hirsch has compared Silverman's concept of "heteropathic recollection" with her own notion of "postmemory" (see esp. 1999). In "postmemory," one also takes on as one's own the suffering of others, specifically those of previous generations. Oftentimes this is done unconsciously, as children or grandchildren of people who have suffered trauma, for example, are marked by the traumatic experiences of their elders even though they have not directly lived those events. This experience of "postmemory" is the focus of the next chapter, as it is a central concern in *El jinete polaco* by Antonio Muñoz Molina. The problematics of "postmemory" are relevant to Norma's difficulty in finding the appropriate way to present the stories of suffering that she is investigating, for she has not directly lived those experiences. They belong to a previous generation. At one point, the ex-deportee she is interviewing wants to give her all his lists with information about his fellow inmates at Mauthausen, but Norma feels she cannot accept them, for she has not lived that experience. She recognizes how important it is that the old man wants to pass his information on to someone else, but asks herself "aquest algú ¿era ella, que havia nascut un any més tard de l'alliberament dels camps, que no tenia ningú a prop que hagués patit la deportació, i que només sabia que existien camps d'extermini gràcies a algun reportatge i a les pel·licules, poques, que havien arribat al seu país durant el franquisme?" (Roig 1993, 193) [Was that someone her, she who was born one year after the camps were liberated, she who did not have any relative that had suffered deportation and that only knew of the existence of the extermination camps thanks to some documentary and to a few movies, very few, that had arrived in her country during Francoism?] (¿Ese alguien era ella, que había nacido un año después de que los campos fuesen liberados, que no tenía ningún pariente que hubiera padecido la deportación y que sólo sabía que existían los campos de exterminio gracias a algún reportaje y a algunas películas, pocas, que llegaron a su país durante el franquismo? (Roig 1980a, 221)). It is only once she is told that the ex-deportee has died, and that he still wanted to give her some of his documents, that Norma realizes she can, indeed, accept them. This is only possible, however, once she accepts the full implications and disruptions inherent in the process of "heteropathic recollection," or "postmemory."

75. "creo que la historia de la deportación de nuestros compatriotas tiene que ser contada, no la podemos desterrar de la memoria colectiva" (Roig 1980a, 214).

76. "sólo era una esbozo de novela, que no había ido hasta el fondo"; "eran pasado y nada más" (Roig 1980a, 265).
77. "Hay que recordar y olvidar al mismo tiempo. La memoria también es olvido" (Roig 2001, 31).
78. "No, no hace falta inventar, sólo imaginar. . . . Había que imaginar, la imaginación es una buena aliada del recuerdo" (Roig 1980a, 250).
79. "el orden de la imaginación se sale de todos los datos, de todos los hechos. Ésta es la venganza de la literatura contra la historia" (Roig 1980a, 103).

5. Antonio Muñoz Molina

1. *El jinete polaco* also won the Premio Nacional de Narrativa (National Narrative Prize) in 1992. In 1995, Muñoz Molina was elected the youngest member of the Real Academia Española de la Lengua [Royal Spanish Academy of Language], adding the literary prestige accompanying such membership to the fame he has gained due to the blockbuster sales of his novels. In 2004, Muñoz Molina was named Director of the prestigious Instituto Cervantes in New York City, a position he held for three years.
2. For more on historiographic metafiction, see Linda Hutcheon 1988 and 1989.
3. Muñoz Molina belongs to what has been called by some the generation of 1981 (see Pope 1990). It is the first generation that did not experience the civil war or the postwar years, but grew up during the later years of the Franco regime and started publishing in the 1980s. This is a generation emerging after the so-called Generation of 1968, to which Montserrat Roig belonged. That generation began writing toward the end of the Franco regime and was an active participant in the transition to democracy.
4. Even his inaugural address, as he was being inducted into the Real Academia Española de la Lengua in 1996, became a platform for Muñoz Molina to reiterate his conviction regarding the need to recover, or invent, the history of Spain that the regime had not allowed to flourish, as well as his ethical vindication of the victims of the regime's view of history. Muñoz Molina evoked, in his address, an apocryphal speech that Max Aub had written in exile in 1956 in which Aub himself was supposedly being inducted into the Real Academia. The idealized Academy that Aub imagined himself joining in 1956 housed such members as Antonio Machado, Federico García Lorca, and Rafael Alberti, among others. Aub thus dared to imagine his fictional ceremony as if the civil war had never occurred, as if Lorca had never been executed, as if Machado had not already died, as if he and his friends had never gone into exile. Aub's fictitious speech embodies a rebellion against history and the belief in the power of the imagination to recall not just what *did* happen in the past, but what *could have* happened. Muñoz Molina thus again "mixes memory and desire" in his acceptance speech. His address presents an idea central to several of his novels, especially *El jinete polaco:* the conviction that his own voice is but the echo of those voices that have existed long before his, but that have not been allowed, like his own, to be raised freely.
5. It is likewise not coincidental that Manuel Vázquez Montalbán is the author who extolled Muñoz Molina's novel when he was presented the Planeta Prize, recognizing the political urgency and subversive nature of Muñoz Molina's exploration of memory:

> *El jinete polaco* es un libro de memoria, una memoria en gran parte heredada y sometida a una lectura desde el presente. . . . La memoria es en sí misma una novela que cada cual falsifica, pero que todos necesitamos. . . . Los dotados de la capacidad del lenguaje podrán transmitir su

memoria. Los que no gozan de ese privilegio tendrán la memoria como un quiste, y no siempre benigno. *El jinete polaco* no es una novela de la nostalgia, sino de la memoria. El sentimiento está usado como forma de conocimiento, y no sensiblería. (E.F.S. 1991)

[*El jinete polaco* is a book of memory, a memory in large part inherited and submitted to a reading from the present.... Memory itself is a novel that each individual falsifies, but that we all need.... Those who are gifted with the capacity for language will be able to transmit their memory. Those who do not enjoy that privilege will bear memory like a cyst, and not always benign. *El jinete polaco* is not a novel of nostalgia, but of memory. Feeling is used as a form of knowledge, and not of sentimentality.]

The exploration of memory as a political strategy against the amnesia predominant in post-Franco Spain is a topic that Vázquez Montalbán has consistently pursued in his own literary career. It is no surprise, therefore, that Eliot's verse, "mixing memory and desire," is also a favorite of Vázquez Montalbán's, one he was fond of quoting, orally as well as in his texts (a 1986 anthology of his poetry, for example, is entitled *Memoria y deseo* [*Memory and Desire*]).

6. For a comparison of the concept of "postmemory" developed by Marianne Hirsch and Silverman's use of the term "heteropathic recollection," see Hirsch 1999.

7. *El jinete polaco* contains many autobiographical elements, from the place and date of birth of the protagonist as well as the conditions of his upbringing, to a similar personal trajectory as both author and protagonist, Manuel, distance themselves from their past only to return to it later in life. The turn, after having written predominantly nonautobiographical fiction, to a more autobiographical, yet still fictional, narrative that Muñoz Molina initiated with *El jinete polaco* is somewhat like Manuel's experience within the plot of *El jinete polaco*. In a 1995 conference entitled "Memoria y ficción" [Memory and Fiction], Muñoz Molina commented on his need to turn from purely fictional writing to more autobiographical texts. He highlights that this turn, while signaling a change in his narrative, likewise underscored the fundamental similarities in both kinds of writing. Not surprisingly, the "mixing [of] memory and desire," as well as the imbrication of history and fiction, reappear in his explanation:

Hubo un tiempo en el que yo no sabía o no me atrevía a convertir la literatura en una desnuda confesión personal y me veía abocado a escribir novelas. En los últimos años, lo que me ocurre es que queriendo escribir novelas cada vez se me interpone más imperiosamente el flujo de la memoria personal, y renuncio, contra los consejos de mi inteligencia, a inventar tramas, y me dejo llevar por el puro impulso de la rememoración. Sospecho entonces que el azar y la disciplina, la intuición y la técnica, pueden aliarse, que es posible una literatura en la que se sumen el recuerdo y la ficción, la memoria y el deseo, la reflexión y la aventura, la belleza del mito y la intensidad de la pura experiencia de ahora mismo. (1998d, 189)

[There was a time when I did not know how to, or dare to, convert literature into a naked personal confession, and I preferred to write novels. In the last few years, what has happened is that when I want to write novels, the flow of personal memory imposes itself on me ever more imperiously, and I desist, against the best advice of my intelligence, from inventing plots, allowing myself to be led by a pure impulse to remember. I suspect then that chance and discipline, intuition and technique, can become allied, and that it is possible to have a literature that combines remembering and fiction, memory and desire, reflection and adventure, the beauty of myth and the intensity of the pure experience of the here and now.]

8. See Moreno-Muño 2006 for a reading of *El jinete polaco* that also focuses on how younger generations inherit the trauma of the civil war.

9. As in Roig's *L'hora violeta,* it is the death of those who were responsible for passing on their memory to the protagonists that partly serves as a catalyst for them

to take up the rememorative process themselves. In Roig's case, the death of Natàlia's parents and of the Catalan ex-deportee who shared his memory of Mauthausen with Norma contribute to Natàlia and Norma's assuming the responsibility for productively working through memory. Both these novels, therefore, reflect a phenomenon mentioned in the introduction to this book. One of the reasons for the sense of urgency with which the problem of memory is being raised in Spain, in the latter part of the twentieth century and the beginning of the twenty-first, is the recognition that the generation that has lived the civil war and the postwar years is rapidly disappearing. Carlos Elordi's book of oral interviews with people who lived these experiences, entitled *Antes que el tiempo muera en nuestros brazos* [*Before Time Dies in Our Arms*], is one manifestation, among others, of this sense of urgency in recovering a memory that will soon be available to us only as postmemory.

10. We encounter, here, the same problem that Semprún explores recurrently in writing about his Buchenwald experience: the difficulty in conveying the memory of a traumatic experience to those who have not suffered it.

11. Maria Torok, in "Story of Fear," raises a point, concerning the experience of the "transgenerational phantom," that resonates with this comment on Manuel's part. She describes how this experience necessarily implies a questioning of the purely individual nature of the first person singular pronoun. With respect to the experience of the transgenerational phantom, "when people say 'I' they might in fact be referring to something quite different from their own identity as recorded in their identification papers" (1994, 179).

12. In a review of *El jinete polaco*, Santiago del Rey appropriately explains this opening up of the first person singular pronoun to a plethora of voices by evoking the famous verse by French poet Rimbaud: "Je est un autre" [I is another]. As Santiago del Rey explains, this verse "tal vez quiere decir: el yo, sede-irreductible-de-la-identidad, me es ajeno y no me pertenece, es un lugar colonizado—y no soberano—habitado, como quiere el psicoanálisis, por voces medio olvidadas; un lugar poblado de palabras, de amenazas y sermones, de leyendas y mentiras familiares y de principios sacrosantos con los que, efectivamente, nos pasamos media vida disputando" (1992, 67) [perhaps means: the I, the irreducible-center-of-identity, is alien to me, and does not belong to me, it is a colonized—and not sovereign—place, inhabited, according to psychoanalysis, by half-forgotten voices; a place inhabited by words, threats and sermons, legends and family lies, and by sacrosanct principles against which, in fact, we spend half our life battling]. This description of a self "colonized" by the voices of the past is a perfect image of the experience of postmemory analyzed here.

13. We may recall that Norma, in *L'hora violeta*, has a similar reaction when the Catalan ex-deportee she is interviewing wants to give her his information about Mauthausen. She wonders whether she is the most appropriate person to receive such material, since she has not experienced anything close to what he is narrating: "¿Ese alguien era ella, que había nacido un año después de que los campos fuesen liberados, que no tenía ningún pariente que hubiera padecido la deportación y que sólo sabía que existían los campos de exterminio gracias a algún reportaje y a algunas películas, pocas, que llegaron a su país durante el franquismo?" (Roig 1980a, 221) [Was that someone her, she who was born one year after the camps were liberated, she who did not have any relative that had suffered deportation and that only knew of the existence of the extermination camps thanks to some documentary and to a few movies, very few, that had arrived in her country during Francoism?]. In both novels, therefore, the younger generation can only imagine the traumatic experiences of their elders through the mediation of literary or filmic texts they have seen. Both of these novels thus explore the problem of how to work through a traumatic past to which one has only indirect access.

14. There are many other instances in the novel in which an event is shaped by some form or another of textual mediation. When Don Mercurio, for example, tells Ramiro Retratista a false story of the mummified woman (not wanting to admit that he was the man with whom the young woman had had an affair many years before), the narrator mentions that the tale "fue cobrando un torvo romanticismo de litografía y de folletín" (1991, 128) [slowly took on a grim romanticism as of a lithography or a serial novel]. Don Mercurio himself compares the tales he is telling to "leyendas," "novelas por entregas," (1991, 131) [legends, serial novels] and the end he invents to "el último pliege del folletín" (1991, 132) [the last issue of the serial novel]. Later on, the adolescent Manuel will imagine adventurous futures for himself far from Mágina, based on the American rock songs to which he listens. He imagines himself as a mysterious, Jim Morrison-like "rider on the storm," or a Lou Reed-like loner "taking a walk on the wild side." These fantasies are further modeled on his readings, for he sees himself as "una figura solitaria y novelesca concebida en la infancia, hecha irresponsablemente de personajes de películas, de aventureros de novelas y de tebeos" (1991, 255) [a solitary and novelesque figure conceived in his youth, irresponsibly crafted from movie characters, as well as novel and comic book heroes]. The textual mediation of reality is thus ever-present within the text. For more on some of the intertextual resonances within the novel, see Elizabeth Amann 1998.

15. In "La invención de un pasado" [The Invention of a Past], Muñoz Molina explicitly mentions the fact that contemporary Spanish culture has a debt with those who were forced to suffer exile, both external and internal. Recovering and vindicating these experiences from oblivion, as Muñoz Molina does in many of his texts, are an important task that Spanish authors must still face:

> Ya no hay razón para que los españoles vivan, escriban y mueran obligatoriamente lejos de su país, o enquistados dentro de sí mismos, en la claustrofobia de lo que se llamó el exilio interior: tal vez lo que todavía nos falta es abolir también el destierro en el tiempo, y ofrecer por fin la plena ciudadanía del presente a quienes fueron confinados a un pasado de exilio y desconocimiento. Sospecho que sólo entonces, cuando convierta en presencia viva lo que ahora es abandono y olvido, podrá adquirir la cultura española el vigor necesario para merecer una cierta universalidad. (1998c, 219)

> [There is no longer any reason for Spaniards to have to obligatorily live, write, and die far from their own country, or enclosed within themselves, in the claustrophobia of what was called interior exile: perhaps what we still need to abolish is also the exile in time, and finally offer a full citizenship in the present to those who were confined to a past of exile and namelessness. I suspect that only then, when Spanish culture has transformed into a live presence what is now still forsaken and forgotten, will it be able to acquire the necessary vigor to merit a certain universality.]

By re-creating the stories of their family past together, Nadia and Manuel are effectively "offering full citizenship in the present" to those members of their family who had been confined to exile, both external, in the case of Commander Galaz, and internal, in the case of Manuel's family. Memory is the vehicle for this politically significant act. It is also highly significant that this process is taking place in New York, the site of Commander Galaz's exile. Again, Muñoz Molina is indicating that the re-creations of Spanish history that will "offer full citizenship in the present" to those who experienced exile must in part take place from within that site of their banishment, a site that will be reconnected with Spain itself when Manuel and Nadia meet in Mágina at the end of the novel.

16. Manuel has earlier compared the Polish rider of the painting to his hero Miguel Strogoff, highlighting the fact that Strogoff had only apparently lost his sight: "en el

grabado del jinete que estaba colgado enfrente de la cama fue como si también cayera otra vez la noche y se avivara el fuego que alguien había encendido junto a un río y en el que unos tártaros sublevados contra el zar calentaban hasta el rojo vivo el filo del sable que en apariencia cegaría a Miguel Strogoff" (1991, 14) [it was as if the night also fell again on the painting of the rider that hung in front of the bed, and as if the fire was re-ignited, the fire that someone had lit near a river, and in which some rebel Tartars were heating the blade that would supposedly blind Miguel Strogoff]. The intertextual resonance that Muñoz Molina's novel establishes with adventure novels such as Verne's, or the entangled folletines mentioned recurrently throughout the text, are further established by the pattern of unlikely coincidences in the storyline. Nadia and Manuel's chance encounter at an international conference in Madrid in 1991 is an example. Another is the fact that Manuel visits the Frick collection in New York, and stops in front of the original painting of the Polish rider (which he vaguely remembers but cannot place in his memory), immediately before he returns to his hotel in New York where Nadia finally arrives to meet him. She, of course, arrives just as he is about to leave for good, after he has left numerous messages on her answering machine and has received no reply. As in many adventure tales, the plot here often advances due to almost magical coincidences.

17. The photographs are not the only elements mediating Manuel and Nadia's access to their past that are copies, and somewhat false to boot. The reproduction of Rembrandt's painting, "The Polish Rider," is also but a copy of the original. In the case of the original artwork, moreover, the play between original and copy is even more complex, since the painting is in all probability a copy, painted by William Drost, one of Rembrandt's disciples, and not the master himself. For more information on the history of the painting, see Bailey 1990.

18. This understanding of memory as inexorably connecting truth and falsehood, as well as of the inextricable connection between memory and forgetting, are recurrent themes in Muñoz Molina's critical writing. His article "Memoria y ficción" [Memory and Fiction] among many other examples, argues for the fundamental role of memory in all literary creation. This memory, however, has to be understood as a creative process that does not exclude, but necessarily incorporates, the dynamics of forgetting and falsehood:

> La literatura está hecha de memoria en la misma medida en que el primer hombre de la Biblia estaba hecho de barro, o en que el halcón maltés estaba hecho de plomo y también de la materia de los sueños. Digo literatura y no las novelas ni los libros de versos o de confesiones personales; y digo que está hecha de, y no que tiene que ver con o trata de la memoria, y menos aún del recuerdo, pues la literatura también está hecha de olvido.... Otro oficio de la memoria es la edificación del pasado, en cuyos materiales constructivos suelen mezclarse la verdad y la mentira, y en la que no hay experiencia no desfigurada por la lejanía, no modificada y perdida igual que la materia orgánica en la tierra fértil. Ya dijo William James que a lo que principalmente se dedica la memoria es a olvidar: en un movimiento doble y simultáneo la trama de la vida se teje y se deshace.... Recordando y olvidando, escribiendo y borrando, casi siempre en la arena, la memoria actúa sobre nosotros y dentro de nosotros de un modo tan incesante como late el corazón o se nos ensanchan los pulmones. (1998d, 175)

> [Literature is made of memory in the same way as the first man of the Bible was made of earth, or as the Maltese falcon was made of lead and also of the stuff of dreams. I say literature and not novels or books of verse or personal confessions; and I say that it is made of, and not that it deals with or relates to memory, and even less remembering, for literature is also made of forgetting.... Another task of memory is the edification of the past, where truth and falsehood mix, and where there is no experience that has not been disfigured by distance, nor modified and lost, as the organic matter in fertile land. William James said that what memory pri-

marily does is to forget: in a double and simultaneous movement, the story of our lives is woven and unraveled.... Remembering and forgetting, writing and erasing, almost always in the sand, memory acts upon us and within us as incessantly as our heart beats or as our lungs expand.]

This echoes Roig's claim in her critical writing that "hay que recordar y olvidar al mismo tiempo. La memoria también es olvido" (2001, 31) [We have to remember and forget at the same time. Memory is also forgetting]. Both authors, therefore, establish very close connections between their literary and critical writings.

19. The parallels between Muñoz Molina's creative and critical writing are again underscored when he makes a similar analogy, in "La invención de un pasado" [The Invention of the Past], between memory (as well as the representation of time in the novel), and the process of developing a photograph: "En literatura tiempo se escribe con mayúscula porque casi siempre se escribe sobre el tiempo y se trabaja con él en la misma medida en que el alfarero trabaja con la arcilla o el fotótografo con los procesos químicos de la fijación de la luz" (1998c, 166) [In literature, time is capitalized because one almost always writes about time and one works with it in the same way a potter works with clay, or a photographer with the chemical processes that fix light].

20. In "El hombre habitado por las voces" [The Man Inhabited by Voices], an essay on the work of William Faulkner, Muñoz Molina mentions a famous quote by the American author which has had an enormous influence on him: "The past is not dead, it is not even past" (1998b, 146). This quote is very relevant to the exploration of memory and postmemory presented in *El jinete polaco*, and to its recognition of the weight of the past in the present. It is no coincidence that this quote from Faulkner was also a favorite of Juan Benet's who cited it often, and who, as has been studied, made the exploration of memory one of the central themes of his writing. Manuel also echoes this notion that the past is not past, but part of the present, when he thinks about the fact that the very term "pasado" [past] seems terribly inappropriate to describe what he is remembering in Nadia's apartment: "aunque tampoco le gusta esa palabra, le parece inexacta, probablemente mentirosa, no puede ser pasado lo que está viviendo ahora mismo en él, es el mismo presente que nota latir con una apaciguada suavidad en el pulso de Nadia" (1991, 152) [although he doesn't like that word either, it seems inexact, probably false, something cannot be past if it is living right now within him, if it is the very present that he feels beating with a peaceful softness in Nadia's pulse].

21. In this respect, *El jinete polaco* is representative of novels of the last two decades that deal with the history of the Spanish civil war and Franco regime, but that do so without necessarily reproducing the ideological discourse of the "Dos Espanãs" [Two Spains] that permeated novels exploring these historical experiences in earlier decades. *El jinete polaco*, for example, has been productively compared with Juan Goytisolo's *Señas de identidad* (originally published in 1967) [*Marks of Identity*] in this light. For more on such comparisons, see Benson 1994 and Oropesa 1999. Herzberger summarizes this difference in attitude when he explains: "In contrast to many characters in Spanish novels of the 1950s and 1960s, Manuel here turns not *against* the prevailing discourses of the nation but *away* from them" (1998, 31).

Conclusion

1. The Galician original of Rivas's novel, *O lapis do carpinteiro*, was published in 1998.

2. The Basque original of Atxaga's novel, *Soinujolearen semea*, appeared in 2003.

3. For more on myth and recent novels about the Spanish Civil War see Moreno-Nuño 2006.

4. Semprún makes the same point close to the end of *L'écriture ou la vie* [*Writing or Life*], a fact that shows this is truly a major concern for the author:

> Un jour viendrait, relativement proche, où il ne resterait plus aucun survivant de Buchenwald.... Plus personne n'aurait dans son âme et son cerveau, indélébile, l'odeur de chair brûlée des fours crématories.... Un jour prochain, pourtant, personne n'aura plus le souvenir réel de cette odeur: ce ne sera plus qu'une phrase, une référence littéraire, une idée d'odeur. Inodore, donc. (1994a, 301–2)

> A day would come, relatively soon, when there would no longer be a single survivor of Buchenwald left.... No longer would anyone be indelibly marked, body and soul, by the smell of burning flesh from the crematory ovens.... A day is coming, though, when no one will actually remember this smell: it will be nothing more than a phrase, a literary reference, an idea of an odor. Odorless, therefore. (1997, 292–93)

> Llegaría un día, relativamente cercano, que ya no quedaría ningún superviviente de Buchenwald.... Ya nadie tendría en su alma y en su cerebro, indeleble, el olor a carne quemada de los hornos crematorios.... Un día cercano, no obstante, ya nadie tendrá el recuerdo real de este olor: será sólo una frase, una referencia literaria, una idea de olor. Inodoro, por tanto. (1995b, 311–12)

Works Cited

"A treinta años del siglo XXI, mesa redonda: novela." 1970. *Cuadernos para el Diálogo* 23 (Dec.): 45–52.

Abraham, Nicolas. 1994. "Notes on the Phantom: A Complement to Freud's Metapsychology." In *The Shell and the Kernel*, ed. and trans. Nicholas T. Rand, vol. 1, 171–76. Chicago: Chicago University Press.

Adorno, Theodor W. 1973. *Negative Dialectics*. Trans. E. B. Ashton. New York: Continuum.

Aguilar, Paloma. 2001. "Justice, Politics and Memory in the Spanish Transition." In *The Politics of Memory: Transitional Justice in Democratic Societies*, ed. Alexandra Barahona de Brito, Carmen González-Enríquez, and Paloma Aguilar, 92–118. Oxford: Oxford University Press.

———. 2002. *Memory and Amnesia: The Role of the Spanish Civil War in the Transition to Democracy*. Trans. Mark Oakley. New York: Berghahn Books.

Aguilar, Paloma, and Carsten Humlebaek. 2002. "Collective Memory and National Identity in the Spanish Democracy: The Legacies of Francoism and the Civil War." *History and Memory* 14.1-2 (Fall): 121–64.

Alfaya, Javier. 1976. "Españoles en los campos de concentración nazis." In *El exilio español de 1939*, ed. José Luis Abellán, vol. 2, 91–120. Madrid: Taurus.

Alighieri, Dante. 1897. *The Divine Comedy*. Ed. Oscar Kuhns. Trans. Henry F. Cary. New York: Thomas Y. Crowell.

———. 1995. *La divina commedia*. Ed. Antonio Lanza. Anzio: De Rubeis.

Amann, Elizabeth. 1998. "Genres in Dialogue: Antonio Muñoz Molina's *El jinete polaco*." *Revista Canadiense de Estudios Hispánicos* 23.1 (Fall) 1–21.

Amnesty International. 2005. "España: poner fin al silencio y a la injusticia. La deuda pendiente con las víctimas de la guerra civil española y del régimen franquista." http://www.es.amnesty.org/esp/docs/victimas_franquismo.pdf.

Anderson, Benedict. 1983. *Imagined Communities*. London: Verso.

Apter, Emily. 1991. *Feminizing the Fetish: Psychoanalysis and Narrative Obsession in Turn-of-the-Century France*. Ithaca, N.Y.: Cornell University Press.

Aranguren, José Luis. 1976. "El mundo novelístico de Juan Benet." In *Estudios Literarios*, 282–93. Madrid: Gredos.

Armengou, Montse, and Ricard Belis. 2004. *Las fosas del silencio: ¿Hay un holocausto español?* Madrid: Plaza y Janés.

Armengou, Montse, Ricard Belis, and Ricard Vinyes. 2003. *Los niños perdidos del franquismo*. Barcelona: Random House Mondadori.

Atxaga, Bernardo. 2003. *Soinujolearen semea*. Irún, Spain: Pamiela.

———. 2004. *El hijo del acordeonista.* Trans. Asun Garikano and Bernardo Atxaga. Madrid: Santillana.

Aub, Max. 1995. *La gallina ciega: diario español.* Ed. Manuel Aznar Soler. Barcelona: Alba Editorial.

Aznar Soler, Manuel. 1993. "María Teresa León y el teatro español durante la guerra civil española." *Anthropos* 148 (Sept.): 25–51.

Bailey, Anthony. 1990. "A Young Man on Horseback." *The New Yorker,* March 5, 45–77.

Bakhtin, M. M. 1981. *The Dialogic Imagination.* Ed. Michael Holquist. Trans. Caryl Emerson and Michael Holquist. Austin: University of Texas Press.

———. 1986. *Speech Genres and Other Late Essays.* Ed. Caryl Emerson and Michael Holquist. Trans. Vern W. McGee. Austin: University of Texas Press.

Bal, Mieke. 1999. "Introduction." In *Acts of Memory: Cultural Recall in the Present,* ed. Mieke Bal, Jonathan Crewe, and Leo Spitzer, vii–xvii, Hanover, N.H.: University Press of New England.

Balibrea, Mari Paz. 1999. *En la tierra baldía: Manuel Vázquez Montalbán y la izquierda española en la postmodernidad.* Madrid: El Viejo Topo.

———. 2000. "El exilio republicano y la historiografía literaria española." In *Las literaturas del exilio republicano de 1939,* ed. Manuel Aznar Soler, vol. 2, 185–94. Barcelona: GEXEL.

———. 2003. "El paradigma exilio." *Nuevo Texto Crítico* 29–32: 17–39.

Barthes, Roland. 1981. *Camera Lucida: Reflections on Photography.* Trans. Richard Howard. New York: Hill and Wang.

Bellver, Catherine G. 1991. "Montserrat Roig and the Creation of a Gynocentric Reality." In *Women Writers of Contemporary Spain: Exiles in the Homeland,* ed. Joan L. Brown, 217–39. Newark: University of Delaware Press.

Benet, Juan. 1967. *Volverás a Región.* Barcelona: Destino.

———. 1970a. *Puerta de tierra.* Barcelona: Seix Barral.

———. 1970b. "Reflexiones sobre Galdós." *Cuadernos para el Diálogo* 23 (Dec.): 13–16.

———. 1970c. "Respuesta al señor Montero." *Cuadernos para el Diálogo* 23 (Dec.): 75–76.

———. 1976a. *El ángel del Señor abandona a Tobías.* Barcelona: La Gaya Ciencia.

———. 1976b. "Breve historia de *Volverás a Región.*" *Revista de Occidente* 134: 160–65.

———. 1976c. *Del Pozo y del Numa: un ensayo y una leyenda.* Barcelona: La Gaya Ciencia.

———. 1976d. *En ciernes.* Madrid: Taurus.

———. 1985. *Return to Región.* Trans. Gregory Rabassa. New York: Columbia University Press.

———. 1987. *Otoño en Madrid hacia 1950.* Madrid: Alianza.

Benjamin, Walter. 1969. "Theses on the Philosophy of History." In *Illuminations,* ed. Hannah Arendt, trans. Harry Zohn, 253–64. New York: Schocken Books.

———. 1986. "A Berlin Chronicle." In *Reflections: Essays, Aphorisms, Autobiographical Writings,* ed. Peter Demetz, trans. Edmund Jephcott, 3–60. New York: Schocken Books.

———. 1999. *The Arcades Project.* Trans. Howard Eiland and Kevin McLaughlin. Cambridge, Mass.: Harvard University Press.

Benson, Ken. 1994. "Transformación del horizonte de expectativas en la narrativa posmoderna española: de *Señas de indentidad* a *El jinete polaco.*" *Revista Canadiense de Estudios Hispánicos* 19.1 (Fall): 1–20.

———. 2000–2001. "La memoria en ruinas: narrativa, memoria y olvido en la postguerra española según la cosmovisión de Juan Benet." *Anales: nueva época* 3–4: 21–56.

———. 2004. *Fenomenología del enigma: Juan Benet y el pensamiento literario postestructuralista.* Amsterdam: Rodopi.

Benstock, Shari. 1989. "Expatriate Modernism: Writing on the Cultural Rim." In *Women's Writing in Exile,* ed. Mary Lynn Broe and Angela Ingram, 19–40. Chapel Hill: University of North Carolina Press.

———. 1998. "Authorizing the Autobiographical." In *Women, Autobiography, Theory: A Reader,* ed. Sidonie Smith and Julia Watson, 145–55. Madison: University of Wisconsin Press.

Bergson, Henri Louis. 1970. *Essai sur les données immédiates de la conscience.* Paris: Presses Universitaires de France.

Bertrand de Muñoz, Maryse. 1996. "Novela histórica, autobiografía y mito (la novela y la guerra civil española desde la transición)." In *La novela histórica a finales del siglo XX: Actas del V seminario internacional del instituto de semiótica literaria y teatral de la Uned,* ed. José Romera Castillo, Francisco Gutiérrez Carbajo and Mario García-Page, 19–38. Madrid: Visor.

Blanchot, Maurice. 1986. *The Writing of the Disaster.* Trans. Ann Smock. Lincoln: University of Nebraska Press.

Blanco, Alda. 1991. " 'Las voces perdidas': silencio y recuerdo en *Memoria de la melancolía* de María Teresa León." *Anthropos* 125 (Oct.): 45–49.

Blanco, Amalio. 2003. "El deber de la memoria." *El País,* Dec. 31. http://www.elpais.es.

Bravo, María Elena. 1985. "Ensanchando el horizonte del discurso literario." In *Faulkner en España: perspectivas de la narrativa de postguerra,* 279–302. Barcelona: Península.

———. 1986. "Región, una crónica del discurso literario." In *Juan Benet,* ed. Kathleen Vernon, 177–91. Madrid: Taurus.

———. 1993. "De Modernismo a Posmodernismo." *Insula* 559–90 (July-Aug.): 5–7.

Butler, Judith. 1990. "Performative Acts and Gender Constitution: An Essay in Phenomenology and Feminist Theory." In *Performing Feminisms: Feminist Critical Theory and the Theatre,* ed. Sue-Ellen Case, 270–82. Baltimore: Johns Hopkins University Press.

———. 1993. *Bodies That Matter: On the Discursive Limits of "Sex."* New York: Routledge.

Campbell, Federico. 1971. "Juan Benet o el azar." In *Infame Turba,* 293–310. Barcelona: Lumen.

Carr, Raymond. 1987. "Introduction: The Spanish Transition to Democracy in Historical Perspective." In *Spain in the 1980's: The Democratic Transition and a New International Role,* ed. Robert P. Clark and Michael H. Haltzel, 1–14. Cambridge, Mass: Ballinger.

Carrier, Peter. 2000. "Places, Politics and the Archiving of Contemporary Memory." In *Memory and Methodology,* ed. Susannah Radstone, 37–57. New York: Berg.

Carroll, Lewis. 1998. *Alice's Adventures in Wonderland and Through the Looking-Glass*. New York: Penguin.

Caruth, Cathy, ed. 1991. "Unclaimed Experience: Trauma and the Possibility of History." *Yale French Studies* 79:181–92.

———. 1995, ed. *Trauma: Explorations in Memory*. Baltimore: Johns Hopkins University Press.

———. 1996. *Unclaimed Experience: Trauma, Narrative, and History*. Baltimore: Johns Hopkins University Press.

Castellet, José María, Pere Gimferrer, and Julián Ríos. 1973. "Encuesta: nueva literatura española." *Plural: Revista Mensual de Excelsior* 25: 4–6.

Castresana Fernández, Carlos. 2001. "Transición, memoria y justicia." *El País*, May 1. http://www.elpais.es.

Caudet, Francisco. 1997. *Hipótesis sobre el exilio republicano de 1939*. Madrid: Fundación Universitaria Española.

Celan, Paul. 1980. *Poems*. Trans. Michael Hamburger. New York: Persea.

———. 1986. *Collected Prose*. Trans. Rosemarie Waldrop. Manchester, England: Carcanet.

Cercas, Javier. 2001. *Soldados de Salamina*. Barcelona: Tusquets.

Chacón, Dulce. 2002. *La voz dormida*. Madrid: Santillana.

Chamorro, Eduardo. 1976. "Intento de aproximación a los textos de Juan Benet." *Cuaderno de Norte: Revista Hispánica de Amsterdam*, 110–20.

Chapa, Ana. 1989. "Jorge Semprún dice que su obra lucha contra el olvido." *El País*, Sep 14. http://www.elpais.es.

Cibreiro, Estrella. 1993. "Juan Benet: memoria e irracionalidad en tres obras regionatas." *Ojáncano: Revista de Literatura Española* 7: 28–39.

Cicero. 1970. *On Oratory and Orators*. Trans. and ed. J. S. Watson. Carbondale: Southern Illinois University Press.

Colmeiro, José. 2005. *Memoria histórica e identidad cultural: de la postguerra a la postmodernidad*. Barcelona: Anthropos.

Colomer, Josep María. 1998. *La transición a la democracia, el modelo español*. Barcelona: Anagrama.

Corcuera, Álvaro. 2004. "La memoria recuperada." *El País*, Nov. 7. http://www.elpais.es.

Cornejo-Parriego, Rosalía. 1999. "Exilio y muerte de la amistad femenina en la narrativa de Montserrat Roig." *Letras peninsulares* 12.2–3 (Fall): 255–77.

Corominas, Joan. 1981. *Diccionario crítico etimológico castellano e hispánico*. Madrid: Gredos.

Corrales Egea, José. 1971. *La novela española actual: ensayo de ordenación*. Madrid: Editorial Cuadernos para el Diálogo.

Cortanze, Gérard de. 2004. *L'écriture de la vie*. Paris: Folio.

Costa, Luis F. 1979. "El lector-viajero en *Volverás a Región*." *Anales de la Narrativa Española Contemporánea* 4: 9–19.

Crossland, Zoë. 2000. "Buried Lives: Forensic Archaeology and the Disappeared in Argentina." *Archaeological Dialogues* 7.2:146–59.

———. 2002. "Violent Spaces: Conflict Over the Reappearance of Argentina's Disappeared." In *Matériel Culture: The Archaeology of Twentieth-Century Conflict*, ed.

John Schofield, William Gray Johnson, and Colleen M. Beck, 115–31. London: Routledge.

Cué, Carlos. 2002. "La tierra devuelve a sus muertos." *El País*, July 1. http://www.elpais.es.

———. 2003. "El PP, contrario a un homenaje a víctimas del franquismo." *El País*, Nov. 24. http://www.elpais.es.

———. 2004. "El gobierno rehabilitará 'jurídica y moralmente' a las víctimas del franquismo." *El País*. Sept. 10. http://www.elpais.es.

———. 2005a. "De la Vega frena la ley de memoria histórica para acoger a ambos bandos." *El País*, Sept. 12. http://www.elpais.es.

———. 2005b. "Qué hacer con el panteón del franquismo." *El País*. April 3. http://www.elpais.es.

———. 2005c. "La reconstrucción de un pasado vergonzante." *El País*, May 15. http://www.elpais.es.

———. 2005d. "Treinta años sin Franco." *El País* Nov. 20. http://www.elpais.es.

———. 2006a. "El consejo de Europa condena el franquismo e insta a España a honrar a sus víctimas." *El País*, March 18. http://www.elpais.es.

———. 2006b. "El Gobierno suaviza su ley más delicada, la de Memoria Histórica, para aplacar al PP." *El País*, July 17. http://www.elpais.es.

———. 2006c. "Proyecto de ley de las víctimas de la Guerra Civil y la dictadura: un consejo de cinco notables rehabilitará a las víctimas del franquismo en el BOE." *El País*, July 29. http://www.elpais.es.

———. 2006d. "La ley de víctimas del franquismo no permitirá la publicación de los nombres de los verdugos." *El País*, July 31. http://www.elpais.es.

———. 2006e. "El Gobierno quitó de la ley de la memoria el consejo de suprimir símbolos franquistas: el último borrador del proyecto hacía una recomendación dirigida a municipios y comunidades." *El País*, Aug 25. http://www.elpais.es.

Davies, Catherine. 1994. *Contemporary Feminist Fiction in Spain: The Work of Montserrat Roig and Rosa Montero*. Oxford: Berg.

Davis, Colin. 1991. "Understanding the Concentration Camps: Elie Wiesel's *La Nuit* and Jorge Semprun's *Quel Beau Dimanche!*" *Australian Journal of French Studies* 28: 291–303.

De Lauretis, Teresa. 1990. "Eccentric Subjects: Feminist Theory and Historical Consciousness." *Feminist Studies* 16.1 (Spring): 115–50.

Delbo, Charlotte. 1968. *None of Us Will Return*. Trans. John Githens. New York: Grove.

Derrida, Jacques. 1981. "Plato's Pharmacy." In *Dissemination*, trans. Barbara Johnson, 61–155. Chicago: University of Chicago Press.

———. 1986. *Memoires for Paul de Man*. Trans. Cecile Lindsay, Jonathan Culler, and Eduardo Cadava. New York: Columbia University Press.

———. 1991. *Cinders*. Trans. Ned Lukacher. Lincoln: University of Nebraska Press.

———. 1993. *Spectres de Marx: L'État de la dette, le travail du deuil et la nouvelle Internationale*. Paris: Galilée.

———. 1994. *Specters of Marx: The State of the Debt, the Work of Mourning, and the New International*. Trans. Peggy Kamuf. New York: Routledge.

———. 1995. "Passage—from Traumatism to Promise." In *Points . . . Interviews, 1974–1994*, ed. Elisabeth Weber, trans. Peggy Kamuf et al., 372–95. Stanford, Calif.: Stanford University Press.

Díaz, Elías. 1999. "Con Aranguren." *El País,* Oct 6. http://www.elpais.es.

Díaz, Janet. 1976a. "Origins, Aesthetics and the 'Nueva Novela Española.' " *Hispania* 59:109–17.

———. 1976b. "Spain's Senior 'New Novelist,' Juan Benet." In *Studies in Language and Literature. Proceedings of the 23rd Mountain Interstate Foreign Language Conference,* ed. Charles L. Nelson, 137–42. Richmond: Eastern Kentucky University.

Draaisma, Douwe. 1995. *Metaphors of Memory: A History of Ideas about the Mind.* Trans. Paul Vincent. Cambridge: Cambridge University Press.

Dupláa, Christina. 1996. *La voz testimonial en Montserrat Roig.* Barcelona: Icaria.

Durán, Manuel. 1986. "Juan Benet y la nueva novela española." In *Juan Benet,* ed. Kathleen Vernon, 229–42. Madrid: Taurus.

Dyson, John, and Anita Rozlapa. 1977. "Entrevista con Juan Benet." *The American Hispanist* 3.22:19–21.

E.F.S. 1991. "Vázquez Montalbán: la novela de Muñoz Molina es un libro de memoria." *El País,* Nov 19. http://www.elpais.es.

Egri, Péter. 1969. *Survie et réinterpretation de la forme proustienne: Proust – Déry – Semprun.* Debrecen: Kossuth Lagos Tudományeguetem.

El País. 1991. "Antonio Muñoz Molina gana el Planeta con una 'ficción en forma autobiográfica.' " Oct 16. http://www.elpais.es.

———. 2003. "Cultura del Holocausto." Nov 22. http://www.elpais.es.

———. 2005a. "El Gobierno concede una pensión anual de 6,090 euros a 603 'niños de la guerra.' " Jan 22. http://www.elpais.es.

———. 2005b. "Un funeral en La Almudena cierra los actos en recuerdo de las víctimas del 11-M.' " March 11. http://www.elpais.es.

———. 2006a. "Proyecto de ley de las víctimas de la Guerra Civil y la dictadura: Catedráticos de derecho e historia creen que la ley es 'insuficiente.' " July 29. http://www.elpais.es.

———. 2006b. "Proyecto de ley de las víctimas de la Guerra Civil y la dictadura: las asociaciones de represaliados, el PP, IU y ERC critican la propuesta del gobierno." July 29. http://www.elpais.es.

———. 2006c. "El historiador Paul Preston se muestra en contra de la retirada de todos los símbolos franquistas." Aug 2. http://www.elpais.es.

———. 2006d. "IU pedirá cambios en el proyecto de ley de la memoria histórica." Aug 19. http://www.elpais.es.

———. 2006e. "El Gobierno dice que buscará el consenso en la ley de memoria." Aug 26. *http://www.elpais.es.*

Eliot, T. S. 1999. *The Waste Land and Other Poems.* London: Faber and Faber.

Elordi, Carlos. 1996. *Antes que el tiempo muera en nuestros brazos: Recuerdos y reflexiones de quienes vivieron con Franco.* Barcelona: Grijalbo.

Epps, Brad. 1997. "The Cold Furnace of Desire: The Site of Sexuality in *Volverás a Región.*" In *Juan Benet: A Critical Reappraisal of His Fiction,* ed. John B. Margenot, 33–91. West Cornwall, England: Locust Hill.

———. 2000. "Writing in Accessible Language: Benet, Goytisolo, Galdós." *Revista de Estudios Hispánicos* 34.4 (May): 351–90.

———. 2003. "Questioning the Text." In *The Cambridge Companion to the Spanish Novel: From 1600 to the Present,* ed. Harriet Turner and Adelaida López de Martínez, 193–211. Cambridge: Cambridge University Press.

Espada, Arcadi. 2000. "Jorge Semprún, escritor. ¿Qué haces con el olor a carne quemada?" *El País,* Aug 19. http://www.elpais.es.

———. 2001. " 'Habría que ver cuándo se ha prohibido hablar una lengua en España': Entrevista: Pilar del Castillo, Ministra de Educación, Cultura y Deportes." *El País,* May 5. http://www.elpais.es.

Estébanez Gil, Juan Carlos. 1995. *María Teresa León: estudio de su obra literaria.* Burgos: Editorial "La Olmeda."

Felman, Shoshana, and Dori Laub. 1992. *Testimony: Crises of Witnessing in Literature, Psychoanalysis, and History.* New York: Routledge.

Fernández de Mata, Ignacio. 2005. "The Rupture of the World and the Conflict of Memories." Paper presented at the conference "Franco's Mass Graves: An International, Interdisciplinary Symposium," organized by the Department of Romance Languages and Literatures, University of Notre Dame, South Bend, Indiana, Oct. 28–29.

———. 2006. "The 'Logics' of Violence and Franco's Mass Graves. An Ethnohistorical Approach." *International Journal of the Humanities* 2.3: 2527–35.

Ferrán, Ofelia. 2000. "Memory and Forgetting, Resistance and Noise in the Spanish Transition: Semprún and Vázquez Montalbán." In *Disremembering the Dictatorship: The Politics of Memory in the Spanish Transition to Democracy,* ed. Joan Ramon Resina, 191–222. Amsterdam: Rodopi.

———. Forthcoming. "El destierro y el destiempo del exilio en Max Aub: entre 'un pasado que no fue, . . . [y] un futuro imposible.' " In *Tercer Congreso Internacional: Escritores, Editoriales y Revistas del Exilio Republicano de 1939,* ed. Manuel Aznar Soler. Barcelona: GEXEL.

Ferrándiz, Francisco. 2005a. "The Intimacy of Defeat: Exhumations in Contemporary Spain." Paper presented at the conference "Franco's Mass Graves: An International, Interdisciplinary Symposium," organized by the Department of Romance Languages and Literatures, University of Notre Dame, South Bend, Indiana, Oct. 28–29.

———. 2005b. "La memoria de los vencidos de la guerra civil: El impacto de las exhumaciones de fosas comunes en la España contemporánea." In *Las políticas de la memoria en los sistemas democráticos: Poder, cultura y mercado,* ed. S. Narotzky and J. M. Valcuende, 109–32. Sevilla: ASANA-FAAEE.

Foster, Hal. 1996. *The Return of the Real: The Avant-Garde at the End of the Century.* Cambridge, Mass.: MIT Press.

Foucault, Michel. 1977. *Language, Counter-Memory, Practice: Selected Essays and Interviews.* Ed. Donald F. Bouchard. Ithaca, N.Y.: Cornell University Press.

Frazier, Lessie Jo. 1999. " 'Subverted Memories': Countermourning as Political Action in Chile." In *Acts of Memory: Cultural Recall in the Present,* ed. Mieke Bal, Jonathan Crewe, and Leo Spitzer, 105–19. Hanover, N.H.: University Press of New England.

Freud, Sigmund. 1958a. "Mourning and Melancholia." In *The Standard Edition of the Complete Psychological Works of Sigmund Freud,* trans. and ed. James Strachey, Anna Freud, Alix Strachey, and Alan Tyson, vol. 14, 237–58. London: Hogarth Press.

———. 1958b. "Remembering, Repeating and Working-Through." In *The Standard Edition of the Complete Psychological Works of Sigmund Freud,* trans. and ed. James Strachey, Anna Freud, Alix Strachey, and Alan Tyson, vol. 12, 145–56. London: Hogarth Press

———. 1961a. *Beyond the Pleasure Principle.* Trans. and ed. James Strachey. New York: Norton.

———. 1961b. "Fetishism." In *The Standard Edition of the Complete Psychological Works of Sigmund Freud,* trans. and ed. James Strachey, Anna Freud, Alix Strachey, and Alan Tyson, vol. 21, 152–57. London: Hogarth Press.

Friedlander, Saul, ed. 1992. *Probing the Limits of Representation: Nazism and the "Final Solution."* Cambridge, Mass.: Harvard University Press.

———. 1993. *Memory, History, and the Extermination of the Jews of Europe.* Bloomington: Indiana University Press.

Frisby, David. 1986. *Fragments of Modernity: Theories of Modernity in the Work of Simmel, Kracauer and Benjamin.* Cambridge, Mass.: MIT Press.

Gabilondo, Joseba. 2003. "Historical Memory, Neoliberal Spain, and the Latin American Postcolonial Ghost: On the Politics of Recognition, Apology, and Reparation in Contemporary Spanish Historiography." *Arizona Journal of Hispanic Cultural Studies* 7: 247–66.

Galaz, Mabel. 2005. "El regimen franquista sigue vivo 30 años después en 167 calles de la capital." *El País,* Nov 20. http://www.elpais.es.

Gamman, Lorraine, and Merja Makinen. 1994. *Female Fetishism.* New York: New York University Press.

Gartland, Patricia A. 1983. "Three Holocaust Writers: Speaking the Unspeakable." *Critique: Studies in Contemporary Fiction* 25: 45–56.

Gimferrer, Pere. 1986. "Sobre Juan Benet." In *Juan Benet,* ed. Kathleen Vernon, 45–58. Madrid: Taurus.

Ginzburg, Carlo. 1997. "Shared Memories, Private Recollections." *History and Memory* 9.1–2: 353–63.

González, Felipe. 2001. "Chile, Argentina y las Comisiones de la Verdad." *El País,* April 22. http://www.elpais.es.

Goytisolo, Juan.1980. *Señas de identidad.* Barcelona: Seix Barral.

———. 1986. *En los reinos de taifa.* Barcelona: Seix Barral.

———. 1999. *Coto vedado.* Madrid: Alianza Editorial.

Gracia, Jordi. 2004. "Cuando el pasado se convierte en novela." *La Vanguadia,* Dec. 5. http://www.lavanguardia.es.

Graham, Helen. 2005. *The Spanish Civil War: A Very Short Introduction.* Oxford: Oxford University Press.

Graham, Helen, and Antonio Sánchez. 1995. "The Politics of 1992." In *Spanish Cultural Studies: An Introduction,* ed. Helen Graham and Jo Labanyi, 406–18. Oxford: Oxford University Press.

Granados Nieto, Antonio José. 2004. *Historia de la historia 10,000 años de aventuras.* July 26. http://www.iespana.es/historiadehistoria/AntonioNavidad03.htm?.

Grobbel, Michaela M. 2004. *Enacting Past and Present: The Memory Theaters of Djuna Barnes, Ingeborg Bachmann, and Marguerite Duras.* Lanham, Md.: Lexington Books.

Grosz, Elizabeth A. 1991. "Lesbian Fetishism?" *Differences: A Journal of Feminist Cultural Studies* 3.2: 39–54.

Guelbenzu, José María. 1969. "Dos libros de Juan Benet." *Cuadernos para el Diálogo* 73: 48.

Gullón, Ricardo. 1973. "Una región laberíntica que bien pudiera llamarse España." *Insula* 319: 3,10.

———. 1985. "Sombras de Juan Benet." *Cuadernos Hispanoamericanos* 417: 45–70.

———. 1986. "Esperando a Coré." In *Juan Benet,* ed. Kathleen Vernon, 127–46. Madrid: Taurus.

Halbwachs, Maurice. 1980. *The Collective Memory.* Trans. Francis J. Ditter. New York: Harper & Row.

———. 1992. *On Collective Memory.* Trans. Lewis A. Coser. Chicago: University of Chicago Press.

Herzberger, David K. 1976. *The Novelistic World of Juan Benet.* Clear Creek, Ind.: The American Hispanist.

———. 1980. "Theoretical Approaches to the Spanish New Novel: Juan Benet and Juan Goytisolo." *Revista de Estudios Hispánicos* 14: 3–17.

———. 1984. "Numa and the Nature of the Fantastic in the Fiction of Juan Benet." *Studies in Twentieth Century Literature* 8: 185–96.

———. 1995. *Narrating the Past: Fiction and Historiography in Postwar Spain.* Durham, N.C.: Duke University Press.

———. 1998. "Writing Without a Grain: Identity Formation in Three Works by Muñoz Molina." *Arizona Journal of Hispanic Cultural Studies* 2: 23–40.

———. 1999. "Nuevo historicismo: 'Construyendo la disidencia: historia y ficción en *Volverás a Región* de Juan Benet.' " In *El hispanismo en los Estados Unidos: discursos críticos/prácticas textuales,* ed. José M. del Pino and Francisco la Rubia Prado, 133–47. Madrid: Visor.

———. 2000. "Oblivion and Remembrance: The Double Desire of Muñoz Molina's *El jinete polaco.*" In *Disremembering the Dictatorship: The Politics of Memory in the Spanish Transition to Democracy,* ed. Joan Ramon Resina, 127–38. Amsterdam: Rodopi.

Hirsch, Marianne. 1996. "Past Lives: Postmemories in Exile." In *Exile and Creativity: Signposts, Travelers, Outsiders, Backwards Glances,* ed. Susan Rubin Suleiman, 418–46. Durham, N.C.: Duke University Press.

———. 1997. *Family Frames: Photography, Narrative, and Postmemory.* Cambridge, Mass.: Harvard University Press.

———. 1999. "Projected Memory: Holocaust Photographs in Personal and Public Fantasy." In *Acts of Memory: Cultural Recall in the Present,* ed. Mieke Bal, Jonathan Crewe, and Leo Spitzer, 3–23. Hanover, N.H.: University Press of New England.

———. 2001. "Surviving Images: Holocaust Photographs and the Work of Postmemory." *Yale Journal of Criticism* 14.1: 5–37.

Hobsbawm, Eric, and Terence Ranger, eds. 1983. *The Invention of Tradition.* New York: Cambridge University Press.

Hutcheon, Linda. 1988. *A Poetics of Postmodernism: History, Theory, Fiction.* New York: Routledge.

———. 1989. *The Politics of Postmodernism.* New York: Routledge.

Huyssen, Andreas. 1995. *Twilight Memories: Marking Time in a Culture of Amnesia.* New York: Routledge.

———. 2003. *Present Pasts: Urban Palimpsests and the Politics of Memory.* Stanford, Calif.: Stanford University Press.

Ilie, Paul. 1980. *Literature and Inner Exile: Authoritarian Spain, 1939–1975.* Baltimore: Johns Hopkins University Press.

Irwin-Zarecka, Iwona. 1994. *Frames of Remembrance: The Dynamics of Collective Memory.* New Brunswick, N.J.: Transaction.

J.V. 2004. "El recuerdo de la censura del régimen de Franco." *El País,* March 27. http://www.elpais.es.

Jay, Martin. 1999. "Against Consolation: Walter Benjamin and the Refusal to Mourn." In *War and Remembrance in the Twentieth Century,* ed. Jay Winter and Emmanuel Sivan, 221–39. Cambridge: Cambridge University Press.

Jelin, Elizabeth. 2003. *State Repression and the Labors of Memory.* Trans. Judy Rein and Marcial Godoy-Anativia. Minneapolis: University of Minnesota Press.

Johnson, Kathleen Ann. 1989. "Narrative Revolutions/Narrative Resolutions: Jorge Semprun's *Le Grand Voyage.*" *Romanic Review* 80: 277–87.

Juliá, Santos. 1999a. "Rastros del pasado." *El País,* July 25. http://www.elpais.es.

———, ed. 1999b. *Víctimas de la guerra civil.* Madrid: Ediciones Temas de Hoy.

———. 2002. "Echar al olvido." *El País,* June 15. http://www.elpais.es.

———. 2003. "Echar al olvido: memoria y amnistía en la transición." *Claves de razón práctica* 129: 14–24.

Junta Interministerial Conmemoradora del XXV Aniversario de la Paz Española. 1964. *25 aniversario de la paz española: el gobierno informa.* Madrid: Imprenta Héroes.

Kaplan, Brett Ashley. 2003. " 'The Bitter Residue of Death': Jorge Semprún and the Aesthetics of Holocaust Memory." *Comparative Literature* 55.4 (Fall): 320–37.

Kolbert, Elizabeth. 2003. "Looking for Lorca: A Country Begins To Disinter Its Painful Past." *The New Yorker,* Dec. 22 and 29. 64–75.

Kristeva, Julia. 1989. *Black Sun: Depression and Melancholia.* Trans. Leon S. Roudiez. New York: Columbia University Press.

Kuhn, Annette. 2000. "A Journey Through Memory." In *Memory and Methodology,* ed. Susannah Radstone, 179–96. Oxford: Berg.

Labanyi, Jo. 1989. *Myth and History in the Contemporary Spanish Novel.* Cambridge: Cambridge University Press.

———. 1995. "Postmodernism and the Problem of Cultural Identity." In *Spanish Cultural Studies: An Introduction,* ed. Helen Graham and Jo Labanyi, 396–418. Oxford: Oxford University Press.

———. 1999. "Narrative in Culture, 1975–1996." In *The Cambridge Companion to Modern Spanish Culture,* ed. David T. Gies, 147–62. Cambridge: Cambridge University Press.

———. 2000. "History and Hauntology; or, What Does One Do with the Ghosts of the Past? Reflections on Spanish Film and Fiction of the Post-Franco Period." In *Disremembering the Dictatorship: The Politics of Memory in the Spanish Transition to Democracy,* ed. Joan Ramon Resina, 65–82. Amsterdam: Rodopi.

———. 2002. "Introduction: Engaging with Ghosts; or, Theorizing Culture in Modern Spain." In *Constructing Identity in Contemporary Spain: Theoretical Debates and Cultural Practice,* ed. Jo Labanyi, 1–14. Oxford: Oxford University Press.

Lacan, Jacques. 1977. *Écrits: A Selection.* Trans. Alan Sheridan. New York: Norton.

LaCapra, Dominick. 1994. *Representing the Holocaust: History, Theory, Trauma.* Ithaca, N.Y.: Cornell University Press.

———. 1998. *History and Memory after Auschwitz*. Ithaca, N.Y.: Cornell University Press.

———. 2001. *Writing History, Writing Trauma*. Baltimore: Johns Hopkins University Press.

———. 2004. *History in Transit: Experience, Identity, Critical Theory*. Ithaca, N.Y.: Cornell University Press.

Lang, Berel, ed. 1988. *Writing and the Holocaust*. New York: Holmes and Meier.

Langer, Lawrence. 1991. *Holocaust Testimonies: The Ruins of Memory*. New Haven, Conn.: Yale University Press.

———. 2001. "Pursuit of Death in Holocaust Narrative." *Partisan Review* 68.3 (Summer): 379–95.

Lejeune, Philippe. 1977. "Autobiography in the Third Person." Trans. Annette Tomarken and Edward Tomarken. *New Literary History: A Journal of Theory and Interpretation* 9.1 (Fall): 27–50.

León, María Teresa. 1944. *La historia tiene la palabra: noticia sobre el salvamento del tesoro artístico de España*. Buenos Aires: Patronato Hispano - Argentino de Cultura.

———. 1950. *Las peregrinaciones de Teresa*. Buenos Aires: Botella al mar.

———. 1959. *Juego Limpio*. Buenos Aires: Goyanarte.

———. 1998. *Memoria de la melancolía*. Ed. Gregorio Torres Nebrera. Madrid: Castalia.

———. 2003a. *Obras Dramáticas y Escritos sobre teatro*. Ed. Gregorio Torres Nebrera. Madrid: Publicaciones de la Asociación de Directores de la Escena Española.

———. 2003b. *Teatro: La libertad en el tejado y Sueño y verdad de Goya*. Ed. Manuel Aznar Soler. Sevilla: Renacimiento.

López, Helena. 2004. "Algunas claves para una lectura feminista de *Memoria de la melancolía* de María Teresa León." *Journal of Iberian and Latin American Studies* 10.2:147–67.

López-Aranguren, Eduardo. 1999a. "Que el lector juzgue." *El País*, July 17. http://www.elpais.es.

———. 1999b. "Réplicas. " *El País*, July 3. http://www.elpais.es.

Loriga, Ray. 2005. "Caramba con Franco." *El País*, March 27. http://www.elpais.es.

Loureiro, Angel. 2000. *The Ethics of Autobiography: Replacing the Subject in Modern Spain*. Nashville, Tenn.: Vanderbilt University Press.

Lyotard, Jean-François. *La condition postmoderne: rapport sur le savoir*. Paris: Éditions de Minuit.

Mangini, Shirley. 1995. *Memories of Resistance: Women's Voices From the Spanish Civil War*. New Haven, Conn.: Yale University Press.

———. 2001. *Las modernas: Las grandes intelectuales españolas de la vanguardia*. Barcelona: Península.

Mannoni, Octave. 1969. "Je sais bien, mais quand même . . ." In *Clefs pour l'imaginaire ou l'autre scène*, 9–33. Paris: Seuil.

Manteiga, Roberto C. 1984. "Time, Space, and Narration in Juan Benet's Short Stories." In *Critical Approaches to the Writings of Juan Benet*, ed. Roberto C. Manteiga, David K. Herzberger, and Malcom A. Compitello, 120–36. Hanover, N.H.: University Press of New England.

———. 1993. "El lector-viajero de Juan Benet." *Insula* 559–560 (July-Aug.): 23–24.

Manteiga, Roberto C., David K. Herzberer, and Malcom A. Compitello, eds. 1984. *Critical Approaches to the Writings of Juan Benet.* Hanover, N.H.: University Press of New England.

Marcos, P., and E. Company. 2001. "La afirmación del Rey de que 'nunca se obligó a hablar en castellano' provoca una tormenta política." *El País,* April 25. http://www.elpais.es.

Marías, Javier. 1999a. "El artículo más iluso." *El País,* June 24. http://www.elpais.es.

——. 1999b. "Con desagrado respondo." *El País,* July 10. http://www.elpais.es.

——. 1999c. "Con hastío respondo." *El País,* July 24. http://www.elpais.es.

Martí, Octavi. 1995. "La literatura como memoria: Jorge Semprún, Premio de la Paz de los editores y libreros alemanes." *El País, Babelia,* Oct. 1, 6–7.

Martin, Biddy, and Chandra Talpade Mohanty. 1997. "Feminist Politics: What's Home Got To Do With It?" In *Feminisms: An Anthology of Literary Theory and Criticism, (Rev. Ed.).* Ed. Robyn R. Warhol and Diane Price Herndl, 293–310. New Brunswick, N.J.: Rutgers University Press.

Martín Gaite, Carmen. 1978. *El cuarto de atrás.* Barcelona: Destino.

Martín-Santos, Luis. 1993. *Tiempo de silencio.* Barcelona: Seix Barral.

McCole, John. 1993. *Walter Benjamin and the Antinomies of Tradition.* Ithaca, N.Y.: Cornell University Press.

McDonough, Peter, Samuel H. Barnes, and Antonio López Pina. 1998. *The Cultural Dynamics of Democratization in Spain.* Ithaca, N.Y.: Cornell University Press.

Medina Domínguez, Alberto. 2001. *Exorcismos de la memoria: políticas y poéticas de la melancolía en la España de la transición.* Madrid: Libertarias.

Mertens, Pierre. 2003. *Ecrire après Auschwitz: Semprún, Levi, Cayrol, Kertész.* Tournai, Belgium: Renaissance du livre.

Moa, Pío. 2003. *Los mitos de la guerra civil.* Madrid: La Esfera de los Libros.

Monedero, Juan Carlos. 2004. "Nocturno de la transición." In *La memoria de los olvidados: un debate sobre el silencio de la represión franquista,* ed. Emilio Silva, Asunción Esteban, Javier Castán, and Pancho Salvador, 133–52. Valladolid, Spain: Ámbito Ediciones.

Montero, Isaac. 1970. "Acotación a una mesa redonda (Respuestas a Juan Benet y defensa apresurada del realismo)." *Cuadernos para el Diálogo* 23 (Dec.): 65–74.

Mora, Miguel. 2003. "Hay que repensar la política, la ética y la historia con la mirada de las víctimas." *El País,* Nov. 24. http://www.elpais.es.

Morán, Gregorio. 1991. *El precio de la transición.* Barcelona: Planeta.

Moreiras Menor, Cristina. 2002. *Cultura herida: literatura y cine en la España democrática.* Madrid: Libertarias.

Moreno-Nuño, Carmen. 2006. *Las huellas de la Guerra Civil. Mito y trauma en la narrativa de la España democrática.* Madrid: Libertarias.

Morrison, Toni. 1988. *Beloved.* New York: Penguin Books.

Muguerza, Javier. 1999a. "Por alusiones." *El País,* July 17. http://www.elpais.es.

——. 1999b. "Réplicas." *El País,* July 3. http://www.elpais.es.

Muñoz Molina, Antonio. 1986. *Beatus Ille.* Barcelona: Seix Barral.

——. 1991. *El jinete polaco.* Barcelona: Planeta.

——. 1998a. "Destierro y destiempo de Max Aub." In *Pura alegría,* 87–118. Madrid: Alfaguara.

———. 1998b. "El hombre habitado por las voces." In *Pura alegría*, 139–52. Madrid: Alfaguara.

———. 1998c. "La invención de un pasado." In *Pura alegría*, 191–219. Madrid: Alfaguara.

———. 1998d. "Memoria y ficción." In *Pura alegría*, 175–90. Madrid: Alfaguara.

Naharro-Calderón, José María. 2000. "Falacias de exilios." In *El exilio literario de 1939: actas del Congreso Internacional celebrado en la Universidad de la Rioja del 2 al 5 de noviembre de 1999*, ed. María Teresa González de Garay Fernández and Juan Aguilera Sastre, 350–58. Barcelona: GEXEL.

———. 2005. "Los trenes de la memoria." *Journal of Spanish Cultural Studies* 6.1 (March): 101–22.

Nash, Mary. 1983. *Mujer, familia y trabajo en España (1875–1936)*. Barcelona: Anthropos.

———. 1999a. *Rojas: las mujeres republicanas en la Guerra Civil*. Madrid: Taurus.

———. 1999b. "Un/Contested Identities: Motherhood, Sex Reform and the Modernization of Gender Identity in Early Twentieth-Century Spain." In *Constructing Spanish Womanhood: Female Identity in Modern Spain*, ed. Victoria Lorée Enders and Pamela Beth Radcliff, 25–49. Albany: State University of New York Press.

Navarro, Vicenç. 2001. "Los costes de la desmemoria histórica." *El País*, June 16. http://www.elpais.es.

Nelson, Esther W. 1984. "Narrative Perspective in *Volverás a Región*." In *Critical Approaches to the Writings of Juan Benet*, ed. Roberto C. Manteiga, David K. Herzberer, and Malcom A. Compitello, 27–38. Hanover, N.H.: University Press of New England.

Nichols, Geraldine C. 1989. *Escribir, espacio propio: Laforet, Matute, Moix, Tusquets, Riera y Roig por sí mismas*. Minneapolis, Minn.: Institute for the Study of Ideologies and Literatures.

Nicoladzé, Françoise. 1997. *La deuxième vie de Jorge Semprún: une écriture tressée aux spirales de l'histoire*. Castelnau-Le-Nez, France: Climats.

Nora, Pierre. 1989. "Between Memory and History: *Les Lieux de mémoire*." Trans. Marc Roudebush. *Representations* 26: 7–25.

Nussbaum, Felicity A. 1998. "The Politics of Subjectivity and the Ideology of Gender." In *Women, Autobiography, Theory: A Reader*, ed. Sidonie Smith and Julia Watson, 160–67. Madison: University of Wisconsin Press.

O'Meally, Robert, and Geneviève Fabre. 1994. "Introduction." In *History and Memory in African-American Culture*, ed. Robert O'Meally and Geneviève Fabre, 3–17. New York: Oxford University Press.

Oropesa, Salvador A. 1999. *La novelística de Antonio Muñoz Molina: sociedad civil y literatura lúdica*. Jaén, Spain: Universidad de Jaén.

Ortega, José. 1986. "La dimensión temporal en *Volverás a Región* de Juan Benet." In *Juan Benet*, ed. Kathleen Vernon, 61–92. Madrid: Taurus.

Osiel, Mark. 1997. *Mass Atrocity, Collective Memory, and the Law*. New Brunswick, N.J.: Transaction.

Padilla, Mar. 2004. "La memoria del himno de Riego." *El País*, April 15. http://www.elpais.es.

Paez, D. et al., eds. 1998. *Memorias colectivas de procesos culturales y políticos*. Bilbao, Spain: Universidad del País Vasco.

Pensky, Max. 2004. "Method and Time: Benjamin's Dialectical Images." In *The Cambridge Companion to Walter Benjamin*, ed. David S. Ferris, 177–98. Cambridge: Cambridge University Press.

Pérez Magallón, Jesús. 1991. "Tiempo y tiempos en *Volverás a Región*, de Juan Benet." *Hispanic Review* 59: 281–94.

Perlman, Michael. 1988. *Imaginal Memory and the Place of Hiroshima*. Albany: State University of New York Press.

Pope, Randolph D. 1984. "Benet, Faulkner, and Bergson's Memory." In *Critical Approaches to the Writings of Juan Benet*, ed. Roberto C. Manteiga, David K. Herzberger, and Malcom A. Compitello, 111–19. Hanover, N.H.: University Press of New England.

———. 1990. "Writing after the Battle: Juan Goytisolo's Renewal." In *Literature, the Arts, and Democracy: Spain in the Eighties*, ed. Samuel Amell, 58–66. Rutherford, N.J.: Fairleigh Dickinson University Press.

Preston, Paul. 1993. *Franco: A Biography*. New York: HarperCollins.

———. 2005. "Un Memorial Democrático en Catalunya." *El País*, Feb 24. http://www.elpais.es.

Radstone, Susannah. 2000. *Memory and Methodology*. Oxford: Berg.

Radstone, Susannah, and Katharine Hodgkin, eds. 2003. *Regimes of Memory*. New York: Routledge.

Rahola, Pilar. 2005. "Enric Marco, el fraude." *El País*, May 14. http://www.elpais.es.

Ramos, Ramón. 1989. "Maurice Halbwachs y la memoria colectica." *Revista de occidente* 100: 63–81.

Real Academia Española de la Lengua. 1956. *Diccionario de la lengua española*. Madrid: Real Academia Española de la Lengua / Espasa Calpe.

Renan, Ernest. 1990. "What Is a Nation?" In *Nation and Narration*, ed. Homi K. Bhabha, 8–22. New York: Routledge.

Resina, Joan Ramon. 2000a. "Introduction." In *Disremembering the Dictatorship: The Politics of Memory in the Spanish Transition to Democracy*, ed. Joan Ramon Resina, 1–15. Amsterdam: Rodopi.

———. 2000b. "Short of Memory: The Reclamation of the Past Since the Spanish Transition to Democracy." In *Disremembering the Dictatorship: The Politics of Memory in the Spanish Transition to Democracy*, ed. Joan Ramon Resina, 83–125. Amsterdam: Rodopi.

Rey, Santiago del. 1992. "La memoria a dos voces." Quimera: Revista de literatura 109: 67.

Reyes Mate, Manuel. 1991. *La razón de los vencidos*. Barcelona: Anthropos.

———. 1993. "Walter Benjamin ¿una filosofía política de la historia? O Atenas y Jerusalem ante la identidad europea." In *En torno a Walter Benjamin*, ed. Claudia Kerik, 155–72. Mexico City: Universidad Autónoma Metropolitana.

———. 2002a. *La filosofía después del Holocausto*. Barcelona: Riopiedras.

———. 2002b. "Políticas de la memoria." *El País*, Nov. 12. http://www.elpais.es.

———. 2003a. *Memoria de Auschwitz. Actualidad moral y política*. Madrid: Trotta.

———. 2003b. *For los campos de exterminio*. Barcelona: Anthropos.

———. 2003c. "¿Recordar para mejor olvidar?" *El País*, Sept. 27. http://www.elpais.es.

———. 2004. "Lugares de la memoria." *El País*, March 12. http://www.elpais.es.
Richard, Nelly. 1998. *Residuos y metáforas (ensayos de crítica cultural sobre el Chile de la Transición)*. Santiago, Chile: Cuarto Propio.
———. 2004. *Cultural Residues: Chile in Transition*. Trans. Alan West-Durán and Theodore Quester. Minneapolis: University of Minnesota Press.
Richards, Michael. 2000. "Collective Memory, the Nation-State and Post-Franco Society." In *Contemporary Spanish Cultural Studies*, ed. Barry Jordan and Rikki Morgan-Tamosunas, 38–47. London: Arnold.
Ricoeur, Paul. 1975. *The Rule of Metaphor: Multi-Disciplinary Studies of the Creation of Meaning in Language*. Trans. Robert Czerny, with Kathleen McLaughlin and John Costello. Toronto: University of Toronto Press.
———. 1984. *Time and Narrative*. Trans. Kathleen McLaughlin and David Pellauer, vols. 1–3. Chicago: University of Chicago Press.
———. 1999. "Memory and Forgetting." *Questioning Ethics: Contemporary Debates in Philosophy*. Ed. Richard Kearney and Mark Dooley, 5–11. London: Routledge.
———. 2004. *Memory, History, Forgetting*. Trans. Kathleen Blamey and David Pellauer. Chicago: University of Chicago Press.
Ridell, María Carmen. 2000. "Última etapa del exilio de María Teresa León: la escritura reparadora." *Donaire* 14 (June): 38–46.
Rivas, Manuel. 1998. *O lapis do carpinteiro*. Vigo, Spain: Edicións Xerais de Galicia.
———. 2000. *El lápiz del carpintero*. Trans. Dolores Vilavedra. Madrid: Santillana.
Rivkin, Laura. 1984. "Literary Questing in Juan Benet's *Una meditación*." *Anales de la Literatura Española Contemporánea* 9: 97–115.
Roig, Montserrat. 1977a. *El temps de les cireres*. Barcelona: Edicions 62.
———. 1977b. *Els catalans als camps nazis*. Barcelona: Edicions 62.
———. 1978. *Noche y niebla: los catalanes en los campos nazi*. Trans. C. Vilaginés. Barcelona: Península.
———. 1980a. *La hora violeta*. Trans. Enrique Sordo. Barcelona: Argos Vergara.
———. 1980b. *Ramona adiós*. Trans. Joaquim Sempere. Barcelona: Argos Vergara.
———. 1983. *La ópera cotidiana*. Trans. Enrique Sordo. Barcelona: Destino.
———. 1985. *Isabel-Clara Simó, Montserrat Roig: Diàlegs a Barcelona*. Ed. Xavier Febrés. Barcelona: Ajuntament de Barcelona / Laia.
———. 1989a. "Mare, no entenc els salmons." In *El cant de la joventut*, 105–12. Barcelona: Edicions 62.
———. 1989b. "Voces y diálogos." In *El oficio de narrar*, ed. Marina Mayoral, 69–80. Madrid: Cátedra.
———. 1990. "Madre, no entiendo a los salmones." In *El canto de la juventud*. Trans. Joaquim Sempere, 85–91. Barcelona: Península.
———. 1991a. *Digues que m'estimes encara que sigui mentida*. Barcelona: Edicions 62.
———. 1991b. *La voz melodiosa*. Trans. José Agustín Goytisolo. Barcelona: Destino.
———. 1993. *L'hora violeta*. Barcelona: Edicions 62.
———. 1996. *Tiempo de cerezas*. Trans. Enrique Sordo. Barcelona: Plaza & Janés.
———. 2001. *Dime que me quieres aunque sea mentira: sobre el placer solitario de escribir y el vicio compartido de leer*. Trans. Antonia Picazo. Barcelona: Península.

Rojo, José Andrés. 2004. "De vuelta al pasado sin miedo ni culpa: un seminario recupera la memoria de la guerra y el franquismo desde otras perspectivas." *El Pais,* Oct. 31. http://www.elpais.es.

Rubin Suleiman, Susan. 2004. "Historical Trauma and Literary Testimony: Writing and Repetition in the Buchenwald Memoirs of Jorge Semprún." *Journal of Romance Studies* 4.2:1–19.

Samuel, Raphael. 1997. *Theatres of Memory.* London: Verso.

Scanlon, Geraldine M. 1976. *La polémica feminista en la España contemporánea (1868–1974).* Madrid: Siglo XXI.

Scarry, Elaine. 1985. *The Body in Pain: The Making and Unmaking of the World.* Oxford: Oxford University Press.

Schacter, Daniel L. 1995. *Memory Distortion: How Minds, Brains, and Societies Reconstruct the Past.* Cambridge, Mass.: Harvard University Press.

Schechner, Richard. 2002. *Performance Studies: An Introduction.* New York: Routledge.

Schor, Naomi.1995. "Fetishism and Its Ironies." In *Bad Objects: Essays Popular and Unpopular,* 101–7. Durham, N.C.: Duke University Press.

Schudson, Michael. 1995. "Dynamics of Distortion in Collective Memory." In *Memory Distortion: How Minds, Brains, and Societies Reconstruct the Past,* 346–64. Cambridge, Mass.: Harvard University Press.

Scott, Joan. 1992. "Experience." In *Feminists Theorize the Political,* ed. Judith Butler and Joan Scott, 22–40. New York: Routledge.

Semprún, Jorge. 1963. *Le grand voyage.* Paris: Gallimard.

———. 1964. *The Long Voyage.* Trans. Richard Seaver. New York: Schocken Books.

———. 1967. *L'Evanouissement.* Paris: Gallimard.

———. 1976. *El largo viaje.* Trans. Jacqueline Conte and Rafael Conte. Barcelona: Seix Barral.

———. 1977. *Autobiografía de Federico Sánchez.* Barcelona: Planeta.

———. 1979. *El desvanecimiento.* Trans. Javier Albiñana. Barcelona: Planeta.

———. 1980. *Quel beau dimanche!* Paris: Grasset et Fasquelle.

———. 1981. *Aquel domingo.* Trans. Javier Albiñana. Barcelona: Planeta.

———. 1982. *What a Beautiful Sunday!* Trans. Alan Sheridan. New York: Harcourt Brace Jovanovich.

———. 1986a. *La montagne blanche.* Paris: Gallimard.

———. 1986b. *La montaña blanca.* Madrid: Alfaguara.

———. 1993a. *Federico Sánchez se despide de ustedes.* Barcelona: Tusquets.

———. 1993b. *Federico Sánchez vous salue bien.* Paris: Grasset et Fasquelle.

———. 1994a. *L'Écriture ou la vie.* Paris: Gallimard.

———. 1994b. *Una tumba en las nubes: discurso con la ocasión del Premio de la Paz.* Barcelona: Tusquets.

———. 1995a. *L'Écriture et la vie.* Dirs. Patrick Rotman and Laurent Perrin. Production Cinétévé and Fabienne Servan-Schreiber.

———. 1995b. *La escritura o la vida.* Trans. Thomas Kauf. Barcelona: Tusquets.

———. 1995c. *Mal et modernité suivi de ". . . Vous avez une tombe au creux des nuages . . ."* Paris: Climats.

———. 1997. *Literature or Life*. Trans. Linda Coverdale. New York: Viking Press.
———. 1998a. *Adieu, vive clarté*. . . . Paris: Gallimard.
———. 1998b. *Adios, luz de veranos*. . . . Trad. Javier Albiñana. Barcelona: Tusquets.
———. 2001a. *Le mort qu'il faut*. Paris: Gallimard.
———. 2001b. *Viviré con su nombre, morirá con el mío*. Trans. Carlos Pujol. Barcelona: Tusquets.
———. 2003. *Veinte años y un día*. Barcelona: Tusquets.
Shaw, Christopher, and Malcolm Chase, eds. 1989. *The Imagined Past: History and Nostalgia*. Manchester, England: Manchester University Press.
Showalter, Elaine. 1985. *The Female Malady*. New York: Pantheon Books.
Silk, Sally Margaret. 1992. "Writing the Holocaust/Writing Travel: The Space of Representation in Jorge Semprun's *Le Grand Voyage*." *CLIO: A Journal of Literature, History, and the Philosophy of History* 22: 53–65.
Silva, Emilio, and Santiago Macías. 2003. *Las fosas de Franco: los republicanos que el dictador dejó en las cunetas*. Madrid: Ediciones Temas de Hoy.
Silverman, Kaja. 1996. *The Threshold of the Visible World*. New York: Routledge.
Sinnigen, Jack. 1982. *Narrativa e ideología*. Madrid: Nuestra Cultura.
Smith, Sidonie. 1987. *A Poetics of Women's Autobiography: Marginality and the Fictions of Self-Representation*. Bloomington: Indiana University Press.
———. 1998. "Performativity, Autobiographical Practice, Resistance." In *Women, Autobiography, Theory: A Reader*, ed. Sidonie Smith and Julia Watson, 108–15. Madison: University of Wisconsin Press.
Sobejano, Gonzalo. 1970. *Novela española de nuestro tiempo: en busca del pueblo perdido*. Madrid: Prensa Española.
———. 1983. "Teoría de la novela en la novela española última: Martín-Santos, Benet, Juan y Luis Goytisolo." In *Aspekte der Hispania im 19. und 20. Jahrhundert: Akten des Deutschen Hispanistentages*, ed. Dieter Kremer, 11–31. Hamburg: Buske.
———. 1986. "Dos estilos de comparación: Juan Benet, Luis Goytisolo." In *Juan Benet*, ed. Kathleen Vernon, 254–80. Madrid: Taurus.
Solé Tura, Jordi. 1987. "The Spanish Transition to Democracy." In *Spain in the 1980's: The Democratic Transition and a New International Role*, ed. Robert P. Clark and Michael H. Haltzel, 25–34. Cambridge, Mass.: Ballinger.
Sontag, Susan. 1990. *On Photography*. New York: Anchor Books, Doubleday.
Soria Olmedo, Andrés. 2004. "Lorca en Víznar: memoria pública, memoria privada." *El País*, Sept. 17. http://www.elpais.es.
Soto-Fernández, Liliana. 1996. *La autobiografía ficticia en Miguel de Unamuno, Carmen Martín Gaite y Jorge Semprún*. Madrid: Pliegos.
Spires, Robert. 1984. "Juan Benet's Poetics of Open Spaces." In *Critical Approaches to the Writings of Juan Benet*, ed. Roberto C. Manteiga, David K. Herzberger, and Malcom A. Compitello, 1–7. Hanover, N.H.: University Press of New England.
Steiner, George. 1967. *Language and Silence: Essays on Language, Literature, and the Inhuman*. New York: Atheneum.
Subirats, Eduardo. 1990. "Moderna España." *El País*, Dec. 3. http://www.elpais.es.
Summerhill, Stephen J. 1984. "Prohibition and Transgression in *Volverás a Región* and *Una meditación*." In *Critical Approaches to the Writings of Juan Benet*, ed. Roberto

C. Manteiga, David K. Herzberger, and Malcom A. Compitello, 93–108. Hanover, N.H.: University Press of New England.

Todorov, Svetan. 2000. *Los abusos de la memoria.* Barcelona: Paidós.

Torok, Maria. 1994. "Story of Fear: The Symptoms of Phobia—The Return of the Repressed or the Return of the Phantom?" In *The Shell and the Kernel,* ed. and trans. Nicholas T. Rand, vol. 1, 177–86. Chicago: Chicago University Press.

Torres Nebrera, Gregorio. 1996. *Los espacios de la memoria: la obra literaria de María Teresa León.* Madrid: Ediciones de la Torre.

Tsuchiya, Akiko. 1998. "Reflections on Historiography in Montserrat Roig's *L'hora violeta.*" *Arizona Journal of Hispanic Cultural Studies* 2:163–74.

Tusell, Javier. 1999. "La memoria y el encono." *El País,* Sept. 11. http://www.elpais.es.

———. 2003. "La reconciliación española." *Claves de razón práctica* 132: 32–39.

Ugarte, Michael. 1998. "Women and Exile: The Civil War Autobiographies of Constancia de la Mora and María Teresa León." *Letras Peninsulares* 11.1 (Spring): 207–22.

Valdes, Mario J., ed. 1991. *A Ricoeur Reader: Reflection and Imagination.* Toronto: University of Toronto Press.

Valenzuela, Javier. 2002. "El despertar tras la amnesia." *El País,* Nov. 2. http://www.elpais.es.

Vásquez, Mary S. 1984. "The Creative Task: Existential Self-Invention in *Una meditación.*" In *Critical Approaches to the Writings of Juan Benet,* ed. Roberto C. Manteiga, David K. Herzberger, and Malcom A. Compitello, 64–71. Hanover, N.H.: University Press of New England.

Vázquez Montalbán, Manuel. 1991. "La literatura española en la construcción de la ciudad democrática." *Revista de Occidente* 122–23: 125–33.

———. 1992. *Autobiografía del general Franco.* Barcelona: Planeta.

Vallespín, Fernando. 1999. "Pretérito imperfecto." *El País,* Sept. 11. http://www.elpais.es.

Verdery, Katherine. 1999. *The Political Lives of Dead Bodies: Reburial and Postsocialist Change.* New York: Columbia University Press.

Vernon, Kathleen M., ed. 1986. *Juan Benet.* Madrid: Taurus.

———. 1989. "El lenguaje de la memoria en la narrativa española contemporánea." In *Actas del IX Congreso de la Asociación Internacional de Hispanistas,* ed. Sebastian Neumeister, vol. 2, 429–37. Frankfort: Vervuert.

Vilá, Dani. 2003. "La transición española se basó 'en la amnistía y en la amnesia,' dice Semprún." *La Vanguardia,* April 26. http://www.lavanguardia.es.

Vilarós, Teresa. 1998. *El mono del desencanto: una crítica cultural de la transición española (1973–1993).* Madrid: Siglo Veintiuno.

Vitzthum, Carlta, and John Carreyrou. 2004. "The General's Ghost: Among Spaniards, Al Qaeda Attacks Awaken Old Feuds; In Anger, Voters Linked Conservative Government With Franco's Regime." *The Wall Street Journal,* March 26. http://www.wsj.com.

Vosburg, Nancy. 2001. "The Tapestry of a Feminist Life: María Teresa León (1903–88)." In *Recovering Spain's Feminist Tradition,* ed. Lisa Vollendorf, 260–77. New York: The Modern Language Association of America.

Wescott, Julia Lupinacci. 1984. "Subversion of Character Conventions in Benet's Trilogy." In *Critical Approaches to the Writings of Juan Benet,* ed. Roberto C. Manteiga,

David K. Herzberger, and Malcom A. Compitello, 72–87. Hanover, N.H.: University Press of New England.

Winter, Ulrich. 2005. " 'Localizar a los muertos' y 'reconocer al Otro': Lugares de memoria(s) en la cultura española contemporánea." In *Casa encantada: lugares de memoria en la España constitucional (1978–2004)*, ed. Joan Ramon Resina and Ulrich Winter, 17–39. Frankfort: Vervuert.

Wright, Elizabeth. 1989. *Postmodern Brecht: A Re-Presentation*. New York: Routledge.

Ximénez de Sandoval. 2004. "La memoria histórica tras las rejas." *El País*, Oct. 17. http://www.elpais.es.

Yates, Frances A. 1966. *The Art of Memory*. London: Pimlico.

Young, James E. 1993. *The Texture of Memory: Holocaust Memorials and Meaning*. New Haven, Conn.: Yale University Press.

———. 2000. *At Memory's Edge: After-Images of the Holocaust in Contemporary Art and Architecture*. New Haven, Conn.: Yale University Press.

———. 2004. "Teaching German Memory and Countermemory: The End of the Holocaust Monument in Germany" In *Teaching the Representation of the Holocaust*, ed. Marianne Hirsch and Irene Kacandes, 274–85. New York: The Modern Language Association of America.

Zambrano, María. 1990. *Los bienaventurados*. Madrid: Siruela.

Zatlin, Phyllis. 1988. "Passivity and Immobility: Patterns of Inner Exile in Postwar Spanish Novels Written by Women." *Letras Femeninas* 14.1–2: 3–9.

Zelizer, Barbie. 1998. *Remembering to Forget: Holocaust Memory through the Camera's Eye*. Chicago: University of Chicago Press.

Index

Abellán, José Luis, 314 n. 40
Abraham, Nicolas, 236–37, 244–245
absence, 54, 96–97, 193, 196, 201–2, 209, 223, 248
act(s) of memory, 46, 146, 175, 243–45, 256
Adorno, Theodor W., 71
Aguilar, Paloma, 24, 32–33, 35, 39, 306 n. 19, 307 nn. 21, and 24
Alberti, Rafael, 142–43, 147, 162, 321 n. 18, 322 n. 23, 331 n. 4
Alcazar, 118, 316 n. 16
Alianza de Intelectuales Antifascistas, 147, 318–19 n. 7
amnesia, 331–32 n. 5; collective, 24, 39; culture of, 23, 171, 176; transition to democracy and, 143. *See also* forgetting.
Amnesty International, 41, 301 n. 7; 2005 report on Spain, 30–31, 306 n. 20
Amnesty Law (1977), 23, 31, 39
Andalucía, 305–6 n. 19
Anderson, Benedict, 317 n. 22
"angel del hogar," 152
Anteproyecto de ley por la que se reconocen y amplían derechos..., 281–98, 306–7 n. 21
Apter, Emily, 199–200
Aranguren, José Luis, 303–4 n. 15
Archivo de la Guerra Civil, 305 n. 19
Argentina, 14, 20, 48, 323 n. 27
Armengou, Montse, 33–34, 37, 300 n. 4, 301–2 n. 10
ARMH. *See* Asociación para la Recuperación de la Memoria Histórica
ars memorativa, 66–67
ashes, 95–96, 138
Asociación de Directores de Escena de España, 319 n. 7
Asociación de Familiares y Amigos de la Fosa Común de Oviedo, 300–301 n. 6, 323 n. 27
Asociación para la Recuperación de la Memoria Histórica (ARMH), 29, 31–32, 41, 300–301 n. 6, 301–2 n. 10, 306–7 n. 21; exhumation and, 20–22, 36–38, 44–45, 280, 299–300 n. 3, 321 n. 21
Atocha bombings, 13–14, 28, 60, 299 n. 1
Atxaga, Bernardo, 273, 336 n. 2
Aub, Max, 320 n. 16, 331 n. 4
Auschwitz, 168
autobiographical writing, 86, 269; ethical nature of, 86; gender and, 154–55; León and, 149, 157–58, 164, 166, 319 n. 9, 320 nn. 13 and 15; Muñoz Molina and, 332 n. 7; Semprún and, 310–11 n. 6; shifting pronouns in, 319 n. 9; unified self in, 90, 91–92
awakening, 242, 254–55, 313 n. 27
Aznar, José María, 27, 321–22 n. 22
Aznar Soler, Manuel, 318 n. 5

Bakhtin, Mikhail, 153, 155, 203, 234
Bal, Mieke, 47, 146, 243–44
Balibrea, Mari Paz, 144–45, 170, 172, 322 n. 24
Barral, Carlos, 92
Barthes, Roland, 201, 249, 252–53
Basque region, 26, 305 n. 19. *See also* ETA (Euskadi Ta Askatasuna)
Belis, Ricard, 33, 34, 37, 300 n. 4, 301–2 n. 10
Bellver, Catherine, 185, 325–26 n. 18
Benet, Juan, 102–41, 179, 316 nn. 12 and 13; ambiguity in, 109; chronology and, 131–32, 136; exile and, 145; the fantastic in, 111–12; Faulkner and,

Benet, Juan (*continued*)
336n. 20; history and, 132; language and, 103–4, 107, 129–31, 137; lyricism and, 111; memory and, 103–4, 106, 132–33, 160; narrative and, 109, 316n. 9; the *nouveau roman* and, 315n. 4; order and, 123–24, 126, 131–32, 136, 137; the *pharmakon* and, 315nn. 1, 326n. 29; progress and, 134; realism and, 104, 107, 110–11, 130, 315n. 3; ruins and, 132–33, 140; self-reflexivity in, 108; Spanish civil war and, 107–8, 118, 325–26n. 18; subversivity of, 63, 109, 118–19; temporality and, 106, 122–23, 131–32, 136, 138, 315nn. 1 and 5, 316nn. 9 and 14; trauma and, 326n. 29; *Volverás a Región*, 63, 107–41, 145, 157–58, 160, 169, 211, 226–27, 269, 270, 325–26n. 18, 313n. 27, 315n. 1, 316n. 20, 326n. 29; "wounded spaces," 107, 129, 136, 141; writing and, 103–5, 115

Benjamin, Walter, 18, 137, 252; "angel of history," 133–34, 179, 215–16, 260; *The Arcades Project*, 253–54; "Copernican turn of remembrance," 253–54, 257–58; *eingedenken*, 17; on history, 16–17, 55–56, 133, 134–36, 177, 179, 215, 229; on memory, 16–17, 57, 178, 253, 259–60, 271; on photography, 257; on progress, 133–34, 177, 215, 261–62; "Theses on the Philosophy of History," 16–17, 133

Benson, Ken, 125–26, 132
Benstock, Shari, 153, 155
Bergson, Henri, 105–6, 121, 315n. 5
Bermejo, Benito, 88
Bertrand de Muñoz, Maryse, 275
Blanchot, Maurice, 53–55, 71, 82–83, 92, 107, 131, 136, 201
Blanco, Alda, 168, 319–20n. 11
Bosnia, 49
Brecht, Bertholdt, 165, 321n. 18
Brodsky, Joseph, 220
Buchenwald, 63, 67
burial, 14, 37–39, 212–13, 300–301n. 6, of exiles, 167–70; improper, 271, 308n. 26; mass graves, 14, 49, 179, 268–69, 279–80; symbolic, 271; text as cemetery, 168–70, 180, 212–13, 271. *See also* exhumation; ghosts; mass graves

Butler, Judith, 152–53

"Camp de la Bota," 305n. 19
canon formation, 144–45
Carrier, Peter, 98
Carroll, Lewis, 182
Caruth, Cathy, 161–62, 209, 311n. 9
Casanova, Julián, 300n. 4
Castilla, 26
Castillo, Pilar del, 26
Castor, 66–67, 91, 96
Castresana Fernández, Carlos, 14
Cataluña, 26, 305n. 19
Causa general, 306n. 20
Cebrián, Juan Luis, 327n. 39
Cela, Camilo José, 303–4n. 15
Celan, Paul, 68–69, 72, 82, 84, 96
Celaya, Gabriel, 229
cemetery, text as, 168–70, 180, 212–13, 271
censorship, 92–>94
Cercas, Javier, 273
Cervantes Saavedra, Miguel de, 162
Chacón, Dulce, 273
Chile, 20, 38, 52, 54–55, 61, 323n. 27
chronological order, 131; death and, 82; in *El jinete polaco*, 259–60; in *El largo viaje*, 75–76, 78–79; mastery and, 81; in *Quel beau dimanche!*, 80–81; in *Volverás a Región*, 109–10, 121–22, 131–32, 136–37
Cicero, 66–67, 91, 309nn. 1 and 2
cinders, 96, 138. *See* ashes
civil war. *See* Spanish civil war, the
Claudín, Fernando, 67
collective amnesia, 24, 39
collective memory, 272, 309n. 38; *dissensus* and, 42; in *El jinete polaco*, 231, 236; in *L'hora violeta*, 208, 219, 221–22; in *Memoria de la Melancolía*, 155–56, 160, 168, 174–75, 177, 320n. 14; personal memory and, 48, 60, 155–56; in Spanish society, 14, 40, 304n. 16. *See also* postmemory
Colmeiro, José, 23, 25–27
Comité de Agitación y Propaganda Interior, 147
Communism, fall of, 47
Communist Party. *See* Spanish Communist Party
concentration camps, 63, 67, 88, 93, 269, 310n. 5, 313n. 32; Auschwitz, 168;

Buchenwald, 98; in *El jinete polaco*, 240; in *El largo viaje*, 80–81; in *L'hora violeta*, 210; Semprún and, 314 n. 42; Spaniards in, 94, 168, 314 n. 40; in *Volverás a Región*, 114–115. *See also* Semprún Maura, Jorge
congressional decree of 2002, 22–23
congressional decree (proposed) of 2003, 22–23
Consejo Central del Teatro, 147
consejos de guerra, 306–7 n. 21
consensus, 41–42, 43
Constitution of 1978, 303 n. 14
control. *See* mastery
Cornejo-Parriego, Rosalía, 328 n. 44
Corominas, Joan, 171
countermemory, 15, 176–77, 195–96, 213
countermourning, 38, 45, 323 n. 27. *See also* "effective memory"
Crossland, Zoë, 323 n. 27
Cuadernos de Ruedo Ibérico, 67
Cuéntame como pasó, 275
culture of amnesia, 23, 176
culture of memory, 14–15, 60–61, 100–101, 262–63, 267

Dante Alighieri, 84–85
Davies, Catherine, 194, 327 n. 32
death: chronological order and, 82; in *El largo viaje*, 80, 85, 89; in *L'Évanouissement*, 82; photography and, 201–2, 248–51; in *Quel beau dimanche!*, 81–82; self and, 83; survival and, 210; temporality and, 82; in *Volverás a Región*, 138–39
De Lauretis, Teresa, 149
Delbo, Charlotte, 71
deportation. *See* concentration camps; exile
Derrida, Jacques, 93, 96, 138; on the *pharmakon*, 103, 113, 114, 119, 127, 159; *Specters of Marx*, 172, 219, 251–53
desaparecidos, 20–21, 48–49, 54–55, 300 n. 4, 301–2 n. 10,
desire, memory and, 226–28, 230, 232, 243, 266, 331 n. 4, 332 n. 7
desencanto, 31, 183, 204
"desmemoria," 143
disidentification, 63–64, 146, 149, 154–60, 162–63, 165–66, 170, 174,

176–77, 270, 314 n. 45, 319 n. 9, 320 nn. 12, 13, and 16, 322–23 n. 26
dissensus, 42–44, 47
"dos Españas," 33, 336 n. 21
Drost, William, 335 n. 17
Dupláa, Christina, 324–25 n. 8
durée (Bergson), 105–6, 121, 130

"echar en en olvido." *See* forgetting
"effective history," 176–77, 195. *See also* countermourning
eingedenken, 17
Eliot, T. S., 182, 225, 227, 323 n. 3, 332 n. 5
Elordi, Carlos, 332–33 n. 9
"empathic unsettlement," 52–53, 55, 175–77, 184, 220, 272, 275, 277
Epps, Brad, 108, 317 n. 20
Escuela Técnica Teatral, 147
ETA (Euskadi Ta Askatasuna), 28
European Council, 307 n. 23
exhumation, 14, 43, 47, 54, 170, 179, 279, 300 n. 5, 304 n. 16; the ARMH and, 21, 29, 36–38, 44–45, 280, 299–300 n. 3, 321–22 n. 22; debates about, 300–301 n. 6, 323 n. 27. *See also* mass graves
exile, 64, 92, 100, 142–43, 269; burial and, 167–70; canon formation and, 144–45; consciousness of, 321 n. 20; eternal, 73; under the Franco regime, 142–44, 164–67, 170–71, 173–74, 303 n. 14, 318 n. 5, 322 n. 23; gender and, 148–49, 163, 319 n. 8, 328 n. 44; inner, 137–38, 141, 145, 208; in *L'hora violeta*, 208, 214; literature of, 94–95, 170, 322 n. 24; as living death, 167; in *Memoria de la Melancolía*, 149, 153, 156–57, 159, 163, 167–69, 173–80, 319 n. 8; memory and, 176, 208, 270; multiplicity of, 318 n. 3; nation formation and, 144–45, 166–67, 318 n. 3; as *pharmakos*, 159–60; Semprún and, 310 n. 3; in Spanish history, 166–67, 334 n. 15; traumatic memory of, 176, 270. *See also* "homelessness"
"Exilio" exhibit, 317–18 n. 1, 303 n. 14

Fabre, Geneviève, 309 n. 36
Faulkner, William, 45, 104, 228, 266, 336 n. 20
fear, 235–36

Felman, Shoshana, 70, 311 n. 9
feminism. *See* women
Fernández de la Vega, María Teresa, 321–22 n. 22
Fernández de Mata, Ignacio, 44–45, 54
Ferrándiz, Francisco, 44–45
fetishism, 64, 185, 196–201, 203–4, 207, 317 n. 19, 326 n. 29, 327 n. 32
fiction, 87–88; history and, 78, 83–84, 107, 126–27, 133, 186, 210, 223–24, 269, 277–78, 332 n. 7; memory and, 277, 335–36 n. 18; trauma and, 70
figurative language: memory and, 52, 56–60; religious imagery, 135; sewing metaphors, 136; symbolic language, 61; theatrical imagery, 126, 149, 162, 164; in *Volverás a Región*, 130–32
fissures, 170–73, 322 n. 23
forgetting, 39, 41–42, 49, 53, 96, 158, 171, 184, 308 n. 27; amnesia, 23, 39, 143, 171, 176, 331–32 n. 5; historical, 143; memory and, 35, 188, 202, 304 n. 16, 335–36 n. 18; nation formation and, 167; "pact of forgetting," 24, 40; politically imposed, 171, 173–74, 176–78; in Spain, 19–45; theories of, 45–61
"Foro por la Memoria," 299–300 n. 3, 300–301 n. 6
Fort-Da game, 70, 72, 128–29, 160, 317 n. 20
Foster, Hal, 49–50
Foucault, Michel, 15, 146, 176–77, 195, 213
Fraga Iribarne, Manuel, 124
fragmentary objects, 57, 135–37. *See also* newspapers
frames, 187–88, 195, 201, 204
Franco, Francisco, 14, 19–20; death of, 204, 304 n. 16; in *L'hora violeta*, 191–92; pseudoautobiography of (*Autobiografía del General Franco*), 278–79; statues of, 304–5 n. 18
Franco regime, the, 14, 24, 28; 1964 commemeoration, 35–36; "25 años de paz" (1964), 123–24, 172; censorship by, 92–94; condemnation of, 21–23, 307 n. 23; contemporary perception of, 33–35; crimes against humanity by, 30–31; exile under, 142–43, 170–71, 173–74; the family under, 118–19; forgetting and, 176; as genocidal, 300 n. 4; historiography and, 132, 139, 190, 317 n. 21; ideology of, 63, 118–19, 137, 157–58, 191–92, 227, 317 n. 21; last phase of, 34; in literature, 336 n. 21; memory of, 52, 171, 273–76, 278, 301–2 n. 10, 302–3 n. 11, 305–6 n. 19, 306–7 n. 21; monuments of, 307 n. 21; mythologized view of, 275–77; progress and, 157–58; religious rhetoric of, 135; repression by, 17–19, 24–26, 29, 300 n. 4; rhetoric of, 33–35, 118, 124, 135, 157–58, 172–74, 271, 317 n. 21; slogans of, 33–35; symbols of, 307 n. 21; transition to democracy and, 301 n. 8, 325 n. 15; victims of, 17–18, 29; violence by, 26; women's plight under, 193–94
Frazer, James George, 113–14, 316 nn. 12 and 13
Frazier, Lessie Jo, 38, 323 n. 27
Freud, Sigmund, 16, 72, 96, 268, 316 n. 13; *Beyond the Pleasure Principle*, 69–70, 317 n. 20; on the fetish, 196–98; on the *Fort-Da* game, 70, 72, 128–29, 160–61, 317 n. 20; on melancholia, 172–73; "Remembering, Repeating and Working-Through," 50–51; on repetition, 69–70, 75; on "the return of the repressed," 69–70; on trauma, 69
Friedlander, Saul, 16, 50, 53–55, 58
Frisby, David, 134, 137, 257, 259–60

Galdós, Benito Pérez, 166
García Lorca, Federico, 300–301 n. 6, 331 n. 4
Garzón, Baltasar, 20–21
gaze, the, 189, 191, 215–17, 252–53. *See also* vision
gender, 148–49, 320 n. 12; autobiography and, 154–55; exile and, 148–49, 163, 319 n. 8, 328 n. 44; the fetish and, 198–99; in *L'hora violeta*, 186, 193, 198–99, 324–25 n. 8; madness and, 194; in *Memoria de la Melancolía*, 149, 151, 163, 319–20 n. 11, 319 n. 8; nationalism and, 323 n. 4; patriarchy and, 319–20 n. 11, 320 n. 12; performative nature of, 152–53; in post-Franco Spain, 183; in Spanish

society, 319–20 n. 11; vision and, 189–90, 216
generación de los nietos de los vencidos, 32–34, 36–37, 42–43, 99, 265, 272–73, 280
Generation of 1968, 331 n. 3
Generation of 1981, 331 n. 3
ghosts, 38–39, 176–77, 229–30, 239, 244–48, 253, 268–69; in *El jinete polaco,* 235–36, 239, 249, 251–52, 255, 266, 317 n. 23, 322 n. 23; exiles as, 144, 176–77; Labanyi on, 169, 260, 268; in *L'hora violeta,* 196, 212–14, 219–20; in *Memoria de la Melancolía,* 146, 167, 169–70, 172, 176–77, 180; "philosophy of the phantasm," 146, 167, 176; photography and, 249–50; in *Volverás a Región,* 138–39
ghost stories, 236
Ginzburg, Carlo, 48
globalization, 274–75
González, Felipe, 67, 303 n. 12
Goya y Lucientes, Francisco José de, 166
Goyri, Jimena, 320 n. 12
Goyri, María, 150, 320 n. 12
Goytisolo, Juan, 319 n. 9, 320 n. 13, 336 n. 21
Gracia, Jordi, 272–73
Graham, Helen, 32, 280
Grosz, Elizabeth, 198–99
Grup d'Estudis de l'Exili Literari, 318 n. 5
Guerillas del Teatro, 147, 160, 162–63, 180, 318–19 n. 7
Guerra, Alfonso, 303 n. 14
Gulf War (1991), 262–63, 274

Halbwachs, Maurice, 155–56, 222, 309 n. 38
Haro Tecglen, Eduardo, 303–4 n. 15
"heritage industry," 46, 275
Herzberger, David, 94–95, 111, 124, 132, 241–42, 264, 315 n. 7, 316 n. 11, 317 n. 21, 336 n. 21
"heteropathic recollection," 221–23, 229, 241, 330 n. 74, 332 n. 6
Himno de Riego, 27
Hirsch, Marianne, 229–30, 237–38, 245, 248–49, 330 n. 74
Historians' Debate of 1986, 48

historiographic metafiction, 226. *See also* metafiction
history, 130; alternative versions of, 185–90, 195, 223–24, 227–28, 254–55, 257; ambiguity and, 132; Benjamin on, 16–17, 55–56, 133; countermemory and, 176–77; family, 229; fiction and, 78, 83–84, 107, 126–27, 133, 186, 210, 223–24, 269, 277–78, 332 n. 7; forgetting and, 143; imagination and, 195, 223–24; in *L'hora violeta,* 185–89, 215; literature and, 277–78; memory and, 143, 222; myth and, 275–76; performativity and, 92; in *Volverás a Región,* 134–35, 213
Hodgkin, Katharine, 311 n. 8
Holocaust, the, 16, 67, 84, 100; ethical memory of, 92; interest in, 47–48; literature and, 70–71, 77–78, 92, 94–95, 311 n. 11; postmemory and, 229–30; representation and, 70–72, 92, 311 n. 11; Spaniards and, 314 n. 40; survivors' discourse, 70; temporality and, 83; writing of, 70–72. *See also* Holocaust studies
Holocaust studies, 16, 49, 50. *See also* Holocaust, the
Holocaust (television series), 48
"homelessness," 153–54. *See also* exile
horror, language and, 104–5
human rights, 21, 31–32, 41; human rights law, 31; human rights violations, 20, 30–31, 38, 41, 306 n. 20
Hutcheon, Linda, 226, 331 n. 2
Huyssen, Andreas, 46–50, 274; on "memory culture," 262–63; "productive remembering," 263–64; on "twilight memories", 183–86, 188, 223

identity: in *El jinete polaco,* 264; individual versus family/national, 154–55; in *L'hora violeta,* 183; in *Memoria de la Melancolía,* 156; memory and, 15–16; performativity of, 153–55; social constitution of, 155. *See also* self
Ilie, Paul, 137–38
imagination, 195; in *El jinete polaco,* 264; history and, 223–24; memory and, 195, 223–24, 264
International Human Rights Law, 21

intertextuality, 185, 187, 334 n. 14, 334–35 n. 16
Irwin-Zarecka, Iwona, 188

Janet, Pierre, 268
Jay, Martin, 177
Jelin, Elizabeth, 32, 42–43
Johnson, Kathleen, 77
Juan Carlos, King, 26
Juliá, Santos, 24–25, 27, 32–34, 39–43, 300 n. 4, 303–4 n. 15, 308 n. 27
Junta de Ampliación de Estudios, 147
Junta de Incautación del Tesoro Artístico, 147

Klee, Paul, 133
Kolbert, Elizabeth, 321–22 n. 22
Kristeva, Julia, 148

Labanyi, Jo, 39, 170, 212–13, 228, 245, 265–66, 316 n. 11, 317 n. 21; on *El jinete polaco*, 245, 257–58; on ghosts, 169, 260, 268; on *Volverás a Región*, 116–17, 134
Lacan, Jacques, 129
LaCapra, Dominick, 16, 50–52, 55, 58, 175, 220
Landera, José Antonio, 37–38
Landera Cachón, José, 37–38
Landman, Thomas, 99
Lang, Berel, 311 n. 11
Langer, Lawrence, 82
language, 54, 68–69; Benet and, 129, 130–31, 137; disenchantment with, 205; as a homeland, 68–69, 73–74; horror and, 104–5; loss of faith in, 206–7; memory and, 103–4, 311 n. 8; opacity of, 104, 107, 311 n. 8; Semprún and, 73–74; silence and, 84; symbolic, 61; trauma and, 69–70, 84, 129. *See also* figurative language
Latin America: *desaparecidos* in, 48–49; mass graves in, 323 n. 27; Pinochet affair, 20–21. *See also specific countries*
Laub, Dori, 70, 220, 311 n. 9
law of historical memory, 29–30, 280–98, 306–7 n. 21, 307 n. 23, 321–22 n. 22. *See also Anteproyecto de ley por la que se reconocen y amplían derechos . . .*
Lejeune, Philippe, 90

León, María Teresa, 63–64, 142–81; act(s) of memory in, 175; Alberti and, 147, 321 n. 18, 322 n. 23; Alzheimer's and, 181; audience and, 165–66; autobiographical writing and, 149, 157–58, 164, 166, 320 nn. 13 and 15; biography of, 146–47; Brechtian acting and, 165–66; childhood and adolescence of, 149–54, 157–58, 162–63, 174; death of, 181; dialogic narrative in, 153; disidentification and, 146, 149, 154–60, 162–63, 165–66, 170, 174, 176–77, 270, 314 n. 45, 319 n. 9, 320 nn. 12, and 16, 322–23 n. 26; "El teatro internacional," 319 n. 10; ethical responsibility and, 164, 168–69, 174; exile and, 148, 153, 156–57, 159–60, 163–69, 174–80, 319 n. 8; family history of, 153–54; feminism and, 319 n. 7, 322–23 n. 26; gender and, 148–49, 151–53, 319 n. 8, 319–20 n. 11; "homelessness" and, 153–54; identity and, 154–55; *Juego limpio*, 318 n. 4, 318–19 n. 7, 320 n. 13; *La historia tiene la palabra*, 318 n. 4; mastery and, 320–21 n. 17; melancholia and, 173, 320–21 n. 17, 323 n. 27; *Memoria de la Melancolía*, 63–64, 144, 203, 211–13, 269–70, 314 n. 45, 318 n. 4, 325–26 n. 18,; memory and, 148, 158–61, 174–76, 180–81, 203, 220–21, 314 n. 47, 320 n. 13, 320–21 n. 17, 322–23 n. 26; narrative and, 160–61, 316 n. 15; performativity and, 63–64, 146, 152–53, 161–62, 165–66, 180; point of view and, 154–55; political activism of, 147; Premio María Teresa León para Autoras Dramáticas, 319 n. 7; ruins and, 148, 178; Spanish civil war and, 325–26 n. 18; Spanish Communist Party and, 147, 321 n. 19; subversivity of, 157–58, 173, 175, 177; temporality and, 148; theater and, 146–47, 153, 160, 162–66, 318–19 n. 7, 319 nn. 8 and 10; theatrical imagery in, 149, 162, 164, 175; theatricality and, 153, 180; theatrical works of, 318–19 n. 7; "transmemoria" and, 174–75, 178, 184, 229; traumatic memory and, 160–61; "vigilant memory" and, 168; writing and, 159–60; writing as elegy in, 168

Les Temps Modernes, 67
Levi, Primo, 72, 311 n. 13
Levinas, Emmanuel, 86
"Ley de memoria histórica." *See Anteproyecto de ley por la que se reconocen y amplían derechos . . .;* law of historical memory
lieux de mémoire, 16, 59–60, 97–100, 168–70, 176, 179–80, 247–48, 269–70, 273, 309 nn. 36 and 37. *See also* places of memory
López, Helena, 322–23 n. 26
Lorca, Federico García, 147
Loriga, Ray, 304–5 n. 18
"Los campos de concentración de Franco," 303–4 n. 15
Loureiro, Angel, 86, 148, 164, 174, 310–11 n. 6, 311 n. 13, 313 n. 27, 318 n. 4, 320–21 n. 17, 321 n. 19
lugares de reconocimiento, 43–45, 47, 98–100
Lyotard, Jean-François, 46

Machado, Antonio, 331 n. 4
madness, 117, 119, 194
Madres de la Plaza de Mayo (Argentina), 323 n. 27
Maetzu, María de, 320 n. 12
Mannoni, Octave, 207
Manrique, Jorge, 242
March 11, 2004, bombings, 13–14, 28, 60, 299 n. 1
Marcha Real, 27
Marco, Enric, 88
Marías, Javier, 303–4 n. 15
Martin, Biddy, 154
Martín Gaite, Carmen, 186
Martín-Santos, Luis, 94
Martín Villa, Rodolfo, 301–2 n. 10
mass graves, 14, 18–21, 47, 49, 54, 169–70, 179, 268–69, 271, 279–80, 300 n. 5, 304 n. 16, 321 n. 21, 321–22 n. 22; exhumation; the ARMH and, 20, 29, 36–38, 43–45, 299–300 n. 3; debates about, 300–301 n. 6, 323 n. 27. *See also* burial
mastery, 79–80; chronological order and, 81; in *El largo viaje,* 75–76, 79–80, 88–89; the fetish and, 199–200; in *L'écriture ou la vie,* 87–88; in *Memoria de la Melancolía,* 320–21 n. 17; in *Quel beau dimanche!,* 80–81; repetition and, 75–76; trauma and, 92, 161–62, 320–21 n. 17. *See also* order
Mauthausen, Amical, 88
McCole, John, 17
McDonough, Peter, 31–32
Medina Domínguez, Alberto, 204–7, 327 n. 39
melancholia, 148, 172–73, 237–38, 320–21 n. 17, 322 n. 24, 323 n. 27
"memoria insatisfecha." *See* "unsatisfied memory"
"memoria vigilante." *See* "vigilant memory"
Memorial democrático, 305
memory, 15, 44, 50–51, 223, 268–69, 277, 309 n. 1; affective dimension of, 175–76; awakening and, 242, 254–55; in *Beatus Ille,* 225–26; Benjamin on, 178; Bergson on, 105–6; blindness and, 194–95; cognitive dimension of, 52–53; collective, 14, 40, 48, 60, 155–56, 174–75, 219, 221–22, 231, 272, 304 n. 16, 309 n. 38, 320 n. 14; commodification of, 265–66; creative nature of, 127, 246; crisis of, 183–84; desire and, 226–28, 230, 232, 243, 331 n. 4, 332 n. 7; distortion of, 58, 309 n. 35; in *El jinete polaco,* 230–236, 238–39, 241, 243–49, 252, 254–56, 258–60, 263–64, 266, 331 n. 4, 332 nn. 5 and 7, 332–33 n. 9, 335–36 n. 18, 336 n. 20; in *El largo viaje,* 74–80, 83, 85, 88–92, 94–99, 139–40, 316 n. 17; ethical, 86–87, 92; exile and, 176, 208, 270; fiction and, 335–36 n. 18; forgetting and, 35, 188, 202, 304 n. 16, 335–36 n. 18; frames and, 188; hierarchies of, 40; history and, 143, 222; identity and, 15–16; imagination and, 195, 223–24, 264–65; intergenerational, 229, 231, 236–37, 239–40, 314 n. 47, 322 n. 25, 330 n. 74; language and, 103–4, 311 n. 8; in *L'hora violeta,* 18, 184–224, 190–91, 194–95, 202–3, 208, 214, 218–23, 247, 323 n. 4, 327 n. 32, 328 n. 43, 332–33 n. 9; mediation of, 49–50, 183, 239–40, 245–48, 253, 264–65, 311 n. 8, 333 n. 13; melancholia and, 172–73; in *Memoria de la Melancolía,* 148,

memory (*continued*)
157–61, 174–76, 180–81, 203, 320n.
13, 320–21n. 17, 322–23n. 26, 314n.
47; multivocal, 202–3, 234; Muñoz
Molina, Antonio, 225–36; Muñoz
Molina on, 227–28, 336n. 19;
narrative and, 58; performativity and,
142–81, 164; *pharmakon* of, 102–41,
106–7, 109–10, 113, 116, 127, 159,
315n. 7; photography and, 247–51,
256–57, 336n. 19; repetition and,
50–51; rhetoric and, 66–67; Roig on,
336n. 18; self-reflexivity and, 51,
59–60; Semprún and, 66–101; in Spain,
19–45, 32, 50–51, 98; subversivity of,
125, 190–91, 195; "theatre of
memory," 180; theories of, 45–61;
transmission of, 15, 231, 236–37,
239–40, 314n. 47, 322n. 25, 330n. 74,
332–33n. 9, 333n. 13; trauma and,
66–101, 160–61, 184, 209–10, 218–21,
243–44, 269–70, 277–78, 309n. 2,
311n. 9, 314n. 47, 333nn. 10 and 13;
traumatic, 14; "twilight," 182–86, 188,
223, 243; vision and, 242–43; in
Volverás a Región, 125, 132–33,
139–40, 315n. 1; working through,
15–16, 50–55, 58, 73, 238–39, 271;
writing and, 103–4. *See also* "act(s) of
memory"; "heteropathic
recollection"; "unsatisfied memory";
"vigilant memory"; culture of
memory; memory practices; places of
memory; postmemory; remembrance
memory practices, 46–47, 52, 262–63,
271; figurative language and, 52;
metaphors for, 56–60, post-
Holocaust, 55; self-reflexivity of, 47
memory studies, 15–16, 48, 299n. 2
Menéndez Pidal, Ramón, 150
metafiction, 15, 226, 331n. 2. *See also*
meta-memory texts; self-reflexivity
meta-memory texts, 15, 53–54, 58,
60–62, 87, 101, 202, 268, 273, 659; *El
jinete polaco*, 243, 267; *El largo viaje*,
93, 100; *L'écriture ou la vie*, 73, 100;
L'hora violeta, 223; *Memoria de la
Melancolía*, 145, 169, 173, 177;
politically transformative potential of,
268, 276; self-reflexivity of, 268;
twenty-first century, 64–65, 273–75,
279; *Volverás a Región*, 107. *See also*
self-reflexivity
meta-narrative, 73, 75, 77. *See also* self-
reflexivity
metaphor. *See* figurative language
Miguel Strogoff, 240–43, 334–35n. 16
mise en abîme, 77, 185, 200–201, 312n.
22. *See also* self-reflexivity
mirada bòrnia, 215
Misiones Pedagógicas, 147
Moa, Pía, 300n. 4
modernism, 46
Monedero, Juan Carlos, 307–8n. 24
Montero, Isaac, 315n. 3
Morán, Gregorio, 143
Moreiras Menor, Cristina, 171–73, 175,
215, 308n. 26
Moreno-Nuño, Carmen, 301n. 9, 332n.
8, 337n. 3
Morrison, Toni, 18
Moscardó, General, 118, 316n. 16
mourning, 237–38, 322n. 24. *See also*
countermourning
multivocality, 333n. 12
Muñoz Molina, Antonio, 225–67, 322n.
25; autobiographical writing and,
332n. 7; *Beatus Ille*, 225–27, 249;
desire and, 226–28, 230, 232, 266,
331n. 4, 332n. 7; "El hombre habitado
por las voces", 336n. 20; *El jinete
polaco*, 64, 225–26, 228–29, 232–67,
269–72, 274–75, 330n. 74, 331nn. 1
and 4, 331–32n. 5, 332nn. 7 and 8,
334n. 16, 335n. 17, 336n. 20; *El
porvenir de los vencidos*, 229; on exile,
334n. 15; on Faulkner, 336n. 20; fear
and, 235–36; fiction and, 332n. 7;
Generation of 1981 and, 331n. 3;
history and, 332n. 7; identity and,
264; imagination and, 264;
intertextuality in the work of, 334n.
14, 334–35n. 16; "La invención de un
pasado," 227–28, 334n. 15, 336n. 19;
"Memoria y ficción," 335–36n. 18;
memory and, 225–36, 234, 238–39,
241, 243–49, 252, 254–56, 258–60,
263–66, 331n. 4, 331–32n. 5, 332n. 7,
335–36n. 18, 336n. 19; multivocality
and, 234, 333n. 12; narrative and, 244;
photography and, 247–53, 256–57,
270–71, 336n. 19; Planeta Prize and,

225, 228–29, 331–32 n. 5; point of view and, 238–39, 245; postmemory and, 229–30, 232, 238–39, 241, 260, 262, 330 n. 74, 333 n. 12; Premio Nacional de Narrativa and, 331 nn. 1; Real Academia Española de la Lengua and, 331 n. 1 and 4; songs and, 260; temporality and, 255, 258–63; vision and, 252–53
mythology: in *Volverás a Región*, 113–14

Naharro-Calderón, José María, 303 n. 14, 318 n. 3
narrative, 244, 316 nn. 9 and 15; intergenerational, 239–40; memory and, 58; postmodernity and, 46, 49; self-reflexive, 53–54, 73, 312 n. 22; as therapy, 243–44; trauma and, 83–84, 91–92, 94, 209–10, 272, 311 n. 13. *See also* storytelling
Nash, Mary, 152
Nationalist regime. *See* Franco regime
nation formation, 144–45, 166–67
new novel, 104. *See also nouveau roman*
newspapers, 135–37, 157–58, 317 n. 22
Nichols, Geraldine Cleary, 325 n. 15
Nora, Pierre, 16, 59–60, 97–98, 137, 180, 309 nn. 36 and 37
nouveau roman, 104, 315 n. 4
"novel of memory," 95
Nueva Escena, 147
Numancia, 162
"Nunca Más" report (Argentina), 14, 48
Nussbaum, Felicity, 149

O'Meally, Robert, 309 n. 36
order, 115–18, 123–26, 137. *See also* chronological order; mastery
Osiel, Mark, 42
Otto, Rudolf, 84

"Pactos de la Moncloa," 204
Paez, Darío, 304 n. 16
pain, 79, 221–22
palimpsests, 57, 93, 96–97, 139–40, 179, 211–12, 221, 264, 317 n. 23
Pardo Bazán, Emilia, 320 n. 12
Partido Popular, 21–23, 26–28, 306 n. 21, 321–22 n. 22

past, the. *See* history; memory; temporality
Patino, Basilio Martín, 62
Pensky, Max, 257
performativity, 63–64, 313 n. 27; gender and, 152–53; history and, 92; of identity, 153–55; in *Memoria de la Melancolía*, 146, 153, 161–62, 164–66, 180; memory and, 142–81, 164; trauma and, 71, 92, 161–62
Perlman, Michael, 309 n. 2
phantoms. *See* ghosts
pharmakon, the, 63–64, 102–41, 127–29; of memory, 109, 113, 127–28, 134–35, 139–40, 159, 315 n. 7; myth of, 102–3, 114–15; of reading, 140; subversivity of, 119–20; in *Volverás a Región*, 315 n. 1, 326 n. 29; of writing, 113
pharmakos, the, 119–20, 138, 159–60; exile as, 159–60, 166; in *Volverás a Región*, 129
"philosophy of the phantasm," 146, 167, 176
photography, 187, 190–91, 200–201, 231, 245, 252–53, 336 n. 19; death and, 201–2, 248–51, in *El jinete polaco*, 247–49, 250–51, 253, 256–57, 270–71, 335 n. 17; ghosts and, 249–50; in *L'hora violeta*, 270, 327 n. 32; memory and, 250–51, 256–57, 336 n. 19; subversivity of, 257; temporality and, 249
Pinochet, Augusto, 20–21
places of memory, 14, 16, 43–44, 59–60, 97–100, 273, 308–9 n. 31, 309 n. 36; in *El jinete polaco*, 247–48; Francoist, 29, 304–5 n. 18, 305 n. 19, 307 n. 21; in *L'écriture ou la vie*, 99–100; in *L'hora violeta*, 221; in *Memoria de la Melancolía*, 176, 179–80, 220–21; in Spain, 269–70; text as place of memory, 169–70; in *Volverás a Región*, 137–39. *See also lieux de mémoire*;
places of recognition, 43–45, 47, 98, 99–100
Plato, 102–3, 113
point of view, 74, 90, 154–55, 238–39, 245
politics, 205–7
Pollux, 66–67, 91, 96

Pope, Randolph, 316 n. 23
"Portal del Exilio," 142–44, 146, 317–18 n. 1, 322 n. 23
Portelli, Alessandro, 236
postmemory, 64, 225–67, 330 n. 74, 332 n. 6; in *El jinete polaco*, 229–30, 232–36, 238–39, 241, 245, 248, 260, 262–64, 266–67, 330 n. 74, 333 n. 12, 336 n. 20; in *L'hora violeta*, 330 n. 74; origin of the term, 229–30; in post-Franco Spain, 231–32. *See also* collective memory
postmodernism, 46, 228
postmodernity, 46, 49, 274
power. *See* mastery
Prado de Paradiña, 37
Premio María Teresa León para Autoras Dramáticas, 319 n. 7
presence-as-absence, 201–2, 213, 248
Preston, Paul, 304–5 n. 18, 300 n. 4, 316 n. 16
Priaranza del Bierzo, 19, 21
progress: Benjamin on, 133–34; discourse of, 51, 56; Francoist ideology of, 33–35, 157–58, 316 n. 21; questioning of idea of, 46, 48, 133–34, 177, 257, 260–62; in *Volverás a Región*, 136
Proust, Marcel, 312 n. 22
psychoanalysis, 69–70, 128–29, 196–200, 313 n. 27. *See also* Freud, Sigmund
punctum, 252–54

Quinto Centenario del Descubrimiento de América, 25–26

Radstone, Susannah, 311 n. 8
Rajoy, Mariano, 306 n. 21
Ramos, Ramón, 222–23
reading, 140
realism, 94–95, 107, 110–11, 130
recognition, 43–45, 98–100. *See also* places of recognition
reconocimiento. *See also lugares de reconocimiento*
recordar, 17, 53
Reixa, Antón, 273
Rembrandt (Harmensz van Rijn), 232, 335 n. 17
remembrance, 16–19, 45, 53, 57, 173, 212–13, 269, 271, 280. *See also* memory
remembranza, 17, 45. *See also* remembrance
remembrar, 17, 55, 271
rememorar, 17, 55, 271
rememory, 18
Renan, Ernest, 166–67
reparations, 31, 212
repetition, 50–51, 69–70, 160–61, 313 n. 27; mastery and, 75–76; trauma and, 72, 173, 313 n. 27
repression (of the past), 26–28, 42, 69–70, 125, 138–39
Resina, Joan Ramon, 146, 167
responsibility, 86–87, 164, 174, 313 n. 32
Rey, Santiago del, 333 n. 12
Reyes Mate, Manuel, 13–14, 16–17, 36–38, 56–57, 60, 100, 254, 258, 269, 280, 299 n. 1, 314 n. 40
rhetoric, 66–67
Richard, Nelly, 52, 54–56, 61
Ricoeur, Paul, 16, 130–31, 140, 280; on *dissensus*, 42; *Memory, History, Forgetting*, 41–43, 50, 58, 60–61, 169, 308 n. 27; *Time and Narrative*, 78, 83–84, 94
Ridell, María Carmen, 320 n. 15
Rimbaud, Arthur, 333 n. 12
Rivas, Manuel, 273, 336 n. 1
Rodríguez Lozano, Juan, 28
Rodríguez Zapatero, José Luis, 28–29, 32, 39, 321–22 n. 22
Roig, Montserrat, 182–224, 226, 322 n. 25, 323 n. 2; ambivalence and, 208, 215; blindness and, 194–95; Catalan nationalism and, 323 n. 4; concentration camps and, 210; disillusionment and, 205; *Els catalans als camps nazis*, 186, 210, 211, 314 n. 40; *El temps de les ciceres*, 186, 192–93, 323 n. 4; exile and, 208, 214; fetishism and, 196–98, 203–4, 327 n. 32; Franco regime and, 325 n. 15; the gaze and, 215–17; gender and, 186, 193, 323 n. 4, 324–25 n. 8; Generation of 1968 and, 331 n. 3; history and, 215; identity and, 183; intertextuality in the work of, 185, 187; *La veu melodiosa*, 323 n. 4; *L'hora violeta*, 64, 182–83, 227, 229, 231, 241, 243, 247–48, 252, 264, 269–70, 272, 316 n. 14, 317 n. 19, 323 n. 4, 325–26 n. 18, 332–33 n. 9, 333 n. 13; *L'opera*

quotidiana, 323 n. 4; "L'un i l'altra," 194, 325 n. 9; memory and, 183–24, 202–3, 208, 214, 218–20, 222–23, 247, 323 n. 4, 327 n. 32, 328 n. 43, 332–33 n. 9, 336 n. 18; photography and, 187, 190–91, 200, 270, 327 n. 32; places of memory and, 221; on post-Franco Spain, 328 nn. 42 and 43; postmemory and, 330 n. 74; presence-as-absence in, 201–2, 213; *Ramona adeu,* 323 n. 4; ruins and, 215; Spanish civil war and, 325–26 n. 18; on Spanish youth, 328 n. 42; temporality and, 316 n. 14; testimony and, 217, 219–20, 221–22; text-as-archive in, 219; trauma and, 223; vision and, 195–96, 215–17; "Voces y diálogos," 203; women and, 324–25 n. 8, 325 n. 9
Rubin Suleiman, Susan, 313 n. 27
ruins, 57, 133–36, 138, 140, 148, 178–79, 213, 215. *See also* fragmentary objects; places of memory
Rwanda, 49

Samuel, Raphael, 180
Santayana, George, 23
Saura, Carlos, 62
scapegoat, 159. *See pharmakos,* the
Scarry, Elaine, 79
Schechner, Richard, 165
Schor, Naomi, 202
Schudson, Michael, 309 n. 35
Scilingo, Adolfo, 20
Scott, Joan, 189–90, 212
self, 64, 83, 90–92, 154–56. *See also* identity
self-reflexivity, 14–15, 17, 53–54, 77, 108, 268; memory and, 47, 51, 59–60; in Roig, 185, 200–201; in Semprún, 73, 75, 311 n. 13. *See also* meta-memory texts
Semprún Maura, Jorge, 62–63, 66–101, 67, 169, 179; ". . . Vous avez une tombe au creux des nuage . . .," 68; *Adieu, vive clarté . . .,* 310 n. 4; *Autobiografía de Federico Sánchez,* 310 n. 6; autobiographical writing and, 86, 310–11 n. 6; biography of, 67; Buchenwald and, 63, 67–68, 72–73, 80–82, 86–90, 92–95, 97–101, 107, 137, 145, 153, 209–10, 276–78, 310 n. 3, 313 n. 27, 314 n. 48, 322 n. 25, 333 n.

10; censorship and, 92, 139–40; chronology and, 75–76, 78–81, 107, 131; concentration camps and, 63, 81–82, 93, 310 n. 5, 310–11 n. 6, 313 n. 32, 314 n. 42; death and, 81–83, 85, 89; disidentification and, 90; *El largo viaje,* 63, 74–80, 83, 85, 88–92, 94–99, 139–40, 211, 243–44, 269–70, 312 n. 22, 314 n. 48; embodiment and, 79; exile and, 73, 81, 83, 92, 96, 100, 137, 145, 153, 310 n. 3; *Federico Sánchez se despide de ustedes,* 310 n. 4; fiction and, 87–88; Franco regime and, 100; French literary tradition and, 310–11 n. 6; in the French Resistance, 74; on the future, 276–78; "Gurs: una tragedia europea," 310 n. 5; Hiroshima and, 82–83; the Holocaust and, 82; Holocaust literature and, 310–11 n. 6; José Manuel Lara prize and, 310 n. 4; language and, 68–69, 73–74; *L'écriture ou la vie,* 72–74, 80, 86–88, 92–93, 95, 97, 99–101, 311 n. 13, 313 n. 27, 337 n. 3; *L'Évanouissement,* 82–83; mastery and, 75–76, 79–80, 87–89; memory and, 74–80, 83, 85, 88–92, 94–99, 139–40, 160, 314 n. 48, 316 n. 17, 333 n. 10; meta-narrative in, 73; narration and, 313 n. 27; narrative and, 243–44; narrative strategies in, 312 n. 22; national displacement of, 68–69, 81, 83; Planeta Prize and, 310 n. 4; political activism of, 67–68, 310 n. 4; *Quel beau dimanche!,* 72, 80–83, 88, 99; receives Formentor Literature Prize (1964), 92; responsibility and, 86, 313 n. 32; self-reflexivity and, 311 n. 13; as Simonides, 314 n. 42; social realist tradition and, 94–95; the Spanish civil war and, 314 n. 48; Spanish Communist Party and, 81–82, 310 n. 4; within the Spanish literary tradition, 94–95; Stalinism and, 100; temporality and, 75–76, 78–81, 107, 131; transition to democracy and, 310 n. 4; "transmemoria" and, 322 n. 25; traumatic memory and, 82, 88, 90, 93, 107, 313 n. 27, 333 n. 10; "unsatisfied memory" and, 83; *Veinte años y un día,* 273, 310 n. 4, 314 n. 48; works of, 309–10 nn. 3 and 4
Shakespeare, William, 194

Showalter, Elaine, 194
Silk, Sally, 83
Silva, Emilio, 19–20, 29, 32, 36–39, 300 n. 4, 301–2 n. 10, 304 n. 16, 307–8 n. 24,
Silva Faba, Emilio, 19
Silverman, Kaja, 221–22, 229, 330 n. 74, 332 n. 6
Simonides of Ceos, 66–67, 91, 97, 99, 168–69, 309 nn. 1 and 2
Smith, Sidonie, 153, 166
Sobejano, Gonzalo, 123, 316 n. 9
Socialist Party (Spanish), 28
social realist tradition, 94–95, 104, 315 n. 3. *See also* realism
Socrates, 113
Solé Tura, Jordi, 31
songs, 236, 260
Sontag, Susan, 249
South Africa, 14
Spain: 2003 Davis Cup and, 27; "25 años de paz" (1964), 123–24, 172; "25 años de vida española" (1936–61), 35; *Anteproyecto de ley por la que se reconocen y amplían derechos...*, 281–98, 306–7 n. 21; autonomous regions of, 305–6 n. 19; Basque region, 26; Castilla, 26; Cataluña, 26; civic organizations in, 31–32, 36; collective memory in, 14, 40, 304 n. 16; concentration camps in, 303–4 n. 15; confrontation with the past in, 19–45, 50–51, 100, 171, 177–79, 222–23, 266–67, 269–71, 273–80, 299 n. 1, 299–300 n. 3, 300 n. 4, 301 n. 8, 301–2 n. 10, 302–3 nn. 11, 303 nn. 12, 14 and 15, 304 n. 16, 304–5 n. 18, 305–6 n. 19, 306–7 n. 21, 308 n. 26, 321–22 n. 22, 331–32 n. 5, 334 n. 15; congressional decree of 2002, 22–23; congressional decree (proposed) of 2003, 22–23; Constitution of 1978, 303 n. 14; culture of amnesia in, 23, 171, 176; "dos Españas," 33, 336 n. 21; education about the past in, 37–38; elections in, 28, 206–7; Expo in Sevilla, 25; *generación de los nietos de los vencidos,* 32–34, 36–37, 99, 265, 272–73, 279–80; Generation of 1968, 331 n. 3; Generation of 1981, 331 n. 3; government of, 21–23, 28, 29–30, 34–35; history of, 166, 227–28; human rights violations in, 306 n. 20; law of historical memory, 29–30, 280, 281–98, 306–7 n. 21, 307 n. 23, 321–22 n. 22,; modernization of, 25–26, 261, 302–3 n. 11; national anthem of, 27; Olympics in (1992), 25; Partido Popular in, 21, 22–23, 26–28, 321–22 n. 22, 306 n. 21; places of memory in, 269–70; politics in, 205–6; post-Franco, 23, 50, 169–71, 222–23, 231–32, 261, 269, 271, 301 n. 8 and 9, 301–2 n. 10, 302 n. 11, 331–32 n. 5, 332–33 n. 9, 328 n. 43; postmemory in, 231–32; reconciliation in, 40–42, 303 n. 12, 303 n. 14, 318 n. 2; Second Republic, 24; Socialist government of the 1990s, 34–35; Socialist Party in, 28; transition to democracy in, 24–25, 31–32, 36, 171–72, 177–79, 183, 187–88, 204, 205–7, 215, 222–23, 229, 261–62, 266–67, 300 n. 4, 301 n. 8, 303 n. 14, 304 n. 16, 307–8 n. 24, 310 n. 4, 318 n. 2, 325 n. 15; war tribunals in, 306–7 n. 21; younger generation in, 33–35, 99, 101, 262, 266–67, 272, 276–77, 328 n. 42, 332 n. 8, 332–33 n. 9, 333 n. 13. *See also specific autonomous regions; See also* Asociación para la Recuperación de la Memoria Histórica (ARMH)
Spanish civil war, the, 107–8, 118, 299–300 n. 3, 325–26 n. 18, 332 n. 8; anniversary of, 27; crimes against humanity during, 30–31; exiles from, 164–65; in literature, 336 n. 21, 337 n. 3; memory of, 14, 23–25, 48, 52, 164–65, 171, 273–78, 301 n. 9, 304 n. 16, 305–6 n. 19, 306–7 n. 21; mythologized view of, 275–77, 301 n. 9; repression during, 18, 24–25; women and the, 325–26 n. 18
Spanish Communist Party, 67, 147, 204, 299–300 n. 3, 300–301 n. 6, 310 n. 4, 321 n. 19
Spanish society: collective memory in, 14
Spires, Robert, 107, 136
Steiner, George, 84–85
storytelling, 239, 243, 244
studium, 252–53
Suarez, Adolfo, 301–2 n. 10

Subirats, Eduardo, 302–3 n. 11
sublime, the, 84
Summerhill, Stephen, 114, 316 n. 18
survivors, 67, 70, 71, 94, 210–11, 229–30

Talpade Mohanty, Chandra, 154
tears, 54
Teatro de Arte y Propaganda, 147
temporality, 47, 258, 274, 275; Bergson on, 105–6; calendars, 136; chronological, 75–76, 80–82, 106, 109–10, 121–22, 131, 136–37, 259–60; death and, 82; *durée* (Bergson), 105–6, 121, 130; in *El jinete polaco*, 255, 258–63; in *El largo viaje*, 75–76, 78–79, 131; of the Holocaust, 83; liminal, 316 n. 14; linear; in *Memoria de la Melancolía*, 148; photography and, 249; in *Quel beau dimanche!*, 80–81; in *Volverás a Región*, 109–10, 121–23, 125, 130, 131–32, 136–38, 315 nn. 1 and 5, 316 n. 9. *See also* progress
Terminus, 114, 119
testimony, 164, 217, 219–22
text as cemetery, 168–69, 180, 212–13, 271
Thamus, 103
"theatre of memory," 180
theatrical imagery, 126, 149, 162, 164
theatricality, political, 205–6, 207
therapy, 50–51
Theuth, 103, 105
time. *See* temporality
Tiresias, 182, 189, 323 n. 3
Torok, Maria, 236–37, 333 n. 11
Touraine, Alain, 304 n. 16
"transgenerational phantom," 236–39, 251–52, 333 n. 11
transition to democracy, 24–25, 31–32, 36, 171–72, 183, 204, 207, 229, 261–62, 266–67, 301 n. 8, 303 n. 14, 304 n. 16, 307–8 n. 24,; amnesia and, 143; disillusionment of, 183, 187, 204–7; exhumations during the, 300 n. 5; forgetting and, 176, 222–23, 301–2 n. 10; Generation of 1968 and, 331 n. 3; in *L'hora violeta*, 187–88, 204–5, 215, 325 n. 15; memory and, 222–23; memory work and, 32, 98; "pact of amnesia" and, 318 n. 2; politics in, 206–7; reconciliation and, 41–42; right of equality under the, 143; Semprún and the, 310 n. 4; in Spain, 179, 223; theatricality of, 205–6; underrepresentation of Francoist repression during the, 300 n. 4
"transmemoria", 174–75, 178, 184–85, 229, 322 n. 25
trauma, 16, 49, 268; absence and, 209–10; collective, 272; dynamics of, 49–50, 69, 92, 128–29; in *El largo viaje*, 90; embodiment of, 221; of exile, 270; intergenerational, 229, 236–37, 330 n. 74; language and, 69, 70, 84; in *L'écriture ou la vie*, 88; in *L'hora violeta*, 184, 209, 218–23; mastery and, 92, 161–62, 320–21 n. 17; memory and, 66–101, 160–61, 184, 209–10, 218–22, 243–44, 269–70, 277–78, 309 n. 2, 311 n. 9, 314 n. 47, 333 n. 10, 333 n. 13; narration and, 311 n. 13; narrative and, 83–84, 91–92, 209–10, 272; performativity and, 71, 92, 161–62; postmemory and, 229–31, 236–37; repetition and, 69–70, 72, 160–61, 173, 313 n. 27; representation and, 70–71; repression and, 69–70; self and, 90; signification and, 53; silence and, 84; survivors and, 210–11; theories of, 16, 63, 71, 84; therapy and, 50–51; transmission of, 333 n. 13; victims of, 212; in *Volverás a Región*, 326 n. 29. *See also* traumatic memory
traumatic memory, 14, 39, 49–50, 70–71, 93, 161–62, 175; danger of, 72; of exile, 176; León and, 160–61; narrative and, 91–92, 94; Semprún and, 72–73, 82, 88, 90, 93, 107, 313 n. 27, 333 n. 10. *See also* trauma
tremendum fascinosum, 84, 85
tremendum horrendum, 84, 94
Trueba, David, 273
Truth and Reconciliation Commission (South Africa), 14
Tsuchiya, Akiko, 185–86
Tusell, Javier, 40–41
"twilight memories," 182–86, 188, 223, 243

Ugarte, Michael, 322–23 n. 26
Umbral, Francisco, 26

United Nations Work Group on Forced Disappearances, 21
"unsatisfied memory," 55–56, 59, 83, 92, 127–28, 202, 223, 271
Uruguay, 20

Valle de los Caídos, 29
Vallespín, Fernando, 303–4 n. 15
Vázquez Montalbán, Manuel, 278–79, 331–32 n. 5
Verdery, Katherine, 279, 308 n. 28
verfremdungsfekt, 165
Verne, Jules, 240–43, 334–35 n. 16
"vigilant memory", 56–57, 59, 87, 168, 264, 271
Vilarós, Teresa, 301 n. 8
violet hour, the, 182–83, 185–86, 243
vision; blindness, 194–95; in *El jinete polaco*, 252–53, 256–57; the fetish and, 200–201; gender and, 189–90, 216; ideological constitution of, 189–91; in *L'hora violeta*, 189–91, 195–96, 200–201, 215–17; memory and, 242–43. *See also* photography
void. *See* absence

Wescott Lupinacci, Julia, 109
Wiesel, Elie, 71
Winter, Ulrich, 43–44, 59, 270
women; cult of, 152; femininity, 154, 194, 319 n. 7, 322–23 n. 26, 324–25 n. 8; under the Franco regime, 193–94; in *L'hora violeta*, 324–25 n. 8–9; patriarchy and, 319–20 n. 11–12; Spanish civil war and, 325–26 n. 18. *See also* gender: female domesticity; feminism
Woolf, Virginia, 194
World Warr II, anniversary of, 48
Wright, Elizabeth, 165
writing: contradictory nature of, 103, 105; frames and, 187; as illness, 159–60; in *L'hora violeta*, 218–20; memory and, 103–4; *pharmakon* of, 113, 115; in Plato's *Phaedrus*, 103; as testimony, 219–20; in *Volverás a Región*, 115. *See also* autobiographic writing

Yates, Frances, 309 n. 1
Young, James, 231

Zambrano, María, 159–60, 179–80, 321 n. 20
Zatlin, Phyllis, 328 n. 44
Zeus, 91